D1526974

THE ANXIETIES OF
PLINY THE YOUNGER

AMERICAN PHILOLOGICAL ASSOCIATION
American Classical Studies

Series Editor

Harvey Yunis

Number 43

THE ANXIETIES OF
PLINY THE YOUNGER

by
Stanley E. Hoffer

Stanley E. Hoffer

The Anxieties of
Pliny the Younger

Scholars Press
Atlanta, Georgia

THE ANXIETIES OF PLINY THE YOUNGER

by
Stanley E. Hoffer

Library of Congress Cataloging in Publication Data

Hoffer, Stanley E.
    The anxieties of Pliny, the Younger / Stanley E. Hoffer.
        p.   cm. — (American classical studies ; no. 43)
    Includes bibliographical references and index.
    ISBN 0-7885-0565-3 (cloth : alk. paper)
    1. Pliny, the Younger—Criticism and interpretation. 2. Rome—
History—Domitian, 81–96 Biography. 3. Rome—History—Trajan,
98–117 Biography. 4. Latin letters—History and criticism. 5. Authors,
Latin—Rome Biography.   6. Lawyers—Rome Biography.
    I. Title. II. Series.
    PA6640.H64   1999
    873'.01—dc21
    [B]   99-27448
                                                     CIP

08 07 06 05 04 03 02 01 00 99   5 4 3 2 1

Printed in the United States of America
on acid-free paper

CONTENTS

1. Introduction: The Anxieties of Pliny the Younger   1
    The First Book: Introduction and Epitome   3
    The Ideal Emperor and the Ideal Senator   5
    Friendship and Exchange: The "Virtuous Circle"   10
    Ideology and Literary Style   13

2. No Regrets? Literary and Political Programmatic Elements in 1.1   15
    Literary Favors and Self-Fulfilling Prophecies   17

3. Villas: Factories of Literature (1.3)   29
    Utopias in the Villa Description   31
    Representations of Literary Value   38
    Literary Value and Immortality   40
    The Internal Friendly Cycle of the Self   43

4. The Material Conditions of Life: New and Old Slaves (1.4, 1.21)   45
    Letter 1.21: Judging New Slaves With Eyes and Ears   45
    Letter 1.4: Mild Masters and Slaves Waking Up   50

5. Models of Senators and Emperors: Regulus, the Bad Senator (1.5)   55
    Regulus: The "Eloquence" of the Collaborator   64
    Spurinna: Communications Among Good Senators   76
    The Meeting with Regulus: Satisfied with Our Era?   83

6. Pliny's Three Children (1.8)   93
    The Directions of Pliny's Anxieties: Downwards,
        Sideways, and Upwards   97
    Containing the Rhetoric of Blame   104
    Bitter Medicine for Raising Children   105

7. Literary Leisure in the Life of Politics (1.9)   111

8. Pliny's Tame Philosopher (1.10)   119
    Praising the Tame Philosopher   126

9. The Death of Corellius: Pain and Loss, Consolation and Gain (1.12)   141
    The Philosophical Reckoning of Grief and Loss   145
    The Two Sickbed Scenes   152
    A Great New Consolation   157

10. The New Freedom of Speech, along with the Freedom Not
        to Listen (1.13)   161

11. Producing the Next Deserving Generation of the Ruling Class (1.14)   177

12. Creating Imperial Meaning out of Republican Forms (1.23)   195

13. Establishing Friendly Ties and Hierarchies: Suetonius (1.18, 1.24)   211
    Letter 1.18: Pliny's Dream: Bravery under the Prior Regime   211
    Letter 1.24: No Regrets: Real Estate and the Circulation of
        Symbolic Capital   221

14. Conclusion: A Personal Note   227

    Appendix: Marriage and Child-rearing among the Roman Elite   229

    Bibliography   235

    Index   241

INTRODUCTION
THE ANXIETIES OF PLINY THE YOUNGER

The leading trait in Pliny's epistolary self-portrait is his confidence: confidence in himself and his friends, in their writings and activities, in the Roman government, and in the emperor. Pliny presents a man and a world that have the fewest possible anxieties. This very absence of anxiety invites us to look at the opposite side of the picture, at Pliny's anxieties, to help us understand his aims in putting together and publishing the letters. Pliny evidently protests too much; his cheerful and confident picture is designed to wish away the basic tensions and contradictions of his upper-class Roman life.

Several kinds of anxieties appear despite the dominant confident tone of the letters. First, there are the explicit anxieties. In certain well-defined areas, Pliny allows himself to express his worries openly, as over a friend's health, over a young friend's candidacy, or over reciting or publishing (e.g. 1.22, 2.9, 9.34). The question of unexpressed anxieties is more difficult, but also more fruitful. When we find tensions, gaps, or contradictions in Pliny's rhetoric, or when we find passages that seem to confront political or social pressures attested in other texts, we can suspect that Pliny is hiding troubling aspects of his life. Yet we can rarely be sure whether Pliny the expert orator is carefully glossing over anxieties, or whether the rhetorical fault lines reflect underlying social tensions that creep into Pliny's text without his knowledge. I will use the term "anxiety" to cover both categories, both the consciously felt concerns and the unconscious expression of social contradictions, which we might call the anxieties of the collective unconscious of the ruling class. This of course differs from Pliny's own usage, in which words such as *aestus, angor, anxietas, cura,* and *sollicitudo* signify conscious worry.

I use the word "anxiety" in this way for two reasons, both to emphasize the inherent gradations in the concept and to assert that Pliny's anxieties are very often conscious. As for the first point, the two terms "conscious anxiety" and "unfelt social pressures and contradictions" are not mutually exclusive opposites but rather the end points of a continuum filled with subtle gradations. The inevitable social contradictions in the conditions of life often leave some mark, even a faint or suppressed mark, on one's mental awareness, and one can feel general anxiety without fully understanding the underlying causes. Second, I believe that many of the half-expressed tensions in Pliny's text reflect conscious anxieties, or at least lie near the conscious end of the spectrum. We can never look straight into the subconscious mind of Pliny, or even of a living person, or of ourselves. But external evidence often confirms that a certain anxiety was in the air, so to speak, and thus likely to have been in his mind. Whether in Tacitus' criticisms of imperial government, in Juvenal's condemnations of luxury expenditure, or in Stoic attacks on the desire for power, fame, and wealth, we often find in Pliny's own milieu a clear expression of an anxiety which Pliny seems to ignore or suppress.

The works of many writers connected with Pliny happen to survive, including those of his uncle Pliny the Elder, his teacher Quintilian, and his friends Tacitus and Suetonius. Philosophical writings, especially Epictetus', will be especially revealing, since some philosophers undertook to challenge conventional values and to uncover, mock, and cure false pretensions and needless anxieties. Many of Epictetus' views may have been known to Pliny, since Pliny professes admiration for Musonius Rufus (3.11.5) and Euphrates (1.10), both of whom were teachers or role models for Epictetus (Epict. 1.7.32, Fronto 2.50 Haines; Epict. 3.15.8, 4.8.17–20). To be sure, I am not suggesting that the letters perpetrate a complete deception, covering up agonizing terrors with a completely false self-portrait, any more than I would suggest that the real Trajan behind the flattering praises was no better than the real Nero who received similar praise from his courtiers.[1] On the other hand, our evidence, though indirect and inconclusive, suggests that Pliny was more aware of the tensions in the political, social, and economic conditions of his life than the letters reveal on the surface. As an expert orator, he knew well how to argue on both sides of a question, and how to pitch an argument or narrative in such a way as to suppress opposing interpretations.

I will concentrate on four primary areas of anxiety in Pliny's life, politics, friendship, literature, and material conditions. I use these terms in a broad sense, with "friendship" including all Pliny's idealized personal relationships with friends, relatives, slaves, and even the emperor; "literature" including all formal utterance from political speeches to private letters; and "material conditions" including money, land, slavery, and so on. Thus defined, these four areas are closely connected, virtually being four ways of looking at the same phenomenon, the lives of Pliny and his friends, as seen from the point of

---

[1] Bartsch (1994:148–87) shows how these ambiguities underlie the *Panegyric*.

view of power, personal relations, conceptual expression, and material basis. The interconnection among these areas will therefore be a fruitful topic of investigation. For example, Pliny's literary production depends on his estates with their study chambers, supplies, slaves and tenants; his secure ownership of property, in turn, depends on a stable imperial government controlled by a well-established emperor; his writing also depends on his supportive circle of friends, who are connected through the mutual channels of political activity, promotion, and patronage; and so on.

The linchpin of the entire system is the ideal emperor; the *Panegyric* makes explicit what is implicit throughout the letters.[2] The good emperor makes it possible for his subjects to carry out meaningful and honorable political activities (44.5–7, 45.2, 76), to have loyal friends rather than false flatterers (42.2, 85.1), to devote themselves freely to meaningful literature (47.1–3), and to have secure enjoyment of their wealth, villas, and slaves (42, 50.4). The anxiety-free pose which Pliny maintains throughout the letters offers continuous implicit praise not only of the ideal statesman (Pliny) but also of his counterpart, the ideal emperor who makes his upper-class life possible. The letters dramatize Pliny's ideal circle of friends with their open and mutually beneficial cycles of exchange. They also show how Pliny justifies his material wealth by transforming it into higher literary and political value. And above all, they claim positive moral value for the newly restored imperial system and for Pliny's place within it.

THE FIRST BOOK: INTRODUCTION AND EPITOME

The first book of letters lets us see especially clearly how Pliny deals with his central concerns. Like the dedication letter 1.1, which implicitly dedicates all nine books to Septicius Clarus, Book 1 as a whole acts as an introduction to the rest of the collection, revealing to us the basic topics and aims of all nine books. Murgia points out that the collection was published in its final form as a unified whole, with Book 1 functioning as an introduction and Book 9 as a conclusion; even the opening words correspond (1.1.1 *frequenter hortatus es,* 9.1.1 *saepe te monui*).[3] The opening book offers a panorama of the topics and viewpoints that will dominate the entire corpus. Literature and politics, friendship and money, leisure, villas, and banquets, patronage and munificence, emperors and senators, relatives, lesser friends, and slaves, Senate and courtroom, Rome, Italy, and the provinces—all these topics are

---

[2] Trisoglio aptly names a section of his work "L'imperatore come valorizzatore" (1972:94–96), but he merely summarizes and echoes Pliny's enthusiastic praise of Trajan.

[3] Murgia 1985:198–99, Fantham 1996:299 n. 40. "When Pliny published the last book, what he published was books 1 through 9" (Murgia 1985:201).

treated in Book 1, and treated in a way that sets the tone for the remaining books. The first book is also rich in the programmatic treatment of the meaning and value of literature, and implicitly of letter-writing as well. A deeper understanding of Book 1 therefore offers us a deeper understanding of the whole collection.

The opening dozen or so letters in particular function as a thematic showcase introducing the major topics and letter types of the collection, rather like Horace's first nine odes that introduce the nine principal meters of his collection. Letter 1.7 introduces the sequence of major letters on trials involving provincial administration (2.11–12 Priscus; 3.4, 3.9 Classicus; 4.9 Bassus; 5.20, 6.5, 6.13, 7.6, 7.10 Varenus; 7.33 Massa). The short villa letters 1.3, 1.4, and 1.9 anticipate the long villa letters 2.17 and 5.6 (compare 9.7, 36, 40). The letters on Regulus, perhaps the most memorable character in the collection, are introduced by letter 1.5. Letter 1.12 is the first of the obituary letters, and introduces the first of the senior senators who were Pliny's patrons (such as Verginius Rufus, Spurinna, and Frontinus). Two letters, 1.5 and 1.14, introduce the "opposition" group with which Pliny is so eager to associate himself, a group including Helvidius Priscus, Herennius Senecio, Rusticus, Mauricus, Arria, and Fannia (e.g. 2.18, 3.11, 7.19, 9.13), and going back all the way to Paetus and Arria the Elder (3.16, 6.24). Two letters in the opening sequence give detailed programmatic discussions on literary style and content (1.2, 1.8), and three others (1.3, 1.9, and 1.10) investigate the relationship between *negotium* (business and politics) and *otium* (leisure and literature). Even the casual joke letter 1.6 serves to introduce Tacitus, the most prominent of the friends, who receives the most letters (eleven) as well as two of the major set-pieces, the Vesuvius letters (6.16 and 6.20).[4] Thus the first half of Book 1 covers all the important topics of the collection and adumbrates most of the major set-pieces.

The implicit setting of Book 1 in the years 96–98 heightens the panegyric aspect which permeates the entire collection. The letters as a whole praise the new emperors both through their contents and through their very existence; like Tacitus' *Agricola* and *Histories,* they are new works that it is finally possible to write and publish in the new and happier age. The opening book is especially rich in this restoration propaganda that runs throughout the collection, and can give us special insight into the rhetoric of imperial restoration in the letters. Each of the topics introduced in Book 1 establishes the panegyric meaning of that topic. For example, letter 1.5 demonstrates that

---

[4] Sherwin-White, in detecting Pliny's growing intimacy and self-confidence towards Tacitus, seems to me to be accepting the ostensible chronology of the letters too literally (1966:100). In the final books Pliny deliberately and explicitly stresses his close association with Tacitus the literary great (7.20, 9.14, 9.23) to impart a tone of completion and success to the collection.

Domitian's insidious tool, Regulus, no longer poses political dangers for Pliny and his ideal circle of friends. Similarly, letter 1.1 shows that they can publish letters freely now, 1.3 and 1.4 that they can control their luxury villas and slaves safely now, and 1.10 and 1.13 that they can indulge in literature and philosophical moralizing safely now. Even a seemingly apolitical letter on prolixity in oratory (1.20), to the concise Tacitus of all people (Riggsby 1995:127), is an implied rebuke to the *Dialogus*: oratory is not dead under the imperial system, but still has an important public function.[5]

THE IDEAL EMPEROR AND THE IDEAL SENATOR

Pliny's political anxieties focus on the emperor, whose idealized figure pervades the collection both in person and as an implied parallel to the ideal upper-class men of the collection, Pliny and his friends. The letters are a counterpart to the *Panegyric* in a more discreet form, praising the ideal emperor of the new regime (in contrast to his opposite, the bad emperor), who both models himself after, and serves as a model for, the ideal ruling-class man (in contrast to *his* opposite, the bad senator, the bad man of power, the *delator*).[6] The stresses of the years of transition 96–98 heighten the anxieties surrounding this neat pattern. Pliny must work especially hard to maintain the fragile distinctions on which government under a "good emperor" depends. He must ignore the opening turbulence under Nerva; he must sharply distinguish good emperors from bad emperors despite their many apparent similarities; he must distinguish himself, a prominent and successful senator under Domitian, from the loathed collaborators; he must distinguish the all-powerful emperor from the leading senators, any of whom

---

[5] Ironically, the acerbic and taciturn Tacitus appears next in the most imperial and prolix of oratorical roles, the lavish eulogist (2.1.6). Tacitus seems to have given up oratory soon afterwards (Syme 1958:103, 116; Kennedy 1972:516). One wonders how pleased he could have been at Pliny's praise for this performance. Syme also speculates at Tacitus' dissatisfaction at the outcome of the Priscus trial at which he spoke (1958:112), and detects possible barbs at Pliny in the *Dialogus:* scorn of Pliny's voluble teacher Nicetes, of Pliny's main arena, the Centumviral court, and of part-time poetry-writing by orators (*Dial.* 15.3, 38.2, 21.6; 1958:115).

[6] The letters have often been recognized as a portrait of the ideal ruling-class member. "The *Letters* are, and are meant to be, a handbook for the perfect Roman senator" (Veyne 1990:9); "the closest that was decent or possible to the autobiography of an orator and statesman" (Syme 1958:98). Compare Fantham (1996:201): "a full representation of Pliny's life and world as he wished to display it... midway between essay and autobiography." The process of modeling one's personal identity after an ideal figure is called by Greenblatt "self-fashioning" (1980:1–9); compare, for example, Pliny 1.14.4 *formari... et institui, Pan.* 47.1 *formas.* On the idea of the emperor as "an example to his citizens," see Woodman 1975:292 ("an idea of great antiquity").

could have occupied his position; and he must ignore the likelihood that conspiracies, executions, and civil war could return at any time given the inherent instability of the imperial system, especially in non-hereditary transfers of power.

The boundary between emperor and senator remained blurry because by a mutually acceptable fiction, the role of emperor scarcely existed. In principle the emperor was merely a high-ranking senator with supplementary powers and honors, including *imperium,* tribunician *potestas,* the position of Pontifex Maximus, control of the imperial wealth, and especially control of the armies and praetorian guard. Hence the good emperor was constantly playing the role of a high-ranking senator, and more dangerously, senators played at being a lesser emperor.[7] Only a bad emperor refuses to play the game, and emphasizes titles and honors that cannot be shared or imitated, especially deification. Pliny is fond of using imperial nomenclature in a generic meaning, especially the standard word for emperor, *princeps.*[8] For example, by tending to his "fatherland" Comum (e.g. 3.6.4 *patria*) as to a "daughter" (4.13.5), Pliny gets to play at "father of the fatherland," a favorite imperial title.[9] And as "father" of his household of slaves or ex-slaves (5.19.2), the Roman aristocrat is always playing at being ruler of a "republic."[10]

Since Pliny's official speech of thanks to the emperor survives, we can compare the official modes of imperial praise with the implicit praise of the Letters. Like coin titles, which the *Panegyric* often resembles, the speech praises imperial virtues, traits of the ideal emperor: *simplicitas, moderatio, humanitas, comitas, providentia, securitas,* and so on.[11] These traits recur throughout the Letters, and I will often refer to them as "imperial virtues," and to their opposites as "imperial vices." I do not mean to imply that every use of these standard Roman moral terms is a conscious allusion to the emperor, but that the machinery of imperial propaganda tended to arrogate to itself all moral values. Octavian's arrogation of the word *augustus* is a

[7] Hopkins emphasizes the significance of the emperor exchanging social visits as if with equals (1983:121 n. 2). On the other hand, Riggsby argues that one normally received visits from an equal or slightly inferior guest in one's *cubiculum,* and points out that emperors did not normally visit the *cubicula* of their "friends," but received them in their own *cubicula* (1997:41).
[8] For example, Pompeius Iulianus and Euphrates (1.10.8), Macrinus (1.14.5), Arrianus (3.2.2), and Frontinus (4.8.3) are all "leading citizens."
[9] See Veyne 1990:175 n. 166 for bibliography on the inscriptional use of the honorific titles "parent" or "nourisher" of the city.
[10] 8.16.2 *res publica*; compare Sen. *de Ira* 3.35.1. The tag with which Pliny gives Homeric support to the Roman concept *paterfamilias* (5.19.2 = *Od.* 2.47, 234, 5.12) implicitly supports the Roman concept *pater patriae* as well: Odysseus was as "gentle as a father" to his people.
[11] "Many chapters of that speech could bear coin legends for their title" Syme 1958:754; see also Ramage 1989:652.

notorious example, and Pliny flatteringly predicts that the word "best" will hereafter remind everyone of Trajan (*Pan.* 88.10). The emperor was the focus about which all moral and political discourse tended to gather, like a grain around which a crystal forms.

Pliny does his best to generate sincerity in the *Panegyric* by using *recusatio,* by *refusing* to praise abundantly, just as the emperor tries to generate legitimacy by refusing powers and titles ("le refus de pouvoir," Béranger 1953:137). Even as he trots out the usual fulsome praise he claims that he is praising modestly, unlike the way prior Bad Emperors were given excessive forced praise. Bartsch has shown how Pliny struggles to restore sincere meanings to the names of virtues and to the rituals of legitimacy, which had become debased by years of false adulation.[12] The speech of thanks was to be sure an unavoidable obligation which you had to perform, even if it killed you, as it did Verginius Rufus (2.15). But the earnest Pliny exceeds even the ordinary consul giving a speech of thanks, by his expanding it, reciting it (3.18.6), and publishing it.

Not only is the distinction between a good emperor and a bad emperor unstable, with the same praises offered to both; in addition, the lists of virtues and vices themselves cannot easily be kept apart by anyone trained in the technique of *distinctio,* by which the same trait can be given a positive or negative name.[13] For example, justice can be called "harshness," and clemency can be called "laxness" (*rigidam duramque... dissolutam,* 4.9.19). Throughout Pliny's praise of the ideal emperor and society we can detect a continual effort to enforce distinctions, to separate good patronage from bad, good ambition from bad, good leisure from bad, and so on. For example, the good name for patronage is "friendship"; the bad name is "factionalism" or "favoritism" (1.5.15 *factiosus,* 3.20.6 *gratiosi*).[14]

Pliny constantly makes the effort to preserve his self-image by reinforcing the distinction between the good senator and the bad senator, between good obedience and bad obsequiousness, between good inheriting and bad *captatio,* between good and bad eloquence. The good aristocrat is represented by senior colleagues (who appear mostly in the early books), equals, and lesser friends

---

[12] See Bartsch's chapter on Pliny's *Panegyric* for the difficulty of distinguishing between sincere praise of a "good emperor" and insincere praise of a "bad emperor" (1994:148–87). The terms "good" and "bad" emperors reflect the ancient phraseology (e.g. 9.13.23, *Pan.* 4.1, Suet. *Tib.* 29.1, Tac. *Agric.* 42.5, 43.4).

[13] Quint. *Inst.* 9.3.65; see Bartsch 1994:171.

[14] What upsets Pliny most about the frivolous secret ballots in the Senate is that someone makes explicit what everyone knows, that he is really voting not for the candidate but for the powerful patron (*in una <scil. tabella>... pro candidatorum nominibus suffragatorum nomina inventa sunt,* 4.25.1). He is making a farce (*ista ludibria, scaena et pulpito digna,* 4.25.5) by showing the elections to be a farce.

(portrayed as ideal young aristocrats, often in recommendation letters). Pliny's self-portrait combines all three aspects, as if in a perfect union of ages (as at 5.16.2). He shows us his earlier self as a successful young politician (e.g. 1.18), and gives an anticipated view of his dignified retirement (e.g. 3.1.11; compare Quint. *Inst.* 12.11.1–7). Pliny combines the three cardinal political roles all in one, the loyal follower, the autonomous colleague, and the leading senior statesman, to constitute the ideal Roman imperial statesman. On the other hand, just as the good statesman is the image of the good emperor, to the bad emperor corresponds the bad statesman. The most prominent bad statesman is Regulus; other bad lackeys of the past are Veiento, Certus, Catullus Messalinus, and even the ex-slave Pallas. Pliny is at pains to show that essentially, under a good emperor there are no bad statesmen. Bad statesmen can arise only under bad emperors. Under good emperors they become harmless, as Veiento and Regulus (4.22.6, 6.2.4). Italicus, whose offenses were still further in the past, can even redeem himself and almost be admitted into the ranks of the honorable senior statesmen (3.7.3), though we can suspect that his death was a relief not only to himself (3.7.2), but also to others, with the disease of Neronian times finally being put to rest with the death of the last of the Neronian consulars.

The transition from "bad" to "good" emperor is a particularly anxious time in a senator's career. This is the moment commemorated in Book 1. Bad senators such as Regulus and Veiento have to survive under the new regime, and survive with high status, or else another reign of terror would destabilize the senators' position even further and give the "good" regime an uncomfortable resemblance to the "bad" one. Only Certus is accommodating enough to have a natural death during this awkward period; the others live on and must be dealt with. Conversely, there must be good senators under a bad emperor to provide a power base for the new good emperor (cf. Tac. *Agric.* 42.4). The good emperor himself has to have been a high-ranking senator under the bad emperor, as Nerva and Trajan under Domitian.[15] A political non-entity, such as Piso the returned exile in 69, does not have the power and status to become emperor. On the other hand, returning exiles have great symbolic value as proven opponents of the bad emperor, and thus Pliny places great emphasis on his close and loyal friendship with the returned exile Mauricus, and with the martyrs' wives Arria, Fannia, and Anteia (9.13.4–5), who carry their husbands' prestige. Pliny himself struggles to demonstrate his status as an opponent and near-victim of Domitian, and to hide the continuing high patronage he received until the end. Only from inscriptions do we know of his treasury position in Domitian's last years (*CIL* 5.5262, 5.5667).

[15] As Otho tells the praetorians, emperors arise from senators (Tac. *Hist.* 1.84.4).

An understanding of Pliny's rhetorical aims can also help us date the
letters, even if only negatively to warn us against making too much historical
use of passages that have a mainly rhetorical function. An extreme example is
the death of Corellius (1.12), which is presented as if it occurred right after
Domitian's death, although in reality Corellius lived on for a year or more.
Similarly, Pliny's political anxiety over popularity-seeking (1.8.17) is a
widespread imperial trope that cannot be used to suggest a Domitianic date for
the *alimenta* speech (as does Sherwin-White 1966:105). As we shall see, other
features of letter 1.8 from which Sherwin-White argues for an early date
(tentativeness in a new friendship with Saturninus? lack of more recent major
writings to send?) derive from Pliny's overriding aim in the letter, to present
the rhetoric of self-praise in the best possible light. A full understanding of the
historical and chronological aspects of the letters requires a careful literary
and rhetorical appreciation.

An investigation of the rhetorical aspects of Book 1 confirms the widely
held view that they were edited and published many years later than their
dramatic date of 96–98, at least after the death of Regulus. Although Pliny
may well have sent real letters in 96–98 resembling those of Book 1, he
evidently selected, revised, and rewrote them with great care, maintaining the
fiction of authentic letters by avoiding explicit anachronisms.[16] Unlike in the
explicitly retrospective letter 9.13, Pliny has almost completely suppressed the
dangers and anxieties of the time, and has produced a confident and optimistic
persona. Even Regulus is portrayed as being weak, laughable, and almost
pitiable despite Pliny's claim that he is still dangerous (1.5.15). The terrified
senators and ominous military prospects of 9.13 (9.13.7, 11), the campaigns of
vengeance (9.13.4) and the uprising of the praetorians and near breakdown of
Nerva's authority (*Pan.* 6.2, 10.1) all go unmentioned, as do the possible
uncertainties associated with the time between Trajan's adoption in October
97, his accession in January 98, and his return to Rome in the latter part of 99.
The need to maintain a confident persona has also induced Pliny to omit
personal details such as his serious illness (10.5.1, 10.8.3) and the death of his
wife in 97 (9.13.4). Other features appear only in later books, such as his
interests in writing poetry, his remarriage to Calpurnia, his methods of
agricultural management, or his shift in obituaries away from old men and
towards women and young people. I would prefer to attribute at least some of

[16] As Murgia observes, the pointed reference to Regulus calling down the gods' wrath onto his
unfortunate son's head (2.20.6) was almost certainly written after and not before the son's
death (1985:193, cf. 201; *contra,* Sherwin-White 1966:203). Of course, Pliny never explicitly
claims that the letters are unrevised, but the epistolary framework of greeting, occasional
message, and farewell "guarantee" their authenticity—though Pliny knows enough to be
suspicious about the letters of his friend's wife (1.16.6).

these changes not to actual changes in Pliny's life and attitudes between 96–100 (the setting of the early books) and 105–108 (the setting of the later books), but rather to his feelings for the literary shape of the collection as a presentation of his life and his times, when he was making his final revisions to the entire collection in about 107–109. I therefore consider it legitimate and appropriate to see whether material in later books can help us understand earlier passages. A notorious example is the use that we should make of letter 4.2 on the death of Regulus' son, as the background to letter 2.20 with Regulus swearing falsely by his son's life (2.20.6). Though we can never know how much of Book 1 is original and how much is later recomposition, Pliny's own comments on revising for the sake of oratorical exercise provide a suggestive guide. The ideal revision keeps much but adds more, inserts some and rewrites some, adding new limbs to a complete body without disturbing the original limbs (*multa retinere plura transire, alia interscribere alia rescribere... nova velut membra peracto corpori intexere nec tamen priora turbare*, 7.9.5–6).

FRIENDSHIP AND EXCHANGE: THE "VIRTUOUS CIRCLE"

Pliny's letters are above all an ideal record of friendship. Sent to his friends, responding to his friends' letters, and describing or recommending other friends, they show friendship in its cardinal aspects, at business and at leisure, in politics and in literature, in Rome, in country villas, and in travels. Here, too, if we look beneath the anxiety-free surface, we find numerous signs of the problems of upper-class friendship which Pliny's portrait suppresses or resolves: the problems of competition, resentment, and envy, of subservience and equality, of patronage and merit, and of the competing pressures of family and patronage that impinge on a "new man" in imperial society.

Envy is endemic to a zero-sum system in which one person can only gain at the expense of another. Though Pliny and his associates have no shortage of necessities, the basic items of value in upper-class life are in limited supply. There is only a limited number of positions in the Senate, and of forms of valuable patronage that the emperor can dispense.[17] A town can only support so many landlords with vast estates and luxury villas. Even literary success is competitive, and subject to the envy of others (e.g. Callim. *Epigr.* 21.4, *Hymn* 2.105–13, Hor. *Odes* 2.20.4, Mart. 1.91, 4.27, 5.10). The more widely-read books other people write, the less widely one's own books will be read.

Pliny therefore emphasizes the mutual benefits that arise from friendly exchange, what one might call a "virtuous circle" of friendship. Rather than being stuck in a vicious circle of envy, detraction, and revenge, they eagerly

---

[17] For bibliography on envy and "zero-sum games," see Barton 1993:150, 186. Seneca mentions the envy people feel when someone is appointed consul (*Ep.* 104.9).

and selflessly help each other, and they incidentally derive benefit for themselves as a side-effect. Pliny and his friends spur each other to mutual literary glory (e.g. 3.7.15, 7.20.3); their mutual visits increase the pleasure they take in their leisure hours (e.g. 1.15.3, 2.17.29); and they receive mutual benefit from their exchange of political favors in the Senate and law courts, and especially in their hierarchical relationships, receiving benefits from the emperor and more powerful leaders and dispensing benefits below to rising young leaders, lesser friends, and townspeople. Pliny often uses the trope of the linked analogy to express this hierarchical relationship: as A is to B, so B is to C. For example, as Rusticus and Mauricus formed Pliny, so Pliny forms Acilianus (1.14.4). After Pliny wins his suit for Suetonius, Suetonius will win for his client (1.18.6). Suetonius will be indebted to Pliny as Pliny will be indebted to Baebius Hispanus (1.24.4). This trope rhetorically dramatizes mutual benefits as a self-perpetuating cycle that reaches from the past to the future, and from above to below on the social ladder. The trope also allows Pliny to display an awareness of the real hierarchies in status, and of his own rising position within it, while maintaining the obligatory fiction of gifts freely given between equals.[18] I should emphasize that I often echo Pliny's laudatory point of view merely as an ironic shorthand; my intention here and throughout this work is to warn us against being deceived by it.

Even material gifts can be understood as mutual gain, according to the principle of "symbolic capital," or the intangible benefits in gratitude and prestige that are gained by donating one's wealth or labor (Bourdieu 1977). Symbolic capital is the glue that holds the patronage system together, that makes it more than worthwhile for the patron to give "generously" to the client. Mauricus and Corellius gained more than they lost for their efforts in "forming" and recommending Pliny, just as Pliny will gain more than the HS 300,000 he loses by making Romatius Firmus a knight: he gains a more loyal ("mindful," 1.19.3) and more powerful friend who can do local political and financial favors for Pliny. Conversely, Corellia can cash in on her deceased husband's patronage of Pliny when she gets a discount of HS 200,000 on land at Comum (7.11.1, 7.14.1).[19]

Symbolic value is generally more valuable that the cash and material goods into which and out of which it can be transformed. It is more flexible than cash, it can buy more kinds of things, and it does not have the negative

---

[18] See Dixon on the tendency to express unequal exchange relationships among the elite in the language of friendly equality (1993:451). Dixon also discusses the tension between the real function of gift-giving in creating social debt and social hierarchies, and the ideal of altruistic gift-giving that is urged by moralizing treatises such as Cicero's and Seneca's (452–56).

[19] Pliny may yet receive a repayment for this gift to Corellia. Although her powerful brother is dead, she still has access to useful patronage through his daughter, married to one of the Neratii (Raepsaet-Charlier 1987:238).

connotations of peddlery and bribery; it is enshrined in lovely moral
terminology such as gratitude, friendship, duty, loyalty, reverence, sacred
memory, and so on (e.g. 1.13.6 *gratia,* 1.17.1 *fides, officium,* 7.11.3
reverentia, memoria sacrosancta). Under cover of these positive names, both
parties to the exchange can gain honor, just as the donor Titinius Capito gets
as much glory from the statue as does the honorand, the dead Silanus
Torquatus (1.17.4).[20] And best of all, unlike simple cash purchases, exchanges
involving symbolic capital create lasting obligations and reinforce hierarchical
power relations. Despite the appearance of equality, friendly exchanges up and
down the social scale reinforce the difference in power. A more powerful
friend can dispense larger favors that can only be reciprocated through deeper
and deeper indebtedness and more loyal subservience. The extreme example is
the emperor, who displays and reinforces his dominance by dispensing
political favors, which can never be repaid (10.51.2). Unless the relationship
is broken by disloyalty, death, or disaster (and sometimes even despite these),
the superior gains more in symbolic capital, and thus ultimately in real profit,
than the cost of the gift.[21]

A certain tension existed among the Roman elite between this system of
friendly reciprocity and kinship networks, a tension that was epitomized by
the widely maligned figure of the inheritance hunter, the *captator*.[22] People
were suspecting of offering ingratiating friendly services to rich and childless
Romans in order to profit from inheritances; conversely, upper-class Romans
were suspected of deliberately remaining childless in order to receive such
ingratiating services. I will argue that a more subtle version of this
phenomenon took place on the level of political patronage, and partially
explains why there are relatively few siblings and offspring to be found
among Pliny's circle: the system of political patronage seems to have acted as a
disincentive to child-rearing.[23] It has been recognized that having too many
children made it more difficult for any one of them to have a successful
career.[24] More importantly, however, it may have made it more difficult for
the father to attract patronage in well-placed circles. Being saddled with too
strong a natural kinship network was apparently a disadvantage in establishing

---

[20] Merwald 1964:26.

[21] On patronage in traditional societies of the twentieth century, see for example Scott
(1977:25): "The generosity [of wealthy patrons] redounds to their growing prestige and serves
to surround them with a grateful clientele which helps validate their position in the community.
It represents, in addition, a set of social debts which can be converted into goods and services
if need be."

[22] See Champlin 1991:87–102, 201–02.

[23] Parkin merely confesses that "precise causes for the decline in fertility are not readily
apparent" (1992:133).

[24] Hopkins 1983:78.

a very different kind of network, the delicate, artificial bonds of friendship, loyalty, and patronage.

Captatio was simply a crass version of a widespread tendency in the upper reaches of imperial patronage. The childlessness both of the emperor and of so many of his courtiers is one more sign of how the emperor and the courtiers are reflections of each other, shaped by similar pressures and ideologies. Moreover, the conflict between actual childlessness and the official encouragement of child-rearing points to yet another fundamental tension in upper-class life. By seeing how Pliny's letters confront the competing pressures of kinship and patronage, we can understand better how these pressures worked and how they affected upper-class life and discourse. We will see marks of these pressures throughout Book 1, from the family of the Greek philosopher Euphrates to that of the Roman statesman Corellius, and from the donation of child-support payments to the marriage of Rusticus' daughter.

IDEOLOGY AND LITERARY STYLE

Pliny's style has been widely admired, but less often analyzed.[25] As we shall see, Pliny's brilliant style often expresses or cloaks deeper concerns and tensions, which we can better understand through analyzing his literary style. Conversely, examining the tensions beneath the carefree surface can help us see more accurately just how Pliny's rhetoric works. For example, the use of ring composition often gives an important clue to the underlying tensions in a letter.[26] A letter often returns to its opening topic at the end, but usually with significant alteration. The opening lines often give a retrospective look to a prior letter from the addressee, a request, or a problem, and the closing lines give us another view of the same topic, but looking forward to an outcome or solution. By seeing how the course of the letter has transformed the opening topic we can get an indirect look at what the rhetoric of the letter is doing, and how Pliny is using the rhetoric to confront the ideological contradictions of his world. Similarly, another typical device, the interweaving of boasting and modesty, often serves not only to let Pliny praise himself without incurring ill

---

[25] For examples, see Mommsen 1869:32 ("Klarheit und Anmuth der Sprache"), Syme 1958:96 ("for graciousness of style... variety... delicacy... tact, the correspondence of Pliny has no rival"), and Fantham 1996:220 ("Pliny was more of a stylist, notoriously molding conventional content into brilliant form").

[26] See the chapters on letters 1.12, 1.18, and 1.23. Guillemin compares Martial's use of ring composition (1929:147–48).

will, but also to confront specific objections to various aspects of his laudatory picture of ruling-class life.[27]

Finally, I hope to call greater attention to the numerous fine points of Pliny's style. Pliny the careful stylist often makes significant use of single words, in etymological wordplay (e.g. 1.5.16 *prudens–providere*), significant metaphors (e.g. 1.24.4 the "dowered" estate), and poeticisms (1.3.1 the "jeweled" watercourse). He sometimes seems to give special point to the meaning of names (e.g. 1.5 Modestus, 1.14 Rusticus) or dates (e.g. 1.12 Corellius' illness, 1.13 Nonianus' reading). His frequent use of Greek, taboo in more formal genres, often has a specific point beyond displaying the prestigious bilingual culture of Pliny and his friends.[28] Greek can give learnedness, distance, lightheartedness, or philosophical weightiness; often a quoted passage has deeper bearing on Pliny's meaning (as the Homeric passages in 1.18). Above all we need to be alert to Pliny's often casual and subtle insertion of significant terms such as jealousy, regret, shame, complaint, advice, obedience, and so on. Not everyone will agree with each of my interpretations of such fine points. I hope, however, that the collective weight of evidence, in passage after passage, will convince readers to be more alert both to the brilliance and subtlety of Pliny's style, and to the contribution the style makes to his overall political and ideological purposes.

---

[27] See the chapters on letters 1.8, 1.10, and 1.23. Rudd's discussion of this device, which he aptly calls "stratagems of vanity," stays on the general level of showing how Pliny manages his self-praise (1992:26–32).

[28] Pliny's subtle use of Greek, though admired by many critics (e.g. Sherwin-White 1966:182, Hutchinson 1993:270), has not been adequately examined.

NO REGRETS? LITERARY AND POLITICAL
PROGRAMMATIC ELEMENTS IN 1.1

The first letter is a dedication letter, with an explanation of how the collection came into being. It is therefore the obvious place to look for programmatic claims about Pliny's intentions in publishing the collection. Two explicit claims have been widely noted. Pliny claims that he has selected "rather carefully written" letters (*si quas... curatius scripsissem,* 1.1.1), and that he has not put them into chronological order *(non servato temporis ordine),* but rather, into the random order in which "each one had come into [his] hands" *(ut quaeque in manus venerat).*

Both claims are disingenuous, but they do contain a grain of truth. The letters *are* carefully written, though we can probably reject Pliny's implied assertion that he is publishing them unrevised and unselected, with their (original) stylistic excellence being the only criterion for including them. And they are indeed out of order (within each book, that is), though we can reject the implication that they are in random order.[1] Yet in addition to these two topics, literary style and chronological order, this little letter provides much more programmatic material about the purpose and meaning of the collection.

First, we should note that this dedication letter differs from ordinary dedicatory epistles since it introduces a book of other letters. In form it is merely one letter among many, though of course its content displays the conventional dedicatory motif of explaining how the book came into being through the initiation or encouragement of the dedicatee.[2] Each of the letters is above all the record of a friendship, and therefore this first letter,

---

[1] Merrill, for example, observes that the letters show "a skilful selection and a careful arrangement in all the books" (1912:160 ad loc.); see also Mommsen 1869:31.

[2] Prose examples are *ad Herenn.* 1.1, Cic. *de Orat.* 1.4; see Janson 1964:116–18, Curtius 1953:85. A poetic analogue is Catullus 1, which Pliny's uncle actually cites at the start of his own dedicatory epistle (*NH* praef. 1).

portraying the ideal friendship between Pliny and Septicius Clarus, will serve as a model for the entire collection. The friendship that generated this book and that is commemorated on its opening page will be a representative friendship in this book of friendships. The letter presents several aspects of this friendship. First, it is a self-perpetuating cycle of encouragement and favors, a cycle that is embodied by the self-perpetuating exchange of the letters themselves. It is therefore essentially equal in spite of whatever public power each friend possesses, and in spite of who is giving the favor and who is receiving it at a particular time, since the sincere friendship makes the friends' powers and favors mutually beneficial. Moreover, because of this sincere circulation of favors, which transforms social ranking into friendly equality, there is no place for regret in the lives of Pliny and his friends. And finally, their friendships generate a higher value out of their everyday activities, just as Pliny's friendship with Clarus generated this book of literary value out of nugatory everyday letters.

The dedication letter thus establishes an idealizing portrayal of Pliny's social circle, a portrayal that will continue throughout the corpus. Pliny suggests that between himself and his less powerful but rising friend there exist perfectly harmonious, reciprocal, and mutually beneficial relations that ignore differences in status and that do not calculate the specific value of individual favors. Pliny and his friends interact as free and equal individuals, without any prior calculation of the mutual benefits that arise, as if fortuitously, from their interactions. These relations are epitomized by the reciprocal exchange of the letters themselves, seemingly valueless tokens of friendly exchange that are actually loaded with the pricelessly valuable symbolic capital of political favors and social status.[3] Furthermore, in suggesting that both Clarus and himself will have "no regrets" over their decision to publish the letters (1.1.2), Pliny is tactfully proclaiming that he and his friends have no regrets, neither for their writings nor for their actions. On the literal level, Pliny is confronting the problem of the literary value of a nugatory genre, private letters, claiming that the future literary success of the letters will prove their value. But also, since the letters purport to reflect the lives of Pliny's circle, Pliny hints that he and his friends live exemplary lives

---

[3] Cicero's programmatic letter to Curio on letter-writing suggests the mutual benefit of epistolary exchange: *ut certiores faceremus absentis, si quid esset, quod eos scire aut nostra aut ipsorum interesset* ("to inform those who are absent, if there is anything which is *in our or their own interest* for them to know," *Fam.* 2.4.1). On "equality" in friendship between unequals, see Cic. *de Amicit.* 69. On mutual benefits in friendship, see e.g. Cic. *de Amicit.* 30, 51, Sen. *Ep.* 7.8, 48.2–3. Of course, the notion that one gives *for the purpose* of receiving must be repudiated (e.g. 9.30.2, Cic. *de Amicit.* 27–32, Sen. *de Benef.* 1.1.9–1.2.3; cf. Aristot. *EN* 8.4 1157A15 and Dixon 1993:452–56).

with no regrets for their actions; therefore they can all face the publication of casual letters between close friends with eagerness rather than fear.[4]

LITERARY FAVORS AND SELF-FULFILLING PROPHECIES

In choosing a knight rather than a leading senator for the dedication, Pliny does more than avoid offending other senators (as Sherwin-White claims, 1966:85 on 1.1). He also advertises that he is near the top of the Roman world, and in no need of a flattering dedication upwards to solicit or repay patronage. Though Pliny still stands very much in need of patronage from the inner imperial circle, he pretends that his position in a free and powerful Senate is secure, and that unlike a lower-status writer such as Martial or Statius, he can afford to offer the dedication purely out of friendly sentiment. Actually, the entire corpus will serve as a flattering tribute to the emperor and the existing power structure. Pliny has no need of so coarse a gesture as a flattering dedication upwards on the social scale; scattered letters of praise will do the job more discreetly.[5]

We happen to know enough about Clarus, however, to get a closer idea of the real power relations between him and Pliny. He was a knight, but one with brilliant future prospects under Hadrian, and the uncle of a young man who, under Pliny's patronage (2.9), was just starting a highly successful senatorial career.[6] He might therefore be considered an example of Pliny's "knack of preselecting the leaders of the next generation."[7] Other such rising or future leaders are Catilius Severus (1.22), Pompeius Falco (1.23), Rosianus Geminus (7.1), and the two promising youths of 6.11, Fuscus Salinator and Ummidius Quadratus.

But the ranks of future leaders in Pliny's letters are more probably a *vaticinium ex eventu,* a prophecy after the fact. The presence in Book 1 of so

---

[4] Philosophical diatribe also advocated living a life without regret, e.g. Sen. *Ep.* 92.29, 115.18, *de Vita Beata* 7.4, Epictetus 2.22.35, *Encheir.* 34, fr. 25 (Stob. 3.20.67), M. Aurelius *Med.* 3.4.2, 8.2, 8.53, 11.19, Cic. *Muren.* 61, *Tusc. Disp.* 5.53, 81; Guillemin 1929:90. The ideal emperor also lives without regrets (Suet. *Tit.* 10.1; compare Piso at Tac. *Hist.* 1.15.3).

[5] As Zelzer observes (1964:160), most of the letters are aimed at knights and North Italians rather than to members of the highest political class. Yet Pliny includes enough intimate letters to current leaders such as Servianus (3.17, 6.26) to flaunt his closeness to the power set. His numerous letters to lesser friends, on the other hand, flaunt how unpretentious he is to stay on an "equal" footing with the class from which he has risen.

[6] Clarus was praetorian prefect under Hadrian until he was dismissed around 122 C.E., along with Suetonius the secretary *ab epistulis,* because of palace intrigue or scandal (*HA Hadr.* 11.3; see Syme 1958:779). He also received the dedication of Suetonius' *Lives of the Caesars* (Joh. Lydus *de Magistratibus* 2.6).

[7] Sherwin-White 1966:157 on 2.9.1.

many future leaders is probably due not so much to his amazing prescience in the opening months of the new regime, as to his judicious editing years later. Moreover, in a relatively closed hierarchical system such as the Roman political system, future success can be predicted with good accuracy. We might compare trying to predict future leaders 10 or 20 years in advance in a modern closed system such as a military or academic hierarchy. Clarus may well have already had enough progress in his political career, or enough intimacy with Hadrian, to mark him out for future success. The choice of Hadrian as heir apparent, a taboo topic in Pliny's letters, may have become increasingly clear over the years 97 to 108.[8]

Pliny, then, is dedicating his book to a possibly lower-ranking but probably up-and-coming colleague. Dedicating a book is a political act, just as offering or accepting an invitation to dinner (the subject of Pliny's next letter to Clarus, 1.15) is a political act. Pliny's choice of dedicatee reveals something of the ambiguities of his own status as a high-ranking senator. On the one hand, he is near the pinnacle of Roman politics. He comes from a prominent family of Comum, his uncle Pliny the Elder rose to the upper reaches of an equestrian career as a "friend" of the Flavians, and he himself rose quickly through the senatorial *cursus* to the consulship under the patronage of three emperors and of high ranking senators such as Corellius Rufus and Verginius Rufus. A "new man," like his model Cicero, he was an outsider who had made it to the top.[9]

Under the imperial system, however, the position of "new man" had acquired counterbalancing advantages, because now all patronage was ultimately controlled by the emperor. The emperor could promote a new man and trust him precisely because he had no independent prestige and power which could interfere with his loyalty—like the notorious ex-slaves for which Bad Emperors were reviled (e.g. 6.31.9, *Pan.* 88.1). Similarly, many critical positions in running the empire were entrusted to equestrian men who owed their position directly to the emperor's patronage.[10] In sum, it might not have

---

[8] The *Historia Augusta* indicates a special relationship between Trajan and Hadrian starting with Trajan's guardianship in 86 C.E. and rising to hints of imperial succession from the year 105—although many of these signs of future success could have been invented after the fact. Syme notes the "remarkable" absence of Hadrian and his circle of kin and friends from the letters (1958:88); Servianus "is the nearest he gets to Hadrian" (1985:358 on 6.26). Pliny broaches the sensitive topic of the heir only at *Pan.* 94.5, praying that after a long reign, Trajan may be succeeded by a natural *or adopted* son.

[9] Pliny's boast that he attained the consulship at a "much younger" age than did Cicero (4.8.5) is disingenuous. Cicero was elected to a year-long and powerful position, whereas Pliny was appointed by the emperor among about eight suffect consuls to a brief and powerless term of office.

[10] Hopkins (1983:171 n. 66) cites the memoirs of Louis XIV in relation to the new man in imperial politics. "It was not in my interest to seek men of more eminent rank... [Since] those

been certain whose position was, or was likely to become, more powerful, a senator or an imperial favorite with a successful equestrian career.

While superficially condescending to an inferior, Pliny is also investing in a family of future promise; the dedication is comparable, in a small way, to his uncle's dedication letter to Titus the heir apparent in 77 C.E. (*NH* praef. 3). Neither uncle nor nephew could have known, of course, that they would not live to reap the benefits of their investments. Pliny's actual investment, a letter opening his book, is of course trivial, but it can offer Clarus something that Titus, by contrast, already had, the prospect of immortal fame. Clarus was apparently interested in literature (as Pliny's literary banquet suggests, 1.15.2–3), but not a writer himself (as the implied contrast with his "eloquent" brother-in-law suggests, 2.9.4). He may therefore have been especially eager for help from writers such as Pliny and Suetonius to immortalize his name. To Titus, the most that the Elder could offer was public testimony of his easygoing, untyrannical ways in condescending to an "equal" friendship with the author. Conversely, Pliny's display of his intimate friendship with Clarus gives public testimony of Clarus' intimate friendship with the more famous Pliny. Hence, both dedications emphasize the intimacy between the writer and his friend.[11] The Elder, dedicating a scientific treatise, must portray the intimacy of the friendship in the dedicatory letter, and in writing to the powerful Titus, the job is best done by simply announcing that he is being jauntily informal (*NH* praef. 1 *licentiore epistula,* 2 *alia procaci epistula,* etc.). Pliny, on the other hand, can simply *be* bold and easygoing with Clarus, and in a book of letters he can wait until later to display their intimacy fully—in letter 1.15, by far the most casual and intimate letter of the opening book, with its colloquial opening *(heus tu!)* and mock angry lawsuit.[12] So free and easy are their relations that Clarus can feel free about standing Pliny up for dinner (1.15) even though he will need Pliny's future patronage (as for his

---

whom I chose to serve me... were conscious of who they were, they had no higher aspirations than those I chose to permit." On the other hand, established senior senators such as Spurinna, Frontinus, or Arrius Antoninus could help establish a new, insecure emperor precisely because of their independent prestige (see Sherwin-White 1966:154).

[11] We can compare Augustus' complaint that Horace was ashamed that posterity would know that he was Augustus' friend (*an vereris ne apud posteros infame tibi sit, quod videaris familiaris nobis esse?* Suet. *de Poetis* fr. 40 Reifferscheid).

[12] Compare Iulius Victor on letter-writing: *lepidum est nonnumquam quasi praesentem alloqui, uti 'heus tu' et 'quid ais' et 'video te deridere': quod genus apud M. Tullium multa sunt* (448.32–33 Halm). Victor's warning against joking with a superior confirms that jokes can convey social equality: *Epistola, si superiori scribas, ne iocularis sit; si pari, ne inhumana; si inferiori, ne superba* (448.16–17 Halm).

nephew, 2.9). That Clarus can risk offending Pliny, and that Pliny can pretend to be angry in such a touchy situation, are public proofs of their intimacy.[13]

The dedication letter not only ignores the official ranking of Pliny and Clarus, but even seems to invert it. Clarus has often exhorted Pliny *(hortatus es),* giving advice *(consilii)* to publish his letters. "Exhortation" and "advice" can go upwards or downwards on the social ladder, but they fit the downward direction better, from a superior to an inferior. Even the emperor, to be sure, can receive "advice" from advisers (his *consilium*), but this is clearly a charade of freedom and equality: he is not likely to obey against his wishes, nor are advisers likely to oppose his known wishes.[14] Pliny, though, is "obeying" Clarus' advice (1.1.2 *obsequii*), apparently reluctantly, since Clarus has had to exhort "often."[15] The trope of reluctant obedience allows Pliny to praise his own book through the voice of someone else (Clarus), in a typically modest cloak for his boastful self-praise (Rudd 1992:26–27). For example, in 1.2 he attributes news of his literary success to the booksellers' flattery, and in 1.10 he has Euphrates the philosopher (the ostensible *laudandus*) praise Pliny's political activities as being the "most splendid part" of philosophy.

Pliny's report of Clarus' actual exhortation similarly combines self-praise with self-deprecation. "You have often exhorted me that, *if* I have written *any* letters *a little more* carefully, I should collect and publish them" *(si quas paulo curatius...).* The deprecatory tone shows the same (insincere) pairing of the author's low opinion with the patron's high opinion, as in Catullus 1, with the "trifles" (in Catullus' reckoning) that are "something" in Nepos' reckoning. The conditional *si quas* stands in for the relative *quas.*[16] But it also suggests uncertainty about whether any letters *are* well written.[17] Furthermore, the comparative "rather well-written" serves as a diminutive.[18] The word *paulo*

---

[13] See Cic. *de Amic.* 66 on lightheartedness in friendship (*amicitia* remissior *esse debet et* liberior...). Janson's claim that dedications to superiors and to inferiors have very much the same form (1964:116) does not apply to emperors.

[14] Pliny makes much of the free expression of advice by privy counselors (4.22.3, 6.31.12) and senators (8.14.10, *Pan.* 76.3), as opposed to "the servility of prior times" (8.14.2; cf. Juv. 4.85–86). Trajan "obeys" the Senate in accepting consulships (*Pan.* 60.4, 78.1); he even became emperor through this ultimate imperial virtue, obedience (*Pan.* 9.3, 9.5).

[15] Pliny seems to be the first to mention "obedience" in a dedication (Janson 1964:119).

[16] *OLD* s.v. *quis* 1a; manuscripts BF omit *si* by error.

[17] Döring (1843) comments on the modesty in *si* ("Bescheidenheit"). Compare 3.9.21 *si quam haberem in dicendo facultatem,* and Gamberini 1983:133.

[18] For the "diminutive" use of the comparative see Kühner-Stegmann 1966:II.2.475 §225 Anm. 19: "... ziemlich, etwas, ein wenig ... entweder überschreitend oder nicht erreichend." Quintilian's example of comparative for positive (*Inst.* 9.3.19 *infirmiorem,* "rather unwell") seems to be a diminutive comparative. Janson notes that dedications often express modesty through actual diminutives, such as *opusculum* or *lucubratiuncula* (1964:146).

("a little bit") reinforces the diminutive, modest tone: there may be some letters written more carefully, even if only by a little bit.

Pliny has nevertheless shown us from the first word *(frequenter)* that Clarus' opinion was enthusiastic; the diminutive, deprecating terms in Clarus' indirect command were evidently not Clarus' own words. Pliny has elegantly conflated the two voices of Catullus 1.3–4, the diffident author and the enthusiastic patron, into a single phrase, in which the friend's praise shows through the author's modest screen, which toned down Clarus' enthusiastic praise of Pliny's magnificent letters. Pliny's and Catullus' modesty is conventional in a dedication, and it deflects the blame for publishing a bad book from the diffident author to the confident dedicatee, who picks up the symbolic tab of blame if the book is a failure. With his dedication Catullus repays Nepos for symbolically extending a line of credit by "reckoning" that his "trifles were something." If the book proves to be worthless, it was the dedicatee's fault for encouraging its publication against the author's initial wishes. Conversely, Pliny's "obedience" to Clarus gives Clarus the credit for the success of the book.[19] Clarus' encouragement is a self-fulfilling prophecy, a typical motif in the letters. The circulation of praise is credited with the practical function of encouraging Pliny and his friends to fulfill the praise (Trisoglio 1972:143).

What is the value of the letters? This question can arise in any literary or even political activity, but it arises most pressingly in low-prestige, nugatory genres such as Catullus' short poetry or Pliny's letters. The opening letter is the first of Pliny's many attempts to deal with the nagging question of the value of his literary activities, and the related question of the value of his political activities. In the next letter he continues to deal with this anxiety, by reporting the booksellers' assurances that his earlier works are still popular (1.2.6). At the end of 1.1, Pliny expresses this anxiety over value briefly: it remains for neither of us to have regrets, you for your advice, and me for my compliance (1.1.2). They will *regret* the publication if the book turns out to be a failure; conversely, the success of his hendecasyllables (7.4.9) keeps him from *regretting* that he published them *(nec paenitet,* 7.4.8). Pliny banishes the specter of literary failure by future action, the publication of later volumes, which he is evidently already planning. These future volumes will prove that neither Clarus nor Pliny have regrets over this one *(ita enim fiet,* 2). Behind

---

[19] The request theme "frees the writer from a certain amount of the responsibility for the work" (Janson 1964:124). The usual version, that the friend gave the writer the confidence or motivation to *write* the book (Janson 1964:116, White 1974:54), obviously cannot be used for the letters, which are theoretically already written.

Pliny's anxious pose lies the optimistic hope that by continuing to publish further volumes, Pliny is proving the lasting value of his work.[20]

Pliny's prediction of future volumes also serves as an elastic clause in the dedication. By encouraging the publication of this first volume, the "patron" has earned the honor of having it dedicated to him. Then the success of the first volume will by itself encourage future publication, replacing the function that Clarus fulfilled for the first volume. Indirectly, then, all volumes will have been published because of Clarus' encouragement, and will all be dedicated to him through this elastic clause. The elastic clause not only dedicates all future volumes to Clarus, but also demonstrates why he earns these future dedications.[21] The circulation of symbolic capital through the exchange of friendly favors is a mutually beneficial and self-perpetuating process, and not a closed barter of finite goods in a zero-sum system.[22] In bringing literary fame to Pliny, Clarus brings reflected fame to himself, and the successful literary enterprise thus initiated grows on its own success, bestowing unlimited benefit to both partners. These private letters, ostensibly written to be read by one person on one occasion, will bestow lasting fame both on the writer Pliny and on the representative addressee Clarus. An epistolary correspondence, in which writer and addressee trade places by turns, is the perfect symbol for this mutually beneficial cycle of friendly favors. But the artificial one-way nature of the published collection, which includes no return letters, dramatizes the fact that the center of fame is Pliny himself, whereas Clarus is merely an empty place-holder, who could be replaced by any other friend.

Pliny's modest claim that the letters are in random order (*ut quaeque in manus venerat,* 1.1.1) is characteristic for a genre of minor, shorter works, which differ from major genres such as history, epic, or oratory in having no temporal or logical connection from beginning to end.[23] Indeed, continuous narrative is rare in the letters; the three narrative letters to Tacitus are explicitly aimed outside the epistolary genre, towards history (6.16, 6.20, 7.33). But again Pliny's modest pose conceals self-praise. He "was not

---

[20] Sherwin-White claims that Pliny's modesty "rings true" (1966:333 on 5.8); but it is merely a consistent persona that tells us little about his "true" feelings. He is certainly eager to rival Cicero in his speeches (e.g. 1.5.12, 4.8.4, Riggsby 1995:130), and perhaps in his letters (9.2.2), and thus clearly hopes for immortality like Cicero's (or Demosthenes', 4.5, 6.33, 7.30); see Bütler 1970:34 36. Pliny's pose of modesty fits Quintilian's warnings against boasting of one's oratorical skill (*Inst.* 11.1.15–22).

[21] As Murgia points out, letter 1.1 serves as a dedicatory preface for all nine volumes in Pliny's final edition (1985:181).

[22] Here as elsewhere I am merely elucidating Pliny's rhetoric, not agreeing with it.

[23] Similarly, Martial modestly suggests that the reader can make the book shorter by stopping anywhere (10.1; cf. 4.89.6–7).

composing a *history"* (1.1.1), which might be read out of human curiosity for information or narrative interest. Oratory and poetry must be of the "highest eloquence" to win favor, but history can please simply by satisfying people's curiosity about the facts (5.8.4; cf. 3.13.2, Vitruv. 5 praef. 1, cited at Syme 1958:117 n. 2). Each letter, Pliny suggests, stands on its own, deserving to be read not only as a record of Pliny's and his friends' lives, but also as a miniature of stylistic perfection. Pliny may even be suggesting a contrast with his great predecessor, whose letters to Atticus, published in chronological order, might well be read out of historical curiosity, as Nepos remarks (*Atticus* 16.3–4).[24] Pliny's later apologies for the comparative lack of political excitement in his times and letters (3.20.10, 9.2.2–3) have the same double edge of self-deprecation and self-praise: if his letters are less exciting in their contents, they are all the more impressive in being worth reading for their literary value.

The contrast with Cicero's letters highlights a more important aspect of letter-publication that the dedication ignores, or rather, suppresses: the problem of privacy. The most pressing problem in publishing one's own letters is neither "is this written carefully enough?" nor "what order should I use?" but "am I willing for this to become public?" In pretending to consider only the first two problems, Pliny elegantly disguises his biggest pretense, the pretense that nothing has been omitted or rewritten out of the fear or shame of public exposure. Pliny's epistolary persona has no secrets, no bad conscience, in a word, no regrets. Pliny does nothing to cause regret, is not ashamed of his actions, and does not need to apologize. Thus all his letters can be freely displayed in public, and by implication, Pliny's entire private and political life, which the letters symbolize and reveal, can also be displayed in public. Pliny only confesses to shame or regret with disingenuousness, to reveal a "flaw" that the reader sees to be a virtue, as, for example, when he "confesses" to feeling human grief over his slaves' deaths rather than maintaining "wiser" philosophical equanimity over the mere financial loss (8.16.3).

The contrast with Cicero's letters is clear. Cicero frequently worries about the secrecy of his letters (e.g. *Att.* 10.11.1, 10.18.1–2, 11.4a), and his accidental discovery of his brother's letters (11.9) led to a devastating break in their relations.[25] He sometimes resorts to tricks of disguise, such as writing sensitive matters in Greek, or in riddling phrases, or both, as in the

---

[24] Döring comments on the implied contrast to the chronological Atticus letters of Cicero (1843 on 1.1.1), which apparently became a definitive model for later letter-writers (Cugusi 1983:188).

[25] On the secrecy of private letters, see e.g. Cic. *Phil.* 2.7, Quint. *Inst.* 1.1.29, Suet. *Jul.* 56.6, Aul. Gell. 17.9.2; Cugusi 1983:188.

"tyrannicide from Croton" (i.e. Milo, 6.4.3).[26] Furthermore, Cicero often asks Atticus for advice, not in Pliny's casual manner of asking a question to which he already knows the right answer, but in the agonizingly torn mood of a man who is genuinely undecided—or rather, who knows what he must do and will do, but who has unavoidable second thoughts because the choice he knows he must take will have unacceptable results. In a word, Cicero experiences his regrets in advance, even before he performs the action. Should I give my brother the burden of taking over my province, or should I endanger the province in the hands of an incompetent quaestor (e.g. 5.21.9, 6.3.1–2, 6.6.3–4)? Should I go over to Caesar's side or declare myself for Pompey (e.g. 7.1.2–4, and throughout books 7–10)? This dilemma, and other major decisions, give Cicero deep regrets (e.g. 11.6.2 *consili paenitet,* 8.12.5 *ingemiscens sum recordatus*).[27]

We can recognize this difference between Cicero's anxious letters and Pliny's regret-free letters as the difference between authentic letters and artificial letters from which all messy, difficult decisions have been left out. Pliny himself, however, presents his letters as the authentic record of an ideal person in an ideal time, in which neither agonizing decisions nor regrets ever arise. Pliny's optimistic, regret-free persona implies praise of the new emperors, under whom this ideal life is possible. In truth, though, there *is* a contrast between Cicero's times and Pliny's: the pressures of open civic strife generate Cicero's agonizing decision-making, whereas the imperial system tends to flatten out personal and political expression into a single authorized voice. To this change Tacitus attributes the decline of oratory (*Dial.* 40–41) and Pliny the lack of political news (3.20.10–12). At most, imperial politics could create a pair of simple but opposite voices, either under a "bad emperor" or in retrospective denigration of a "bad emperor." Hence it is during the flashbacks to Domitianic times that Pliny shows himself facing real decisions; and it is here that he must be most careful to show that he has no regrets even for his successful career under Domitian.

Even under Domitian Pliny managed to get out of potentially dishonorable decisions, as when the "gods" helped him out on the witness stand when Regulus kept pressing a dangerous question onto him about a man banished by Domitian, Mettius Modestus (1.5.7). His Senate under Domitian sounds less guilty than in Tacitus' comparable description (8.14.8–9, Tac. *Agric.* 45.1–2):

---

[26] Riepl 1913:316–18, Nicholson 1994:43–52. Iulius Victor (448.5–9 Halm) advises making secrets clear to the addressee by using *notae,* as do Caesar, Augustus, and Cicero.

[27] Seneca criticizes a letter (no longer extant) to Atticus in which Cicero laments the past, complains about the present, and is in despair about the future, instead of having the proper philosophical contentment (*Brev. Vit.* 5.2–3): regret, complaint, and despair are three versions of the same vice. At *Ep.* 118.1–2 Seneca rejects the anxieties over political matters that fill Cicero's letters to Atticus, in favor of looking within oneself for peace and freedom.

Pliny rejects the charge of collaboration in Domitian's crimes, to which Tacitus confesses. Under the new regime, however, he never has to make the choice between saving his skin or choosing the honorable course of action, or worse, between two dangerous *and* dishonorable courses, as Cicero's dilemma in 50–49 B.C.E. When he asks for advice, he generally shapes the terms of the question to make the "correct" answer clear. For example, Aristo is evidently supposed to admire the legal quibbles by which Pliny forced a humane, "lenient" decision out of a harsh Senate that was inclined to execute the ex-slaves of a consul who died in suspicious circumstances (8.14.21 *mitius*). Pliny is not in despair or even indecision: he already knows the correct answer. Even in his official letters to Trajan, Pliny tends to slant the question to produce the desired answer, or to display foreknowledge of the anticipated answer, making Trajan's answers rarely a surprise. This process of second-guessing was an inevitable feature of political advice-giving between a monarchical ruler and his deputies.

When Pliny does portray himself as caught in a conflict of obligations or a conflict of desires, it is in order to dramatize how he always resolves such conflicts smoothly. When his friend asks if he would act against the people of Baetica, his client province, he can appeal to his friend's own better judgment, against his friend's immediate desire (1.7.3).[28] Rufus' alternative request (either to act against them or not to act for them) was already designed to elicit this honorable response. Similarly, Pliny can sit in judgment in a testamentary dispute which pits his friend's interests against his own, and at his friend's own request (5.1); although he decides against Curianus, he later donates his share to Curianus to free his co-heirs from a dangerous suit, and nevertheless he later inherits from this very Curianus. Pliny can also smoothly resolve his perennial conflict between obligation and desire, between his political obligations and his desire for leisure and literature. He always chooses to fulfill his political obligations, and he has enough time for leisure as well; indeed, he is able to transmute the dross of political obligation into the gold of literature, since his two major genres, oratory and epistolography, derive much of their content from his political activities. In sum, Pliny only confesses regrets and vices in his generalizing philosophic diatribes, in which he eagerly joins in the collective guilt of humanity, predominantly in the later books, when he has already established his virtuous persona (especially 7.26, 8.22, 9.12, 9.30.4).

Pliny is not the only one to live without regrets and embarrassments. Neither Clarus will regret his advice to publish, nor will Pliny regret obeying

---

[28] See Nichols 1980:376: "The conflict of coinciding obligations is not... uncommon... Pliny devotes a number of letters to resolving such painful choices (e.g. 1.7 and 4.17)." Seneca also advises consulting the friend's better judgment (Sen. *Ben.* 6.33.1; Guillemin 1927:7 n. 2).

it (1.1.2). The fact that Clarus, the representative addressee, is urging the
reluctant Pliny to publish suggests that Pliny's friends have even less to fear
than does Pliny from the published letters. Indeed, Clarus is not even
embarrassed for letter 1.15 to be published, potentially the most embarrassing
letter in the book. The broken dinner appointment shows that Clarus had to
manage conflicting obligations of his own. Despite Pliny's teasing, it is likely
that Clarus was not lusting after oysters, or dancing-women of Gades (1.15.3)
with their quivering buttocks (Mart. 5.78.27, 6.71.2, 14.203, Juv. 11.162–64),
but that he felt it necessary to cultivate another powerful patron.[29] The teasing
tone suggests that Clarus shares Pliny's high-minded scorn of luxury, but felt
obliged to attend the boorish banquet anyway.[30] With Pliny's support already
in his pocket, Clarus felt it necessary to stand him up and endure an evening
with a *nescio quem* (3) whose patronage he will also need, to further his
nephew's or his own career. Thus, even this, seemingly a rare example of a
discreditable letter, actually redounds to Clarus' credit. Clarus is intimate
enough with the powerful Pliny to stand him up without offense, moderate
enough to prefer Pliny's "simple fare" in good Trajanic style (e.g. 6.31.13),
but dutiful enough to endure an evening of boorish luxury to fulfill a social
obligation.

   The last line of the dedication letter, the elastic clause that stretches into the
past and future, generalizes this lack of regret onto the whole life of Pliny and
of his friends. Pliny will offer the rest of his letters, past and future, to the
public without worrying about the publication of private secrets, just as he
published this first volume without worries. Old letters which are lying
around neglected he will seek out, presumably whether they are in his files or
in his friends'. Neither side will be reluctant to have them made public. Still
more bold is his statement on future letters: he will not "suppress" them.[31]
Pliny can already guarantee that he and his friends will live their lives in such
a way that they will continue to have no regrets to impede the publication of
personal letters in the future.

   We might skeptically assume that once Pliny has started to publish his
correspondence, he will pre-censor all future letters with an eye toward

---

[29] On the political importance of dinner parties for creating alliances and demonstrating status,
see Ellis 1991:119. Gunderson comments that the prurient connotations of *Gaditanae* might be
intensified by the preceding mention of sow's wombs (1.15.3 *vulvas*) on the menu of the
supposititious rival dinner party (1997:220).
[30] Martial has a more satirical description of someone refusing a friend's invitation in order to
seek more expensive meals (5.44).
[31] The term *(supprimam)* can be used simply of avoiding publication (as of Proculus' poems,
3.15.3), but it is also used of political suppression, as when emperors "suppress" opponents'
wills (Suet. *Calig.* 16.3, *Nero* 34.5) or news of Vitellius' or Vespasian's revolts (Tac. *Hist.*
1.50.1, 2.96.2). Compare Curtius Rufus 3.7.15, on suppressing a letter out of political fears.

publication, making sure he writes nothing that could cause embarrassment. But that may be little different from the letters of Book 1; even here the pose of authentic, unedited letters need not be entirely fictitious. Much of Pliny's careful self-crafting of his public image could have been already present in the original versions of the letters. Even Cicero's authentic private letters can be as complacent and self-congratulatory as those of Pliny, when he is not faced with the crushing pressures of late Republican civic strife. For example, the letters on his proconsulship have more unmitigated self-praise than anything in Pliny (*Att.* 5.16.2–3, 5.21.5, 6.2.4–5, 6.3.3 are just a few of many such passages). In sum, every member of the ruling class, whether emperor or citizen, carries out all activities of life, even private activities, with their public impact in mind. This constant discipline makes the self-fashioning "natural," and Pliny himself may well have considered these letters the authentic record of his private life and inner thoughts.

Just as the pose of an ideal life without regrets implicitly praises the ideal emperor, so the elastic future clause projects that praise indefinitely into the future. The most pressing anxiety during the reign of a "good emperor" is the uncertain future of the emperor. Will the good emperor Trajan be replaced by a bad emperor, or turn into one? All that is needed to make a "bad emperor" are a few conspiracies and senatorial executions, followed by a rough transition to a successor who has more to gain by denigrating than praising his predecessor. The greatest praise Pliny can offer Trajan is not merely that he makes it possible for the ruling class to live honorably and securely. Pliny even pretends that the fundamental anxiety of the imperial system, the total dependence on the life and whim of one person, is gone. The fear of future "bad emperors" is absent from Book 1, where it belongs because of the disturbances of imperial transition at the time. Only in Book 9 does Pliny venture to mention the fears of the time (9.13.10–12)—fears that have presumably died out after years of security.

VILLAS
FACTORIES OF LITERATURE (1.3)

Letter 1.3, to a fellow townsman, deals with two cardinal areas of value in Pliny's life, real estate and literature. The wealthy lifestyle of Pliny and his circle exploited a disproportionate share of land and resources, and the labor of numerous workers, free and slave.[1] Though we are surely not to imagine that the typical wealthy person was constantly tormented by guilt over this inequitable distribution of resources, the widespread criticism of luxury in Roman moralizing discourse may have reflected or even caused a certain amount of anxiety, and the luxury villa was often the focus of such criticism.[2] We can discern in Pliny's letter traces of anxiety concerning this expensive item from the way he minimizes both the luxury materials out of which the villa is built, and the slave labor that supports and maintains it. Instead, he inverts or displaces the real conditions of luxury expenditure, ownership, and slavery: the villa "owns" the man, the landowner is a slave to his financial concerns from which he must "free himself," the lake acts as the landowner's "slave," the watercourse is metaphorically "bejeweled" with natural colors, and so on. On the other hand, Pliny justifies villa life by giving it transcendent meaning, above mere material exploitation and empty leisure. The villa is

---

[1] Pliny's wealth has been estimated at HS 20,000,000 (Duncan Jones 1974:20, 24), mostly invested in landholdings at Comum and Tifernum. His slave force alone, not counting free tenants, counted over 500, since his will mentions support for 100 ex-slaves, apparently the statutory limit freed at his death (*CIL* 5.5262): the *lex Fufia Caninia de manumissione* prohibited an owner from freeing more than one-fifth of his slaves by testament, up to a limit of 100 slaves. Labor estimates also suggest many hundreds of agricultural workers (18 *iugera* per worker for olives, Cato *Agr.* 10.1, 7 *iugera* per worker for viticulture, Col. 3.3.8; Duncan-Jones 1974:327–28), not to mention non-productive house slaves.

[2] For example, Hor. *Odes* 1.1.33–37, Sen. *Ep.* 86.4–11, 90.9, 115.8–9, Juv. 7.178–83, 14.86–95, 140–72; Edwards 1993:139–47. At one point Seneca holds Zeno up for admiration for having owned no slaves (*ad Helv.* 12.4).

itself a utopian setting, a work of art as well as the highest expression of natural beauty. It therefore symbolizes the higher value of literature, as well as providing the necessary conditions for literary creation.

Yet the value of literature is itself uncertain. Here Pliny allows his anxieties to run closer to the surface. Behind the complex interweaving of modesty and boasting throughout the letters, we can sense anxiety over whether his writings really deserve and will obtain the attention of future generations. Even his most confident statement at 9.14 *(nos certe meremur)* is surrounded by doubts. His speeches may become lost in the river of oratory that is constantly pouring forth, his imperial panegyric may be made obsolete by another dynastic revolution, and his nugatory works, his letters and poems, may turn out to be nugatory indeed.[3] Is literary achievement nothing but a house of cards, an unstable investment pyramid? Is it merely an empty collection of symbolic markers by which the ruling class perpetuates its political dominance through a display of cultural superiority, achieved through reading and imitating the "masters"? Is there a central core of worth for which the writings deserve to be remembered? Pliny himself contrasts the lasting value of *deeds* to the more uncertain value of mere literary achievement (3.7.14, to the same Caninius Rufus; compare 9.19.3–6).[4]

As often, Pliny solves two problems by joining them together. The two fragile structures, the life of wealth and the life of literature, support each other, and both are grounded on the supporting foundation of friendship. Wealth has higher value because it makes possible literary leisure. Hence Pliny uses the diction of possession and price throughout the literary exhortation in the second half of the letter (4 *perpetuo tuum,* 5 *tanti quanti*). Pliny in turn implicitly upholds the value of literature by enmeshing it in the upper-class life and especially in his own circle of friends. The cycles of friendship and friendly exchange will inspire Rufus' self-confidence and guarantee the value of the writer and his writings (5). The villa of Rufus, which he and Pliny love and share, becomes an example both of the aesthetic artifice which they are creating as writers, and of the shared esteem which ensures the value of their work.

On both counts, though, both in property and in literature, Pliny exceeds his lesser friend, because his own life has a further mainstay, political activity.

---

[3] On the competition for literary and oratorical fame as a zero-sum game, see Gleason 1994:xxiii.

[4] Attacks on the pursuit of literary fame, though less prevalent than attacks on luxury, also appeared in philosophic discourse (e.g. Epict. 3.23.17–26). See Syme 1958:99 on the anxieties of "some of the less enthusiastic among the friends of Pliny" about whether it was still possible to achieve meaningful fame. "Were the means adequate? Did the Empire in its mature season offer scope for distinction in the arts of peace or war?... was it not too late, even for oratory?"

Pliny's own wealth is justified by the public offices for which it qualifies him, and his principal writings (his speeches and even his letters) are given additional value because they commemorate meaningful political deeds. If even a local leisured poet can give real meaning and value to his estate and his writings, all the more can the high-ranking Roman senator and orator, whose political life underwrites his financial and literary existence. To be sure, Pliny avoids mentioning here that Rufus is a poet, so as not to disrupt the parallelism between Rufus' and Pliny's literary activities. Still, we can already surmise that the literary works that Rufus can create in rural seclusion are pure belles-lettres, unlike Pliny's political oratory.

UTOPIAS IN THE VILLA DESCRIPTION

Quid agit Comum, tuae meaeque deliciae? quid suburbanum amoenissimum, quid illa porticus verna semper, quid platanon opacissimus, quid euripus viridis et gemmeus, quid subiectus et serviens lacus, quid illa mollis et tamen solida gestatio, quid balineum illud quod plurimus sol implet et circumit, quid triclinia illa popularia illa paucorum, quid cubicula diurna nocturna? Possident te et per vices partiuntur? an, ut solebas, intentione rei familiaris obeundae crebris excursionibus avocaris? Si possident, felix beatusque es; si minus, 'unus ex multis'. (1.3.1–2)

How is your darling and mine, Comum, doing? How is the most delightful estate near town, how is that colonnade that is forever springlike, how is the shadiest sycamore arboretum, how is the lush aquamarine canal, how is the lake, low-lying and serviceable, how is that riding-course, yielding and yet firm, how is that bathhouse that so much sun fills and surrounds, how are those dining halls for mass entertainment and those for the few, how are the private chambers for daytime and night? Do they own you and share you in turn? Or are you making frequent journeys, as you used to do, summoned by your attention to surveying your household property? If they own you, heavenly bliss is yours; otherwise, you are one of the crowd.

The opening of 1.3 personifies Comum and Rufus' estate. "How is Comum doing, how is your most lovely estate near the city doing?" The same trope opens letter 2.15: "How are your old Marsian estates [treating] you? ... My mother's estates are treating me none too nicely."[5] Indeed, the entire letter can be considered an elaboration of the epistolary frame, "Pliny wishes Rufus well... Farewell." Just as Seneca can claim that the *real* meaning of the epistolary frame is "if you are philosophizing, it is well" (*Ep.* 15.1), so Pliny

---

[5] Niemirska-Pliszczynska 1955:79. In 2.15.1, the missing verb *tractant,* which Pliny supplies in the following section *(me praedia materna parum commode tractant),* is normally used of people ("handle"), and in fact can be used of a person "managing" property (*OLD* s.v. 6). As often Pliny mystifies property relations by imagining the owner "owned" by his property (cf. 1.3.1 *possident te,* 1.3.3 *adseris*).

elaborates the basic letter frame to mean "How are you enjoying and managing your estates? How is your writing?" These are the fundamental aspects of the life that Pliny and Rufus share. Pliny's personal interest in both town and estate, as if they are mutual friends of himself and Rufus, also helps to diffuse the idea of private ownership. Pliny and Rufus are as fond of their hometown, their *deliciae* (1.3.1), as they are of their estates (compare 2.17.20 *amores,* 5.6.41 *amori*); the warm personal diction imparts a patriotic aura to their love of their estates.

The opening question develops into a sequence of ten questions, inquiries about Comum and the various parts of the estate. The questions mark out a spatial journey, starting from the town Comum and proceeding through the villa grounds to the inner rooms. They also mark out a temporal schedule of activities in the villa, first exercising in the riding grounds, then having a bath and dinner, and finally withdrawing to the bedrooms, where the serious business of studying and writing goes on (2.17.23, 3.1.7–9, 9.36.4, 9.40.2).[6] The sequence of questions displays to the public that Pliny knows Rufus' villa well. Like Comum, "your delight and mine," the villa is shared between close friends, as in the next letter (1.4.2). As a close friend, Pliny has enjoyed the entire villa, the inside as well as the outside, the intimate dining room as well as the huge public dining room (1 *illa popularia illa paucorum*; compare 9.36.4 *paucis*). Perhaps he has even used the bedchambers for shared studies or overnight stays (as at 3.1.8).[7]

Pliny is tracing out not only Rufus' typical day in the villa and Pliny's memories of sharing it, but also Pliny's own experiences in his *own* villas, for the basic elements of upper-class Roman architecture and lifestyle were relatively uniform throughout Italy and beyond.[8] Pliny, who owns his own villa at Comum, does not need to stay at Rufus' villa the way he needs to stay

---

[6] The letter thus anticipates both the great villa letters (2.17 and 5.6) and the "daily routine" letters (especially 3.1, 3.5, 9.36, 9.40).

[7] "The most intimate receptions took place in the bedroom *(in cubiculo)*... The depth to which the guest penetrated the building... emphasized his degree of intimacy with the owner" (Ellis 1991:123). On the conceptually concentric "circles" of privacy culminating in the *cubiculum,* see Riggsby 1997:48, Wallace-Hadrill 1988:54, 86. To Pliny and his associates, who did much of their reading and writing in bed, often before and after sleeping, the *cubiculum* was naturally associated with *studia,* an association not listed by Riggsby (2.17.22–24, 9.36.2, 9.40.2; cf. Spurinna 3.1.7, Pliny the Elder 3.5.8, and Gaius Fannius the historian of Nero's crimes 5.5.5). "The ancients were not well supplied with comfortable chairs" (Sherwin-White 1966:321).

[8] By the second century, "an architectural style... was rapidly acquiring international status all over the coastal provinces of the central and eastern Mediterranean and the Black Sea," Ward-Perkins 1988:147; cf. D'Arms 1981:94. To be sure, there was a great deal of adaptation within the "vocabulary of forms" that had been inherited from Greece and Hellenistic Asia (McKay 1975:157).

at the villas of his mother-in-law, but the detailed list advertises that he knows it as well as his own. In fact, only at the end of the list does Pliny make it explicit to the outside reader that he is describing Rufus' villa and not his own (*possident te,* 1); we could have imagined that all these features and rooms belonged to Pliny's own villa, which Rufus has been enjoying. The villa life is a common "language" that belongs to all members of the upper class, just as literature (Greek as well as Latin literature) is their common cultural language.[9]

Yet Pliny and his friend Rufus have very different relations with their hometown Comum. Rufus is a local gentlemen who lives among his income-producing estates and devotes himself to poetry, whereas Pliny the senator and officeholder can make the lengthy trip to Comum only on rare occasions, less than once a year. Comum is about as remote as one can be from Rome and still be in Italy. Even a visit to his Tifernum estate requires thirty days, and special permission during a term of office (10.8.9). The letter therefore advertises Pliny's close connection, after all these years of separation, with his "fatherland" (*patria,* 3.6.4, 4.13.3–4) and his "fellow citizens" (*municipes,* 1.8.2, 4.13.3). Pliny's material connections with Comum—his own income-producing estates, his marriage connection, and his political connections with local aristocrats—are turned into a purely sentimental connection, a shared "delight" (*deliciae,* 1); elsewhere the word has a light, even condescending tone, the opposite of *seria* (8.1.2), close to "whim" (1.20.23, 2.3.4, 5.19.9, *Pan.* 59.2). Pliny implicitly flaunts his high position at Rome, which keeps him away so much that he has to ask how his own town is doing, while at the same time boasting that in his heart his "real" home is Comum, which he shares *equally* with the full-time resident Rufus.

The description of Rufus' villa is a miniature version of the long villa letters.[10] It embodies in words the essential significance of the villa, with its artistic and poetic style, its emphasis on leisurely delight with a corresponding de-emphasis on the slave labor supporting it, and its ideal union of opposites. In his brief but exquisitely crafted description, Pliny shows how the villa unites artifice and nature, indoor and outdoor, winter and summer, crowds and intimacy, possession and subservience, even Greek and Latin.[11] The union of artifice and nature reappears throughout the long villa letters, especially in 5.6. In the midst of a carefully planned *city-like* garden is a patch of imitation "natural" *countryside* (*in opere* urbanissimo *subita velut inlati* ruris *imitatio,*

---

[9] We learn that Rufus writes Greek poetry at 8.4.3, and perhaps at 7.25.4 (if that is to the same Rufus).

[10] Guillemin 1927:I.5 n. 1 ad loc.

[11] The union of opposites is a conventional rhetorical device, e.g. Quint. *Inst.* 10.1.46.

5.6.35).[12] The inside walls are painted with birds on branches (5.6.22), while the outside vegetation is clipped into animal or word shapes, even "uttering the name of its owner"—Pliny's name in topiary (*in... litteras... quae... nomen domini dicunt...*, 5.6.35). The entire scene looks like a natural "amphitheater" or "painting" (5.6.7, 13).[13]

Rufus' year-round residence combines the virtues of Pliny's winter residence at Laurentum and of his summer residence at Tifernum, and thus the description combines the literary emphases of the two great villa letters, with their descriptions of the indoor architecture enhanced by nature (2.17) and the outdoor beauty of nature enhanced by artifice (5.6). The outdoor grove offers "the highest degree of shade" for the summer (1.3.1 *opacissimus*), while the indoor bath "is filled and surrounded" by "the greatest amount of sun" for the winter *(plurimus sol implet et circumit).*[14] This union of opposite seasons results in "eternal spring" *(verna semper),* like the "spring warmth" during the winter at Laurentum (2.17.3).

Eternal spring without extremes of temperature is also a feature of the ideal worlds of the past (Golden Age) or future (Isles of the Blessed). Homer's Elysian plain has no snow or storms but only eternally cool breezes *(Odyss.* 4.566–68), Pindar's afterlife has equal days and nights, as at the equinox *(O.* 2.61–62), and Ovid's Golden Age has eternal spring *(Metam.* 1.107). Pliny's own description of the mild summers at Tifernum calls subtle attention to the Golden Age significance of temperate climate. The extremely aged people of this healthy site do not merely tell old stories from another age, but could even make you think that you were *born* "in another age" *(putes* alio *te* saeculo *natum,* 5.6.6). Though literally Pliny means an earlier generation, the combination of utopian weather, longevity, and the idea of being reborn, as it were, into a prior world suggests myths of the Golden Age, and perhaps a political golden age before Domitian, the Civil War, and the later years of Nero.[15] Just as mythical utopias tend to be given attributes of upper-class life (especially leisure and bountiful resources), so Pliny gives upper-class life a utopian veneer to divert attention from the all-too-human

---

[12] Compare the juxtaposition of "natural" and "artificial" fields at 5.6.18, *pratum inde non minus natura quam superiora illa arte visendum.*

[13] In Statius' villa poems, too, nature and artifice cooperate, with nature outdoing art, and art imitating nature *(Silv.* 1.3.15–17, 48, 2.2.15, 52–53); see Van Dam 1984:251, and compare Sen. *Contr.* 2.1.13. For earlier villa descriptions in Latin literature, see Guillemin 1929:141.

[14] The ideal of temperature control in villas in order to moderate the seasons is a frequent topic of praise (e.g. Sen. *Ep.* 55.7, Statius *Silv.* 1.2.156–57, 1.3.5–8, 3.5.83), though occasionally a topic of blame (Sen. *Ep.* 86.8, Juv. 7.183).

[15] On "Golden Age" propaganda at the start of a reign see e.g. Sen. *Apocol.* 4, Syme 1958:217 n. 1, Williams 1982:22. For good health and long life in utopian ages, see Hes. *Op.* 92, 114.

conditions of labor and exploitation that create and maintain the villa, the portico, and even the plane grove and the watercourse.[16] The springlike coolness in the summer comes from the natural shade of plane trees, and the springlike warmth in the winter is maintained not by the luxury of piped heating (2.17.9), but by a design that exploits the sun's natural motion (*sol implet et circumit*; cf. 5.6.31 *ut circumit sol,* 2.17.6–8, 12–13, 17–19, 5.6.24). In reality, both the natural warming and the natural shade are made possible by expensive artifice, the bath which was built to concentrate the sunlight and the plane grove which was either planted or incorporated into the luxury architecture.[17]

This shaping of nature through expensive artifice (as in the plane grove and the solar-heated bath) is echoed by Pliny's rhetorical description, which transfers the luxury materials and slave labor from the villa to the natural surroundings. The only luxury materials mentioned are in the metaphorically "bejeweled" watercourse (*euripus viridis et gemmeus*), which is sparkling with gemlike colors, like the flower-dotted meadows at Tifernum (*prata florida et gemmea,* 5.6.11).[18] Pliny's elegant style bestows expensive embellishments on the natural surroundings for free, as it were, whereas the actual marbles, metals, gems, and artworks that adorn luxury villas receive little attention.[19] Pliny also uses metaphor to describe the amenities of the lake. Like the (unmentioned) staff of slaves that do the owner's will, the lake

---

[16] Utopia is often imagined as a slightly improved version of real upper-class life (Baldry 1952:86). On the myth of timeless leisure in utopian ages see Humphreys 1981:275. Comic versions exaggerate the connection between utopian ages and wealth, with banquets and luxury items springing up automatically (see the Old Comic fragments of Crates' *Theria,* Telecleides' *Amphiktyones,* and other plays at Athenaeus 6.267E–270A). Roman moralizing literature, on the other hand, usually emphasizes pristine simplicity (e.g. Tibull. 1.10.7).

[17] The plane grove was a typical feature of villas, e.g. 5.6.20, 22, 32, Sen. *Ep.* 55.6. Vatia's villa even has two *artificial* caves to provide sun and shade (*Ep.* 55.6), an upper-class version of Philoctetes' all-season cave (Soph. *Phil.* 17–19). Some seasonal variety in dining rooms has been detected at Pompeii (Wallace-Hadrill 1988:90).

[18] The Romans seem to have believed (wrongly) that the original meaning of *gemma* was "jewel," with the meaning "bud" being a rustic metaphor (Cic. *de Orat.* 3.155; Quint. *Inst.* 8.6.6).

[19] Poetry often uses metaphors of luxury materials to describe natural beauty, e.g. Ovid *Metam.* 3.407 *nitidis argenteus undis.* Statius, in contrast with Pliny, dwells at length on luxury materials (*Silv.* 1.3.35–36, 47–57, 2.2.85–93), including gems (1.3.49); see Van Dam 1984:246–47 on Stat. *Silv.* 2.2.85–93. On artworks in villas, see Van Dam 1984:233. Pliny displaces the numerous expensive artworks that are so prominent in Statius (e.g. *Silv.* 2.2.63–69) onto variously disreputable characters such as Silius Italicus (3.7.8), Regulus (4.2.5), and Domitius Tullus (8.18.11). "Pliny's description, however [as opposed to Statius'], focuses on [the] refinement [of the villas] rather than *luxuria*" (Edwards 1993:142 n. 11); see Trisoglio 1972:152.

is literally "under" him, and is "acting as his slave" *(subiectus et serviens);* the same metaphor recurs at 5.6.23 *(piscinam quae... servit ac subiacet).*

The elegance of the villa letters, with their great length and poetic elaboration, is clearly meant to reflect the artistic and natural elegance of the villa life itself. Pliny compares reading the letter to strolling around the villa (5.6.41), and he cites as models for his lengthy ecphrasis the descriptions by the supreme poets, Homer and Vergil, of consummate works of art, the arms of Achilles and Aeneas, along with Aratus' description of the natural sky (5.6.43). The upper-class estate is itself a kind of poetry, the poetry of nature and the poetry of artifice, and is therefore the perfect site for a poet to create something of lasting beauty, even more lasting and more his own than the estate which will have owner after owner (1.3.4). Thus the villa letters implicitly defend the luxury expense of the villa in several ways: they represent the luxury as a work of nature, they represent the villa itself as a meaningful work of art, and they represent it as the necessary precondition for more meaningful artifice, the writing of literature.

The list of opposites also helps present the villa as an embodiment of political and literary ideals. There are dining rooms for "mobs" and for the "few." The term *popularis* has a negative connotation, like the *unus ex multis* in the next section (1.3.2), and thus gives a slight preference to the second term of the pair *(paucorum).*[20] The upper class villa had areas that were public, private, and more private, ranging from large halls for morning *salutatio* to large dining-rooms, to small dining-rooms, to intimate *cubicula* for close friends of similar status to the owner. The sociable delights of the villa, like the recherché delights of Rufus' Greek poetry, are fully enjoyed and appreciated by Rufus' select few friends.[21] This trope of the climax of privacy gives a positive political twist to the aristocrat's practice of arrogating for his private use huge resources of land and labor, a standard topic of satiric and philosophic invective (e.g. Sen. *Ep.* 90.39). In restricting access to the ordinary riffraff of Comum, the aristocrat is upholding proper status distinctions and imperial prestige: his wealth will not be used to gain inordinate popularity and establish an independent local power base. This disparagement of the mob contributes to the focusing technique in the letter, from the town to the estate to the crowded banquet to the small private dinner

---

[20] Elsewhere Pliny uses the word *popularis* of his "not populist" gift (1.8.12), of a "harmlessly populist" defendant (6.31.3), and of Trajan himself *not* trying to be "populist" (*Pan.* 77.4).

[21] Indeed, Wallace-Hadrill points out that the proliferation of real and painted columns, peristyles, and porticoes, as well as the display of marble statues and panel paintings, aimed at arrogating and privatizing the prestige of Greek *public* architecture (1988:66, 76); the most prestigious architectural paintings and displayed artworks were often placed in the most private part of the house (1988:76, Riggsby 1997:38).

and finally to the "deep and lush seclusion" where the writer in solitude can be eternal "lord" (*dominum,* 4) of his literary realm, "freed" from external constraints (*adseris,* 3). Even the "soft but firm" riding ground *(mollis et... solida),* like the sandy beach at 2.17.27 *(mollit... indurat),* may have literary and political undertones. *Mollis* is a programmatic term for light verse, like the elegies of Catullus and Passennus Paulus.[22] It is also a political term for "leniency."[23] The ideal poet and the ideal governor, like the ideal horse track, need to balance softness and toughness. For example, the "soft" sentence proposed for Priscus at 2.11.21 is too lenient and does not prevail (compare Saturninus' poetry, *inserit... mollibus... duriusculos,* 1.16.5).

The stylistic combination of the two languages, Greek and Latin, also reflects the union of opposites, of nature and artifice. The villa description anticipates the long villa letters in their prominent use of Greek words. Aside from the ordinary, naturalized Greek words for bath and dining room (*balineum* < βαλανεῖον, *triclinium* < τρικλίνιον), he uses rarer words that stick out with their non-Latin phonology (the noun ending of *platanon* and the opening diphthong of *euripus*).[24] The long villa letters abound in uncommon and un-Latinized Greek terms, mostly for architectural entities (e.g. 2.17.8 *hapsida* [accus.], 5.6.25 *hypocauston* [nomin.]). Pliny is almost forced to borrow such words to describe his elaborately wrought villa because of the "neediness of the paternal language," which is deficient in technical and scientific vocabulary (4.18.1 = Lucret. 1.832; compare Quint. *Inst.* 12.10.34). These Greek names for the plane grove and watercourse help suggest that these "natural" outdoor features are artificially constructed.

In this context, Latin is the language of nature, and Greek is the language of artifice. Although Pliny is perfectly capable of writing a long letter without using a single Greek word (for example, a weighty Roman marriage recommendation, 1.14), Greek is almost unavoidable in a villa letter. We should distinguish this incidental use of single Greek technical words, common in all Latin writings, from Pliny's frequent use of phrases and quotations, which is taboo in "serious" Latin writing.[25] The Greek terms

---

[22] 4.14.5 *molliculi* = Catull. 16.4; 9.22.2 *molle.*

[23] See 2.11.21, 4.11.14, 8.24.5. Pliny's also treats his slaves and ex-slaves "leniently" (5.19.1 *molliter;* compare 5.19.2 *durior,* 8.16.3 *durior*), and a household is like a "republic" (8.16.2 *re publica;* compare Sen. *de Ira* 3.35.1).

[24] Quintilian lavishes praise on the beautiful-sounding Greek final "n" in contrast to the ugly Latin final "m" (*Inst.* 12.10.31). Niemirska-Pliszczynska notes that Pliny uses Latinized Greek words mostly for describing villas and literary studies (1955:56).

[25] In formal Latin writing, Greek is only admitted in single words (Townend 1960:98). In the *Panegyric,* Pliny uses Greek sparingly (Gamberini 1983:460). Pliny seems to be imitating Cicero's letters in his frequent use of Greek in the letters, and even in some of the actual Greek

indicate that upper-class architecture belongs to the same lofty tradition as upper-class literature, whose models and critical terminology are Greek even when the text is Latin (and indeed Rufus himself writes Greek poetry, 8.4.3).

Pliny's casual use of Greek throughout the letters flaunts the distinction between educated aristocrats and their uneducated local townspeople. Pliny, Rufus, Trajan, and Euphrates are "cosmopolitan" fellow citizens of the larger civilized world more than Pliny and Rufus are fellow citizens with the working class of Comum. It is no shame for Romans to be imitators of the great cultural tradition of their conquered Greek subjects if they know and use Greek as well as, or better than, the Greeks. As Pliny later says, probably to this same Rufus, "you would think the fellow lives in Athens, not in an Italian villa" (*Athenis vivere hominem, non in villa putes,* 7.25.3). Similarly, Antoninus' Greek is "more Attic than Athens" (*non... ipsas Athenas tam Atticas dixerim,* 4.3.5). Pliny does not really "envy the Greeks" (invideo *Graecis quod illorum lingua scribere maluisti,* 4.3.5). Rather, he implies that the Greeks should envy the Romans for mastering and taking over their language and cultural tradition. The Italian aristocrat derives international cachet from his Greco-Roman villa, and a similar but greater cachet from his poetry, whether it is in Greek, or in Latin but following Greek models.

REPRESENTATIONS OF LITERARY VALUE

Pliny ends the opening sequence with a pair of alternate questions. "Does the villa in all its parts own you and share you out in turns? Or are you following your past practice of letting yourself be called away on frequent trips, focused on visiting your property?" Although Pliny elsewhere denounces the greed that makes one paradoxically "owned by one's wealth" (9.30.4), here being "owned" by one's property is the desirable state of "blessedness" that is *opposed* to excessive concern about money. Pliny presents this state as a total surrender to the villa's various charms in "blissful" abandon, away from "lowly and dirty concerns" that one would have as an over-controlling landlord (*felix beatusque... humiles et sordidas curas,* 2–3). But in the reality behind the slanted rhetoric, being "owned" by one's property means being all the more firmly in control of the property and the overseers who manage the "filthy" cash details of extracting agricultural profits. Pliny himself, the absentee landlord at Rome, is an implicit model for Rufus; his secure network of friends, relatives, and slave and ex-slave overseers keeps the profits rolling in, freeing him to devote himself to the

---

phrases (Guillemin 1929:78). Compare Iulius Victor's advice: *Graece aliquid addere litteris suave est, si id neque intempestive neque crebro facias* (448.30 Halm).

literary and political activities that will bring him immortality. Furthermore, through the idealized lives of the aristocrats of Comum and of Rome, Pliny implies praise of the good emperor, who is in firm control of his own power and of his dependent slaves and ex-slaves, and who makes possible for the upper class the secure life of luxury villas, obedient slaves, loyal friends, and literary immortality.

Pliny's exhortation thus creates a discreet distance between the leisured author and the agricultural laborer who supports him, a distance that is peopled by the unnamed "others" who will literally take care of matters of the ground and the dirt (*humiles et sordidas curas*, 3) while the author recedes into his private utopia. There he will create an eternal possession, a work of literature that will sublimate the merely physical villa to a higher order of value. The description of ideal leisure builds on the opening hint of utopian imagery, the "eternal spring" *(verna semper)*. Being possessed by the villa will make Rufus "fortunate and blessed" *(felix beatusque*, 2). These terms are often associated with utopian settings such as the Golden Age or the Isles of the "Blessed" (e.g. Cic. *Fin.* 5.53 *in beatorum insulis,* Verg. *Aen.* 6.639 *sedesque beatas,* 6.669 *felices animae,* Hor. *Epod.* 16.41 *arva beata,* Sen. *Apoc.* 4.1 *felicia vellera*). Rufus will go beyond the temporary "blessedness" of the villa to reach the immortal "blessedness" of literary fame.[26]

The alternate questions form a pivot from the starting topic, the villa (1), to the final topic, literature (3–5), by portraying the villa as an island of transcendent value above the ordinary life of upper-class moneymaking (2). Pliny explains that this transcendent value comes from literature (3). A diligent moneymaker is merely an ordinary person, one of the "many," of the hoi polloi (*unus ex multis;* see *OLD* 1143 s.v. *multus* 2b). The rich landowner is ironically a mere proletarian until he cuts himself off from dirty profits and creates real value from literature. The terms *adseris* (3) even suggests that as a mere landlord Rufus is a "slave," owned by his property and his dirty financial worries, until he "lays claim to his freedom" and becomes a writer.[27]

Only if the rich landlord gives over his moneymaking pursuits can he devote himself to studies in his "deep, lush" retreat (*alto... pinguique secessu,* 3). The word *pinguis,* like the earlier word *felix,* has agricultural undertones (as at 7.21.4 "plump" chickens, 3.19.5 "rich" soil, 2.17.15 a "lush" garden).[28]

---

[26] The ideal felicity of literary leisure in the villa, which is possible thanks to the happy new age, echoes the imperial virtue *felicitas* (e.g. 8.14.10, 10.2.2, 10.12.2, 10.58.7, 10.102.1 and throughout the *Panegyric*; see Syme 1958:755).

[27] The metaphor of "freeing" someone from the oblivion of death occurs at 2.10.4 (Octavius Rufus, reluctant to publish) and 3.5.4 (Drusus, in the Elder's dream); see 10.66.2 (Trajan) for an example of the legal meaning of *adsero.*

[28] In the corresponding letter in book 9, the "fat deep otium" is an *alternative* to the struggle for immortality (*pingue illud altumque otium,* 9.3.1). For the scholarly Rufus, the life of literary

Elsewhere Pliny plays explicitly on the idea that literary production is more valuable than agricultural produce (e.g. 4.6, 9.16; compare 1.6.1).[29] To be sure, the trope has a literal truth as well, as the (refused) offer of HS 400,000 for the Elder's notebooks shows (3.5.17); Pliny finds it worth mentioning that Atilius Crescens practices literature for pleasure and glory only, not for profit (6.8.6). By sinking his investments into the symbolic capital of literature, an author may well be able to recoup them materially through the cash value of the prestige and patronage that he gains. The ostentatious costs of the villa and of literature pose as a rejection of "lowly" financial concerns, but they actually contribute to solidifying the financial and political dominance of the upper-class in the face of the laboring masses. Someone who has an elegant villa has the leisure and the environment needed to create meaningful literature, and someone who creates meaningful literature shows that he deserves to live in the elegant villa. The impoverished masses are excluded from this magic, self-reinforcing cycle of money, elegance, literature, and friendship, as surely as they are turned back from the gates of the villa or the city council (as at 1.8.17).

LITERARY VALUE AND IMMORTALITY

Hoc sit negotium tuum hoc otium; hic labor haec quies; in his vigilia, in his etiam somnus reponatur. Effinge aliquid et excude, quod sit perpetuo tuum. Nam reliqua rerum tuarum post te alium atque alium dominum sortientur, hoc numquam tuum desinet esse si semel coeperit. Scio quem animum, quod horter ingenium; tu modo enitere ut tibi ipse sis tanti, quanti videberis aliis si tibi fueris. Vale. (3–5)

Let this be your business, this your leisure, let this be your work, this your rest; stay awake in these pursuits, in these lay your sleeping hours for safekeeping. Mold and forge something to be yours for eternity. The remainder of your property will fall to the lot of another owner and yet another, but this will never cease being yours if once it has begun. I know what a mind, what a

---

leisure is an absolute ideal, but for two high-ranking senators (Pliny and probably Valerius Paulinus at 9.3), it is a slightly disreputable alternative to serious political activity at Rome, and needs to be excused with a disingenuous reference to "laziness" (*desidia*, 2.2.2, to Paulinus). Similarly, the "soft, fat" life for which a sick man longs sounds a bit too inert to be a serious ideal (*mollemque... et pinguem,... hoc est innoxiam beatamque... vitam*, 7.26.3). Elsewhere Pliny concedes boastfully that his continuous devotion to literature would have been "blessed" but perhaps not "proper" (*non audeo dicere rectius, certe beatius erat*, 7.15.1). Bütler discusses Pliny's rather apologetic presentation of leisure and even *studia* as opposed to *negotia* (1970:54–55). See Riggsby 1998:86 n. 27 on the tension in values between political duties performed at the Roman center and leisured study performed at the rural margins.
[29] Bütler 1970:49.

talent I am encouraging. Just make the effort yourself to be as valuable to
yourself as others will think you are, once you are to yourself. Farewell.

Pliny's catalogue in praise of literature counterbalances his earlier praise
of the villa, with forms of *hic* replacing forms of *illa.* Pliny is now inviting
Rufus into "this" world, Pliny's own world of supreme literary value, instead
of looking off with wistful delight at "that" world, the small-town aristocratic
life that he has left far behind. Further on, too, Pliny dismissively calls the
material life of the villa "the rest of your affairs" in contrast to "this," the
world of literature (*reliqua rerum tuarum... hoc,* 4). Like the earlier list in
praise of the villa, this list is organized as a union of opposites, and it also
culminates in Rufus' private chambers at night (*in his vigilia, in his etiam
somnus reponatur,* 3). Literature is work that is restful, and it is rest that is
productive work (*hic labor haec quies,* 3). Literature will keep one awake at
night, as it does Pliny the Elder (3.5.8), Fannius (5.5.7 *vigiliarum*),
Athenodorus (7.27.7), and Pliny himself (9.40.2). It is something at which
one can continue even during sleep, as Pliny the Elder's dream of Drusus
illustrates (3.5.4).[30] This paradoxical union of opposites allows one to enjoy
the benefits of literature continuously, just as the opposites in the villa allow
one to enjoy the villa day and night, summer and winter. Furthermore, unlike
the villa, a mere temporary imitation of the Isles of the Blessed, literature
offers true immortality (*perpetuo tuum,* 4).

Pliny's diction even suggests that literary fame is an improvement over the
immortality of traditional myth and belief. "This will never stop being yours
if once it begins" (4). With literature, you can start enjoying the beatific
existence of immortality *today.* It starts to be yours during your life, and
continues after death. The successful author is like Verginius Rufus, who read
the poems and histories written about himself and "participated in his own
hereafter" (*posteritati suae interfuit,* 2.1.2).[31] On the other hand, this
description of Verginius suggests that normally one does not participate in
one's afterlife, apparently because one is not conscious of one's posthumous
fame. Elsewhere Pliny shows no great confidence in a personal afterlife,
except in a few honorific allusions to members of the imperial house (e.g.
Pan. 89; compare Drusus' ghost at 3.5.4). Certainly his uncle did not hesitate
to heap scorn on the belief (*NH* 7.188–90). Perhaps not even the hope of

---

[30] Pliny started writing light verse during a sleepless nap time (7.4.4). Quintilian guardedly
recommends night as an ideal time for writing in "seclusion" (*Inst.* 10.3.27; *secessus,*
10.3.28).

[31] By book 9, Pliny can openly aspire to "live together with his coming fame" (*certusque
posteritatis cum futura gloria vivit,* 9.3.1). Quintilian uses the same trope in describing the
retired orator, who will enjoy while alive "the veneration which more usually is offered after
death" (*eam quae post fata praestari magis solet venerationem, Inst.* 12.11.7).

posthumous literary immortality can assuage Pliny's fears that his life will
have been "empty" and "vain" (3.7.14 *temporis futilis et caduci,* 5.5.7
frustra).[32]

Pliny's metaphorical description of literature helps reinforce his praise of
literary immortality. Rufus will produce literature of value by "shaping it"
(effinge) like a sculpture or "hammering it out" *(excude)* like a metal
artwork, or perhaps like a coin (*OLD* ss.vv. *cudo, accudo*). His real property,
on the other hand, will end up in the hands of one owner after another.
Literature is not merely a lump of precious metal that anyone can own, but
metal worked into a shape that gives it lasting identity, like the image on a
coin, or like the shape of a sculpture. The villa, on the other hand, is a generic
piece of upper-class luxury, interchangeable with any other villa and destined
to pass into the control of unnamed heirs who will merely obtain it as if "by
lottery" *(sortientur).*[33] The image suggests that Rufus is childless and perhaps
unmarried: a rural aristocrat without political ambitions has no need of an
early marriage to help him along the *cursus honorum.* If the villa is
bequeathed not to relatives but to friends, by the third owner it may well be
inherited almost randomly, with nothing to do with Rufus at all.

Pliny carefully avoids the idea of *captatio,* the idea that he himself may
inherit some of the estate of his childless friend. Instead, the letter ends with
literary solicitation, a kind of *captatio* in reverse. By paying respect to the
writer Rufus during his life, his friends enrich *him* with posthumous literary
fame. This very letter exemplifies the principle that literary solicitation is
reverse *captatio.* By his friendly attentions and invitations to his powerful
friend Pliny, Rufus has elicited this elegant letter which, when published, will
add to *Pliny's* immortal fame (and incidentally to the addressee's fame as
well). Even after Pliny dispatches it, the letter does not "cease being Pliny's,"
because despite the appearance at the beginning, it is not simply a polite and
formulaic request for information ("how is your villa at Comum doing?").
Rather, it is a virtuoso display piece, both a villa description in a nutshell and
an exhortation to literature. Fundamentally it works as a dedicatory epistle in
reverse, revealing the indebtedness of Rufus the author to his friends'
encouragement, and demonstrating why Pliny has earned a literary dedication
from Rufus (as Clarus at 1.1). Pliny's flattering attentions will lead Rufus to
write and publish a book that will in turn add to Rufus' own fame (and
incidentally to Pliny's).

---

[32] On immortality through literary fame in Pliny, see Bütler 1970:21–27, Trisoglio 1972:181–
82.
[33] Or more literally, the *land* will "obtain" its future owners as if by lottery; these owners also,
qua landlords, will merely be controlled by their possessions unless *qua* writers they create a
true possession of their own.

THE INTERNAL FRIENDLY CYCLE OF THE SELF

The letter closes in typical fashion with an optimistic diminuendo, signaled by the cheerful particle *modo*.[34] Pliny knows that Rufus has the talent to achieve immortality; all Rufus has to do is fulfill his friends' opinions of him, to become as valuable to himself as "others" (his friends such as Pliny) will think he is.[35] Pliny represents literary creation as a self-fulfilling prophecy, as at 1.2.6, 1.8.4, and elsewhere. Rufus will merit immortality because his friends think he merits it. But the future tense and the sandwiched rhetoric puts greater emphasis on Rufus' own view of himself than on his friends' future views of him which they do not yet have *(videberis)*. Rufus must internalize their possible future opinion of him to make it come true. In addition, the sandwiched rhetoric puts him before and after his friends. "Try to be as valuable *to yourself,* as *others* will think you are, if you become so *to yourself."* What really matters is Rufus' own opinion of himself; his friends' future opinions are merely theoretical models of what he should be thinking to himself.

Ultimately the cycle of friends is most important as a model for the self, for one's own mental structure. Pliny urges the individual to internalize the mutually profitable cycle of friendship: become valuable by *considering* yourself to be valuable (as your friends will consider you). The canonical good emotion in the letters, optimistic self-confidence, can thus be thought of as an internalized form of the friendly circle of mutual benefits. Similarly, the taboo emotion in the letters, regret, can be thought of as an internalized form of detraction or envy, a sort of bad friendship with oneself. Instead of being in harmony with oneself, one is resentful at the self that acted wrongly and yearns enviously for a self that would have acted differently, or worse, would even now be acting differently. The ideal good and bad emotions are thus internalized versions of the ideal good and bad friendship.[36]

---

[34] Other examples of the optimistic closing *modo* are 2.9.6, 4.1.7, 4.16.3, 5.6.46, 6.3.2, 8.10.3, 9.14, and 9.21.4. The closing tag *si modo* in the Regulus letter (2.20.14) expresses ironic optimism, of course. Other optimistic closing tags are *dum* (1.2.6), *superest* (e.g. 1.1.2, 1.21.2, 1.22.11, 3.4.9, 7.10.3, etc.), *proinde* (1.6.3, 1.9.7, 1.18.5, 3.3.7, 7.16.5, 8.4.5, etc.), *quin ergo* (7.9.16), and pious phrases such as *faventibus dis* (3.3.7; cf. 1.22.11, 4.8.6, 5.6.46, 8.4.5, etc.). At 8.4.5 the trope marks a false ending.

[35] The opposite is when people come to think "cheaply" of themselves because of their empty labors (*ad vilitatem sui pervenire,* 9.3.2).

[36] The idea of being a "friend to oneself," a conventional paradox (e.g. Sen. *de Ben.* 5.7.2, *Ep.* 6.4, Quint. *Inst.* 10.44.10), is simply the inverse of the idea that a friend is an alter ego, "another I" (e.g. *pro me altero,* 2.9.1). Plato's *Republic* discusses in great detail the inner harmony or inner strife between the parts of the self; his example of severe inner strife is someone who *regrets* what he is doing *while he is doing it* (440A). See Edwards 1997:31 on

This internalized "friendly cycle of the self" is a fitting model for the solipsistic genre in which Pliny is now publishing in the hope of literary immortality, personal letters without their replies. Despite the ubiquitous machinery of exchange between friends, the reader can only look into Pliny's soul; his friends appear only as reflections in his letters and in his thoughts. They are necessary for the letters to be written, but only as instigating causes of Pliny's thoughts; they fade away from the final product. The ultimate intended destination of the letters is also a private, solitary being, the unknown future reader who will read Pliny's immortal letters. Unlike poetry or narrative prose, these letters are unlikely to be recited among groups of people; the most likely context in which the letters may remain known is in private reading by individuals. The portrayals of Pliny and Rufus thus implicitly provide a model for the unknown future reader, presumably a Roman with bilingual upper-class literary training, probably a villa owner, probably male. The ideal life, and the ideal composition of the self, that Pliny holds up for Rufus to follow are also held up as models for the future reader.

Yet the internal friendly cycle of the self and the external circle of friendship are interdependent. Pliny is obviously not proposing a completely solitary, solipsistic ideal in the complete seclusion of the private villa. The rhetorical sandwiching of the final line firmly connects the self and the friends. Although the friends' estimation of Rufus' value is a theoretical future model, it is already realized in Pliny's estimation of him, as this letter shows. Rufus will fulfill his own self-worth and thereby fulfill his friends' expectations and encouragement; his friends, in turn, have high expectations of him because they "know what kind of soul he has," a soul that can spur itself on in internal friendly rivalry (*scio quem animum, quod horter ingenium,* 5). The villa is not merely a place of perfect seclusion but the ideal combination of seclusion and friendly companionship. At the villa literature is not only created in privacy but also shared at visits and at dinners, in conversation, in group reading, and in recitations; Pliny's visit to Spurinna idealizes this feature of villa life (3.1). The letter moves from the shared delight of Pliny and Rufus (1 *tuae meaeque*) to the writer's deep seclusion in his private villa and private literary creation (1 *cubicula... nocturna,* 3 *vigilia... somnus*), but returns at the end to the sharing and exchanging of value, not mere real estate value but the transcendental and lasting value of literature, which will perpetuate the fame of both friends, whether as author and dedicatee of Rufus' poems, or as addressee and author of this letter.

---

interior dialogue as the internalization of interpersonal dialogue in Seneca. For recent psychological writings on how the individual personality internalizes external social relations, see Markus and Cross 1990:576–608.

THE MATERIAL CONDITIONS OF LIFE
NEW AND OLD SLAVES (1.4, 1.21)

LETTER 1.21: JUDGING NEW SLAVES WITH EYES AND EARS

Pliny follows one of his longest letters (on brevity) with one of his briefest, a lighthearted letter on slave-dealing that is likely to revolt the modern reader. Yet if we suspend our revulsion for a moment we can examine what attitudes about slaves Pliny is trying to present, and what anxieties he is hiding. Behind the slave who by eye seems "good" (or subservient) lurks the slave who by ear is "bad" (or insubordinate), and although Pliny's letter seems as light and unconcerned as if he were buying horses, it is precisely because he is buying humans and not horses that the letter is worthwhile for him to publish, and for us to examine.

> Ut animi tui iudicio sic oculorum plurimum tribuo, non quia multum (ne tibi placeas) sed quia tantum quantum ego sapis; quamquam hoc quoque multum est. Omissis iocis credo decentes esse servos, qui sunt empti mihi ex consilio tuo. Superest ut frugi sint, quod de venalibus melius auribus quam oculis iudicatur. Vale. (1.21)

> Just as I assign a great deal of value to your mental judgment, I assign as much to your visual judgment: not because you have great taste (lest you should feel too pleased with yourself), but because you have as much as I have—and yet that too is a great deal. Jokes aside, I believe that those slaves that were bought for me on your advice are suitable. What remains is that they be beneficial, a judgment which, concerning bought slaves, is made better by ear than by eye. Farewell.

The final words contain the core of the letter: one judges better about purchased slaves with the ears than with the eyes. The neat parallelism between the senses, seeing and hearing, hides the real distinction, between seeing for oneself and hearing from others, between seeing their bodily qualities and hearing about their mental qualities. Paternus or Pliny can examine the slaves' external qualities for themselves, even stripping them naked to look for scars and wounds (Sen. *Ep.* 80.9). One might even look for past beatings as a sign of an unreliable slave, unless these have been recently enslaved and have no past history as slaves.[1] But slaves' mental qualities can really be known only in action, from prior owners or above all from one's experience as their owner. Krenkel (1984:358) explains the term "ears" as verbal testimony presented to the buyer at the sale, but the words must primarily refer to the future.[2] The letter moves from the past (Paternus' judgment was good) to the present (the slaves seem suitable) to the future (better judgment is made by ears), marked with a concluding future tag of modest optimism, *superest ut...*[3] Pliny has learned as much as possible about the slaves through Paternus' visual and mental expertise at judging slaves (his sense of sight, *oculorum,* and of "taste," *sapis*). He will now have to find out by ear (that is, from others) about the slaves' qualifications, primarily their mental qualifications. Ironically, the knowledge he gained indirectly, from his friend Paternus, he calls visual, or direct inspection, whereas the knowledge he will gain himself as owner he calls indirect, through verbal report from others.

Why cannot Pliny learn of his slaves' inner qualities himself? Perhaps it is because these new slaves will be careful to be obedient in front of their new owner; the question is how they will behave when they are on their own. Pliny's claim in 1.4 that his slaves behave *worse* in his presence applies to long-established domestic slaves, not newly bought and possibly agricultural slaves, and in any case it should be read as a piece of bad faith, as Pliny's self-flattery for being such a kind slave-owner. Pliny was not a small proprietor working closely with a few slaves that he knew personally, but a member of the richest class of landowners, with estates at Comum, Tifernum, and Laurentum, and a house in Rome. His new slaves will not be laboring under his eye, but maintaining luxury villas, running errands, carrying his letters, and above all extracting profits from the land. Will they work? Will they be loyal? Will they try to escape? Pliny can see over a period of time whether his new slaves have been carrying out their work obediently, but the most direct

---

[1] See *OLD* s.v. *venalis* 1. Laws required the seller to reveal a slave's physical, mental, or moral defects (Gardner 1986:206).
[2] Scheffer's interpretation (in Cortius and Longolius 1734) is similar to Krenkel's: *ex fama et testimonio aliorum de ipsis colligitur, quod sperandum metuendumve sit.*
[3] Compare 1.1.2, 1.22.11, 3.4.9, 5.11.3, 6.26.3, 7.10.3, 7.11.7. Other optimistic closing tags are *modo, dum, proinde, quin ergo, faventibus dis,* etc.

way is to hear from others how the slaves behave in his absence—from friends, household members, and most importantly, from other slaves whose loyalty has been proven, long-established or home-born slaves.[4]

Pliny's complacent comments about excellent judgment concerning slaves cover powerful anxieties, anxieties that come terrifyingly close to the surface in the letter on Macedo's murder. "You see how many dangers, insults, and mockeries we are exposed to, and there is no reason someone could be *without anxiety* just because he is easygoing and mild. For owners are killed not *out of considered judgment* but by criminality" (3.14.5).[5] Upper-class Romans were vastly outnumbered by the slaves they owned, and were totally dependent on their loyalty. A subversive slave could damage property, or subvert the owner's interest, or betray him to a despotic emperor (e.g. *Pan.* 42.2–4, Tac. *Hist.* 1.2.3, *Ann.* 2.30.3), or organize a conspiracy of slaves and kill the slave-owner (as at 3.14 and perhaps 8.14).[6] The upper-class men who disappear with their entourages on journeys may have been murdered by their slaves (6.25.4), or by some of them. The lofty intellectual communion of judgment and reliability from friend to friend, from slave-owner to slave-owner, can only do so much for the owner, since no owner can fully know which slaves are loyal and which are merely acting loyal in his or her presence. Slave-owners can rely, however, on their loyal slaves to inform on other slaves. Since they have one foot in each world, they can gain other slaves' confidence enough to learn their real thoughts and betray them to their owners. Another letter (9.20.2) shows Pliny bringing out his city slaves, of higher status and greater loyalty, to supervise *rustici,* probably farm slaves (cf. 9.37.2–3).[7]

The workings of American slavery may help illustrate Roman slave management. "The slaveholder needed the willing cooperation of some of his bondsmen to make his government work efficiently... he tried to recruit a few [domestics, skilled artisans, and foremen] who would be loyal to him and take

---

[4] On the loyalty of home-born slaves *(vernae),* see, for example, Tac. *Ann.* 14.44.2–3, Bradley 1994:34, 115.

[5] *Vides quot periculis quot contumeliis quot ludibriis simus obnoxii; nec est quod quisquam possit esse securus, quia sit remissus et mitis; non enim iudicio domini sed scelere perimuntur.* Though there were fewer organized slave revolts than in republican times, fear of slaves remained strong (Kudlein 1991:52). Garnsey comments that "fair words" about the kind treatment of slaves may "reflect the moral anxieties and tensions of a slave-owning class engaged in the thoroughgoing and brutal exploitation of their fellow men" (1996:10).

[6] See Bradley 1994:115–16 for the ancient stereotype of the pilfering slave. Scott discusses the strategies of resistance, including theft, shirking, and sabotage, employed by slaves and oppressed peasants (1985:33–37, 248–49, 265–72, 1990:188–97).

[7] De Ste. Croix 1981:257. On an owner having so many slaves that he does not know them, see e.g. Sen. *Contr.* 2.1.26.

his side against the others."[8] This system, however, is based on a shaky foundation, since the one foot that the owners' agents have in the slave world, the foot that affords them true knowledge of the other slaves, may be enough to pull the agents in that direction, to betray the owners to their slaves.[9] The slaves' judgment can be used for or against their owners, despite Pliny's denial that insubordination can ever be by "judgment" (3.14.5). The real problem is not the owners' stable "judgment" with which the letter begins and ends *(iudicio; iudicatur),* but rather the "belief" or "trust" at the center *(credo),* the unstable network of slaves' loyalties on which a slave-owner must rely. The comforting frame of "judgment" at the start and end, reinforcing the cheerful frame of health and well-being *(s[alutem]; vale)* that surrounds each letter, is no more than a formulaic, wishful banishment of anxiety.[10]

Pliny opens with a "joke" *(omissis iocis,* 2), lightly sliding over the deadly serious questions of slavery and loyalty. The line is studded with words for judgment and discernment, *iudicio... tribuo... sapis,* emphasizing perfect mutual discernment and trust. Pliny seasons this flattery of self and addressee with his characteristic understatement through rhetorical alternation. There is perfect understanding and trust among the slave-owner class; only by closing ranks in this way can they control large numbers of slaves securely. Pliny emphasizes the understanding while ignoring the trust. Paternus has evidently had slaves purchased for Pliny without Pliny's direct involvement. As Pliny's agent, he must both discern Pliny's interests and be loyal to them, but the question of Paternus' loyalty would be too insulting even to mention. Hence Pliny omits all mention of belief and trust in the opening: he does not "rely on" or "trust in" Paternus' judgment, but attributes value to it with a firm logical verb, *tribuo.* An explicit assertion of trust or confidence could raise questions, as in the central word *credo* (2): "I *believe* that they are suitable" (but I will have to wait to find out whether we have been duped). *Credo* is a slippery word, often used in contexts of unreliability, false belief, or disbelief.[11]

---

[8] Stampp 1969:151. Stampp calls his chapter on house servants in the American South, "Between Two Cultures" (1969:322–82). Similarly, Genovese calls the slave drivers "The Men Between" (Genovese 1974:365).

[9] "'You have no idea of the corruption to house servants to have a gang of negroes in the yard,' a plantation mistress complained" (Stampp 1969:330). "Uncle Jackson of Virginia, who had virtual immunity from whipping because of his long service to the white family, made the perfect sentry to warn illegally assembled slaves of the approach of white men" (Genovese 1974:342).

[10] Pliny plays openly on the formula at 3.17.3 *(ipse valeo, si valere est...).* Compare Sen. *Ep.* 15.1, 58.37, Ovid *Her.* 4.1, 18.1, *Met.* 9.530, *Trist.* 3.3.88.

[11] E.g. 2.20.5 *illa ut in periculo credula,* 6.22.1 *qui se simpliciter credunt amicis, Pan.* 66.3 *nemini tamen ante te creditum est.* In the earnest Book 10, of course, the confident sense of *credo* predominates.

We might wonder why Pliny is buying an indefinitely plural number of slaves, perhaps a few, perhaps dozens; as we have seen, he probably owned well over 500 (*CIL* 5.5262). Perhaps he is replacing those who have been freed, or who have died off; behind the solicitous veneer, letters such as 8.16 and 8.19 do not suggest a very high life expectancy for his slave labor force. But the vague plural flaunts an insouciance that masks specific concerns about their individual personalities. A single bad slave can do irreparable damage to life and property. With the optimistic tag *superest ut,* Pliny simply imagines them all being successfully broken into his household force, and all turning out "good," profitable, subservient. *Frugi,* often applied to slaves (*OLD* s.v. 1), implies a morally commendable character, whereas *decentes* is a more general word ("suitable"), and sometimes refers to appearances ("becoming"). Pliny's "belief" can only ascertain their general suitability, not their moral character which will determine whether it has been a profitable transaction. This moment, the purchase of new slaves, is the critical one for maintaining the lifestyle of an upper-class Roman, since the home force did not reproduce itself, perhaps due to the preponderance of males. The other possibility, what to do if the "judgment" is negative, if a new slave turns out bad, does not bear mentioning. Sell him at a loss? Endure it philosophically?[12] Beat him into submission?

The final word, recapitulating the opening tone of secure, logical judgment, allays lingering anxieties, with an impersonal passive reinforcing the abstract and logical tone. "Judgment is made about the slaves," either by us or by other slaves (*de venalibus... iudicatur,* 2). It would not do to emphasize who is doing the judging, to emphasize the fact that our slaves have judgment, and that we rely on their judgment. Pliny does not say that we must rely on our ears and *not* on our eyes, but rather, that as good as our eyes (and mind) are, our ears will be even better. In the harmonious household of masters and slaves, and in the harmonious society of cooperating friends, all senses, ears, eyes, and taste, work together harmoniously, and all are governed by judgment, just as all judgments are governed by the master, and all masters are governed by the master of all, the emperor (*dominus* throughout Book 10). The ultimate source of slave-owners' authority is the Roman government, and above all the emperor's power.[13] Though a bad emperor can use slaves to destroy their owner, slave-owners still need the power embodied in the emperor to enforce the hierarchy of the upper class over the multitude and over their slaves.

---

[12] E.g. Diog. Laert. 6.55, Epict. 1.13, 3.19.5; Sen. *de Ira* 1.15.3, 3.12.6, 3.24.2, *Ep.* 47.19, 107.1–5.

[13] This was vividly demonstrated when Nero needed recourse to soldiers to enforce the killing of a murdered man's slaves despite the threats of an unruly mob (Tac. *Ann.* 14.45).

LETTER 1.4: MILD MASTERS AND SLAVES WAKING UP

Letter 1.21 is a counterpart to 1.4: one alludes to the breaking in of new slaves, the other to the behavior of old ones. In one Pliny hopes to hear if his slaves' behavior is worse behind his back; in the other he hopes someone else will come so that his slaves will behave better than they do in front of him. In 1.21, Pliny's bland hopes that the slaves will turn out well suggest that his anxieties about his new slaves' loyalty run close to the surface. In 1.4, by contrast, Pliny's complaints about his house slaves' bad behavior are designed to reveal a true confidence and security, and thus they suggest that his actual anxieties lie further from the surface.

The eventual subject of the letter, Pliny's confident enjoyment of his slaves' labor, hides behind descriptions of inanimate property. He begins with a list of villas and an exclamation over their "furnishings," which include even the bath at Narnia; the *copiae* seem to be physical equipment and supplies. The human aspect of the "supplies" comes up only obliquely in the next line, when he says that "one short old letter," evidently to Pompeia's staff, "is enough" to give him access to these supplies. What is remarkable about the Narnia villa is not that it has a bath but that the slaves were even willing to fire it up specially for Pliny; Sherwin-White (1966:93) compares 2.17.26.[14] The alternation between generic, genderless property and human property (slaves) continues with the varying gender of "mine" and "yours," first neuter *(mea/tua)*, then masculine *(tui/mei)*, then things again *(nostris rebus...)*, and finally people *(mei... servos...)*.[15]

The alternation between human and material property allows Pliny to combine statements about villas and about slaves in one short letter. The slaves of the "mild" Pliny (and Pompeia) serve them not from fear but from eagerness to please, and Pliny and his mother-in-law have a perfectly equal sharing of property and power, as if in a Golden Age paradise before the institution of private property (e.g. Ovid *Met.* 1.135). Just as the individual villa reenacts a Golden Age setting of leisure, abundance, controlled weather, harmony of nature and culture, and so on, so too the upper class of Roman landholders reenacts a Golden Age society of harmonious sharing, a sharing

[14] Mynors' colon at *non est* makes the old letter Pompeia's (1963); Guillemin's parentheses around *nam iam... non est* make it Pliny's (1927). Although we might expect an early switch from exclamatory fragments to full sentences (as at 2.10, 2.15, 3.17, 4.21 e.g.), Mynors' rendering better explains the difference between Pliny's (plural) letters and the one old letter that suffices. Nevertheless, Pliny's and Pompeia's properties and authority are so interchangeable that it does not matter if at first we cannot tell whose initial authorization opened up the homes to Pliny.
[15] Merwald briefly notes the proliferation of pronouns in this letter (1964:22).

which is both symbolized and enacted by the exchange of letters themselves. One old short letter to Pompeia's households was enough to enforce her control over them and to grant Pliny an equal share of control and enjoyment of the villas. Now this letter completes one cycle, reporting back and confirming to Pompeia her control over her households, and begins the other cycle, sending Pompeia to enjoy and confirm Pliny's control over his households. Because of the great distances between households, and between parts of the Empire, the basic hierarchies of power between owner and slave, or between emperor and delegate, had to be enforced by letters, the practical conduits of power.

This letter between "equals" enforces not only their control over their resources but also their equality, which Pliny emphasizes with his characteristic reference to mutual benefit. By staying in each other's villas, they do not take away from each other's wealth, but rather increase it by increasing the level of exploitation of slave labor.[16] Behind the free enjoyment of luxury hotels lurks a kind of unannounced inspection service. Pliny is not inviting Pompeia to *come* stay with him so that he can enjoy improved service along with her; rather, he requests her to *go* visit his estates so that his slaves will "wake up." It turns out that Pompeia is just the right degree of kinship distance, on the border between kin and friend, for this to work best. She is close enough for a perfectly equal sharing of resources, a blurring of *mea* and *tua* (cf. 3.19.8), but distant enough that her visit can be the unannounced visit of a "stranger," not an owner's regular visit with formal inspection of finances and tenants (e.g. 8.2, 9.20, 9.37). Pliny's picture of attentive slaves eager to please, however, hides the fact that their outstanding attentiveness may have been aimed not simply at an ordinary friend of their mistress, but at the powerful Pliny. The same disingenuous modesty hides similar flattery of Pompeia, whose high wealth, status, and consular husband may contribute to putting Pliny's slaves on special alert.[17] Pompeia is not only distant enough, but also important enough, for her inspection to carry weight.

It is no accident that this emphatic portrayal of equal sharing and visiting is written to a woman, one of Pliny's few female correspondents in the collection. Since women were thought to be both physically weaker and mentally more forgiving (8.11.3), Pompeia can be more naturally thought to extract greater service because of the slaves' selfless desire to please her rather than by their fear of physical force or threats. Her high-ranking

---

[16] The only place labor is actually mentioned, at the very last word, cloaks it in bad faith. The slaves are not performing hard labor; their only "work" is to please (cf. 1.10.2 ...*amari*... *laboravi*).

[17] She is generally thought to be the mother of the wife mourned at 9.13.13 (e.g. Merwald 1964:20).

husband goes unmentioned in the letter. In this Golden Age friendship, distinctions of gender and status are absent. Unlike many letters to women, there is no gender marker in the text, no reference to her being a relative (as at 4.19.1), a mother (as at 3.3.1), or "womanly" by nature (as at 8.11.3). The mother-in-law relationship has enough cultural reverence to counterbalance male superior power and make it an ideal relationship of equals. The tense balance of power is neatly expressed in Pliny's dream of her supplication (1.18). Supplication is a role indicating inferiority; a father, for example, would be less likely to beg on his knees. On the other hand, if his mother-in-law *had* supplicated, Pliny would have had to obey and give up the trial because of the obedience she merits. Pliny can ignore her wishes (as Hector does to Hecuba, *Il.* 22.91 or to Poulydamas, *Il.* 12.243 = Plin. 1.18.4) over the trial only because it is just a dream. This even balance of gendered power is simplified by the absence of the two "principals" of the relationship, the father who gives the daughter and the daughter who is given, leaving only the pure relationship that was initiated by the transaction.[18]

The secure possession of villas and slaves is a topic of imperial praise. Under Bad Emperors slaves are suborned to testify against their masters, or even mistresses (e.g. Tac. *Ann.* 14.60, Dio 57.19.2, 60.13.2, 60.15.5, 62.13.4), and wealthy owners of villas are killed because of their property (e.g. Suet. *Calig.* 41.2, Tac. *Ann.* 16.17, Plin. *Pan.* 50.5–7, Plin. *NH* 18.35). The mood at Pliny's estates is conveyed by words such as *secure* (3), *mitium,* and *metus* (4) that have political undertones: this is the mood of the New Age of Nerva and Trajan, with fear gone and security returned.[19] The relation of master to slave was a conventional metaphor for depicting a Bad Emperor such as Domitian, who affected the titles *dominus* and *dominus et deus*; even Trajan is addressed honorifically as *domine* throughout Book 10. The senators themselves now have a "mild" lord (*mitis, Pan.* 80.1), and now that they have "become used to it" their fear, still very much in evidence in 97 C.E. (9.13.7–8), is "fading away" (*ipsa consuetudine metus exolescit,* 4).

The political undertone of the final sentences directs our attention back to the place names in the opening sentence: Ocriculum, Narnia, Carsulae, and Perusia, and again Narnia. The four towns map out an itinerary north from Rome, ending at Perusia, a town whose historical significance is almost as

[18] Conversely, the irascibility that has been detected in Fabatus (Sherwin-White 1966:265, 368, 459) is more a matter of power dynamics than individual personality. Having received Calpurnia from him, her closest male relative, Pliny must be sure to render the proper obedience as a show of his indebtedness.

[19] For *securitas* in propagandistic contexts see 10.52, 10.58.7 (by Nerva), 10.111 (by Trajan), *Pan.* 8.1, 27.1, 34.5, 72.7, etc.; Ramage 1989:652, Fell 1992:28. *Securitas* is also used of the peace of mind of the Emperor himself, *Pan.* 8.4 (Nerva), 24.1, 68.2–4 (Trajan). For *mitis* see *Pan.* 80.1 *mitis severitas.* For *metus* see 10.82.1 (by Trajan), *Pan.* 2.2, etc.

obvious as a Pharsalus or a Cremona: Perusia is the site of the uprising against
Octavian which he defeated in a bloody massacre. Perhaps we can detect
political meaning in the other three towns, especially when we note that *copiae*
can also mean "troops" (e.g. throughout Suetonius and Tacitus). Troops in
Ocriculum, Narnia, Carsulae: this is the Flavians' final march on Rome in the
fateful days of December 69, the most recent civil war Rome had seen. The
Flavians reached Carsulae, while Vitellius' last significant forces had taken up
a stand at Narnia. The peaceful surrender at Narnia led to Vitellius' attempted
abdication on 18 December, and the fatal delay at Ocriculum for the
Saturnalia (Tac. *Hist.* 3.78) led to the anti-Saturnalian scene at Rome, the
massacre of Sabinus and others and the "worst crime in all of Roman history,"
the burning of the Capitoline temple (*Hist.* 3.72; cf. Epict. 1.7.32). The
importance of Narnia in this final chapter of the war would be enough to
explain Pliny's emphatic repetition of Narnia, but there is more: Narnia is also
Nerva's hometown (*epit. de Caes.* 12.1).

The historical map is clear. Perusia, 41 B.C.E., marks the founding crime
of the empire, of the Julio-Claudian imperial dynasty. 19 December 69 is the
real *dies imperii* of Vespasian, who preferred to celebrate the start of his
revolt rather than the bloody end as his *dies imperii* (Suet. *Vesp.* 6.3). And
finally, 96 C.E. marks the founding of the third imperial dynasty, the only
one that was not established through the founding crime of civil war. Pliny's
peaceful and friendly journey reverses the Flavians' bloody march on Rome,
it reverses the bloody crimes of Octavian at Perusia, and it ends up, so to
speak, back at Narnia, whose native son Nerva is removing the moral blots of
the prior dynasties, perhaps washing them off as in a bathhouse, and founding
a new ideal empire where "security" prevails and fear can "go out of fashion,"
though perhaps not disappear entirely. The Senate may have been lulled into
sleep and can only be woken up "by newnesses" (perhaps the transition from
one mild emperor to another), and by working at pleasing their masters
through others (perhaps "friends" of the emperor). But the founding fear
remains. Slave-owners, no matter how mild, retain ultimate power over their
slaves through the possibility of punishment and violence; the slaves' fear may
fade from consciousness, but is always lurking in the background. Similarly,
even "mild" emperors retain the possibility of arbitrary power; Vespasian had
Helvidius Priscus killed for his insubordination (Suet. *Vesp.* 15), and the
Senate cannot discard its prior fear even when the "mild" Nerva comes to
power (9.13.7–8). Nevertheless, it is precisely this residue of fear at the
foundation of society that establishes the security of the present "good" regime
and prevents civil war, which would obstruct the upper class from enjoyment
of its wealth as much as a Bad Emperor does, or more. Pliny's presentation of
his confident, cheerful enjoyment of wealth and status masks the delicate

balance between security and solicitousness, between fear and fearlessness, on which his ideal position in his ideal society depends. The new age has lulled him into a dream world of fearlessness, but even when he wakes up it is not to the harsh reality of power, danger, and fear but to another ideal world of the harmonious strife of cooperation between ranks, between slave and free, and between republican Senate and imperial Princeps.

MODELS OF SENATORS AND EMPERORS
REGULUS, THE BAD SENATOR (1.5)

Letter 1.5 finally gives the keynote of Book 1 explicitly, "after the death of Domitian" (1.5.1), and also introduces one of the most memorable characters of the collection. No one else, no political or literary friend, no relative, no emperor, appears in so many vivid narratives and leaves such a strong impression. No one else is such a consistent butt of Pliny's invective, as well as of his humor. He has been called the only prominent person attacked by name while he was alive (Sherwin-White 1966:55), but the *captatio* letter, with Regulus' false oath by his "unfortunate" son's life (2.20.6), was surely written (or revised) after the son's death at 4.2, and Pliny's confident and light-hearted attitude toward Regulus suggests that both his dangerous power and his misdeeds are over. His tone in 6.2, safe amusement over Regulus verging on longing for him now that he is dead, only slightly exaggerates his attitude throughout the Regulus series.[1] Even in the letters set in Regulus' lifetime the most fear and indignation that Pliny could work up against him was as remote and formalized as is the Greek language with which Pliny expresses, or dismisses, these feelings (1.5.15 δυσκαθαίρετον, 2.20.12 ἀλλὰ τί διατείνομαι; similarly at 4.7.3 and 4.7.6).[2]

Regulus is the antithesis of the ideal orator, a "bad man inexpert of speech" (4.7.5), who is sure to do whatever should not be done (4.2.8). He is thus a parody of the wise senior senator who can be trusted to advise the right thing

---

[1] "...[Plinius Regulus] als einem höchst verächtlichen und lächerlichen Menschen darstellt," Döring 1843; see Trisoglio 1972:112.

[2] Pliny's use of Greek for creating a safe distance has been observed. "L'epistolografo qui si esprime in greco, cercando di smorzare con la ricercatezza della lingua straniera la crudezza di un'ammissione che pure non è possibile eludere" (Trisoglio 1972:4 n.3 on 4.25.5). "The line of Euripides quoted in Greek introduces into the account a slight touch of urbane distance" (Hutchinson 1993:269 n. 22 on 4.11.9).

to do in any situation, as Mauricus (1.5.16) or Corellius (1.12.12, 4.17.8–9).[3] Regulus bears the same relation to Good Senators such as Mauricus, Spurinna, or Pliny that the Bad Emperors Nero and Domitian bear to the Good Emperors Nerva and Trajan. Accordingly his period of greatest power lay in the reigns of Nero and Domitian, and we even have an allusion to his malignant exultation at the accession of the Bad Emperor Otho (over the death of Piso, 2.20.2). Under a Good Emperor, however, he has no power—or rather, no power to harm (6.2.4) as an informer; his inheritance-hunting continues.

Regulus' two cardinal crimes, *delatio* and *captatio,* invert the virtues of the ideal upper-class politician: Regulus the orator uses the justice system for injustice, and Regulus the friend is no friend. His political as well as his social activities are driven by money, not by the abstract noble values which drive the activities of Pliny and his circle. His early delations under Nero were performed (it was said) not to save himself from danger, but out of the desire for money and power, and even the "lust for blood" (Tac. *Hist.* 4.42.1–4). His outrageous exultation over his victims makes it impossible for him to claim that he acted out of fear or imperial command, the usual excuses of *delatores* (as Suillius, another *delator* trapped by the change of rulers, Tac. *Ann.* 13.43.3; cf. *Hist.* 4.8.3, 4.42.3). Instead of the mutually beneficial circulation of favors that Pliny celebrates, Regulus' overriding aim is to amass his private fortune of money (2.20.13–14). Whereas Pliny consults eminent statesmen on serious moral and political questions, Regulus consults entrails to find out whether (or rather, "how soon") his vast wealth will reach HS 60,000,000 (2.20.13 *consuleret*). Perhaps we are to imagine that his son's death punishes him not only for "committing perjury by his son's well-being" (2.20.5) but also for such improper divination; he gets his riches, but only through personal tragedy. To be sure, Pliny avoids gloating directly, and says that this is the one loss Regulus did *not* deserve (4.2.1).

Having become so rich through his crimes and perjuries, Regulus increases his wealth still further by his son's death, which makes him inherit his dead wife's estate which she had originally willed to their son and not to him. Even in itself her will reflects badly on Regulus, as is exemplified by the legal device that was necessary to carry it out, "emancipating" his son from Regulus' paternal authority in order to make him a person legally competent to inherit (4.2.2). Regulus cannot be trusted, as it were, either to carry out his

---

[3] Yet during the Certus affair Pliny's cautious friend attributes to him the same rashness that Pliny attributes to Regulus (*quo audes?* 9.13.11; *audacia,* 4.7.3). See Kaster 1997:16 n. 40 on "good" and "bad" *audacia,* and the difficulties in distinguishing between them.

wife's dying wishes or to carry out his paternal responsibilities.[4] But not even his wife could have foreseen the grotesque perversion of family roles caused by the son's legal emancipation and inheritance of his mother's fortune. Not only has Regulus given up his *patria potestas,* but he has abandoned his paternal responsibility entirely, overindulging his newly rich son, or rather, as Pliny puts it, angling after his son's good graces under the disgusting and unfatherly pretence of being indulgent to his son's faults (4.2.2 *foeda et insolita parentibus indulgentiae simulatione captabat*). Being indulgent to a subordinate's faults is both an imperial virtue and a fatherly virtue, as at 9.12, where the childless Pliny offers expert parental advice on indulging one's son (9.12.1 *indulget*). But in the eyes of the greedy Regulus, the son's new-found wealth has not only removed him from his father's *potestas* but has even made him someone whose favor Regulus must court with false affection as he courts the favor of the childless rich in 2.20 (2.20.7 *captare*).

By using this technical term of inheritance-hunting Pliny manages to raise into the air, without actually asserting, the suggestion that Regulus hoped for his son's death and is now happy about it, though literally Pliny merely says "he may consider it a bad thing—I'm not sure" (4.2.1 *quod nescio an malum putet*).[5] Regulus' irresponsibility towards his son has made it impossible to tell whether he considers his son's death a greater loss than the cash gain that it has brought him. This is indeed a monstrous insult, but Pliny can prove it, not merely by relying on the shifting rhetoric of *distinctio,* between good *indulgentia* and bad *captatio,* but by the vote of the people, as it were, as expressed in a popular derogatory pun.[6] They called his *release* of his son not *emancipatio,* "emancipation," but *mancipatio,* "selling" (we might render it "he *leased* his son at the mother's behest"). And if we are to believe Pliny, this

---

[4] A similar case at 8.18.4 illustrates that it is when the proper family structure has broken down (in that case, a family feud) that the traditional family law of *patria potestas* has to be circumvented (Champlin 191:126). Veyne (1967:750) explains the legal mechanism, with the mother leaving a *fideicommissum* to Regulus to emancipate the son.

[5] Similarly, Pliny hedges his language when he descibes Regulus' excessive show of grief, never quite saying that he was not actually grieved: "that [mass slaughter of pets] was not [caused by] his grief, but [by his wish to make] a public display of his grief" (*nec dolor erat ille, sed ostentatio doloris,* 4.2.4).

[6] Sherwin-White's attitude (1966:266 "monstrous insult," on 4.2.2 *captabat*), is shared by many critics of letters 4.2 and 4.7 (e.g. Bardon 1956.2:207 "injuste"). But Pliny does not openly scorn Regulus' grief for his son's death; he scorns the way Regulus has arranged the maximum profit from the death, and the way he is making an excessive display of his grief. Since *captatio* connoted the "rupture of family ties" and was not normally imagined as being performed by immediate relatives (Champlin 1991:89), here, as at Juvenal 16.51, the *captatio* of an emancipated son epitomizes in itself the rupture of family ties. Compare also Martial's poems on profiting from a relative's death (2.65, 4.70).

joke was popular even before the son died: "people *used to say this* because of the character of the creature" (2 *ita vulgo ex moribus hominis loquebantur*).

Since Regulus "sold out" his son to profit by his wife's death, Regulus is not only cashing in on his successful *captatio* of his own son, but he will continue to profit from it by receiving in his turn flattering favors from the larger crowds of *captatores* which now besiege him since he has become not only richer than ever but also childless.[7] The "unhealthy season" during which he troubles his fellow citizens may help kill some off and enrich his coffers, indeed bringing him further "consolation" for his dead son (4.2.6 *vexat ergo civitatem insaluberrimo tempore et, quod vexat, solacium putat*). Among *captatores* the virtuous circle of favors between friends comes eerily close to revenge killing among family and friends. Regulus' exaggerated display of grief for his son, and the showy expense in precious metals and literary distribution (4.2.3, 4.7.1–2), seem to be a compensation or disguise, public or internal, for the vast profits he has reaped from his son's death—though they also announce that he is now childless and richer than ever, ripe for captatious favors.

As Regulus the senator and Regulus the friend and relative invert Plinian ideals, so too Regulus the man of literature exemplifies bad literature, a counterpart to the bad political situation which fostered it. Regulus' violent aggressive style is perfectly suited to the *delatio* for which it is designed, and letter 1.5 shows us enough of this style to demonstrate that Regulus' "eloquence" (1.5.2) is really non-eloquence.[8] Similarly his "woeful" book on his son's life (4.7.6 *luctuosum... librum*), aimed at proving that he is *not* exulting over this most profitable death, is more likely to arouse laughter than lament (*ut risum magis possit exprimere quam gemitum*, 4.7.7).

Throughout the Regulus series, as elsewhere, Pliny is at pains to maintain the distinctions between good and bad senator, between good and bad emperor, which are always in danger of collapsing. Regulus the *delator* resembles Pliny the prosecutor, Regulus the *captator* resembles Pliny the loyal friend who is always rewarded with legacies from his friends (7.20.6), and Regulus the careful writer and orator resembles Pliny the careful writer and

---

[7] "In ingratiating themselves with Regulus they imitate Regulus" (*in Regulo demerendo Regulum imitantur*, 4.2.4). Pliny likes to damn his villains by making them represent a general and notorious group of anti-values. Of Fabricius Veiento he says, "I've said it all when I've named the creature" (*dixi omnia cum hominem nominavi*, 4.22.4).

[8] Pliny's elegant invective gives a derogatory sense to *eloquentia,* normally a complimentary term (*OLD* s.v.); for example, at 5.20.5 Candidus contrasts (good) *eloquentia* with (bad) *loquentia.*

orator (6.2).[9] Letter 6.2 illustrates the process by which Pliny differentiates virtues from their corresponding vices. Because of his *ambitio,* self-promotion, the bad advocate makes the long and careful speech that the good advocate makes because of his *fides,* loyalty to his client.[10] Even while praising Regulus' care in writing out speeches Pliny disparages it, using it as a comic anti-climax in a scornful list (6.2.2 *timebat pallebat scribebat*), and saying that he cannot memorize them anyway.[11]

Martial's flattering references to Regulus indicate how difficult it was for Pliny to separate himself from the anti-orator Regulus. If we had only Martial's poems by which to judge the two, it would be hard to distinguish the two successful pleaders.[12] In practice, the virtuous advocate acts approximately the same way as does the vicious advocate; he is enlisted to make his client's case sound as good as possible, true or false, and not to apply moral wisdom. Thus Pliny must show how Regulus in arguing his client's case defamed an innocent victim of Domitian (Modestus), even using the opportunity to try to get another senator into trouble (Pliny). A morally conscientious lawyer might possibly have been able to produce a similar benefit for his client in a less harmful way, perhaps by simply reminding the judges that the opponent's case rested on the judgment of an exiled man. The awkward fact remains, however, that Regulus' scheme promises to produce the maximum possible benefit for his client, for what could be better than to force a witness for the other side to support your own case? Under a Bad Emperor, at least, one might imagine that the most unscrupulous advocate is the most effective one. Thus Pliny carefully shows how his divinely inspired self-restraint enabled him to foil Regulus, and even turn the tables on him: even under a Bad Emperor the orator of restraint and honor can be a stronger advocate than the orator of shamelessness and malice.

Pliny elsewhere shows us that when his caution and restraint weaken his advocacy, it thereby makes his advocacy more fair. He refuses to uses his oratorical skill to the hilt to convict Classicus' wife, who may have been

---

[9] "Ironically, it's bad to hunt but good to receive legacies," Saller 1982:125. "It was not easy to distinguish *amicus* from *captator.* Pliny's picture of Julius Naso could apply to a *captator*... VI. 6. 5" (Sherwin-White 1966:204). See Dixon 1993:454.

[10] *O Regule, qui ambitione ab omnibus obtinebas quod fidei paucissimi praestant!* (6.2.7; compare Quint. *Inst.* 12.9.1, 7, 14–15).

[11] Quintilian warns against writing out a speech if you are not going to memorize it, since you will be torn between your imperfect memory and the need to improvise anew (*Inst.* 10.7.32 conj.; 12.9.17).

[12] Both are eloquent (*facundo,* Martial 6.64.11, 10.19.3); both succeed in the Centumviral Court (6.38, 10.19.15); both rival Cicero (4.16, 10.19.17); and both deign to read Martial's trifles (6.64.11, 10.19.21). Martial's praises of Regulus, to be sure, cease with the death of Domitian, whereas the long poem in praise of Pliny is in the revised Book 10, published after Domitian's death.

innocent since the evidence was ambiguous.[13] Pliny's use of his skill is the
inverse of Regulus'. Pliny (modestly) implies that he had enough skill ("such
as it is") to convict Classicus' wife, even if she were innocent, aiming his
oratory "like a weapon against her throat," but his moral scruples held him
back.[14] Regulus, on the other hand, would be perfectly willing to convict and
kill an innocent man, but his skill is not sufficient, at least not against a Pliny.
The "praise and congratulations" Pliny received at 1.5.7 suggest that Regulus
lost the case as well, though in the context of Pliny's mortal danger the
outcome of the financial lawsuit is beneath notice. In sum, even under a bad
emperor a good advocate can do an honest job and succeed by a combination
of talent and decency. Hence, Rusticus' and especially Pliny's successful
careers under Domitian do not taint them morally as Regulus' successful
career does taint him.

Pliny designedly uses a case in which he is a *prosecutor* (the Classicus case)
to illustrate the balance between moral restraint and oratorical skill. Since
punishing the innocent is generally considered worse than acquitting the
guilty, unscrupulous success is worse for a prosecutor than for a defendant.[15]
Pliny only accepted the case reluctantly (with praiseworthy *modestia,* 3.4.4),
having considered that since Classicus himself was dead, he would not be
engaged in endangering a senator—Regulus' specialty (3.4.8 *periculum
senatoris;* cf. 1.5.5 *vides quod periculum*). Since he is prosecuting, Pliny can
act with restraint without violating a bond of *fides* to a client (3.4.4 *fidem*).
He is careful to show us that he first asked his provincial clients whether they

---

[13] Pliny likes to show himself chivalrously defending women (1.5.5, 4.17, 9.13.5). Pliny's
admired friend Herennius also appears as the advocate for the Vestal Virgin, whom Pliny
clearly wishes us to believe innocent (4.11.5–9), although most other sources call her guilty
and most modern scholars follow suit (Suetonius *Dom.* 8.3–4, Juv. 4.8–10, Stat. *Silv.*
1.1.36, 5.3.178, Plut. *Numa* 10.8, Philostr. *Vit. Apoll.* 7.6; Dio 67.3.3–4 seems to consider
the Vestals innocent). The fact that Licinianus was not recalled (Sherwin-White 1966:282)
hardly proves Cornelia's guilt, unless we believe that Nerva and Trajan were infallible. Traub
(1955:217) points out that Tacitus seems to assume that the Vestals were guilty (*Hist.* 1.2.2
pollutae caerimoniae; cf. Vinson 1989:434, Jones 1992:102), but still, it is hard to be certain
about private sexual activities 2000 years ago. Jones even compliments Domitian ("generosity
indeed") for allowing the Vestals to choose their manner of death, apparently without Dio's
irony (Dio 67.3.4). At any rate, we can certainly agree with Pliny that the archaic punishment
was barbaric and hypocritical.

[14] "Then I proceeded to ask advice from the Senate, if it thought that I should hold, against the
throat of an innocent person, whatever skill I may have in speaking, as if it were some
weapon." (*modo consilium a senatu petebam, putaretne debere me, si quam haberem in
dicendo facultatem, in iugulum innocentis quasi telum aliquod intendere,* 3.9.21) The
conditional is Pliny's characteristic way of modestly softening a boast (as at 1.1.1 *si quas
paulo curatius scripsissem*).

[15] E.g. Aristot. *Problem.* 29.951B1, Cic. *de Offic.* 2.14.51, August. *Confess.* 4.2; see David
1992:526, 531.

felt they had proof against Classicus' wife, and then asked the Senate for
permission to refrain from prosecuting her. Pliny "remembers" his faculties
as an impartial judge even when he has been asked to act as an advocate
(3.9.21 *memini tamen me advocatum ex iudicibus datum*). The Senate can still
praise Pliny and his colleague for "diligence, loyalty, and steadfastness"
despite, or perhaps *because* of his refusal to use to the hilt his position as
prosecutor and his skill as orator (3.9.23 *industria fides constantia nostra*).
Although Pliny elsewhere tells us that shamelessness gives strength and
decency causes weakness (4.7.3), letter 1.5 shows how his decency allied with
oratorical skill overcomes Regulus' shamelessness allied with his reckless kind
of anti-eloquence.[16]

This distinction between reckless boldness and cautious restraint also
separates the Good Emperor from the Bad Emperor. The Good Emperor
displays caution and modesty. The familiar game of *recusatio* makes him
decline or postpone accession (*Pan.* 9.2–4, 10.3–4), titles (21), honorary
inscriptions (54.4), and offices (56.3). When requested to show unseemly
favoritism in the Senate he is silent (6.5.5), and he can preside over a trial as
consul without seeming to influence the outcome, his only intervention
concerning the health of Pliny's voice (2.11.15). Nerva even manages to
remain silent while one dinner guest (Mauricus) obliquely insults another
(Veiento, 4.22.6). When Trajan does issue a judgment or decree, it is
described as "moderate."[17] Even Trajan's dinners are restrained (6.31.13
modica).

Domitian is of course the opposite of Trajan throughout the *Panegyric*,
noted for imperial overassertion (*adrogantia principalis, Pan.* 76.7) and
characterized by the same paradoxical combination of fearfulness and
arrogance that Regulus shows (*timore et superbia, Pan.* 49.1; *ut plurimum
audeat plurimum timeat*, 2.11.22). In Domitian's longest appearance in the
collection, at the Vestal trial of Licinianus, we see him as a Regulus on the
throne, extracting incriminating confessions from innocent people and
rejoicing immoderately over their downfall. To the Regulus whose paleness

---

[16] Quintilian warns that invective is often counterproductive (*Inst.* 12.9.8–13), whereas
"restraint" *(modestia)* gives the orator the most authority and credit (*plurimum oratori et
auctoritatis et fidei adfert*, 12.9.12). Winterbottom (1964:94–97) speculates that Quintilian's
emphasis on the moral qualities of the *vir bonus*, and his disparagement of the reckless style,
were inspired by the prominence, and the excellence, of the invective style of the *delatores*, and
are indirect criticisms of Regulus, the "bad man inexpert in speaking" (Plin. 4.7.5).
[17] 5.3.8 *severus et tamen moderatus*, 6.31.11 *summa gravitate, summa moderatione*. For
"moderation" as an imperial virtue, see *Pan.* 3.2, 54.5, 55.1, 56.3, 77.9; Fell 1992:30.
Suetonius praises the *abstinentia* and *moderatio* of the emperors following Domitian (*Dom.*
23.2). Pliny himself often boasts of his own *modestia* (e.g 1.8.5, 3.4.5, 3.18.4, 9.13.4). A
similar topic of praise is *verecundia*, e.g. *Pan.* 24.2, 55.4.

does not quite hide it when he becomes still paler with fear (1.5.13), we may contrast the ruddy Domitian who was immune from blushing with shame.[18] Domitian's only words in Pliny's letters ironically contrast the shameless emperor with the senator endowed with decent restraint. "We must not keep pressing on Licinianus' *sense of shame* (or *self-restraint*)" (*non esse verecundiae eius instandum,* 4.11.13). Assuming the pose of the generous emperor, Domitian is saying that he should not add a harsh punishment onto Licinianus' guilty shame for his misdeed. But *verecundia* is normally a good attribute, proper self-restraint, and Pliny has strongly suggested that Licinianus is innocent. The word "shame" refuses to mean what the shameless emperor tries to make it mean. It comes out almost as Domitian's ironic compliment to the self-restrained senator whose false confession saves Domitian from *invidia* (to be sure, it also saves Licinianus from being beaten). Domitian too might have recognized from its "Homeric" restraint (4.11.12) that the confession expresses not inner guilt but an unwillingness to become a useless martyr—if only he had not been driven by his own sense of guilt to express unrestrained "joy" at being "exonerated" by Licinianus.[19]

Regulus the Bad Senator parallels Domitian the Bad Emperor in this unwholesome combination of shame and shamelessness, of audacity and fearfulness. Like Domitian he persecutes the innocent without compunctions of shame, and only feels guilt when driven to fear the ill will he has aroused. The "odium" (*invidia,* 4.11.5) and "disrepute" (*infamia,* 11) that surrounded Domitian aroused a touch of guilt that he "gave away" *(proderetur)* by his joyful outburst (4.11.13), and correspondingly Regulus' "fear" finally arouses a guilty "memory" for what he has done to Rusticus and Pliny *(reminiscebatur,* 1.5.4). Regulus feels fear *(vereri,* 1.5.1) without shame *(verecundia),* horrified awareness *(conscientia,* 1.5.8) but no sense of moral conscience, as we can see from his weakly inadequate apology (1.5.11).[20] As

---

[18] *Pan.* 48.4, Suet. *Dom.* 18.1, Tac. *Hist.* 4.40.1, *Agric.* 45.3; Kaster 1997:8. Seneca (*Ep.* 40.13) and Martial (11.27.7) even mention producing a fake red complexion to hide shame. Another stand-in for Domitian is Messalinus, whose blindness, like Domitian's ruddiness, makes him immune from blushing (4.22.5 *non erubescat*). A ruddy complexion normally indicates decent bashfulness, as at 5.17.3 and perhaps 1.14.8 (Lilja 1978:57–58); Domitian's was so interpreted—until people learned better (Tac. *Hist.* 4.40.1). Regulus' paleness indicates his tendency to feel cowardly fear rather than moral shame at his misdeeds; see Kaster 1997:4 n. 7, 7 n. 14 on the opposition between the blush of *pudor* and the pallor of *timor*.

[19] The word *verecundia* is normally complimentary, except for two typical contexts, in the predicate dative ("it was shameful") or with a defining genitive ("shame for..."). Another ironic treatment of this traditional laudatory term is at 8.6.12 ("the 'modest restraint' of Pallas").

[20] *Conscientia,* moral self-awareness, is usually "good conscience" at having acted rightly (e.g. 1.8.14, 1.12.3, 1.22.5); it means "bad conscience" at 1.5.8, 2.11.24, 10.30.2, and perhaps 3.20.9.

opposed to the Stoical Pliny who does good for its own sake apart from personal benefit (1.8.14; cf. *Pan.* 44.6), Regulus and Domitian regret wrongdoing only for its bad consequences. Only during the transitions from Bad Emperor to Good Emperor, in 69 and in 96, does Regulus feel a twinge of conscience.

The spectacle of Regulus cringing under a Good Emperor is a half-satisfying substitute for what senators such as Pliny must have really wished to see, Domitian under a Good Emperor. A moment of bloody assassination must have seemed inadequate expiation for the years of humiliations and deaths suffered by the ruling class. Rarely does one get to see a Bad Emperor conquered and confronted with the full force of the hostility he has aroused. Vitellius was the only emperor ever seen publicly giving up office (Tac. *Hist.* 3.67), and led in humiliation to his death (Tac. *Hist.* 3.85, Suet. *Vitell.* 17, Dio 64.20–21). Domitian died too soon for feelings of revenge to play themselves out onto him. Pliny presents the grotesque image of senators hacking away at Domitian's proud statues, as if blood were caused by each blow (*Pan.* 52.4). When death does not offer a satisfying revenge, the avenger takes out further aggression on the corpse.[21]

Regulus himself offers a metaphorical example, "mutilating" Herennius so immoderately as to offend even Herennius' killer himself. He was even accused of the most inhuman mutilation, biting the head of Piso (Tac. *Hist.* 4.42.2), towards whose wife he later performs his flattering *captatio,* 2.20.2.[22] Though Pliny has a vicarious opportunity to mutilate Domitian through the person of Regulus, still he must distinguish himself from Regulus in revenge. If Pliny took the same kind of bestial revenge on his enemies as they took under prior emperors, the two sides would be indistinguishable and in the seesaw of power and revenge there would be no difference between Good and Bad Senator. Hence Pliny's joy is only the discreet moral satisfaction that expresses itself in moderate eloquence, not the aggressive gloating expressed in Regulus' violent "eloquence." The only open invective the letter aims against Regulus comes from Regulus' own mouth, in quoting an insult by Modestus to which Pliny merely assents (1.5.14). Pliny's model for revenge is not Achilles' over Hector, but Odysseus' with his οὐχ ὁσίη φθιμένοισι over

---

[21] Some notorious examples were Cicero, Sejanus, Galba, and Vitellius; people cast down the statues of Sejanus "as if they were abusing the man himself" (Dio 58.11.3; compare 64.21.2 on Vitellius' statues).

[22] Tacitus, to be sure, does not vouch for this charge of cannibalism, which occurs only in Curtius Montanus' "ferocious" speech of accusation (*truci oratione... ut... adpetitumque morsu Pisonis caput obiectaret, Hist.* 4.42.2). Montanus goes on to emphasize the physical brutality of Regulus' eloquence: "in lust for blood you steeped your oratorical skill in aristocratic gore" (*libidine sanguinis... ingenium... caede nobili imbuisti,* 4.42.4). See Plass 1995:144 for other references to cannibalistic rage in Roman history.

the dead suitors ("it is impious [to vaunt] over the dead," 9.1.3; cf. *Od.* 22.412).[23] Once Regulus is dead, Pliny can even afford to "miss" him (6.2.1 *quaerere*).

In the *Panegyric,* too, Pliny shows his restraint in gloating over Domitian even though his rhetorical purpose demands continual contrast between Domitian and Trajan. Pliny himself avoids Regulus' exultant mutilation of the dead, or Domitian's selfish and malignant joy over his enemies' downfall (4.11.13). Even while describing the "bloody" mutilation of Domitian's statues (*ut si... sanguis dolorque..., Pan.* 52.4), Pliny lets show his moral disquiet over the lack of restraint. "No one was so *restrained* in joy and postponed gladness that it did not seem like vengeance to see mutilated limbs, dismembered bodies..." (*Pan.* 52.5 *nemo tam* temperans *gaudii...;* compare Regulus' *lacerat Herennium Senecionem tam* intemperanter..., 1.5.3). Elsewhere Pliny tones down the language of joy from *gaudium* and *laetitia* to *gratus* and *iuvat* in describing the fall of Domitian (e.g. 34.3 *gratius... dignius... fruebamur,* 35.1 *iuvabat,* 36.1, 42.4). Pliny's true "joys" are for the present (*gaudia... laetemur,* 53.6), and if he takes verbal "vengeance" against Bad Emperors (*vindicari,* 53.5; cf. *instar ultionis,* 52.5), it is to praise the present emperor for allowing denigration of past emperors and to warn future emperors by example (53.3, 5–6).

REGULUS: THE "ELOQUENCE" OF THE COLLABORATOR

Vidistine quemquam M. Regulo timidiorem humiliorem post Domitiani mortem? sub quo non minora flagitia commiserat quam sub Nerone sed tectiora. Coepit vereri ne sibi irascerer, nec fallebatur: irascebar. (1.5.1)

Have you seen anyone more fearful or more downcast that Marcus Regulus after the death of Domitian—under whom the crimes he had committed were no smaller than those under Nero, but more hidden. He began to be afraid that I was angry at him, and he was not mistaken: I was angry.

Pliny's first sentence introduces all the essentials: the subject, M. Regulus, the time, after Domitian's death, and the new attitude, fearful and groveling. Pliny's lightheartedly intimate question ("have you ever seen... more...?") implies a superlative. They have never seen anyone more fearful; Regulus is the most. An epistolary parallel and possible model is Caelius' high-spirited romp through the follies of Roman politics, which deserve more mockery

[23] His uncle quotes a similar saying by L. Munatius Plancus, *cum mortuis non nisi larvas luctari, NH* praef. 31.

than indignation.[24] After this light opening Pliny shifts back to describe his grave personal peril under Domitian, and eventually returns to the present Regulus who deserves mockery more than indignation. As in Caelius' letter, the second person address sets the two friends above the muck of political vice and folly. Voconius also sees that Regulus is more fearful than any of Domitian's creatures, and Pliny can tell him why: Regulus is scared after what he did to Pliny and to Pliny's friends. Presumably Pliny is just one of the many Romans Regulus offended by his "hidden crimes." There must be many other "good" Romans who have similar stories to tell of Regulus, and whom Regulus now fears. Yet Pliny gives the impression that Regulus fears him more than anyone else. He began to fear that Pliny was angry; he asks two of Pliny's friends, then Spurinna, to appease his anger; he cannot wait another day, it must be tomorrow morning, early morning. Just as Regulus is more fearful than any of Domitian's agents, Pliny is his object of fear more than any of Domitian's opponents. If Regulus is the worst of senators, then Pliny is the best of senators, or perhaps the best of those who avoided death or exile and maintained high status in Rome.

Regulus' very name ("kinglet") may allude to the hated title *rex* ("king") avoided by those who had become kings again at Rome, the emperors. The king is gone, and his agent the kinglet has been taken down a notch. Keller even detects a mocking allusion to the tiny bird the "kinglet" (βασιλίσκος in Greek) in Modestus' insult "most worthless of *two-legged animals*" (1.5.14; 1887:139–40). But the most prominent echo in the name M. (Aquilius) Regulus is the glorious republican hero M. (Atilius) Regulus, celebrated for remaining faithful and fearless even in facing a death he did *not* deserve, despite the vicissitudes of coming under a different power—in his case, falling into Carthaginian hands. The pathetic spectacle of the fearful, faithless Regulus could arouse a wistful longing for Republican times before civil wars and imperial government, when Romans could hope to serve their country through fearless bravery against foreign enemies, and not have to choose between the useless bravery of a Rusticus, the treacherous cowardice of a Regulus, or at best the cautious prudence of a Pliny or a Spurinna.

The naked names "Domitian" and "Nero" (1.5.1) themselves add to the point, since Pliny normally names emperors with honorific titles, as in *divus Nerva* (4.11.14) or *imperator Nerva* (4.22.4). Pliny never uses the proper names of M. Ulpius Traianus at all, except when he refers to his games, 10.75.2, or his father, *Pan.* 89.2, or when renaming him *Optimus, Pan.* 88.6. He prefers honorific terms such as *Caesar Auguste, Imperator Auguste,* or

---

[24] "Have you ever seen a more incompetent person than this Gnaeus Pompey of yours?" (*Ecquando tu hominem ineptiorem quam tuum Cn. Pompeium vidisti...?* Caelius apud Cic. *Fam.* 8.15.1); Trisoglio 1973:180 n. 56.

Caesare nostro; the groveling *domine* of Book 10 is of course avoided in 1–9 and the *Panegyric*.[25] The personal name of the emperor is too human; using it would be like jostling his body casually. But Nero and Domitian cannot be called *divus,* or indeed any honorific title, since they received not apotheosis but posthumous denigration (see Sherwin-White 1966:128 on 1.18.3). There might even be an echo between the hated term *rex* in Regulus and the lordly *domitor/dominus* in the name Domitianus, also present in the original name of Nero, Domitius.[26]

Regulus' crimes under Domitian and Nero mark these two reigns as the low points of the unfortunate recent period that began after the relatively better times of Claudius' reign and the start of Nero's, and that is just starting to be repaired in the new age of Nerva and Trajan. Furthermore, the manner of Regulus' two periods of *delatio,* open and secret, implies a comparison between these two Bad Emperors, Nero and Domitian. Domitian's crimes, too, were just as bad as Nero's, even if they were less flagrant, and even if he did not roam the streets as a thug or perform on the stage.[27] The two emperors mark the two main periods of Regulus' career. His fears after Domitian's death repeat his vulnerability after Nero's death (Tac. *Hist.* 4.42), and once again reveal his guilt, distinguishing him from a good senator such as Pliny. The regretful Regulus contrasts with Pliny, who behaves at the start of the new regime in such a way that he will feel no regret under future emperors, good or bad (9.13.10). Regulus' obvious change of mood proves that we can distinguish good senators from bad ones despite their similarly successful careers, and good emperors from bad ones despite the similar tone of public adulation.

> Rustici Aruleni periculum foverat, exsultaverat morte; adeo ut librum recitaret publicaretque, in quo Rusticum insectâtur atque etiam 'Stoicorum simiam' adpellat, adicit 'Vitelliana cicatrice stigmosum' (agnoscis eloquentiam Reguli), lacerat Herennium Senecionem tam intemperanter quidem, ut dixerit ei Mettius

---

[25] Similarly, in the many poems on Domitian, Martial uses the name "Domitian" only once (9.1.1). Helvidius Priscus, by contrast, insisted on calling Vespasian by his personal name (Suet. *Vesp.* 15). It is not true that Pliny generally omits the term *divus* when referring to Augustus, Claudius, or Vespasian (Charlesworth 1937:59). They are generally called *divus* (1.14.5, 5.3.5, 8.8.6) or at least *imperator* (3.5.9) or *Caesar* (1.13.3) unless the context is derogatory (3.16.7, 4.9.1).

[26] Ancient etymology derived both *dominus* and *domare/ domitor* from *domus* (Prisc. *Gramm.* 3.506.1–3)—the former correctly, the latter incorrectly. Juvenal equates the two Bad Emperors by calling Domitian the "bald Nero" (4.38), and Martial seems to refer to Domitian by the name "Nero" (11.33.1); see Bartsch 1994:277 n. 23.

[27] *secundum imperatorum ingenium: sub Nerone in propatulo peccabat, sub Domitiano, malitiam dissimulabat* (Catanaeus 1533, on 1.5.1 *tectiora*). I have included a number of references to the early commentators which show their sensitivity to Pliny's sophisticated rhetoric.

Carus 'Quid tibi cum meis mortuis? Numquid ego Crasso aut Camerino molestus sum?' quos ille sub Nerone accusaverat. Haec me Regulus dolenter tulisse credebat, ideoque etiam cum recitaret librum non adhibuerat. (2–4)

He had fostered the persecution of Rusticus Arulenus, and gloated over his death, so much so that he recited and published a book in which he attacked Rusticus, and even called him an "ape of the Stoics," adding that he was "branded with his Vitellian scar" (you recognize Regulus' style of eloquence), and he shredded Herennius Senecio so unrestrainedly that Mettius Carus said to him, "What business have you with my dead ones? I've never troubled Crassus and Camerinus, have I?" (those are people he had accused under Nero). Regulus believed that I had been painfully affected by this, and so he even omitted to invite me when he gave a recitation of the book.

The essence of Regulus' crimes is his attempt to "foster" executions by eliciting actionable statements from his victims for the more open *delatores* to act upon (*periculum foverat;* see Sherwin-White 1966:96). His attempts to entrap Pliny on the stand may indicate what he succeeded in doing to Rusticus. Yet, strangely, the climactic line of the first episode, describing his exultation over Rusticus and Herennius Senecio, is the seemingly bathetic comment that Regulus did not invite Pliny to his reading. The line serves, of course, to give an explicit connection between Regulus' attacks on Rusticus and his later fear of *Pliny's* anger, and it flaunts Pliny's tie with Rusticus as something recognized even by enemies and thus separating the good senator Pliny from the bad senator Regulus. It is no accidental "slip" (Sherwin-White 1966:96) for Pliny to reveal that Regulus normally would invite him, but an acknowledgment of the obvious public fact that senators behave with each other as if they are all colleagues and friends. If Pliny cooperates with Rusticus one day, perhaps as co-advocate (1.5.5 *aderam*), he will act as co-advocate with Regulus another day (1.20.14), and must keep up a friendly façade on all occasions. Pliny's lack of an invitation is a rare public indication of the true alignments. Regulus may not realize that his extreme invective offends even Senecio's killer Mettius Carus, but he does realize that it offends Pliny. If the first episode singles out Pliny as the special friend and mourner of Rusticus, the second episode, back when Rusticus was still alive, singles Pliny out as a possible victim. Pliny and Rusticus are interchangeable here; it might just as well have been Pliny killed, and Rusticus not invited to the reading. Pliny the successful survivor distinguishes himself from Regulus the successful survivor, and identifies himself with Rusticus the heroic martyr.

Pliny presents Regulus' crimes as if they were principally *literary* crimes. To the mere two words on Regulus' role in Rusticus' death (*periculum foverat*) Pliny adds a whole paragraph to describe Regulus' gloating over Rusticus' death. The second episode, Pliny's performance on the stand, is entirely a contest of words, a duel between opposing modes of eloquence. Just as Pliny's characteristic mode is praise, Regulus' characteristic mode is blame. Pliny publishes praise of good men; Regulus publishes blame of good men. Pliny writes almost nothing but praise—of his hometown (2.5), his friends (7.28.1), and Trajan—with the exception of the Regulus letters, though even here Pliny distinguishes his style from Regulus' style of blame. Pliny does not "go for the throat" with violent invective as Regulus does (1.20.14 *iugulum... premo;* cf. 3.9.21 *in iugulum innocentis quasi telum aliquod intendere*), and he even offers Regulus a laudatory obituary of sorts after his death (6.2). We recall that the "crimes" for which Herennius Senecio and Rusticus died were laudatory obituaries of Thrasea Paetus and Helvidius Priscus (Tac. *Agric.* 2, Dio 67.13.2, Suet. *Dom.* 10.3). Though laudation is the staple of oratory under the emperors, Pliny prefers to emphasize the characteristic invective of the *delatores* under the bad emperors in distinction to the praise of virtue under the good emperors.

Pliny's laudatory mode aims at mutual exchange for mutual benefit, whereas harmonious mutual benefit is as impossible among blamers as honor among thieves; Regulus and Carus are reduced to the status of animals fighting over a corpse. The more general metaphors of gloating (*exsultaverat,* "jump up at") and attacking (*insectatur,* "follow after") reach a climax in the vivid term *lacerat,* tearing Herennius to shreds (1.5.2–3), recalling the Tacitean innuendo that Regulus actually bit into the severed head of Piso.[28] Carus is driven to retort, "what business have you with *my* dead ones? Did I ever bother [yours], Crassus or Camerinus?" The victims of *delatores* are "their own dead," following them their whole lives as emblems of dishonor, the opposite of honorific *imagines* of "one's own" people, so to speak. Regulus' attempt to borrow glory by gloating over the victim of another *delator* recoils against himself. Regulus the secret *delator* thinks he can safely gloat over Herennius' death, for which he had no direct responsibility, and flaunt his loyalty to Domitian without suffering obloquy for having caused the death of a fellow senator. Yet Carus the open *delator* can avenge Regulus' attempt to win glory at his expense by pointing to Regulus' own shameful career as open *delator.*[29]

Each of the four episodes (recitation, Arionilla, Spurinna, *praetoris officium*) displays Regulus' actual words. In the first episode Pliny calls attention to the direct quotation by giving us two striking Regulan phrases

---

[28] The similarity between the rhetoric of violent invective and animal violence was enshrined in the proverb of Appius Claudius, "dog's eloquence" (*canina facundia,* Sallust *Hist.* 2 fr. 37D; Quint. *Inst.* 12.9.9).

[29] Though many translators wrongly start a new sentence at *lacerat,* and Keil even altered the text to *lacera<ra>t,* Regulus shreds Herennius and attacks Rusticus *in the same book.* Pliny's recapitulating reference to the recitation (4) shows that Mynors' comma is correct (*in quo Rusticus insectatur..., lacerat Herennium*).

whose very style announces their authorship: "you recognize the 'eloquence' of Regulus." The unflattering tone strips the term *eloquentia* of its usual positive connotation and reduces it to its plain unmarked meaning, "style of speaking," or even to a negative meaning by ironic contrast with its normal meaning.[30] In mocking Regulus, Pliny carefully avoids Regulus' immoral (and ultimately unsuccessful) methods. Instead of attacking him violently, Pliny lets Regulus be damned by the simple facts, by his own words and those of his fellow *delator*. Only with the words *exsultaverat* and *lacerat* does Pliny offer harsh words of his own, but his examples of Regulus' invective show that one can hardly describe such a style accurately without a touch of the same style rubbing off on one's description.

Right from Regulus' opening words we can see how this violent style is ultimately self-defeating. This style is a perfect counterpart to the unrestrained, violent emperors Nero and Domitian under whom it developed—emperors who destroyed themselves by their unrestrained, violent reigns, which led to successful overthrows. Regulus' last words in this letter show most clearly how his words could backfire onto himself. In his vain denial of having tried to entrap Pliny on the stand, Regulus produces the most damning invective against himself ("most worthless of all two-legged creatures," 1.5.14). Regulus' sneer at Rusticus' "Vitellian scar" also shows how his violent style recoils against himself, now that it is no longer supported by the Bad Emperor.

We happen to possess Tacitus' rather anti-Flavian account of this event, which enables us to see how Regulus' rhetoric undoes itself (*Hist.* 3.80.1–2; cf. Suet. *Vitell.* 16, Dio 64.19.1). Regulus mocks the scar that Rusticus received in the final days of the civil war of 69, when as praetor he went on a mission from Rome, which was still held by Vitellian forces. Regulus calls the scar a "brand," as if on a runaway slave, as a permanent mark of its disloyalty.[31] Throughout the Flavian era Rusticus bore a physical mark to show that he belonged to the opposition. No matter how loyally or respectfully he behaved, you could distinguish him from truly loyal senators (such as Regulus) and see that he was unalterably a member of the other side, harboring resentment and treacherous impulses, which come out in his literary support for the Thrasea-Herennius group.[32] But in fact, Rusticus as praetor was using his prestige as a moral authority to preserve peace and decency during the crisis of imperial

---

[30] *Eloquentiam] Ironice, nam erat vir malus dicendi imperitus* (Catanaeus 1533).

[31] *Servili stigmati comparat honestam cicatricem* (Gesner 1739).

[32] Plutarch preserves for us a glimpse of Rusticus as the respected and outwardly loyal (but perhaps too philosophically self-disciplined) senator under Domitian. A message straight from Domitian is delivered to Rusticus while he listens to Plutarch's lecture. Plutarch offers to pause, but Rusticus uses his iron self-control to postpone reading it until the lecture is finished and the audience has dispersed, *de Curios.* 522E.

transition; it is the groveling Regulus who acts as a captured runaway slave during imperial transitions, then and now.

Rusticus' scar is not the brand of a slave but the mark of a heroic wound, earned as if in battle, in trying to save the lives of his fellow citizens. He was not acting as a mere agent of Vitellius against the Flavians, but as praetor, a bearer of "independent" senatorial power, trying to negotiate a halt in the civil war between Vitellius, who was on the verge of surrendering, and the nearly victorious Flavian forces.[33] He is the male counterpart of the Vestal Virgins who were sent for the same purpose, a holder of ancient and sacred power, the highest available "neutral" magistrate, since the chaotic recent sequence of murdered and appointed consuls made them unavailable for this independent, neutral mission.[34] Rather than a reminder of Rusticus' supposed Vitellian leanings, the scar is a memorial to the final horrors of Vespasian's civil war that culminated in the capture of Rome, an utterly useless atrocity that was said to have cost 50,000 lives (Dio 64.19.3). To Tacitus, the wounding and near murder of the praetor Rusticus was an especially appalling crime during the final attack on Rome (*Hist.* 3.80.2).

Mocking bodily defects is always a delicate matter. Early rhetorical writers only allowed it if the defect was the person's fault (Corbeill 1996:25); Regulus was evidently trying for this but missed his aim. Even Cicero, who goes further in allowing joking references to bodily defects, warns that it must not be done like a buffoon (*scurrilis*) or like a clown (*mimicus*).[35] Pliny's own joke about Regulus' paleness (1.5.13) shows how this sort of thing can be done properly. Even more tasteless is to point out the physical defects of a dead man, indeed of a man one has killed, which verges on desecration of the corpse. One thinks of the climactic horror of Nero's matricide, his inspection of the corpse (*atrociora,* Suet. *Nero* 34.4; ἀνοσιώτερον, Dio 61.14.2; Tacitus gives conflicting reports, *Ann.* 14.9.1).

If we turn back to Regulus' first sneer, the "Stoic ape," we find that it too is counterproductive invective that recoils onto himself. Once again we have a hybrid of foreign and native, of Latin and Latinized Greek: *Stoicorum,* like *stigmosum,* is a Latinized Greek word. In the second phrase Rusticus is a

---

[33] Dio and Suetonius, to be sure, make it clearer that the "Senate's" decision to send the delegation was really Vitellius' decision (Tac. *Hist.* 3.80.1 *vocato senatu deliguntur legati... ut praetexto rei publicae concordiam pacemque suaderent;* Dio 64.18.3 καὶ τὴν βουλὴν συναγαγὼν πρέσβεις παρ' αὐτῶν... ἔπεμψεν; Suet. *Vitell.* 16 *suasitque senatui ut legatos... mitterent).* Yet both Dio and Tacitus indicate that they were sent *as senators* (παρ' αὐτῶν, *praetexto rei publicae*), not as Vitellius' agents.

[34] Consuls were appointed well in advance, especially in the year of the four emperors (Plut. *Otho* 1.2, Tac. *Hist.* 3.55, 4.47).

[35] *de Orat.* 2.239; Guillemin 1927:7 n. 2. Corbeill discusses Cicero's theory and use of bodily invective in detail (1996:20–56).

marginal member of the ruling class, an upstart alien slave who was caught running away from the Vitellian side. In the first phrase, Rusticus is a Roman ape in the Greek portico, a Roman who, unlike Tacitus' Agricola (*Agric.* 4.3), went over so wholeheartedly to Greek philosophy as to make himself unfit for Roman politics, and for the proper imperial values of loyalty and obedience. Reducing himself to trying to imitate alien wisdom, he has made himself neither this nor that, neither a politician with Roman *auctoritas* nor a Greek philosopher, but rather a ridiculous ape trying to pretend to be a philosopher by going through the motions of stubbornness, uncooperativeness, and scorn of legitimate authority.[36]

Here too Regulus' invective backfires when it is no longer supported by the Bad Emperor Domitian. Philosophical wisdom is now a compliment, not an insult, not only for Greeks like Euphrates but also for Romans like Attius Clemens and Pliny, who imbibe philosophy in moderation (1.10). Stoic philosophy is rising in prestige, as shown, for example, by the return of the philosophers, the special respect shown Epictetus by Hadrian (*HA Hadr.* 16.10), and finally the reign of the "philosopher-king" Marcus Aurelius (*HA M. Antoninus* 27.7). Furthermore, Tacitus emphasizes the difference between Rusticus the eminent politician well fortified by just enough philosophy and Musonius Rufus, who cuts a rather ridiculous figure pontificating to the impatient troops on a similar mission at the time (*Hist.* 3.81.1). Musonius is presented as a Roman whose excessive devotion to philosophy has indeed made him inept in delicate Roman political transactions.[37] In short, Regulus' excessive invective winds up honoring its intended victim and dishonoring its author, just as his excessive mourning backfires, arousing laughter rather than lamentation (4.7.7). Regulus has too much "force," or whatever his driving desire should be called (4.7.3), and because he is so single-minded and unrestrained he usually misses the mark, attacking the knee or ankle, say, instead of the throat (1.20.15). His invective offends even those such as Carus who might agree with it, and his lamentation provokes mirth even in those who might be inclined to sympathize, such as Pliny (4.2.1 "the only disaster he did not deserve").

The second episode shows another aspect of Regulan "eloquence" in the reign of the Bad Emperor. This, the forensic aspect, is more subtle than his intemperate epideictic oratory, but again shows the single-minded drive for

---

[36] The incisive comment of J. Schefferus (in Cortius and Longolius 1734) deserves to be quoted at length: "*Cur* Stoicorum? ... *quia*... *[ea secta]*... *invisa sub malis principibus tanquam nimis inimica et adversa vitiis, nimis amans libertatis*... *Cur* simiam? *quia imitari cultores eius sectae studeat gravitate vitae, libertateque sermonis, faciat id autem ridicule ac inepte.* Stigmosum, *tamquam cicatrix*... *pro stigmate haberi deberet, quo fuerit inustus ob servitium Vitellio praestitum...*"

[37] Pliny "flatteringly" suppresses the fact that Musonius was a Stoic philosopher, 3.11.5.

accomplishing whatever he desires, good or bad (*intentio quidquid velis optinendi,* 4.7.3), but usually bad (*certum est Regulum esse facturum, quidquid fieri non oportet,* 4.2.8). This time it is less obvious that Regulus is being deliberately malicious to Pliny, so we need to be told that Regulus "remembered this too," how he had harassed Pliny himself in a deadly way (*praeterea reminiscebatur, quam capitaliter ipsum me apud centumviros lacessisset,* 1.5.4). The first incident he obviously recognized to be offensive to Pliny, since he pointedly did not invite him to the recitation. But his behavior in the second episode need not be interpreted as aimed specifically against Pliny, since Regulus might be seen as an overzealous advocate rather than a secret *delator.* In order to press his case against Arionilla, Regulus insistently asked Pliny's opinion about Mettius Modestus, who had once given a related verdict in Arionilla's favor but had since been banished by Domitian. Pliny claims that if he supported Modestus he would risk his life (4 *capitaliter*), but if he attacked Modestus he would not only lose the case, but also lose his honor, his standing among the quietly (and not so quietly) anti-Domitianic members of the ruling elite.

> Nitebamur nos in parte causae sententia Metti Modesti optimi viri: is tunc in exsilio erat, a Domitiano relegatus. Ecce tibi Regulus 'Quaero,' inquit, 'Secunde, quid de Modesto sentias.' Vides quod periculum, si respondissem 'bene'; quod flagitium si 'male'. Non possum dicere aliud tunc mihi quam deos adfuisse. 'Respondebo' inquam 'si de hoc centumviri iudicaturi sunt.' Rursus ille: 'Quaero, quid de Modesto sentias.' Iterum ego: 'Solebant testes in reos, non in damnatos interrogari.' Tertio ille: 'Non iam quid de Modesto, sed quid de pietate Modesti sentias quaero.' 'Quaeris' inquam 'quid sentiam; at ego ne interrogare quidem fas puto, de quo pronuntiatum est.' (5–7)

> In part of our case we were relying on a verdict given by the most excellent man Mettius Modestus. He was in exile then, banished by Domitian. Here goes your Regulus now: "I should like to know, Secundus," he said, "what is your opinion about Modestus." You see what the danger was if I had answered "I think well of him," and the disgrace if I had answered "I think badly of him." All I can say is, at that moment the gods came to my defense. "I will answer," I said, "if it is about him that the Centumviral court is going to pronounce a sentence." He came back again with it: "I should like to know what is your opinion about Modestus." Again I said, "The testimony of witnesses used to be directed at those accused, not at those convicted." For the third time he said, "Well, I am not asking what your opinion is about Modestus now, but about Modestus' loyalty." "You are asking my opinion," I said, "but I think it is wrong even to ask about someone already sentenced."

Is Regulus trying to flush out Pliny's anti-Domitian sentiments and have him executed? Is he trying to get Pliny to commit himself on the record as a collaborator with Domitian's crimes? Or is he just trying to win his case?

Pliny may even be surreptitiously blaming Regulus for bringing the case at all, a prosecution of Timon's wife Arrionilla, a woman who was probably connected with the Roman-political opposition (through Arria and Thrasea) and the Greek-philosophical opposition (through Timon).[38]

To force the worst possible interpretation of Regulus' motives, Pliny explains to us in advance that Regulus realized exactly what he was doing, ensnaring Pliny as a side-benefit to his ostensible aim of helping his client. It is possible, to be sure, that the immoral Regulus does not see that he is trapping Pliny between *periculum* and *flagitium* (5), since he may not recognize defaming a man banished by Domitian as *flagitium* (5). But even Regulus would see that Pliny would at the least be caught between *periculum* and the violation of *fides* towards a client: Pliny can only protect the interests of Arionilla by risking his life through a politically dangerous statement in support of Modestus. The somewhat surprising mention of Rusticus, who does nothing in this narrative, suggests that it could just as well have been Rusticus on the stand facing this dilemma.[39] It was fortunate for Rusticus this time that *he* was not interrogated about Modestus; with his outspoken honesty he may not have waited for "the gods' help" to weasel out of the question like the expert fence-sitter Pliny (5 *deos adfuisse*).

Pliny positions the laudatory epithet in the phrase *Metti Modesti* optimi *viri* to resonate with the name "Modestus": Regulus the petty tyrant, shameless and unrestrained, is attacking Modestus the "moderate," the "best." The same opposition recurs between Spurinna the "best" and Regulus the "most dissimilar," that is, the worst.[40] As we will learn, one reason for Regulus' attack was Modestus' insult ("worst of two-leggeds"). A similar piece of invective ("a bad man inexpert of speech," 4.7.5) came from Herennius, the victim over whom Regulus exulted in the first episode. Again we see Pliny distinguishing between the good senator and the bad senator. Behind the symmetry of invective against invective we have the difference: the good man merely blames, but the bad man kills, and he even "mutilates" the dead or

---

[38] Sherwin-White 1966:97. Jones even wonders whether this was Timon the brother of Plutarch (1971:24).

[39] It seems likely that Pliny is co-advocate with Rusticus, in addition to being challenged to testify about Modestus. Even Sherwin-White, who believes that Pliny was merely a witness, concedes that *aderam* suggests advocacy, 1966:97.

[40] Spurinna the military commander, like Regulus the accused cannibal of Piso, supported Otho (Tac. *Hist.* 2.11, etc.). Spurinna exemplifies how a "best" man can serve under a Bad Emperor with honor. A similar euphemism describes the "most dissimilar father" with whom the "best son" Pompeius Quintianus lived with great dutifulness, perhaps another symbol for dutiful service under a bad emperor (9.9.2 *qua pietate cum* dissimillimo *patre vivebat! ... vir* optimus... optimus *filius*). For another possible pun on a person's name, see Gunderson 1997:227 on 3.3 (Iulius *Genitor*).

harms the exiled. Still more restrained than the "modest" martyrs are the survivors, such as the "best man" Spurinna, his protégé Pliny, and the greatest of the "best" men, the new emperors.[41] The characters in the letter can be divided into three categories, the attackers (Regulus, Carus), the noble victims (Rusticus, Herennius, Modestus, Mauricus), and the cautious survivors (Spurinna, Pliny). Like the "best" senators, the "best" emperors were also cautious survivor-collaborators under the "worst" emperor. Pliny on the stand symbolizes how one could prosper like the attackers while remaining noble like the victims. He can prove his uprightness now by collaborating with the returning Mauricus, and against Certus with the widows of Thrasea and the two Helvidii (Arria, Fannia, and Anteia, 9.13.4–5). Pliny's choice on the stand is between *periculum* (like Rusticus', 2) and *flagitium* (like Regulus', 1), but his god-given answers show a third way through, survival with honor. Thanks to the ability of good senators to survive with honor, the Good Emperors Nerva and Trajan can establish themselves on the throne.[42]

Pliny introduces the three exchanges of quoted dialogue with the vivid *ecce tibi,* "here you go!" He repeats this second person intrusion after Regulus' first question (*vides,* 5). Voconius and the reader are invited into Pliny's position on the stand, as a challenge to see whether we can solve the riddle before Pliny tells us the god-given answer. He even explains the terms of the riddle, *periculum* vs. *flagitium,* to make sure we understand the situation before he gives us the answer. Of course, to the readers the answer comes so fast that we have no time to ponder our answer, but on the other hand it also flows so naturally that it is as if we had thought of it ourselves.[43] Pliny is flattering our understanding and our moral sense. We too understand and sympathize with his dilemma; we too would have come up with the right

---

[41] Pliny even claims that the title "Optimus" asserts that the emperor is an ordinary citizen and senator (as if "best of the citizens, best of the senators," *Pan.* 2.7). He also says that henceforth the title "Best" will be known as Trajan's name just as the term "Augustus" is known as Octavian's name, *Pan.* 88.10. Several times Pliny virtually entitles his *Panegyric* the "Consul's Thanks to the *Best* Emperor": 3.13.1 *librum quo* optimo *principi consul gratias egi,* 3.18.3 *laudare* optimum *principem, Pan.* 1.2 *imperio senatus, auctoritate rei publicae ad agendas* optimo *principi gratias excitamur;* also, more simply, *ut rei publicae nomine principi gratias agerem* (3.18.1). For the title *optimus princeps* see Mattingly & Sydenham 1926, Trajan nos. 91, 94, 96, etc., *ILS* 286 (103 C.E.). *Optimus* was a standard imperial slogan, having been applied to Augustus, Tiberius, Claudius, Nero, Domitian, and Nerva (Kienast 1968:54), although Augustus seems to have avoided it as an official title, since the terms *optimates* and *boni* had been slogans of the republican opposition (Vogt 1933:91).

[42] Trajan had an uninterruptedly successful career under Domitian (Syme 1958:34). Spurinna, along with Frontinus, supported Trajan's adoption (1958:34, *Pan.* 60.5–7).

[43] Pliny elsewhere explains how such clear logical argumentation flatters the readers by making them feel proud of thinking it through on their own (1.20.13); on making listeners feel good about their intellectual skills, compare Aristot. *Rhet.* 3.11.6, Quint. *Inst.* 8.2.21, 9.2.78.

solution if, as he modestly puts it, the gods had come to our help; in short, we too are Good Survivors. Indeed, the gods do appear to us, in the person of Pliny who tells us the answer as a sudden, immediately recognizable illumination. We too can share in the divine favor of the survivors: the letter draws Voconius and the reader into the mutually honoring circle of praise.

In laying his forensic ambush Regulus is studiously polite, but under the surface (*tectiora,* 1) he is just as single-mindedly aggressive as he had been against his dead enemies. He begins with a genteel *quaero.* "I should like to know, Secundus..."[44] Pliny's first response is equally polite, and should show, to someone less single-minded than Regulus, that the plan of entrapment has been foiled and will not succeed.[45] Just as Regulus' evident fear under the Good Emperor betrays his guilt, so Pliny's fearless demeanor and restrained responses protects his reputation under the Bad Emperor. After this first exchange we get to enjoy Pliny's skill, with the danger already averted, as Regulus keeps hammering away in vain, or rather, to his own discredit, for his aggression now forces from Pliny a pair of polite put-downs. Regulus does not see that he has lost; thinking that he is at the throat, he keeps trying to choke the ankle (1.20.15).

In his unthinking attack, he simply repeats the question. Pliny has no further need of special divine "counsel" to deal with the same question a second time.[46] In his first answer he politely refers to the future. The judgment of this trial will not concern Modestus; therefore I will not answer. His second answer refers to the past, now with an insulting edge. "In times past, witnesses used to be interrogated in reference to defendants, not convicted men." You, he implies, are violating good Roman tradition. The sharper defense spurs Regulus to a stronger attack. Unwilling to give up this master plan of getting Pliny into a double-bind, Regulus tries a slightly different approach to the same goal: this is the man who will use "any means" (*quoquo modo,* 8) to reach his aim. Backing off from a question on the *man,* Regulus asks about his *pietas,* his political loyalty and the reliability of his decisions. Pliny's answer shows that he sees through the verbal trick. It is still a question about a man, and one should not ask about a *man* "who has already been sentenced" (Pliny does not say "about his *pietas"*). Pliny finally

---

[44] Quintilian's chapter on humor preserves a comparable scene (*Inst.* 6.3.86), Cicero's felicitous retort to the prosecutor's "repeated, insistent" question (*instaret identidem accusator*) about a damaging witness: *dic, M. Tulli, numquid potes de Sex. Annali?* Cicero finally responds by turning the witness' name into "the sixth book of [Ennius'] *Annals."*
[45] As Merrill puts it (1912), "in his retort Pliny fairly outregulates Regulus."
[46] Pliny uses the same term for "legal assistance" (*aderam,* 5) and for the gods' help (*deos adfuisse,* 5). Quintilian reports this as a rhetorical cliché, referring, however, to a rush of eloquence in the heat of improvisation (*Inst.* 10.7.14 *deum tunc adfuisse... veteres oratores, ut Cicero, dictitabant;* Hutchinson 1993:186 n. 1).

counterattacks, saying that it is "not right" to do what Regulus is doing *(ne interrogare quidem fas puto),* thus accusing Regulus of a legal violation, reopening a closed case (Ulp. *dig.* 48.2.7.2), and perhaps even of political disloyalty.[47] Despite Modestus' banishment his judgments are still valid. Even Domitian's official letters retain their validity and are quoted in Book 10 (10.58, 65, 72).

Regulus might have hoped that Pliny would back down from resting his case on Modestus' judgment, out of political fear, or that he would have incurred political danger by insisting too strongly on Modestus' authority, instead of quietly relying on the narrow legal validity of Modestus' judgment. But Pliny's restrained refusal to discuss the issue makes his answer open to a double interpretation. To Modestus' enemies it could simply mean that Pliny acknowledges the validity of the banishment, though he can still use Modestus' judgment in his case. He can safely refuse to heap gratuitous blame on Modestus since he is bound to help his client, whose case relies on Modestus' (still valid) judgment. But to Pliny's true friends who offer praise and congratulations, his refusal to blame Modestus shows that he considers the banishment unjust, but grudgingly recognizes its legal force. The time to argue for Modestus is not now, but when he was on trial. Even under a Bad Emperor a Good Advocate can do good, but he must work within the corrupt system to the best of his ability. Even if Pliny cannot hope to rescue Modestus from Domitian's unfair punishment, he can still defend the property rights of Arionilla, probably a relation of the Paetus-Arria-Helvidius clan and the wife of a philosopher-friend of Rusticus.[48] Though it is beneath Pliny's mention, we can assume that Regulus lost the case: his silence *(conticuit, 7),* the silence of defeat, ends the matter. It would have made a feeble conclusion for Pliny to have said "I neither *lost the case* nor succumbed to the treachery." To slander Modestus might have been of brief "use" *(utili)* to himself alone, but dishonorable *(inhonesto)* to himself, to Modestus, and to his client Arionilla.

SPURINNA: COMMUNICATIONS AMONG GOOD SENATORS

The third episode comes back to the opening in ring composition. As usual in ring composition, the opening returns but with a difference. With the background explained, Pliny can strengthen the opening description. Regulus

---

[47] J. Schefferus (in Cortius and Longolius 1734): "Respondebo] *ars singularis subterfugiendae responsionis... At ego] Ars alia, qua periculum responsionis vertitur in interrogantem... Nempe qui interrogat videtur dubitare, qui autem dubitat de sententia principis, tacite insimulat eam iniquitatis."* Bartsch gives a similar interpretation in a brief account of Pliny's performance here (1994:64).

[48] Sherwin-White 1966:97 on 1.5.5.

is not merely scared that Pliny is angry (*vereri ne sibi irascerer,* 1); he now
knows it (*efficias ne sibi irascatur,* 8) and asks mutual "friends" to intercede.
He is now more than "timid and lowly" (*timidiorem humiliorem,* 1); he is
terrified (*exterritus,* 8), and now we know exactly why. His involvement in
and exultation over the death of Rusticus was partially aimed at Pliny, and in
the Arionilla trial he tried to drag Pliny down with Rusticus. But the letter
does not end here with the return of the beginning.[49] Rather, it is about to
start in earnest, for the real subject of the letter is Pliny's decision on how to
deal with Regulus, as he puts off Regulus' approaches and waits for Mauricus.
The new section begins with emissaries to Pliny, first Celer and Iustus, and
then Spurinna. The rapid sequence of emissaries illustrates Regulus' new
subordinate status as he fearfully, even "supplicatingly" begs off Pliny's anger
(*suppliciter,* 8). One might think of an enemy defeated in battle supplicating
for his life, or even a defeated emperor, perhaps Vitellius, surrendering his
office and begging to be spared; as we saw, Regulus represents a wish
fulfillment to see Domitian humiliated after his overthrow. The honorable
emissaries symbolize a latter-day Rusticus trying to arrange a peaceful
reconciliation with the winning Flavians after the defeat of Vitellius, though
Pliny, by contrast, respects the emissaries and spares Regulus.

> Nunc ergo conscientia exterritus adprehendit Caecilium Celerem, mox Fabium
> Iustum; rogat ut me sibi reconcilient. Nec contentus pervenit ad Spurinnam;
> huic suppliciter, ut est cum timet abiectissimus: 'Rogo mane videas Plinium
> domi, sed plane mane (neque enim ferre diutius sollicitudinem possum), et
> quoquo modo efficias, ne mihi irascatur.' Evigilaveram; nuntius a Spurinna:
> 'Venio ad te.' 'Immo ego ad te.' Coimus in porticum Liviae, cum alter ad
> alterum tenderemus. Exponit Reguli mandata, addit preces suas, ut decebat
> optimum virum pro dissimillimo, parce. (8–9)

> So now, frightened out of his mind by the awareness of what he had done, he
> gets hold of Caecilius Celer, and right after that Fabius Iustus, asking them to
> bring me back to terms with him. Not satisfied with that, he goes to Spurinna
> and speaks to him beseechingly, since that is the way he is, completely
> groveling, when he is scared. "Please, see Pliny in the morning at his home, I
> mean early morning—I can't bear the worry any longer—and do what you can,
> in any way you can, to make him not be angry at me." I was awake; there is a
> message from Spurinna, "I am coming to your place." "No, I am coming to
> your place." We meet at the Portico of Livia, while we were each hurrying
> towards the other. He lays out the request that Regulus had entrusted to him,
> and puts his own plea on top of it, in the way that was fitting for a most
> excellent man speaking on behalf of one most unlike himself—sparingly.

---

[49] Ring composition is a standard closing device, as at 1.12, 18, 23, and 24, for example.

What does Regulus want? His words speak vaguely of "reconciling Pliny to me" and "making him not be angry at me" (8). Only in the final lines does Pliny touch on Regulus' real fear, when he speaks of "making some attempt" *(temptandi aliquid)* or "keeping his peace" *(quiescendi,* 16). In light of Pliny's senatorial attack on Certus in 9.13 we can understand the "attempt" to be a formal attack or even a prosecution. Regulus must be as eager to extract from Pliny a promise not to attack, as to appease his supposed anger, for even the "perfidious" Regulus (2.20.5 *perfidum... periurum*) knows that a promise from Pliny is reliable.[50] Pliny's ultimate aim against Certus was to strip him of office, and incidentally to promote himself into the vacancy. But Regulus holds no office, and it is unlikely that his "hidden offenses"—such as attempted entrapment of a witness, or unseemly posthumous invective—would justify a prosecution. In any case, Regulus' personal apology is too flimsy to change Pliny's attitude or extract a promise; he pretends that his greatest offense had merely been an ambiguous criticism of Pliny's literary style. On the other hand, the tone of the letter undercuts Pliny's opening assurance that he *was* angry. By section 8, after he has relived the triumphant moment in the Arionilla case, any anger in the letter's tone has dissipated, turning into scorn for the pathetically downcast and suppliant Regulus. Already somewhat ineffectual under Domitian, Regulus is still more ineffectual under Nerva and Trajan.

After Regulus' briefly reported appeals to Celer and Iustus, who may be approximate equals to Pliny, he next turns to the elder statesman Spurinna, in the most abject terms.[51] Again we see the single-minded rashness of Regulus, which shows itself in fear as well as in attack, in mourning as well as in exultation. In trying to appease Pliny in absolutely any way possible, he turns to one of Pliny's most prestigious friends, and his begging appeal extracts from Spurinna a promise to make an evidently unusual early morning visit to Pliny's home. More normally the younger protégé pays his respects at his older patron's home, and we learn elsewhere that Spurinna's daily routine is as fixed as astronomical clockwork, including an extra hour in bed "early in the morning" *(mane,* 3.1.4) and talking on his three-mile morning walk with friends like Pliny who come to pay respects to the old man. If Regulus' groveling request can extract this concession from the aged Spurinna, it could quite possibly have succeeded with Pliny himself. We can easily imagine a successful mission of Regulus himself by combining Spurinna's actions with Regulus' suppliant tone. But Regulus can only grovel before the senior

---

[50] Guillemin discusses the sacrosanct nature of a renewed *amicitia* after a reconciliation (1929:7).

[51] Spurinna, cos. II 98, cos. III 100, is more distinguished and probably older than the unknown Celer and than Iustus, cos. 102 and the dedicatee of Tacitus' *Dialogus.*

statesman, not before the younger senator. In a sense, he is overreaching, hoping for an agreement between equals, not a submissive apology and appeasement. He wants to maintain his dignity, not make a decent reconciliation and win the truer *auctoritas* that decency earns when a Good Emperor is in power (*Pan.* 44.6).

Pliny does not allow Spurinna to come and make his request at Pliny's home. He is awake and alert (*evigilaveram,* 8), not sleepy and indolent as he often pretends to be (e.g. 1.2.3 *longae desidiae indormientem*). He is thus able to prevent a setting in which Spurinna, by going more out of his way, can make Pliny more obliged to obey his request. Even if Pliny does not yet know why Spurinna is coming, he can guess from the unusual visit that it is something out of the ordinary. Pliny then gives a rare topographic detail for their meeting: they meet at the portico of Livia, in a public setting and on equal terms. Their meeting site comes from the origins of imperial government, the time of Augustus (7 B.C.E., Dio 55.8.2). The meeting place is also a Latin translation of the Stoa ("colonnade"), the symbol of the noble political philosophy embraced by Rusticus. These Roman "best men" are putting Greek philosophy into action, an aspiration to which Pliny is about to devote an entire letter (1.10). Spurinna, like Pliny's other senior patrons Corellius, Verginius, and the Elder Pliny, reaches back beyond the evil days of Nero and Domitian, to the healthier origins of the principate.[52] In this letter celebrating restoration, Regulus, who represents the worst of the intervening Bad Emperors, is supplanted while the elder and younger good senators come together on equal terms behind his back and reach an implicit understanding. The symbolic return to Augustan times signals a new beginning of imperial government under the new regime, a beginning marked by reconciliation rather than the vengeance and civil strife by which the Julio-Claudian and Flavian dynasties were founded.[53]

Spurinna's sparing style is the opposite of Regulus' effusive supplication, "as was fitting for a 'best' man acting on behalf of the most dissimilar" (a "worst" man). His style indicates that he himself does not fully support Regulus' request, and undoes the effect of the urgent early morning visit: Spurinna is careful *not* to make the request obligatory for Pliny to obey. Pliny the narrator must be tactful in portraying the conflict of obligations pulling at

---

[52] Like Verginius (cos. III ord. 97) and Frontinus (cos. II 98, cos. III ord. 100), the elderly Spurinna (cos. II 98, cos. III 100) was used to decorate the new regime with his pre-Flavian and even pre-Neronian prestige (cf. Syme 1958:3, Sherwin-White 1966:143). Born about 24 C.E., Spurinna was probably well into his senatorial career by the *quinquennium Neronis*.

[53] The Portico of Livia is a monument to Augustan clemency, being an anti-monument to the notoriously cruel and wealthy equestrian Vedius Pollio, the owner of man-eating eels, whose huge house, bequeathed to Augustus, was torn down so that Pollio would have no monument at Rome (Dio 54.23; cf. Ovid *Fasti* 6.639–46).

the senior senator, who must neither betray his promise to Regulus nor impose an improper demand on Pliny. Hence he arrives early but pleads sparingly. The code of friendship obliges him to agree to attempt a reconciliation (Guillemin 1927:9 n. 1), but it does not oblige him to insist on it with all his authority. Spurinna is a model for the ideal emperor, who carefully avoids throwing his weight around. Spurinna is evidently embarrassed by his mission, as opposed to the bad senator Regulus who has no shame (*verecundia,* 4.7.3), acts unrestrainedly, and then suffers regret. The meeting in a public place shows that they have nothing to hide, that they suffer from no "bad shame" (as the Domitianic *verecundia* at 4.11.13), and their mutual restraint shows the proper modesty, or "good" *verecundia,* that prevents them from suffering regrets. Perhaps another reason for Regulus' original request for such an early meeting at Pliny's home was to avoid airing his shame in front of others.

> Cui ego: 'Dispicies ipse quid renuntiandum Regulo putes. Te decipi a me non oportet. Exspecto Mauricum' (nondum ab exsilio venerat): 'ideo nihil alterutram in partem respondere tibi possum, facturus quidquid ille decreverit; illum enim esse huius consilii ducem, me comitem decet.' (9–10)

> I said to him, "you will have to look into it yourself as to what you think you should report back to Regulus. I must not deceive you: I am waiting for Mauricus" (he had not yet come back from exile), "and so I cannot give you any answer in either direction, since I am going to do whatever he decides. He is the one who should be the leader in this plan, and I should be his associate.

Regulus' characteristic rashness has again backfired. He has reached too high in trying to get the powerful Spurinna to act for him. Spurinna scrupulously *avoids* doing "whatever it takes" (*quoquo modo efficias,* 8) to change Pliny's attitude, or his plans. Pliny can tell from the two facts that Spurinna is actually putting his *auctoritas* behind himself and not behind Regulus. First, the unusual early morning visit shows that the request is out of the ordinary, especially since the messenger does not indicate *why* Spurinna is coming. Second, his sparing request, coming on the heels of such an urgent early visit, shows Pliny that the urgency comes from Regulus, not from Spurinna. Accordingly, Pliny can leave the answer to Spurinna, since he sees that Spurinna is actually on *his* side. "You will decide yourself what you think you should tell him" (10). Pliny will not "deceive" Spurinna (*decipi,* 10): he can trust Spurinna not to tell Regulus his real plans, that he is waiting for Mauricus and will follow Mauricus' wishes. The atmosphere of restraint, trust, and tactful decision-making is brought out by the insistent verbiage of moral judgment: *ut decebat... quid renuntiandum putes... decipi... non oportet... quidquid... decreverit... consilii ducem... comitem decet* (9–10).

Spurinna and Pliny reach decisions together by the half-unspoken exchange of judgment and counsel, not by Regulus' single-minded, unrestrained, driving will. The incident disproves the Thucydidean epigram with which Pliny later describes Regulus.[54] "Decent natures" are *not* weakened by self-restraint; rather, their activity, being properly directed, produces real achievement instead of foiling itself.

In this post-Domitianic portion of the letter, time is foreshortened. Regulus is fearful "now" (8), after Domitian's death (1), and pleads for Spurinna to see Pliny "tomorrow morning, early," since he cannot wait any longer. Pliny gives the impression that this takes place immediately after Domitian's death, with perhaps a few days for the missions of Celer and then Iustus.[55] The meeting with Regulus himself at the *praetoris officium* occurs only "a few days later" (*paucos post dies ipse me Regulus convenit in praetoris officio,* 11), although this "praetor's service" was apparently a New Year's ritual, appropriately enough for a letter about restoration and inauguration, but months after Domitian's September assassination.[56] Within this rapid sequence of foreshortened time we have a striking temporal interruption, telling us that Mauricus "had not yet come from exile" (10). The phrase is generally taken as evidence of later revision because of its anachronism: when this was written, Mauricus *had* already returned (Sherwin-White 1966:14). Perhaps Pliny the careful reviser has actually slipped up for once.[57] Or perhaps between January 1 and the dramatic date of the letter Mauricus had already "come" (10, 15) back to Italy from exile, but Pliny was still "waiting" (16) to talk to him since he had not yet settled into his former position at Rome and reestablished normal contacts with associates such as Pliny.[58] In any case, the temporal

[54] "Upright natures are weakened by self-restraint; twisted ones are strengthened by rashness" (*recta ingenia debilitat verecundia, perversa confirmat audacia,* 4.7.3).

[55] Letter 1.12 gives a similarly false impression of taking place just a few days after Domitian's death.

[56] In 69/70 events were more accommodating to the symbolism of renewal, with the new regime taking over between the Saturnalia of 69 and the Senate meeting of the new year (Tac. *Hist.* 4.39). The start of the year was the customary time for reaffirming one's loyalty to the emperor (Sherwin-White 1966:611–12 on 10.35)—and for revolts, as of Saturninus (Jones 1992:229 n. 2) and Vitellius (Tac. *Hist.* 1.55–56).

[57] The other temporal "error" that has been cited (Sherwin-White 1966:19, Krenkel 1984:xxxix), 3.9.16 *solet,* only requires a few days or weeks for Restitutus' comment to become "habitual"; elsewhere Sherwin-White considers this a sign *either* of revision *or* of a longer interval than the opening sentence (3.9.1) implies (233). Sherwin-White takes this general accuracy to prove that Pliny has not done much revision, but I agree with Murgia that Pliny revises carefully to preserve the original dramatic date of each letter (1985:201). Syme (1958:662) gives several examples where an entire letter is out of sequence, which is another matter, since Pliny himself allows for it (1.1.1).

[58] Elsewhere (1966:117 on 1.14.1) Sherwin-White suggests an interval after the exiles' return for getting their affairs back into order.

interruption reminds us that the letter combines the impression of great haste (tomorrow morning... few days...) with that of long waiting (waiting for Mauricus... until Mauricus comes...), emphasizing the contrast between personal conversation and letter-writing at a distance.

Things happen quickly at Rome, where people can meet and discuss sensitive matters in the half-unspoken style of Pliny's meeting with Spurinna. But Pliny is so cautious that he does *not* write to Mauricus to resolve the matter at a distance, or perhaps Mauricus in his caution (*gravis prudens,* 16) cannot apply his foresight to predict the future without first seeing the past, what has happened at Rome in the momentous years while he has been gone (*et qui futura possit ex praeteritis providere,* 16). Pliny can deal with this difficult decision in a letter to Voconius Romanus because he is not *forming* future decisions but reporting past events and decisions. Even though the letter goes further than reporting the surface of events ("words and deeds"), it is still limited to reporting *consilia,* the plans and motives underlying past events, or plans that have already been made for the future—to do nothing until Mauricus returns (*non solum omnia mea facta dictaque, verum etiam consilia,* 17). Although Pliny does often solve problems of advice by letter, and much imperial business was done by mail (including most of Book 10), the letter form is not fully adequate for the delicate task of reporting and making plans about the complicated recent transition of power, or at least not so adequate as personal conversation. As intimately as the letters bring us into the private conversations of Pliny and his friends, they are still not so intimate as the live conversations themselves. There is still a need, in an empire governed by letter, for councils of "friends" and for senatorial debate.[59]

The limitations of letter-writing explain why Spurinna does not tell Pliny through the messenger why he is coming so early. This delicate situation must be discussed in person, so that he can make sure Pliny understands that he is *not* adding his authority to Regulus' request. To express this awkward and contradictory situation in writing would require the most skillfully written of letters, a disingenuous recommendation letter, so to speak, that is actually a non-recommendation. Regulus also does not approach Pliny by letter. A letter would make a permanent, potentially public record of his groveling supplication—something that this letter of Pliny's nevertheless accomplishes.[60]

---

[59] On the importance of letters in imperial government see Riepl 1913:362–63, Millar 1977:208, 213, 215, 313.

[60] Most surviving ancient letters were written to be sent a great distance (Harris 1989:229). Immediate messages to be sent across town were more often sent on erasable tablets (e.g. 3.18.4, 6.16.8; Sen. *Ep.* 55.11; Riepl 1913:125).

THE MEETING WITH REGULUS: SATISFIED WITH OUR ERA?

The fourth and longest episode takes place at the praetor's ceremony of the New Year, in accordance with the restoration tone of the letter.[61] As we saw concerning Rusticus in 69, the praetorship is the highest traditional Republican office that still maintains a pretense of election and campaigning.[62] Regulus and Pliny meet at the first republican inaugural ceremony of the new regime. At this time Pliny and perhaps Regulus are praetorian senators, the normal rank reached in an average senatorial *cursus,* but Pliny will reach the consulship under the new regime whereas Regulus will not.[63] The *Panegyric* speech of Pliny or of Verginius (2.1.4) is the imperial, consular counterpart to this republican, praetorian ritual.[64] The younger Pliny will enjoy the patronage of the new regime (as well as that of the old regime), but the older Regulus' political influence is coming to an end with the passing of the old regime. Indeed, Pliny reaches the prefecture of Saturn, the launching point for the consulship, by means of a prosecution against Certus similar to the one he is contemplating against Regulus. Although he claims to worry that Regulus is too powerful to attack, in fact he is not powerful enough to be worth attacking, having no office that Pliny can usurp. Pliny never even intended to prosecute Certus officially, and against Regulus he would have no such rhetorical strategy as succeeded against Certus, that he should "return under the Best Emperor the reward he received from the Worst Emperor" (9.13.23).[65] All he could hope for against Regulus would be a vote for a

---

[61] Pliny's meeting with Regulus on the first day of the year is "a few days after" his meeting with Spurinna (1.5.11), which might therefore be set at the time of the Saturnalia. Yet the former meeting serves to reinforce proper status distinctions that had been blurred under Domitian. Pliny, who isolates himself in his aristocratic study during the Saturnalia (2.17.24), dreads any blurring of social distinctions (9.5.3, Barton 1993:111, 145). It may be relevant to compare modern Andalusian landowners, who have taken to leaving town for the duration of carnival rather than endure the insubordinate abuse (Scott 1990:174).

[62] "The consulate was certainly in the personal gift of the emperor" (Millar 1977:308).

[63] Syme's view (1958:102), that Tacitus implies that Regulus reached the consulship (*Hist.* 4.42.5), is not widely followed.

[64] It would seem that Verginius never gave his panegyric, since he was killed by a too massive book (2.1.5 *liber... grandiorem*), perhaps his own massive panegyric (Merrill 1912). His death through stooping to pick up a book while composing his speech of thanks may show symbolically how hard it was for the independent Rufus to "stoop" to flatter even the good emperor Nerva: the old man of liberty and free speech (9.19.5) succumbed to obligatory panegyric. No doubt Tacitus' fulsome funeral eulogy fulfilled the same imperial panegyric function, in the style of *Agricola* 44.5 or Pliny's obituary letters ("he lived to see the Republic flourishing again," 1.12.11, "with the Best Emperor safely established," 2.1.3), and took the place of this missing consular panegyric speech for the momentous New Year of 97.

useless pseudo-censorial mark of moral disapproval, as was proposed against Certus (9.13.16).

Whereas Pliny and Spurinna met in a public colonnade, Regulus needs a private place to talk. The good senator has no secrets, nothing that could lead to embarrassment or regret, but the bad senator must have a private place to deliver even this insincere apology. Both conversations hover discreetly over unstated premises, but in opposite ways. Spurinna and Pliny collaborate in coming to an agreement, the agreement to delay, by sharing unstated moral beliefs. Regulus, however, fails to come to an agreement with Pliny in part because he leaves the essence of the apology unstated, never confessing that he helped kill Pliny's friend Rusticus and tried to do the same to Pliny himself.

> ait timere se ne animo meo penitus haereret, quod in centumvirali iudicio aliquando dixisset, cum responderet mihi et Satrio Rufo: 'Satrius Rufus, cui non est cum Cicerone aemulatio et qui contentus est eloquentia saeculi nostri'. Respondi nunc me intellegere maligne dictum quia ipse confiteretur, ceterum potuisse honorificum existimari. 'Est enim' inquam 'mihi cum Cicerone aemulatio, nec sum contentus eloquentia saeculi nostri; nam stultissimum credo ad imitandum non optima quaeque proponere. Sed tu qui huius iudicii meministi, cur illius oblitus es, in quo me interrogasti, quid de Metti Modesti pietate sentirem?' Expalluit notabiliter, quamvis palleat semper, et haesitabundus: 'Interrogavi non ut tibi nocerem, sed ut Modesto.' (11–13)

> He said he was scared that something was stuck deep in my mind, which he had once said in a Centumviral trial when he was replying to me and to Satrius Rufus: "Satrius Rufus, who does not engage in rivalry with Cicero, and who is satisfied with the style of eloquence of our era." I answered that now I understood that he had said it with evil intent since he was confessing it himself, but it could have been considered complimentary. "I do indeed," I said, "engage in rivalry with Cicero, and I am not satisfied with the style of eloquence of our era. For I consider it very stupid not to hold in front of oneself the best examples for imitating them. But since you remember that trial, why have you forgotten that other one, in which you asked me what my view was concerning the loyalty of Mettius Modestus?" He became noticeably paler, even though he is always pale, and said stammeringly, "I asked in order to harm Modestus, not you."

Regulus' first apology backfires, like the earlier examples of his eloquence. Instead of apologizing for a serious offense, he pretends that the worst he has ever done to Pliny is to give him this relatively harmless backhanded insult. Pliny undoes the pretense by going along with it, pretending that he had not

---

[65] Pliny himself is conveniently out of office in 97. If his own "reward" from the Worst Emperor, the post at the military treasury, ended before Domitian's death, he is now beginning an unsullied Nervan-Trajanic *cursus* (Sherwin-White 1966:75).

noticed the subtlety of Regulus' invective at the time. Pliny thus turns Regulus' apology into a fresh insult, to prepare for his transition to bringing up Regulus' real offense at the Arionilla trial. Or rather, he brings out the latent insult implied by such an inadequate apology. Pliny pretends that only now does he realize that Regulus was insulting him. He thus throws Regulus off-balance by making it seem like giving Pliny a fresh insult to explain that his old comment was an insult. Pliny's wording shows us (and Regulus) that he is only pretending to have taken it as a compliment. He does not say "I thought it was a compliment" but rather "it *could have* been taken as a compliment." No doubt even Regulus sees that Pliny's pretended ignorance cloaks his real point, his change from Regulus' euphemism "it was lingering deep in your mind" (*ne animo meo penitus haereret,* 11) to the plain fact "it was intended maliciously" (*maligne dictum,* 12). Pliny's superficial gesture at reconciliation ("it could have been meant honorifically") serves to deliver the counterattack politely but tellingly.

In the context of the new regime, Regulus' attempted insult is now a compliment. The imperial propaganda of the New Age, already prevalent in Domitian's reign, does not come off well in Regulus' mouth.[66] As Tacitus' *Dialogus* shows, the shift in eloquence from Cicero to Flavian times can be given a political significance (37–41). Cicero is the last orator of the free Republic, and oratory has changed because its political function is subordinate to the emperor. To Pliny, oratory and politics under Domitian are *not* satisfactory. Politics are completely dominated by one man, and oratory is reduced to oblique attacks, such as this very one by Regulus, which are aimed at giving Domitian and his agents pretexts for future executions and banishments. Pliny himself aspires to the restoration of a freer "republic," as under Nerva and Trajan, in which his oratory will have its independent value again. Pliny hopes for the best (*optima quaeque,* 13), for a Trajan, not merely for a Vespasian—for one "better than the best," not merely one "better than the worst" (*Pan.* 92.4 *meliorem optimo;* 44.2 *melior pessimo*). Regulus had been trying to smear Pliny with an insinuation of political discontent under cover of literary imitation. Pliny's philosophical interests were too feeble to admit a charge of aping the Stoics, so his Ciceronian tendencies would have to suffice. Regulus even contrasts Pliny with his own co-advocate Satrius Rufus,

---

[66] For *saeculum* as imperial propaganda for the current "new," "blessed," or "Golden" age, see e.g. 10.1.2, Sen. *Apocol.* 1.1, 4.1, *de Clem.* 2.1.4, Syme 1958:217. Such propaganda tends to infect the style of the entire ruling class. Pliny twice elsewhere presents this propaganda in connection with Domitian's reign. At 4.11.6 *(saeculum suum)* Pliny is giving an ironic report of Domitian's boastful thoughts, and at 7.33.9 *(saeculo est gratulatus, cui exemplum... simile antiquis contigisset)* he shows Nerva as a mouthpiece for Domitian, or rather, as an unwitting "emperor in training" giving preparatory Nervan propaganda even during Domitian's reign.

who reappears later as one of the apologists for the collaborators during the Certus debate (9.13.17). This shows us Pliny the discreet fence-sitter again, willing to share a case with Satrius the "anti-opposition" loyalist, as with Regulus himself at 1.20.13.[67] It also suggests, however, that Regulus' forensic ambushes, such as in the second episode, are more directed against Pliny than in favor of Regulus' client. Regulus is willing to cast possibly dangerous aspersions on Pliny even at the expense of flattering another advocate on the opposing side of the case.

Having forced from Regulus a tacit confession that his innuendo was meant as an insult, Pliny moves directly to his main grievance. "If you remember this case (with its minor insult), why have you forgotten that one (with its major offense)?" Regulus' behavior confesses what the terms of Pliny's question imply, and what Pliny has openly told us, that he *did* remember the second episode (*reminiscebatur,* 4). His extreme pallor, "more than his usual paleness," and his tongue-tied hesitation reveals what his words hide: not only does he remember it, but he *was* trying to harm Pliny by his interrogation. This episode reverses the second episode, with Pliny now interrogating Regulus, but the gods do not come to the aid of Regulus the blasphemous perjurer. His fearful demeanor gives himself away, the opposite of Pliny's fearless self-command that made his ambiguous answer succeed. The fear that gives Regulus away is emblematic of his demeanor in the new age, which proves his "secret" crimes under Domitian and distinguishes him from good senators like Pliny who also prospered under Domitian. Pliny can now afford to indulge in a touch of Regulan exultation because in this setting he is not liable to the ill will Regulus incurred by his tactics. There are no witnesses to this private meeting, so even though Pliny can badger Regulus into embarrassing admissions, Regulus' words cannot be used against him. The only evidence that Regulus said these words is this private letter, which though morally damning is legally useless.

Regulus' final words in the letter also recoil onto himself. This time Pliny explains it in order to make sure we understand how this works. In his eagerness to show that he never meant harm to Pliny when he questioned him about Modestus, Regulus confesses an equally malicious offense, that he intended to harm an exile. In his guilty panic Regulus was unable to find some safe excuse—perhaps the excuse that he was only trying faithfully to do the best for his client, to fulfill his *fides*. In further trying to defend his unwholesome excuse, he goes on to denigrate himself further by providing the most open invective against himself, quoting Modestus' insult. Although we do

---

[67] Satrius' reference at 9.13.17 to the "friends of Arria and Fannia" as opposed to the "friends of Certus" sounds like an anti-Stoic sneer at this clan whose men persist in being convicted of treason.

not believe that Regulus did not want to harm Pliny, we can easily believe that he also wanted to harm Modestus in revenge for this insult. One wonders whether his special "mutilation" of the dead Herennius was also in revenge for his insult "a bad man unversed in speaking" (4.7.5); again, in avenging the insult with his Regulan style of speaking, he proves it true. Pliny flaunts his trust in Voconius, and his security in the new age, by openly agreeing with Modestus' insult, thus making it his own. Unlike Modestus, Pliny can now insult Regulus in a private letter without fearing malicious revenge from him, now weakened under the new regime. Of course, Pliny may have rewritten this letter after Regulus' death; perhaps the original letter was less daringly scornful, just as the attack he did undertake against Certus may have been less risky than he claims (9.13.10–11). Perhaps Pliny was really an agent for people in imperial circles who wanted to remove Certus, Domitian's *delator,* who may have been dying anyway (9.13.24), from the fast track to the consulship, and to make room for a more suitable loyalist, Pliny himself. It is hard to believe that the prudent Pliny acted as independently as he claims.

Pliny voluntarily closes the meeting at this point. The restrained good senator does not press the attack to the end. In particular, he departs without mentioning the first episode, which contains in its opening words the only substantive accusation against Regulus, that he contributed to Rusticus' death (and Mauricus' banishment); the rest of the first two episodes is merely horrifying and entertaining embellishment of no legal standing. Pliny then concludes with a pair of lists summarizing Regulus' and Mauricus' qualities and explaining why Regulus may still be dangerous, and why Mauricus is the person to resolve Pliny's doubts. Pliny sharpens the parallelism between the bad senator and the good senator by omitting the obvious fact that Mauricus, as Regulus' victim and victim's brother, must be consulted to see whether he wants to press for revenge, just as Pliny must consult Anteia, Arria, and Fannia at 9.13.4–5. An attack will hardly stick if Mauricus argues on Regulus' side. But instead of the morally empty seesaw of revenge and counter-revenge, Pliny emphasizes the personal qualities of the two men, as emblematic positive and negative exempla for political power, decision-making, and alliance-formation.

The list of Regulus' qualities opens with a Greek epithet "hard to tear down"; as elsewhere the Greek, later glossed in Latin, gives both a focusing and a distancing effect.[68] The decent concealment of the learned language

---

[68] The subtle nuances of Pliny's use of Greek are asserted but not examined by Sherwin-White ("Pliny never writes pointlessly in Greek," 1966:182) and Hutchinson ("the use of Greek at significant moments... carries varying nuances," 1993:270 n. 24). Pliny suggests a gloss of δυσκαθαίρετον with the following phrase *ut haec concussa labantur* (Schaefer 1805). Similar

keeps at a distance the unseemly image of a jealous, vengeful Pliny trying to tear Regulus down, and partially refutes his assertion that it *is* difficult. A Pliny who has the presence of mind to sport an elegant one-word Greek idiom is not very intimidated by the difficulty of attacking Regulus, and he glosses the term to say that it may *not* be so difficult (*potest tamen fieri ut haec concussa labantur*, 16).[69] What seemed hard in cold Greek logic becomes easier when understood in Roman moral terms of political friendship, gratitude, and loyalty (*amore... gratia... infida,* 15–16). Regulus is not an impregnable fortress, but rather an imposing but hollow sham. Tearing him down would be as easy as demolishing the excessive statuary of Domitian after his death (*strage ac ruina, Pan.* 52.4), or waiting for Philip, the first imperial despot of the Greco-Roman world, to take a tumble (ἀνεχαίτισε καὶ διέλυσε, 9.26.9 = Dem. *Olynth.* 2.9). Certus, Regulus' substitute victim, is indeed quickly abandoned by his imposing but hollow senatorial support (9.13.11 *gratia... amicitiis*).[70] The imposing power of Regulus is a house of cards, held up by the evil despot Domitian; with Domitian dead, the entire structure of money, clientele, and networks of fear is unsupported.

The summarizing catalogue of Regulus' power is uncannily apt for Pliny as well, though Pliny keeps the parallel in abeyance by the use of slanted diction (a kind of *distinctio*).[71] Regulus is rich, so is Pliny. Regulus has an abundant clientele network, so has Pliny. But Regulus is openly called "rich" (*locuples,* 15), whereas Pliny has "resources," modest ones at that (2.4.3 *modicae facultates;* cf. 1.14.9, 3.2.2, 7.18.5, etc.).[72] Pliny elsewhere claims that

---

glosses of Greek are at 1.7.2 *nutu ac renutu,* 1.18.4 *patria,* 1.20.22 *similem nivibus hibernis,* etc.

[69] The rare word δυσκαθαίρετον avoids the more cumbersome and explicit Latin (Niemirska-Pliszczynska 1955:48, who suggests *vinci non possit* in Latin; I would suggest *subverti vix possit*). Quintilian warns that for someone in danger (accused of a capital charge), embellishments such as metaphor, rare words, rounded periods, and so on, all ruin the tone of anxiety (*non perdant haec omnia necessarium periclitanti sollicitudinis colorem...? Inst.* 11.1.49).

[70] Aulus Gellius notes that *gratia* is one of those words which can have a good or bad meaning (*ancipitia,* 12.9.1).

[71] See Bartsch 1994:171 on *distinctio,* the splitting of close synonyms into good and bad opposites.

[72] Compare Syme (1958:84): "He is not averse from explaining that the rich are not really well off [2.4.3, 2.15.2, 4.6.1, 8.2, 9.37.2 ff.]." Pliny generally avoids the term *locuples* except in negative or pejorative contexts (*captatio* of the "rich," 2.20.7, 5.1.3; Artemidorus' "rich" friends hemmed and hawed about loaning him money, 3.11.2; *others* visit their estates to become "richer" [by extracting more money through their presence], but I become poorer [making generous financial arrangements through my presence], 8.2.1; cf. *Pan.* 42.1, 80.1). In the *Panegyric,* on the other hand, it is acceptable to speak of the people being "enriched" by the generous emperor (25.2 *locupletatas tribus,* 27.4).

Regulus' wealth is approaching HS 60,000,000, several times his own, and is "destined" to reach the scandalous sum of HS 120,000,000 (2.20.13). Regulus' *clientela* is a private "faction" (*factiosus,* 15), a dangerously independent power base. Pliny merely has friends, an open network of mutually beneficial and honorable exchange ranging from his lesser friends such as Voconius (17 *amore mutuo*) all the way up to the emperor (e.g. dining with Trajan at 6.31.13). Regulus' lesser associates hold him in "fear" (15 *timetur*) rather than mutual affection; Pliny's hold him in "awe" as well as affection (*diligit, reveretur,* 1.14.3). The Bad Senator's circle of fear imitates the Bad Emperor's rule, just as the Good Senator's circle of affection imitates the Good Emperor's rule, and thus Regulus' circle of fear is an empty relic under the Good Emperor, as out of step with the times as was Pliny's circle of affection with Rusticus, Mauricus, and Modestus under Domitian. The circulation of *gratia* in the circle of affection is more than just a sequence of profitable dealings, since it relies on the moral quality, the "honor" (*fides),* of the participants. The anti-senator has a replica anti-circle of friends, but the structure, lacking the moral glue of affection, loyalty, and goodness, is all façade and no foundation.[73]

In the final lines Pliny brings to a culmination the implicit contrast between the bad senator Regulus and the good senators Pliny and his friends. Parallel to the miniature sketch of Regulus, a list of twisted senatorial qualities, is a contrasting miniature sketch of Mauricus. Just returning from exile, Mauricus can be imagined as having nothing but personal moral qualities, pure *auctoritas* (*auctore,* 16) without faction, fear, or money. Pliny moves from generic political virtues of "weighty integrity" and "prudence" (*gravis prudens,* 16) to the ideal imperial-senatorial virtue "foresight" (*providentia,* an etymological expansion of *prudentia).*[74]

Pliny develops the idea of Mauricus' "foresight" with a characteristic financial metaphor: since Mauricus can foresee the future, "if I act on his authority, *accounts will balance" (illo auctore ratio constabit).* Mauricus'

---

[73] Sallust comments that commonality of feelings is *amicitia* among good men and *factio* among bad men (*Jug.* 31.15; cf. Syme 1958:413). *Factio* can also mean conspiracy against the emperor (Suet. *Claud.* 14). Again, I do not mean for us uncritically to accept Pliny's congratulatory rhetoric, which I echo merely as an ironic shorthand.

[74] *prudens... et qui futura possit...* providere, 16. The generic virtues *gravitas* and *prudentia* appear in other lists, e.g. 1.14.6 *gravitate prudentia fide.* The more concrete term *providentia* is an imperial virtue (6.19.4, 10.54.1, 10.108.2, *Pan.* 25.4, 34.2, 75.5); above all the superlative *providentissimus* belongs to "ceremonial language" (Gamberini 1983:375 n. 2), being used only of the emperor (8.17.2, 10.61.1, 10.77.1) or the ideal senior senator Corellius (4.17.10, 9.13.6). *Providentia* appears in coins and inscriptions, usually of the emperor (e.g. Mattingly & Sydenham 1926, Trajan nos. 28, 357, 661; *ILS* 282 Trajan), although Nerva advertised a new role for the Senate with the coin title *providentia senatus* (Mattingly & Sydenham, Nerva no. 90).

foresight will prevent Pliny from making a bad political "investment" such as attacking Regulus rather than the more powerful and therefore more promising Certus. Regulus has merely money and faction, but no tempting prefecture bestowed by Domitian. On a loftier level, Pliny is using the metaphor of balancing accounts to suggest an ideal of political behavior. The ideal politician is responsible and accountable. His actions can and will be subject to audit, like the financial books of a magistrate at the end of his term of office. The good emperor, too, always acts as if he will have to "turn in his accounts" (*tamquam rationem redditurus, Pan.* 20.5), as Trajan did for his first journey to Rome as emperor, to distinguish himself from Domitian (20.4).[75] This reverses the "unaccountable" practices of the hereditary sequence of emperors from Augustus to Domitian, who could only balance their accounts, ever since the opening crime of Tiberius' reign, if the audits were rendered to the "one man."[76] The fearful Regulus, full of regret and embarrassment, has finally had to show his unbalanced accounts from under Domitian and Nero. But when the good senator grounds his actions on political virtues, on integrity and prudence, then the beneficial circulation of advice, services, and duties always stays "in the black"; he will have no regrets for what he does.

It is suitable in this context that "prudence" is the political virtue that Pliny emphasizes with explanatory detail (*multis experimentis... ratio constabit,* 16). Prudence, or acting with discretion and tact, is an especially important virtue under the Empire. Prudence can even mean doing nothing, or in positive terms, "keeping one's peace" (*quiescendi,* 16), swallowing one's pride or indignation (Tac. *Agric.* 42.4). Thus even the outspoken Mauricus is a prudent survivor in comparison with his executed brother. Regulus seems to have found no Stoic excesses (2) or indiscreet letters (14) for which he could exult over Mauricus tauntingly. Mauricus is the perfect combination of Rusticus' integrity and Pliny's prudence. Pliny, by boasting of subordinating himself to Mauricus' authority, can borrow some of Mauricus' martyrdom prestige to cloak his own prudent collaboration with Domitian.

Pliny's personal letter to his close friend from his youth (2.13.5, 10.4.1) reveals private plans that do not appear to public view through his deeds or even his words.[77] The fact that he is publishing this intimate document is meant to prove that even in his thoughts he has nothing to hide, nothing to

---

[75] Pliny has already suggested a parallel between Mauricus and Trajan by applying the imperial term *dux* to Mauricus, 1.5.10 (*illum... ducem, me comitem...*). On *dux* as an imperial title (the military "leader" par excellence), see for example Plin. *Pan.* 12.1, Mart. 10.6.2, 12.8.6, Béranger 1953:48.

[76] Tac. *Ann.* 1.6 *ut non aliter ratio constet quam si uni reddatur;* compare Pallas' "swearing out of office," 13.14.1 *paresque rationes cum re publica haberet.*

[77] Bütler 1970:100.

cause shame or regret.[78] Of the alternatives Pliny is contemplating, trying something or doing nothing, he evidently chose the latter. For Pliny's post-Domitianic relations with Regulus, there are no public deeds or words, since Pliny did nothing. This letter gives moral significance to "doing nothing," for which Pliny uses the morally positive term *quiescendi,* keeping one's peace, observing proper restraint (cf. 1.23.3, *Pan.* 95.1). Even though Pliny stayed on good terms with Regulus, this was not due to selfish ambition or cowardice, but as a positive decision to keep "quiet," a decision to which even Mauricus assented. Pliny's final comment here has programmatic significance for the entire collection. In the restrained and prudent behavior necessary in the upper reaches of imperial politics, most moral meaning lies beneath the surface. On the surface, good and bad senators and emperors go through the same pseudo-republican forms of virtuous behavior in accordance with traditional ideals of *fides, pietas, officium, gratia,* and so on. Pliny's letters claim to reveal the hidden moral depths beneath the surface, the motives and plans behind the public behavior. The epistolary genre is necessary to show the real meaning of events, in an era in which politics has become a façade. Friendship, including the friendly exchange of thoughts and letters, is the only true guarantee of moral meaning, and of moral continuity across the great divide from regime to regime.

---

[78] Keeping even one's thoughts honorable and free of shame is a commonplace in upper-class ideology (e.g. Sen. *de Tranq.* 17.1, M. Aurelius *Med.* 3.4). Constantly maintaining a false façade involves "anxiety" (Sen. *de Tranq.* 17.1 *si te* anxie *componas...*).

PLINY'S THREE CHILDREN (1.8)

In letter 1.8 we find Pliny donating money to his native town. How splendid—why should that cause anxiety? And yet we find him confessing numerous anxieties, though not, to be sure, all or even the most important of them. The letter is actually constructed as a list of anxieties, or "reasons for hesitation" (*cunctationis... causae,* 5; 18). He begins with the problem of self-praise (5–9); then (10–13; *accedebat his causis,* 10) he turns to the specific problems connected with the gift of food payments for free children, though returning again to the problem of self-praise (13). The next problem (*praeterea,* 14) turns out to be self-praise again. Finally, he has a special problem (*me vero peculiaris quaedam impedit ratio,* 16), which again deals with ostentation and self-promotion.

The master orator has produced a rather confusing letter: the clear rhetorical signposts do not correspond to a clear division in argument, and the essential background information, what the speech was really about, is postponed until late in the letter (*alimenta,* 10).[1] As in other letters, Pliny takes advantage of the epistolary setting to postpone important material. The original reader Saturninus has already read the speech "on the library" (2) and knows that is mainly about *alimenta* (10), that it contains "unpopular" exhortations to raise children (12), and that its original audience consisted of the town decurions (16). In this version of the letter for the general public, the delayed parceling out of the basic facts helps shape the reader's understanding, or rather, helps confuse the reader. Is the speech really self-promotion if it concerns an *unpopular* gift and exhortation? How can a speech about this *unpopular* gift run the risk of ostentatious ambition (17)? It seems that to put the best face on the matter, Pliny has distorted or omitted the real causes of anxiety, presenting only the ones that refute themselves. We need to

---

[1] Rhetorical theory was well acquainted with deceptive openings (e.g. Quint. *Inst.* 10.1.21).

look at the real circumstances of upper-class munificence in order to understand the basic anxieties that underlie the letter and determine its form.[2]

Pliny is making two donations, for a library and for child-support. We know that his gifts to Comum amounted to HS 1,600,000 (5.7.3), including the library, its maintenance (100,000, *CIL* 5.5262), the *alimenta* (500,000, 7.18.2), and presumably a later donation of one-third of teachers' salaries (4.13.5). Finally, after his death he left money for public baths, with 30,000 for furnishing them and 200,000 for maintenance; and 1,866,666 for supporting 100 ex-slaves of his, with the funds later to revert to an annual town banquet (*CIL* 5.5262).

Pliny's gifts are therefore clustered at two moments, the time of 1.8 (about 97–98 C.E.) and the time of his death: the first time gives him the most clout for his money, and the second of course costs him nothing personally.[3] We can attribute the sudden large donations of 1.8 to the critical transition point in the imperial government as well as in his own career. Pliny needed additional prestige with the new rulers Nerva and Trajan, and he needed additional prestige to reach the higher and more selective offices of prefect of the treasury of Saturn and consul. Nerva seems to have been particularly eager to solidify his insecure reign by gaining favor with the people through large-scale benefactions (Syme 1930:63). The library which Pliny is now dedicating (1.8.2) may, to be sure, have been donated earlier, perhaps under Domitian's initiative in patronizing the arts and as a prerequisite for a Domitianic promotion to praetor (c. 93 C.E.) or prefect of the military treasury (94–96).

For all Pliny's high moral tone about noble behavior and liberality on behalf of his home town, the real target of his donations was the imperial government at Rome. Evidently home-town philanthropy on a large scale was an unstated requirement for the consulship or other high imperial favors. By tying local power achieved through popular benefaction to the submission implied by receiving imperial patronage, the emperor reinforces channels of

---

[2] Duncan-Jones (1974:288–319) discusses the evidence and the financial details, and Nichols (1980:365–85) discusses the political motivations, though his awareness of the practical benefits gained by the philanthropist seems to me much too limited. Veyne (1990) treats at length the ideological background of ancient philanthropy, including many of the pressures, sanctions, and temptations that motivated the upper class to euergetism.

[3] Unlike Pliny, who died suddenly, Calpurnius Fabatus was old and weak enough to be anticipating his death (5.11.3, 7.23.1, 8.10.2), which came about five years later (10.120.2). He was therefore able to enjoy his wealth for most of his life and then move his posthumous gifts up into the last years of his life; his portico (5.11) and his freeing of slaves (7.16.4, 7.32) correspond to Pliny's posthumous baths and freeing of slaves. The ones who lose out from Fabatus' near-posthumous benefactions are his heirs (such as Pliny), so Pliny emphasizes not only his pleasure but even his *self-interest* in the donations (5.11.2, 7.32.2).

obligation reaching from individual towns and town councilors through powerful politicians at Rome to himself. Aside from political advancement, the childless Pliny received the "right of three children" at about this time, a valuable grant that allowed him to receive bequests directly from friends. Perhaps by funding child payments Pliny avoided the need to have children of his own. The grant to Comum may therefore have repaid itself not only politically, but even financially.

The speech of Nerva described at 10.8.1 indicates how the emperor can pressure the ruling class to make suitable donations, and magnify what he can accomplish with the imperial fiscus alone. The emperor can thus make use of others' funds without a reign of terror, and without monopolizing the credit. As Pliny puts it, both by his most beautiful speech and by his most noble example Nerva "exhorted all citizens" to munificence (*cum... omnes cives... esset cohortatus,* 10.8.1). By "all" citizens Nerva really means the ruling class, especially the Senate where the speech was probably given, and his "exhortation" was really an implied threat: follow my example or lose imperial patronage. Pliny explicitly attributes his donation of a temple at Tifernum, his other major benefaction at this time, to Nerva's "speech and example."[4] The temple flaunts the link between "private" beneficence and imperial initiative with its statues of the emperors; probably they included only "good" emperors, or perhaps the divine emperors Caesar, Augustus, Claudius, Vespasian, Titus, and Nerva, filled out with Trajan's statue as an informal pre-death apotheosis.[5] Pliny's gift of *alimenta* at Comum fits what was apparently a Nervan innovation, the institution of *alimenta* throughout Italy to complement the *frumentationes* in Rome (*epit. de Caes.* 12.4; Duncan-Jones 1974:291). Nerva and the following emperors seem to have relied on aristocrats to cover the larger towns so that the emperors could concentrate their resources on smaller towns that would have had fewer rich and ambitious patrons.[6] Pliny may even have felt pressure from the emperor, implicit or explicit, to publish this speech in order to publicize the spread of the *alimenta.*

We should note that Pliny's HS 500,000, or about 30,000 in annual income, would have covered only about 150 children at the typical recorded rate of HS

---

[4] Garnsey 1968:379.

[5] We can get a sense of the official "good" emperors from the reissue coinage under the Flavians and Trajan, which honored the deified emperors along with Tiberius and Galba (Mattingly & Sydenham 1926:302–04). Dio has Vindex contrast Nero with Augustus and Claudius (63.22.6), evidently the only two "good" Julio-Claudians.

[6] Duncan-Jones 1974:316. Inscriptions tell us of 47 towns with public *alimenta* and 7 with private *alimenta* (1974:337, 341).

16 per month, a tiny proportion of the population.[7] Pliny's major gifts are devoted to the two places where Pliny's wealth was invested in land; at Laurentum he had only a villa (4.6.2). In a sense, then, these "gifts" are really repayments to the people from whose labor Pliny has been making his money, and small repayments at that. His Comum income of perhaps HS 600,000 per year came from the surplus labor value of many hundreds of workers (perhaps 6,000 *iugera* at 7–30 *iugera* per worker).[8] In return, Pliny is giving minimal support for only 150 children.

Pliny's position as a childless supporter of children is remarkably similar to the position of the childless emperor Nerva, the originator of the *alimenta*. This *pater patriae* was not a father at all, being the only emperor aside from Galba with neither an heir nor plausible prospects of producing one.[9] Nerva, Trajan, and Pliny may all have risen to power partly through being childless, despite the imperial propaganda decrying childlessness. Hence they may have felt the need to exert a special effort to lessen the appearance of hypocrisy. The new emperors favored the appellation "father" (e.g. Nerva, *Pan.* 6.1, 7.4, 10.6; Trajan, *Pan.* 21); Nerva took the title *pater patriae* right from the start (as shown by the coinage); and Trajan seems to have used the child support schemes to bolster his image as the "parent" of all (*Pan.* 26.3, 28.7). Similarly, the childless Pliny acts as a gentle "father" (5.19.2) in his household, his little republic (8.16.2); he is officially addressed as one of the *patres conscripti* in the Senate; and he treats his own *patria* Comum as his *"daughter* or parent" (4.13.5), implicitly making himself the "father of his fatherland."

In this letter Pliny at last deals explicitly with the anxieties relating to self-praise. We might wonder why Pliny needs to publish this speech at all—or whether he in fact did publish it—were it not for the fact that the hierarchical system of his time was based on praise, as much as modern democracies often seem to be based on blame: it takes a great deal of effort to persuade people to support rulers that they did not choose. This letter is Pliny's way of confronting the problems of praise and self-praise, the basic substance of his published letters and of imperial politics.

---

[7] Duncan-Jones gives a very rough estimate of 7000 free children in a total population of 25,000, perhaps 60% free (1974:267). Even if this is off by a factor of five, it demonstrates that the *alimenta* reached only a small number of families.

[8] Sherwin-White 1966:257, Duncan-Jones 1974:325–28.

[9] "A childless prince flattered certain prejudices which the Senate was able to parade from time to time" (Syme 1958:2 on Nerva). The absence of imperial relatives on Nerva's coinage has been noticed (Mattingly & Sydenham 1926:2.222). The young Otho planned to marry (Suet. *Otho* 10.2), and in 90 Martial is still hoping for Domitia to produce an heir (6.3; Jones 1992:37).

Whether or not Pliny published the speech, this letter will accomplish what the speech did, and accomplish it better. In a ceremonial speech at the town hall one is "forced" (5) to give fulsome praise to oneself and one's relatives, but in the letter Pliny can put his "real" private motivations on display instead of his required public stance. Like letter 6.27 on his first speech as *consul designatus,* this letter presents the speech as Pliny would like it to be remembered, not as the occasion forced it to be.

We can therefore identify three principal areas of awkwardness for Pliny to confront: money, self-promotion, and child-rearing. In this letter, one of the richest men of Rome boasts of scorning money, the orator of self-praise deprecates external glory, and the childless man urges the benefits of raising children. Perhaps it is not so noble for the extremely rich Pliny to donate a small portion of his wealth back to his town once in a lifetime (1.8.8). It seems still less noble when we realize that he did it almost entirely for political self-promotion, as a way of "buying" patronage from Nerva and Trajan by subsidizing their Italian public support network. Though he was in a sense "compelled" by these Good Emperors to fork over his wealth, he must make himself seem willing and enthusiastic, and therefore emphasize that he has *no regrets* (1.8.8) for the act, since regret would be a retrospective reflection of having been compelled against his wishes. The good emperor is munificent to his people without "feeding them on slaughter" or "plunder," of the upper class, that is (*Pan.* 27.3–4). Finally, the childless Pliny is trying to get as much of a paternal image out of the donation as he can, and therefore he devotes the central part of his argument to the morality of child-rearing, claiming that the moral statement is even more important than the money itself (which is, indeed, too limited to have much practical effect by itself).[10]

THE DIRECTIONS OF PLINY'S ANXIETIES: DOWNWARDS, SIDEWAYS, AND UPWARDS

Pliny's anxieties can be analyzed by direction as well as by topic, being directed either downwards towards the working-class people of Comum, sideways towards his upper-class colleagues at Comum and at Rome, or upwards towards the inner imperial circle and the emperor himself. In the downward direction, Pliny conceals the fact that he is giving back to the people a small portion of the fruits of their own labor, as a sop to the working

---

[10] Trisoglio speaks more flatteringly of Pliny's frustrated paternity seeking substitute satisfaction ("la sua paternità frustrata cercherà un compenso nell'istituzione di *alimenta,"* 1972:158).

class.[11] Will he succeed in turning latent resentments into warm gratitude? Tenants who are sinking "hopelessly" into debt through oppressive rents, as at 9.37.2 *(desperant),* probably at Tifernum, are probably less than delighted with their landlord. Perhaps some of their boorish petitions and complaints are directed against himself.[12] The people of Comum will have to be satisfied with this one rather limited benefaction until his death, when he can offer gifts that are more popular, baths and banquets, without incurring the charge of populist ambition (1.8.17).

Veyne speaks of the pressure to deflect resentment from below by means of munificence, citing Plutarch's anecdote about the Athenian general Phocion as an example of the political dangers of not making public donations.[13] Similarly, Pliny imagines that prior bad emperors gave popular donations to appease the masses' hatred of them *(Pan.* 28.3). Nevertheless, Pliny emphasizes that his gift is *not* popular, as a gladiator show would be (1.8.10) or as the feast at Tifernum must have been (4.1.6). Perhaps the unpopularity was in fact due not so much to moral reasons, the tedious labor of child-rearing as opposed to the pleasures of eyes and ears (10–11), as to the fact that the gift reached so few people and left out not only the childless (1.8.12, 17) but also most families with children as well. A banquet or a gladiator show might be less useful, but at least it reaches everyone equally. Though upper-class philanthropy did succeed in redistributing some surplus labor value back to the people, it was a limited and inefficient mechanism for collecting and distributing resources. Not only was a large share of resources wasted on private luxury items such as villas, but even the portion that was distributed depended on the whims and plans of "benevolent" (and ambitious) aristocrats.[14]

---

[11] Pliny shows his awareness of the economics of class structure when he praises Trajan's charitable programs: "It does no good for the emperor to neglect the masses and protect the upper class, which will collapse by its own weight like a head cut off from its body" *(frustraque proceres plebe neglecta ut desectum corpore caput nutaturumque instabili pondere tuetur, Pan.* 26.6). Terms such as "working class" and "ruling class" are merely useful simplifications, though more fixed in the Roman world than in ours. "In reality, the social space is a multi-dimensional space, an open set of relatively autonomous fields, fields which are more or less strongly and directly subordinate, in their functioning and their transformations, to the field of economic production" (Bourdieu 1991:245).

[12] 9.15.1 *tam multis undique rusticorum libellis et tam querulis;* cf. 5.14.8 *rusticarum querellarum.* Rents ranged from one-third to two-thirds of agricultural produce (Garnsey 1988:249); compare MacMullen (1974:34) on oppressive rents. A few big landowners might be rich enough to own most of the property in an area (1974:5–6).

[13] Veyne 1990:97; Plut. *Phocion* 9, *Moralia* 188A, 533A, 882D. See also Duncan-Jones 1990:170–71.

[14] Veyne discusses the economic aspects of wasteful sumptuary expenditure (1990:54–58).

Pliny's sideways-directed anxieties involve competitive jealousies with ruling-class colleagues either at Comum or at Rome, although the nature of the competition would be very different in the two cases. On the one hand, being one of the richest and most powerful landowners at Comum makes him subject to local jealousies from his lesser colleagues. But on the other hand, these local colleagues can benefit both from Pliny's local benefactions (especially the library) and from Pliny's own advancement, whereas Pliny's Roman colleagues stand to lose unless they counterbalance Pliny's imperial prestige by donating to their own native and client towns.[15] The better the local son is doing at Rome, the more access to imperial patronage the upper class of Comum enjoys, as Pliny's recommendation of his townsman illustrates (6.25.3). Furthermore, the donated library, which might help attract teachers and establish a local school (4.13), could give real political benefit to the local ruling class: it could help their sons to obtain the upper-class education that will enable them to enter political careers. The library is an example of symbolic (or "cultural") capital, a repository of literary culture, with little practical use but priceless symbolic value in helping the next generation take its place in the ruling class of Comum and the empire. It is in Pliny's own interest, too, to promote his townsmen, since as they rise, Pliny will have a larger network of powerful and indebted friends to draw on. Indeed, even a simple increase in citizen population "strengthens" his hometown (7.32.1 firmissimum *ornamentum*) and therefore his political base. As long as Pliny can spread his patronage without too much invidious favoritism, he and his local colleagues can cooperate smoothly and use imperial patronage for their mutual benefit. Only if Pliny uses his power to undermine his local colleagues does he have to fear their counterattack. For example, will his *alimenta* weaken the dependency of clients on other landowners? Who will decide on the list of beneficiaries? One reason Pliny must give his speech to the town council (1.8.16) is so that the élite can present a united front to the *plebs*.

Pliny's Roman colleagues, however, have little to gain from the rising power of Pliny and his North Italian townspeople. In fact, for provincial senators, who are just now breaking into the upper echelons, Pliny's gift flaunts a kind of prestige from which they are excluded, since Nerva's and Trajan's *alimenta* project is limited to Italy.[16] Pliny's published speech and letter are really directed not at the actual beneficiaries of the *alimenta,* who for the most part probably cannot read anyway, but at his ruling-class colleagues throughout the empire, who are engaged in their own forms of

---

[15] See Nichols 1980:369 on the formal and informal roles of *patronus* of a town.

[16] As Veyne points out, Pliny can only use the *alimenta* for political advantage at Rome because he is an *Italian* senator; Pliny the North Italian is basking in his insider status (1990:375).

munificence in hopes of advancement.[17] Even if Pliny cannot outspend them, he can show them the most eloquent method for cloaking their donations in the appropriate moralizing colors. His colleagues will read his letter, and perhaps his speech, for the same reason they will read his *Panegyric,* not to lap up Pliny's praise of Trajan or of himself, but to learn how to do the job themselves when their turn comes.

Pliny's upward anxieties reach to the emperor's inner circle and to the emperor himself. Pliny must make a substantial enough donation to attract the emperor's attention without arousing political risks through too much local populism, which could disturb the emperor's control and create too strong a local power base. At Rome itself, major building projects and games were the monopoly of the emperor (Veyne 1990:362, 388), and even elsewhere, aristocrats had to be cautious about events such as public shows that could cause populist disturbances (e.g. 4.22.3). Perhaps Pliny even avoided presiding over the games held in his own praetorship because of these dangers (7.11.4). Even a letter commending a gift of gladiator games shows apologetic signs.[18]

Pliny's donation implicitly shows that a good emperor does not need to plunder or kill the rich to feed the poor (*Pan.* 50.5); a harmless speech urging public generosity (10.8.1) will have the same practical effect. All Pliny needs to show is that he does not resent being pressured by the emperor to make donations. His high moral tone therefore emphasizes that he scorns money and delights in the beauty of his noble deeds (1.8.8). Such moral arguments extract him from the political pressures that squeeze him from the top, bottom, and sides, while satisfying his craving for publicity in compensation for his loss of money. We can assume, of course, that he did indeed publish the speech. His rhetoric of self-fulfilling prophecy explains to us the process by which he

---

[17] The proportion of people with enough literacy to read (and to wish to read) formal literature was probably well under 10% (Harris 1989:22, 266). The proportion of "craft literacy," as demonstrated in rudimentary graffiti, simple bookkeeping, Christian liturgical chanting, etc., was higher (e.g. Horsfall 1991:63, 68, 74, Franklin 1991:96–97), but the works of Pliny and his circle are clearly not aimed at people with craft literacy. Pliny, of course, pretends that anyone can read the published speech, that to "publish" (*publicare,* 3) means to speak to the "people" (*apud populum,* 16) or "mob" (*vulgi... plebem,* 17).

[18] "To refuse it would seem *not firm but hardhearted"* (6.34.2 *non constans sed durum*). Sherwin-White, wrongly assuming that this anxiety disappeared at the death of Domitian, implausibly assigns the speech to Domitian's time (1966:105 on 1.8.17) despite evidence that the proliferation of *alimenta* date to Nerva and Trajan (*epit. de Caes.* 12.4, Duncan-Jones 1974:291). The repression of populist events for fear of political disturbances was even stronger in the provinces (e.g. 4.22, 10.116).

created a "meritorious" speech of self-praise out of his meritorious
philanthropy.[19]

Pliny opens the letter with a lengthy treatment of a false anxiety, over
whether Saturninus will resent being bothered again with this speech. We hear
in chiastic repetition about Pliny's anxious fears *(verecundiam... timide uti)*
and Saturninus' resentful refusals *(recusandi laboris... gravari)* which do *not*
exist. Sherwin-White thinks that the awkwardness reflects a new friendship
(1966:103), but actually, Pliny is dramatizing the main point of the letter.
This is a speech of self-praise, but his friend *wants* to read it. We are to
assume that Saturninus commented favorably on the speech when he saw it
last, since he is now asking to see more of Pliny's writing, and since Pliny is
willing to send back this speech that he obviously wants to publish, and
therefore he implicitly expects a favorable reply.[20] Just as the occasion of
announcing donations to the town council "compelled" Pliny to speak in praise
of himself (5), so too Saturninus is in a sense compelling Pliny to send him
self-praise. Hence Pliny uses such strong verbs: Saturninus "pleaded" and
"demanded" that Pliny send him something (1 *flagitabas,* 2 *depoposcisti),* even
though he could have anticipated, knowing Pliny's "laziness," that it was going
to be nothing new *(non est... quod... aliquid novi operis expectes,* 3).
   Saturninus is the ideal recipient for this letter, since he stands outside the
political pressures bearing on Pliny from various directions. He is neither a
fellow townsman nor a senatorial rival, but a lower-ranking advocate and
writer who has nothing to lose from Pliny's further advancement—and
everything to gain, as we will learn later. Pliny reciprocates Saturninus'
flattering encouragement not only with literary publicity to a well-placed
knight, Erucius Clarus (1.16), but also with a valuable political introduction to
a powerful senator, if the Priscus of 7.7–8 is Neratius Priscus, jurist, cos. 97
and governor of Lower Germany and Pannonia *(HA Hadr.* 18.1). In any case,
the Priscus of 7.7–8 is Saturninus' superior, since behind the conventional
protestations of *mutual* affection and obligation (7.7.1) we hear that
Saturninus is telling Pliny in letter upon letter about his deepest gratitude to
Priscus (7.8.1). Saturninus' "constancy" in love *(maximam in amore*

---

[19] "The process of editing, while testing whether the speech is *worthy,* will make it so"
(emendationis ratio... dignum dum id ipsum experitur efficiet, 1.8.4).
[20] In 1.16 Pliny says neither that he has just become friendly with Saturninus, nor that he has
just started to admire his literary talents. What he has just learned is how multifaceted
Saturninus' talents are—not necessarily the sign of a new intimacy. Incidentally, Saturninus
has probably *read* the speech, not *heard* it at a recitation (Sherwin-White 1966:103), since he
has "made notes," 1.8.3 *adnotasse;* compare 3.13.5, Fronto 1.308 Haines. The wording *ut
rursus vaces... iam quaedam adnotasse* (1.8.2) implies that Saturninus will do again what he
has done before.

constantiam, 7.8.3) is like Romatius Firmus' "memory" of Pliny's gift (*memorem huius muneris,* 1.19.3): the lesser friend needs the proper "virtues" (7.8.3) to assure the greater friend that his patronage will be repaid with lasting subservience to his wishes.[21] The most obvious reason Saturninus might be unwilling to receive the speech is that he might not be able to stomach so much self-praise all over again. But Saturninus profits handsomely from his subservient flattery. One would only object to Pliny's self-praise for the same twisted reasons for which one would refuse to praise and love a living author (1.16.9), from the tendency to take things that were done "straight" and make them "twisted" (*recte facta... detorquemus,* 1.8.6), or from a *"crooked* and malicious" attitude (*pravum malignumque,* 1.16.9). If Pliny can overcome the problem of self-praise in this letter (1.8.5–6, 14–15), he can justify the basic structure of his collection of letters, and of his circle of friends. He and Saturninus live in a culture of praise, and they depend on the free circulation of praise for their status and success. Just as the letter shows us how Saturninus can welcome Pliny's self-praise, it similarly shows us how Erucius Clarus and Priscus can welcome Pliny's fulsome praise of Saturninus.

Right from the opening word *peropportune* Pliny dramatizes the mutual benefit in the culture of praise. It was a "fortunate coincidence" that Saturninus asked for what Pliny already wanted to do, and so he has "spurred a horse that was already running on its own" (1 *addidisti ergo calcaria sponte currenti*): Saturninus is as eager as Pliny is for Pliny to send something. Both want it because both will benefit from the friendly transaction. Pliny will get to put the responsibility on Saturninus' tab (on his *auctoritas,* 18) that he is publishing the speech of self-praise, and that he is writing this letter explaining the self-praise to Saturninus, to himself (7), and ultimately to the world. His "obedience" to Saturninus is therefore like his "obedience" to Septicius Clarus (1.8.18 *obsequar... consilio tuo;* 1.1.2 *ut nec te consilii nec me paeniteat obsequii*). Pliny disguises Saturninus' benefit, however, as pure pleasure in reading Pliny's wonderful writings, just as Pliny represents the return favors in 1.16 and 7.7–8 as pure pleasure in Saturninus' writings and loyal friendship.

Pliny's supposed reluctance or "delaying" (*cunctatio,* 4, 5, 18) in publishing a work of self-praise corresponds to the virtues of the good emperor, who creates legitimacy by showing reluctance and delaying in receiving titles, honors, and praises (Béranger 1953:137). "You were refusing

---

[21] On the other hand, Priscus' "affability" (7.15.3 *comitas*) is the virtue of a superior who acts not like a superior but like an equal companion, a *comes.* In particular, it is the imperial virtue of the good *princeps* who acts as if he were merely the equal of his upper-class colleagues (e.g. 6.31.2, *Pan.* 71.6).

to be emperor, which was the mark of someone who was going to be a good emperor" (*Pan.* 5.5 *recusabas... imperare, recusabas, quod erat bene imperaturi*). Trajan is also praised for having postponed the title *pater patriae*, for his reluctance to be praised, and for having postponed his third consulship (21.2, 55.4, 57.1). For the private citizen, too, "delay" is a canonical virtue, appearing in eulogistic lists for Titius Aristo (1.22.3 *cunctatio... haesitat dubitat*) and Pompeius Quintianus (9.9.2 *quanta in sermone cunctatio*). One who speaks or acts only after delaying will avoid making a false step in the treacherous upper reaches of imperial politics, or in the stresses of living obediently with a "most dissimilar father" (9.9.3). Corellius, too, made his significant political pronouncements only after a silent pause (4.17.8), and may have been too "delaying and cautious" to sanction Pliny's bold action against Certus if Pliny had asked for his advice (*erat enim cunctantior cautiorque,* 9.13.6).

Like the good emperor, Pliny speaks in self-praise only because he is "compelled" by the genre. He must give a speech to the councilors when he sets up the *alimenta* system, so that they may give their formulaic consent, just as they must give consent for land to be used for a temple at Tifernum (10.8.2) or for a library at Comum.[22] The genre of announcing a benefaction then "forces" him to speak about his ancestors' and his own munificence (*cogimur,* 5).[23] All he can do is profess that the boastfulness "offends against his modesty" and that he kept the style "restrained and humble" (*onerabit hoc modestiam nostram, etiamsi stilus ipse pressus demissusque fuerit,* 5). Pliny also softens the harsh word "boastful" with a diminutive comparative *(gloriosius),* and pairs it with the kinder synonym *elatius:* "it is a bit on the boastful side, as it were, and on the exalted side" (*est enim paulo quasi gloriosius et elatius,* 1.8.5).

When the emperor accompanies a public benefaction with a "beautiful speech" (10.8.1), he, too, is forced into conventional expressions of self-praise. Nerva's edict at 10.58 gives us a clue to the contents of his beautiful speech (e.g. 10.58.7–8 *felicitas temporum... bonus princeps... indulgentiam meam*). Pliny, too, was "forced" into the groveling flattery of the *Panegyric* by the required delivery of thanks for the consulship (*Pan.* 1.2, 4.1). The imperial style of praise is forced onto him as much as is the public philanthropy.[24] Ideally there should be a division of labor between the doer

---

[22] Sherwin-White 1966:523 on 9.39.1, Veyne 1990:453 n. 241.

[23] Inscriptions mention a public grant of oil donated by a certain L. Caecilius Cilo (*CIL* 5.5279) and a Temple of the Eternity of Rome and Augustus donated by a certain L. Caecilius Secundus (*CIL 5 Supp. Italica* 1.745).

[24] Pliny's use of the modest plural "we" for "I" parallels the imperial plural with which Trajan softens his general commands (e.g. 10.20.1, 10.22.2, 10.32). "Pliny's use of the plural in these sections, following the singular *me* and *meus* in the opening and closing sections of the

and the praiser, as with the emperor, who does his good deeds and leaves most of the job of praising to yes-men such as Pliny. Unfortunately Comum offers Pliny no one talented and prominent enough to provide the praise, so he is saddled with the "awkward and slippery" task himself (*anceps et lubricus*, 6).

CONTAINING THE RHETORIC OF BLAME

Pliny slants his description of the difficulties of self-praise to suggest the solution. A person who cannot tolerate hearing praise of oneself cannot tolerate praise of others (6 alienae *quoque laudes*), or even pious praise of one's ancestors *(de se aut de suis)*. Such a person envies goodness itself *(ipsi honestati)* almost as much as praise of goodness, and will twist and attack good deeds even if they are buried in silence *(recte facta* minus *detorquemus...)*. If we cannot satisfy this captious person even by keeping silent, there is evidently no point in trying. This hostile listener, intolerant of *any* praise at all, is obviously living in the wrong country or wrong century, perhaps unwilling to hear even the Good Emperor praised by loyal subjects.[25]

By a rhetorical twist, however, this captious jealousy is attributed to "us," Pliny and his readers. The loftily modest "we" of Pliny the benefactor ("we are compelled") modulates through an impersonal "one" ("one has trouble getting a fair hearing") to "us" the implacably jealous enemies of good deeds.[26] By exaggerating the critics' jealousy Pliny belittles the seriousness of their attack; but by equating them with ourselves he prepares the ground for his next argument, that the speech is primarily an internal philosophical exercise to persuade ourselves to love goodness and hate stinginess. The purpose of self-praise is not to display it to others, but to convince ourselves. If our human nature is so hostile to noble behavior and pious praise, we are all the more in need of a persuasive speech to convince ourselves that we should indeed pursue noble behavior, and to cure ourselves of retrospective regrets for doing right. The ideal citizen who freely circulates praise and favors has no regrets *(paenitentiam,* 8), no internal self-detraction; his self-praise reflects the fact that he is at peace with himself. By implication, the

---

letter, reflects his embarrassment at his own desire to boast and yet be modest" (Sherwin-White 1966:104); for bibliography on the singular *nos* see Trisoglio 1973:180 n. 53.

[25] Pliny uses the same word *praedicare* for "self-praise" (1.8.15) and for imperial panegyric *(Pan.* 56.2). Moreover, Pliny's forensic diction casts the hostile listener as a biased judge, listening with ears that are not sufficiently fair *(parum aequis)* and not letting the pleader "win his suit" of not having his speech seem bothersome *(obtinere; OLD* s.v. 9–11).

[26] Only at the "private consideration" of 16–17 does Pliny revert to the singular "I" (16 me... peculiaris... impedit ratio).

envious critics who oppose all circulation of praise and of favors, who hate
goodness itself, can never be at peace with themselves.

Pliny argues that the speech has been valuable even if he does not publish
it. It has made him dwell on noble thoughts and look at their beauty; it has
shielded him from the regret that can accompany a sudden benefaction, and
given him practice in despising money (8). In sum, beautifully worded praise
(*stilo,* 8) is not a pretty façade added after the deed is done, but more like the
scaffolding necessary for doing it *(agendae rei necessaria).*[27] The culture of
praise is a necessary precondition for the culture of munificence, and ensures
that the munificence will take place without resentment at the time, and thus
without regret after the fact. Since the speech *precedes* the donation, Pliny can
pretend that it gave him time to deliberate carefully and avoid future regrets:
delay allows the ideal statesman to act without regret (*cunctatio,* 1.22.3,
9.9.2). The proper moral discourse surrounding munificence lifts up the cash
transaction into the lofty realm of virtue and honor. A system of centralized
taxation and disbursement may circulate more money, but at the cost of a
culture of resentment and regret. The culture of praise allows the wealthy to
pretend to "despise money" when they donate it for the public interest—and
for personal prestige.

BITTER MEDICINE FOR RAISING CHILDREN

The importance of avoiding regret becomes clearer when we finally learn
that the speech is really not about the library which he has already donated
(2), but rather about the *alimenta* which he is announcing as a supplementary
donation (10).[28] Unlike the library, this new donation will earn Pliny little
gratitude from the class that counts, the ruling class. And unlike "games or
gladiators," public feasts, or new buildings, all of which appeal to the "eyes
and ears" (10), the *alimenta* may not bring him much popular glory either.
Pliny might easily feel regret for the loss of wealth with only intangible
political advancement to show for it; perhaps his advancement would have
come anyway, without the donation. The political benefits are so intangible
that even Nichols, who recognizes that practical pressures drove aristocrats to
donate lavishly, is hard pressed to explain just what they got out of it

---

[27] Pliny *declines* to give other examples (perhaps scaffolding?) of things "necessary for action
but without use or grace after the action"—(8 *ne longius exempla repetamus*). He evidently
does *not* want to insist too firmly that laudatory rhetoric is useless and graceless once it has
fulfilled its internal psychological task.

[28] Compare 5.11.1, *ut initium novae liberalitatis esset consummatio prioris.* See Veyne
(1967:725) on the practice of capping one piece of munificence with a popular supplement
such as games or a banquet. The opening of one public library was celebrated by a
performance by twelve pairs of gladiators (*CIL* 3.607, Hopkins 1983:12).

(1980:383). Veyne argues that the practical motivation and the moral motivation operate together, each being a valid explanation for philanthropy (1990:11, 375). Pliny of course expresses only his moral reasons, leaving us to guess at the practical ones. In the gift of *alimenta,* though, of the three possible motivating factors (disinterested moral impulse, popular public glory, and intangible personal advancement), the second factor is unfortunately missing. Pliny has no building to show for his money, and instead of grateful townspeople he has an envious majority of childless people and many families with children as well who are receiving nothing. Hence Pliny must emphasize all the more the moral reasons, and incidentally provide himself with some public glory by publishing the speech and the letter.

The actual point of the speech, the *alimenta,* brings up a new problem but also a new excuse for publication. Pliny is not simply supporting children. He is supporting the idea of children, making others "eager" to undertake the "tedium and trouble" of raising children (*ut libenter... taedium laboremque suscipiat,* 11). Pliny presents this as an awkward feature of the speech, but it is also a reason to publish it. As a consolation prize for having given a *useful* donation, Pliny now has an additional moral excuse to advertise his munificence.

To reinforce the paradox that the gift is really aimed at the childless, at those who are *not* receiving it, Pliny adds a striking metaphor, that of a doctor adding charming encouragement to bitter medicine (literally "healthy but pleasureless foods," 12). A sick society would rather eat candy (gladiator shows) than the cod-liver oil it needs (support for raising children). At first sight the metaphor fits naturally, since food payments are being compared to food: Pliny's gift is just what the doctor ordered. But as Pliny explains it, the gift is bitter (or "not so popular," 12 *non perinde populare*) primarily because most people will *not* be receiving it. Pliny's medicinal food is simply food for thought, the healthy moral message to the childless in encouragement of child-rearing. Pliny does confess that *most* people will get nothing, though he pretends that this resentful majority is comprised of the childless whereas everyone with children will be included (17)—a disingenuous pretense, if our population estimates are correct.

Accordingly, Pliny implicitly refutes the accusation that his published speech is ambitious populism (17) by phrasing this accusation in an absurd paradox: he claims to fear that the "mob" who will read the speech will be resentful because they are not the ones receiving the gift. In reality, of course, the terms are reversed. The mob will not be reading his speech, but they, or at least some of them, one hopes, will be receiving the aid. Of course, the rich decurions may well have usurped many slots in this basic payment scheme, even though only for poor recipients were the payments enough to make a

difference in sustaining and encouraging child-rearing.[29] Pliny tells us that
what the non-beneficiaries are likely to resent is the "honor" received by the
few (12 *honoremque*). The term might indicate that the payments will simply
turn into honorific allotments to the town leaders who do not need it; in any
case, it certainly distracts our attention from the hungry children who are or
are not receiving the food. Pliny imagines the money being transformed into
transcendent moral value from the recipient's view as well as from his own.
Similarly, Trajan's good character is said to do more for child-rearing than
his cash presents (*Pan.* 28.7; cf. 27.1). The most important food Pliny is
giving is the food for thought, the "healthful but unpleasant food" of the
moral message in support of child-rearing.

Like his original oration at the town council, Pliny's published speech is
also aimed at a wealthy class, not at the actual or even potential beneficiaries
of *alimenta* schemes. Someone with enough upper-class education to
appreciate the literary "polish" of these "recherché exhortations" is not likely
to change his child-rearing practices for the sake of a subsistence dole of HS
12–16 per month (3 *lima,* 11 *exquisitis adhortationibus*). And if it is true that
subtle incentives and disincentives of the patronage system were the main
causes of childlessness among the wealthy, it is unlikely that Pliny's speech
will have any effect, either. Pliny's actual donation might possibly raise the
birthrate among its poorest beneficiaries, but his carefully wrought speech of
encouragement will not raise the birthrate among its readers. Even the
Augustan marriage legislation seems to have had little effect (e.g. Tac. *Ann.*
3.25.1), despite Pliny's cheerful estimation (*Pan.* 26.5).

Yet imperial propaganda as enshrined in the marriage legislation required
the upper-class to pay lip service to the ideal of a high birthrate, as Pliny's
Panegyric illustrates (22.3, 26.5; cf. 10.2.2). Pliny's real aim in publishing his
speech is neither to appease the childless poor at Comum nor to persuade his
Roman colleagues to have more children, but to bolster his awkward position
between conflicting imperial demands that explicitly required but implicitly
discouraged ruling-class child-rearing.

Pliny's final mention of self-praise (13) brings him back to his opening
topic (5–7), in ring composition. Again Pliny brings the problem of envy to a
logical *reductio ad absurdum,* but this time the rhetoric cooperates with the
logic with a resounding climax. Pliny prepares for the climax with an initial

---

[29] Duncan-Jones (1974:303, 318) assumes that the small size of the payments indicates that the
intended recipients were poor (cf. *epit. de Caes.* 12.4 *puellas puerosque natos parentibus
egestosis*). Pliny implies that the children supported by Trajan were needy (*Pan.* 28.5);
compare the contribution societies at Amisus *ad sustinendam tenuiorum inopiam* (10.93). But
ancient charity schemes rarely discriminated by wealth; they were generally for the "citizens,"
not for the "poor," even if they benefited the poor (Veyne 1990:30, 98). See also De Ste.
Croix 1981:426.

sequence of unexceptionable, good philosophical sentiments. The rewards of goodness should be in good conscience; glory should follow, not be chased; and goodness without glory is still just as splendid (14). Having explained the public benefits of his donation, he can openly state, and quietly mock, his real motive, that he performed his benefactions for the purpose of self-advertisement: "people who adorn their benefactions with words are believed... to have done them in order to boast about them" (*ut praedicarent fecisse creduntur,* 15). Obviously Pliny did make the donation for the sake of publicity, but to put it so baldly, in the midst of this high-sounding moralizing sequence, makes it easy to dismiss this as a motive for donating.

Pliny then reverses his earlier syllogism, quietly contradicting the claim that people resent hearing any praise at all, even of a third person. At the start he argued that if praise of someone else is intolerable, then praise of oneself is even worse (6). Now he suggests that if praise of someone else is glorious, perhaps it should *not* be hollow to talk about what you yourself have done (15). The correct workings of praise have been reestablished, firmly grounded in the praise of others. Pliny can have both his "good conscience" and his "good reputation" (*conscientia... fama,* 14), provided that the fulcrum for his praise is properly situated in others, in his friends, or in the council of Comum.[30] Pliny uses the council of Comum the way the emperor uses the Roman Senate, as an echo chamber that allows him to bask in reflected praise.[31] And Pliny's mutual exchange of letters, advice, and praise with his friends gets him out of the solipsistic conundrum of self-praise and into the profitable circulation of praise.

As he continues, the attitudes of the envious begin to sound more and more absurd, and this time the deployment of grammatical persons does not weaken, but rather strengthens, his argument. There are "people" out there trying to destroy good deeds (*homines enim cum rem destruere non possunt, iactationem eius incessunt,* 15). "You" are blamed for not staying silent *(si laudanda non sileas, ipse culparis).* Whereas the modest "we" of 1.8.6 *(detorquemus)* led into the arguments for not publishing, the confident "you" allies Pliny, Saturninus and the reader in the proper circulation of praise, against an exaggeratedly hostile critic who will attack you whether you do good or bad deeds. "So if you have done *things that should be kept in silence,* the deed itself <is blamed>, but if you do not keep silent about *things that*

---

[30] Some of Pliny's honorary inscriptions at Comum must have been set up as if by the grateful council and townspeople, perhaps with standard formulas such as *optime merito* (Sandys 1927:109). Two inscriptions have Pliny in the dative, one apparently with the nominative *Vercellens[es]* (*CIL* 5.5667, 5263). Compare the inscription for the ex-slave Pallas, *ob fidem pietatemque erga patronos* (7.29.2). See Veyne 1990:124–29 on the "hypertrophy of honours" through public inscriptions and statues.

[31] Letters 7.29 and 8.6 on Pallas show how this procedure goes wrong with a bad emperor.

should be praised, you yourself are blamed" (15). Pliny disguises the third way out (do things that should be praised, and be silent about them) by making the other two possibilities sound like exclusive alternatives. Deeds are either *laudanda* or *silenda,* praiseworthy or unmentionable, but whichever you do, good or bad, the hostile critic will attack you.

The lovely word *laudanda* drives the argument home, grammatically proving Pliny's point. Foul deeds are *silenda,* to be kept in silence, above all, no doubt, by the one who perpetrated them. Good deeds, on the other hand, are *laudanda,* things that should be praised, by others at least, and perhaps by oneself. Whether Pliny publishes his speech or not, this letter has established his main point, that he has acted properly, and that his good deeds should be praised by himself or others. If he has run the risk of arousing resentment, he has also done his best to show that that resentment is baseless hostility. In any case, Pliny concludes this long letter arguing *against* publishing by saying he will "obey" Saturninus even if he thinks Saturninus is *wrong:* "the authority of your advice will be as good as reasoning" (18). Pliny will follow Saturninus' word even if he is not convinced by his reasoning. This final tag, building on the opening depiction of the eager Saturninus, converts the published speech of Pliny's self-praise into someone else's praise of Pliny. Pliny seems not to have wanted to publish it, but Saturninus overruled him. The speech is therefore an expression of Saturninus' opinion, of Saturninus' praise of Pliny.

Pliny's final worry, about mob populism, answers itself. First, Pliny has already explained that the common people who might have roared in dangerous approval are instead resentful at being excluded from this medicinal gift of child support instead of receiving the games or gladiators for which they were hoping. Second, we finally learn that the mob was also excluded from the medicinal speech of encouragement that went with the gift, since Pliny delivered the speech at the town council. Finally, the low rates of literacy and book distribution in the ancient world make it extremely unlikely that the mob will be "shouting in agreement" when the speech is published (*adsentionem vulgi adclamationemque,* 17). The walls of education will exclude the mob as effectively as the walls of the council chamber *(limine... parietibusque).* Pliny's use of lowly synonyms for the "people" (*populum,* 16) highlights the absurdity of his fears (*vulgi... plebem,* 17). Regulus shows us by contrast what someone had to do if he was vulgar enough to want his book to reach the ordinary person. Aside from gathering a "huge" audience at Rome, he had a thousand copies sent throughout the Roman Empire, to be read out loud in each town by the council member with the most notable voice (4.7.2,

6). The ambitious Regulus' showy stunt parodies the emperor's communication system for important announcements.[32]

Pliny concludes by repeating the idea of delay (*cunctationis,* 18), a suitable idea for one of his longest letters. The two other long letters in Book 1 also end in indecision (1.5, 1.20). Length, out of place in this genre (Sherwin-White 1966:4), can dramatize indecision. Whereas Pliny began with the hasty image of spurring a running horse, after this long and repetitive letter he is reemphasizing his delay. Delay, of course, is not repudiation. The fact that Pliny is still delaying implies a positive answer to his question; he will eventually stop delaying and publish the speech. But by the time this letter was published years later, Pliny's small-town display speech must have fallen into oblivion. It is through this letter, more than through the speech, that Pliny hopes to immortalize his local piece of the *alimenta* schemes. Pliny celebrates his munificence not through self-praise, but by giving the arguments against self-praise; he tries to contain the hostile pressures by giving careful expression to a select few of them, the ones most easily dealt with. Pliny attributes the hostility primarily to the gratuitous hatred of noble and useful effort; of the real conflicts of interest and of ideology that motivate the hostility we hear almost nothing, and we must reconstruct them from what we know of Pliny's position. The pure "beauty of noble thoughts" (8) cloaks the hierarchical pressures from the emperor's inner circle above to the impoverished plebs below, and the competitive pressures from Pliny's fellow aristocrats as they too try to convert their lives of financial exploitation and obsequious obedience into something of higher value. For the problematic situations of confronting his working-class townsmen, preaching to the town notables, or publishing to the Roman dynasts, Pliny substitutes his friendly rivalry with his intimates, who "spur each other" on to the love of immortal glory (*cum invicem se mutuis exhortationibus amici ad amorem immortalitatis exacuunt,* 3.7.15; cf. 1.8.1 *calcaria*). Through the circulation of friendly letters, the vicious circle of envious resentment becomes a virtuous circle of mutual praise, which becomes a self-fulfilling prophecy of mutual accomplishment and deserved glory.

---

[32] On the publication of imperial edicts throughout the empire, see Fronto *de Eloquentia* 1, 2.58 Haines, Riepl 1913:362–63, Millar 1977:255.

LITERARY LEISURE IN THE LIFE OF POLITICS (1.9)

Letter 1.9 opens with a financial metaphor, balancing one's accounts for expenses of time. "It is amazing how one's accounts balance (or seem to balance) for individual days in the city, but do not balance for a longer sequence of days." *(Mirum est quam singulis diebus in urbe ratio aut constet aut constare uideatur, pluribus iunctisque non constet.)*[1] Pliny's career centered on finances, and so his opening metaphor is a self-flattering wink at his own political success, much like his opening other letters with allusions to the augurship (7.33.1 *auguror*) and perhaps to the consulship (1.23 *consulis*). Even in Pliny's youthful position as *tribunus militum* he had financial, not military duties, and his two prestigious offices between the praetorship and the consulship were both financial, the *praefectura aerari militaris* (94–96) and the *praefectura aerari Saturni* (98–100).

The letter is apparently set during Pliny's statutory year off between offices, 97, though the date of publication was well after 98. A Pliny who knows that this was merely a year off between prestigious appointments writes in the persona of a Pliny who only knows that he has finished a term of office and is now out of office. Thus the letter presents earlier anxieties in the retrospective light of later success. Perhaps Pliny's career will come to a halt at the rank of praetorian senator. Perhaps his imperial patronage will end under the new emperors.[2] What value will life without high office have? The Senate has very little real function under the imperial system, and in any case even a senator who had reached praetorian rank must have had few opportunities to speak, since the imperial system of suffect consulships had generated dozens of consular senators. Of course, Pliny does not represent his

---

[1] Compare Sen. *Brev. Vit.* 3.1.

[2] Despite Pliny's rapid rise to the consulship, he seems to have suffered a slight loss of imperial patronage afterwards, since his patrons were more influential under Nerva than under Trajan (Syme 1958:83).

current life of relative leisure as a recent change, since he completely suppresses mention of the three-year prestigious position he received during Domitian's final years, the "reign of terror." Rather, his life of leisure stretches an indefinite extent into the past and future, and is shared by an indefinite number of people like Fundanus, another senator waiting for patronage so as to reach the consulate, or their mutual friend Atilius, an "impoverished" scholar (6.8) below senatorial rank.

Pliny justifies the value of his life in two ways, reflecting the two halves of life presented in the letter, life at Rome and life at the villa. Ostensibly only life at the villa gives real value to the upper-class life; indeed, the letter does not really tell us why Pliny and his friends spend any time at Rome at all. On the other hand, though, Pliny slants his description of life at Rome in a way that allows us to see through the description, to see that Rome is the other pole of value in his life, and indeed the more important one. Pliny *will* have a political future, his work as orator and adviser *is* important, and is in fact the source of the literary value that he creates at Laurentum. Pliny's attempts to give the highest value to his leisure at Laurentum, and none to his work at Rome, deal with two awkward problems at once, first, the traditional Roman denigration of leisure and luxury, and second, the need to hide senatorial ambition and imperial patronage.[3] Pliny pursues literary and moral ideals at his villa, not indolence and luxury, whereas his hopes at Rome for patronage to launch him further up the senatorial *cursus* are disguised as selfless performance of minor duties among equals. Meanwhile, in this ideal circulation of political power and literary value, the financial basis, the money on which these two domains depend, is absent. To allow for a balanced reckoning of purely symbolic values, of politics, literature, friendships and favors, all consideration of the cold cash which supports this ideal circulation must be excluded.

Pliny presents life at Rome as a paradox in which the whole is less than the sum of its parts. He offers us one possible way out of the contradiction with the logical warning "seems": each day only *seems* to balance (but in fact even a single day at Rome does not repay the time spent).[4] This is the logic offered by the surface of the letter, by the authorial persona who has rejected Rome entirely for his Laurentum villa and advises Fundanus to do the same. But the real Pliny and the real Fundanus, who do get value from their time at Rome, see through this solution. Another logical solution to the contradiction is

---

[3] Guillemin discusses the growing social acceptability of literary *otium* since the time of Cicero (1929:14); compare Bütler 1970:42, 54, Riggsby 1998:86 n. 27.

[4] Such complaints about social duties are conventional, e.g. Sen. *Brev. Vit.* 2.4, 7.2, 7.7, Quint. *Inst.* 12.11.18, Mart. 10.70, Juv. 1.127–33. "Seneca frequently cites patronal duties as one of the ways people fritter away their lives in Rome," Saller 1982:143 n. 142.

suggested by the emphatically continuous string of days, *pluribus iunctisque, cotidie,* and *quot dies* (1, 3). "These activities, necessary on the day you have done them, *seem* worthless if you reckon that you have done them every day." (*haec quo die feceris, necessaria, eadem, si cotidie fecisse te reputes, inania videntur,* 3). Perhaps the time spent in each single day at Rome *is* necessary and therefore valuable, but too many days in a row make it merely *seem* worthless—again with the slippery reservation of mere "seeming." Business at Rome needs support from leisure at the villa to give it real lasting value, just as mental effort and bodily leisure must alternate to make mental work possible (4).

Yet we can find the most convincing solution to the contradiction if we concentrate on the end of the list of daily tasks at Rome. An endless sequence of weddings and coming-of-age parties does indeed seem a "empty" and "cold" way to spend one's days (*inania... frigidis rebus,* 3), and accounts certainly are unlikely to balance, given the steady stream of required gifts.[5] But the beginning of the list is deceptive, since the list rises step by step, first to the semi-legal responsibility of signing a will, which might even be directly profitable because of a legacy in the will, and finally to solid Roman *negotium,* advocacy, and perhaps even better, counsel, which could even include, for Pliny, serving as adviser in the emperor's *consilium,* one of the most prestigious positions available for an upper-class Roman (cf. 6.31).[6] The list omits its real climax, serving in public office, because the "someone" Pliny imagines asking (*si quem interroges,* 2) reflects Pliny's supposed condition of being out of office, and expecting to remain so in the future.

Just as the list shifts gradually to Pliny's serious work, so the entire letter shifts gradually into Pliny's own voice. It starts with an impersonal statement that accounts do not balance. Next, an indeterminate "you" asks "someone," and "you" realize that you have been wasting your days. This happens to "me," to Pliny, when he has been working at Laurentum, but what Pliny remembers and regrets about his life at Rome is not a list of frigid tasks but its immoral aspect: at Rome, unlike at Laurentum, he *regrets* things that he hears and says (*nihil audio quod audisse, nihil dico quod dixisse paeniteat,* 1.9.5). The contrast with Pliny's usual pose, of handling all aspects of his life (politics, friendship, wealth, literature) without regret, is so striking that we

---

[5] For complaints about burdensome obligatory social gifts, see e.g. Ter. *Phorm.* 40–49, Mart. 7.86, 8.64, Juv. 3.186–89.

[6] Champlin shows that witnesses tended to receive little or nothing from the will (1991:80), but on the other hand, giving a modest legacy was a typical (final) friendly favor (1991:146, Plin. 5.1.1, 7.20.6, 7.31.5). Even before Pliny received the *ius trium liberorum* in early 98 (10.2), he would have been able to profit from friends' wills; the law only took 50%, and could probably be evaded through the setting up of a *fideicommissum* (K. Hopkins 1983:242 n. 54).

can suspect Pliny of being disingenuous. Feigned regret can be useful for the sake of *ethopoiia,* to create a characterization of sincerity (Quint. *Inst.* 9.2.60). Furthermore, Pliny screens himself from the immorality of Rome by his negative formulation. He does not explicitly say that he regrets his improper behavior at Rome, but only that here at Laurentum he does *not* say or hear anything which he later regrets, does *not* listen to left-handed blame (*nemo apud me quemquam sinistris sermonibus carpit,* 5) or bestow reproof, does *not* feel hope or fear.

The second list describing life at Rome by its moral tone (1.9.5) does not quite match the first list describing specific events there (1.9.2), especially the ceremonial events at the start (coming-of-age parties, weddings, and wills). Pliny is not confessing that he regrets his behavior at these parties, and certainly not that he has, like Regulus, cajoled and intimidated shamelessly to profit from will-signing ceremonies (2.20). Pliny's second list suggests that the first list can be divided into two groups of activities, each with its own drawback, empty waste of time for the first half, and morally corrupting political pressures for the second. Empty social ceremonies such as weddings and will signings are a waste of time, whereas real political duties such as advocacy and counsel are fraught with anxiety and political pressures.

In neither case, of course, does Pliny really mean to attribute these negative features to his own activities. Behind the complaints against social ceremonies the reader is supposed to discern Pliny's admirable attentiveness even to lesser social duties, and behind this implied self-flattery we can discern the real meaning of the hollow duties, as ultimately profitable social glue among the members of the upper-class. Pliny's complaints about empty social duties differ greatly from the satirical poets' complaints which they resemble (e.g. Mart. 10.70). Pliny differs from the resentful client who must humbly attend on more powerful patrons, in the often empty hope of winning patronage.[7] Pliny goes to these social functions as an equal who condescends to offer his time freely; as such, his attendance is ennobling, while his reward in gratitude and favors is more certain.[8] Moreover, Pliny emphasizes in his list favors that he is unlikely to ask in return; most obviously, he has no son to bring to manhood or daughter to bestow in marriage. Offering his time to perform unrepayable social favors is an ideal way to lay up symbolic capital for a time when he needs to call in his social credit, to be repaid by return

[7] Pliny later ironically asks a semi-retired senator whether he misses paying salutations in the city rather than receiving them in the country (7.3.3). Epictetus mocks such insincere complaints by aristocrats about the social duties they must endure due to their desire for patronage connections (1.25.15; cf. 1.2.12, 2.6.8, 3.7.31, 3.9.18, 3.24.44–49).

[8] Similarly, Pliny's complaint about differential treatment of dinner guests (2.6) differs from the satirical poets', since Pliny is receiving the better service while the poets are receiving the worse service (e.g. Mart. 3.60, 4.68, Juv. 1.134–38).

favors with real financial or political value. Accordingly, Pliny the patient listener of readings will not give a reading for his friends (1.13.6), at least not in Book 1, since the immediate and equal repayment of a favor undoes its *gratia,* ruining its power in establishing social connections, obligations, and hierarchies. Repaying a cash gift with an equal cash gift is worse than useless; it is an insult (Sen. *de Benef.* 2.21.2, 4.40.4–5; Bourdieu 1977:5–6, 171). *Officium* loses its *gratia* if the *gratia* is demanded back (1.13.6). Pliny is implying, of course, that he goes to readings and weddings out of mere good will, *gratis,* for gratitude. Yet the underlying dynamic of the exchange will make people's good will more useful to him in real favors rather than in filling a lecture room.

The exchange of token social favors is actually not less but more than the sum of its parts. "Someone" thinks that these empty favors have wasted his days, but more goes into the "accounts" than appears at first sight. We may compare the "famous and praised" saying of Emperor Titus after a day in which he did no favors: "friends, I have lost a day" (Suet. *Tit.* 8.1; compare Nerva at 10.58.7–9, Saller 1982:32). In good Roman reckoning, the emperor makes his time worthwhile by doing favors for others, not empty favors like wedding attendance but financial or legal favors, such as Pliny's own favors to his friends of money (e.g. 1.19) or legal loopholes (e.g. 1.18). The emperor, too, is well recompensed for his time and money spent in distributing favors, since the flow of small favors downward through patronage reinforces his position at the summit of the power hierarchy and thus ensures the upward flow of money and power on a large scale.[9] The ideal emperor's daily life is a model for the ideal upper-class citizen, and vice versa. Pliny willingly performs social favors for his equals or inferiors, making himself accessible like the Good Emperor who goes to his friends' houses to dinner (Trajan, Dio 68.7.3, Eutrop. 8.4), visits the public baths (Suet. *Tit.* 8.2), or attends a public reading (the partially good Emperor Claudius, Pliny 1.13.3).[10] Pliny emphasizes that he has a better, more "useful" way to spend half his time, in order to make his willingness to spend the other half at Rome all the more virtuous. Moreover, the fact that he will soon sacrifice most of this idealized leisure to take up the burden of public office for several years makes his political ambition seem like willing self-sacrifice for the public interest, rather than selfish ambition for money, power, and glory. As letter 1.10 will explain, the ideal senator, like the ideal emperor, takes on the burden of political power unwillingly, as a personal sacrifice for the good of the State.[11]

---

[9] Saller 1982:78.
[10] See Hopkins 1983:121 n. 2.
[11] E.g. Tiberius, Tac. *Ann.* 1.12–13, Suet. *Tib.* 24.2; Béranger 1953:137, Plass 1995:159-61.

The second half of the letter has the delicate task of celebrating cultivated leisure without seeming to celebrate luxury and laziness. Pliny is trying to show that even in his year out of office, even if the rest of his life were out of office, even if like Atilius he had never entered office, still his life would be valuable and meaningful. The income-producing estate at Tifernum goes unmentioned here, and is not discussed until later books (3.4, 3.19, 4.1, 5.6, etc.). The intrinsic value of the upper-class life must be firmly demonstrated before Pliny can explain the financial resources that support it.[12] The "laziness" which Pliny flaunts in 1.2 and 1.8 in modestly deprecating his writing skill is absent from 1.9, where every moment is "accounted for" in reading, writing, and (only) such care of the body as is necessary to "support" his higher spiritual faculties (4 *etiam corpori vaco, cuius fulturis animus sustinetur*). The luxurious buildings, landscaping, baths, and banquet halls shrink down to the absolute minimum of sea, shore, and private chamber with books. Instead of numerous slaves, there is only himself and the sacred shrine to the Muses, the natural sea and shore, which "dictates" to him (6). The reality in which Pliny dictates to his slaves (9.36.2; cf. 3.5.15) is replaced by the fantasy in which Nature and the goddesses of the arts are the masters of the estate, and Pliny is their only servant, obediently writing down their inspired literary works.[13] The modesty of this fantasy hides the self-flattery that Pliny the dictator is the real master who produces spiritual value from his own inspiration.

Pliny avoids stressing the positive aspects of the literary life too heavily, so as not to overwhelm too completely the value of Roman political life. The first and largest part of the description of his literary life at Laurentum is in negative terms. He does *not* hear or say anything to regret, and he does not chastise, hope, or worry. The superficial meaning, of course, is that he attributes all these negative qualities to life at Rome, but behind the complaints we can detect implicit guidelines on how he should and does behave in political life at Rome. Pliny does not actually say that he *does* do things at Rome that he regrets; indeed he almost suggests the opposite by putting *hearing* before *saying*. His first complaint is that *other* people say things he wishes he had not heard. The same applies to chastisement and blame. *Others* spread slander with treacherous words, whereas Pliny simply chastises (5 *nemo apud me quemquam sinistris sermonibus carpit, neminem ipse*

---

[12] D'Arms (1981:79–84) points out that whereas most inland villas were centers of income-producing estates, coastal villas were essentially non-productive; cf. Ulp. *dig.* 50.16.198. Later Pliny can even allude to the expensive array of slave labor that supports the luxury villa, 3.19.2–3.

[13] The words *invenitis* and *dictatis* identify "the spirit of the scene with the writer whom it inspires" (Merrill 1912:184; see Trisoglio 1972:222 n. 8). By contrast, Quintilian trenchantly comments that a lovely natural setting will only distract the writer (*Inst.* 10.3.22–24).

reprehendo). The others are clearly more guilty than Pliny.[14] As the letters show, Pliny is chary of attacking the living; Pliny implies that unlike most people, he does *not* spread criticism about others.[15] Even Regulus, Pliny's one consistent object of attack, probably died before Pliny published the letters.

Regret and shame are canonical vices in the letters. The ideal Roman under an ideal emperor does nothing to cause later regret, whether he is ill (7.1.3– 6), donating money (1.8.8), publishing his writings (1.1.2, 7.4.8), or making a bold speech in the Senate (9.13.11–12). The minor regrets to which Pliny confesses are simply the inevitable conflicts of obligations incurred when performing real political duties in a "free republic." The conflicts aroused by Gallus' requests against the Baetici show not only how minor conflicts inevitably arise in political life, but also how the honorable senator can resolve them with an Olympian division of will (1.7.1) and a minimum of regret. The very fact that in 1.9 Pliny can openly (though indirectly) broach the topic of regrets incurred through performing political duties implicitly compliments not only himself but also the new political order. Senators no longer have to choose between acting honorably and staying safe, between acting without regrets and collaborating with the Bad Emperor. Senators can alternate between honorable activity at Rome and meaningful literary work at their villas, thanks to the Good Emperors. Indeed, the safe enjoyment of villas is a topic of panegyric of the new regime (*Pan.* 50.5).

Thus Pliny's list of regrets, listing the vices of Roman political life, implies by reverse a picture of ideal government at Rome. His regret-free life at Laurentum, however, is a still clearer model for good governance. When Pliny has withdrawn from Rome, with its circulation of power among equals, to Laurentum where he has no equals, there are no external restrictions on his life of honor (*rectam sinceramque vitam... dulce otium honestumque,* 6). Pliny is the emperor of his own palace, without even obligations to tenants as at Tifernum (7.30, 9.15, 9.36) or Comum (5.14). Thus the estate at Laurentum, which is pure financial loss, can be reckoned as the purest symbolic profit, bringing in not agricultural produce but creative production (4.6.2). The negative contrast with Rome suggests not only that Pliny lives in perfect solitude, his own mind being a well-governed state, but also that he is in perfect control of a well-governed household (his own private "republic," 8.16.2). He never needs to reprove a slave, and never hears slander, reproof,

---

[14] Similarly, it is not Pliny's illness but his friend's that makes him think of the canonical vices of political life that "one" does not succumb to when sick: greed, lust, ambition, envy, scorn, malicious talk (7.26.2). The last vice, slander, is again displaced onto others: he does not *hearken to* or *batten on* malicious talk (*ne sermonibus quidem malignis aut attendit aut alitur*).

[15] In letter 9.12 Pliny gives the conventional argument against chastising (one's son) too severely, that everyone is only human and has faults.

or dishonorable speech among his household. The ruler of the villa can play the philosopher-king in his household, with perfect philosophic release from hope and fear, because he does not need to engage in an ambitious, competitive scramble to stay in control. In short, he is a model for the good emperor.

Pliny ends in the style of Seneca's first few letters, with a paradoxical tag, which praises "leisure" while redefining it. He invites Fundanus to turn himself over "to studies or to leisure"; as Atilius says, it is better to be at leisure than to be doing nothing" (7–8 *teque studiis uel otio trade. Satius est enim, ut Atilius noster... dixit, otiosum esse quam nihil agere*). Pliny is calling Fundanus away from politics, from the Horatian smoke and noise of Rome (Hor. *Od.* 3.29.12; cf. *Sat.* 2.6.23–39, 59–62), which really means doing nothing, either to studies or to leisure. It might almost seem that Pliny is turning the Roman hierarchy of values on its head, defining an ascending hierarchy of values from politics to studies to leisure. But Pliny calls his own life of study *otium* (6), so the terms *studiis uel otio* are not so much alternatives as synonyms. Fundanus will turn to his studies, his scholarly *otium,* perhaps the philosophic studies which will give him insufficient comfort when his daughter dies (5.16.8). Nevertheless, we can be skeptical when one high-ranking senator quotes to another the words of a mere gentleman-scholar in praise of the non-political life of literary leisure. Whereas Atilius may promote his own life of cultivated leisure above the empty social scurrying of low-ranking politicians at Rome, we can be sure that Pliny sees through this Epicurean persona, and understands that literature and leisure comprise only one part, and not the most important part, of the perfect Roman life. Pliny immediately turns to an outstanding example of the life of pure *studia,* Euphrates' life, to explain where the highest Roman values lie.

PLINY'S TAME PHILOSOPHER (1.10)

Letter 1.10 forms a contrasting pair both with the prior letter 1.9 (1.9 leisure over politics, 1.10 politics over leisure) and with the next substantial letter, 1.12 (1.10 praise of the Greek philosopher, 1.12 praise of the Roman politician). The letter also introduces the first provincial Greek in the collection, and makes him an example and teacher of the value of politics as opposed to leisure. Pliny claims to rank the philosopher Euphrates above himself in wisdom, virtue, eloquence, and activities, but he puts into Euphrates' mouth the highest praise of the Roman politician's active life, in contrast with the Greek philosopher's theoretical life. In his elegant and subtle manner Pliny both sets forth and lays to rest two basic anxieties, first, anxieties over whether the machinery of Roman law and politics has any real value, and second, Roman feelings of inferiority to the older and more prestigious cultural achievements of Greece. Throughout the letter, the implied oppositions and dialogues between Pliny and Euphrates, between Pliny and Clemens, and even between Pliny and his authorial persona, promote Pliny's continuing project of self-praise through the allaying of cultural anxieties.

Euphrates is the first Greek in the collection, aside from the canonical orator Demosthenes (1.2.2) and poet Homer (1.7.1), who, being long dead, can be praised and assimilated at a safe distance. Euphrates, by contrast, is a philosopher, one of the least Romanized and most challenging figures of the Greek tradition.[1] At a time when the Greek world was subject to Roman rule, its philosophers maintained the tone of confident superiority to worldly goods and power that had been set by the founding figure Socrates, the paradigmatic

---

[1] Compare the restraining by Agricola's mother (and the reservations of Tacitus) at *Agric.* 4.3. Tacitus increasingly shuns the very word *philosophia* (Syme 1958:553).

philosopher.[2] The rather threatening image of the self-sufficient philosopher with beard and knapsack was both admired and scorned by the Romans. Furthermore, the image of the philosopher-king or of the Stoic sage always had a potentially subversive meaning against despots, and had contributed to the "Stoic opposition" under the Flavian emperors that had led to several executions of "Stoic" senators such as Helvidius Priscus and Arulenus Rusticus, and to the wholesale banishment of the philosophers from Italy.

The revocation of the banishment under Nerva forms the background to this letter, which thus alludes to the Flavian oppression and praises the "New Age" of Nerva and Trajan through the standard trope of denigration of preceding emperors, a recurring trope in Book 1, most obviously in letters 5, 10, 12, 14, and 17. In contrast to the Flavian age, in which philosophers resisted the political hierarchy and were punished, Pliny opposes a picture of the current age in which philosophy and politics are in perfect harmony. Moreover, whereas the philosophers come off as morally superior to the rulers who oppress them in Flavian times, Pliny is careful, despite his effusive praise of Euphrates, to rank politicians even higher than the philosopher, making Euphrates himself assert this superiority over the protests of Pliny's authorial persona, which despises Roman politics. Accordingly, Pliny never praises the Roman opposition to Domitian *qua* philosophers. Even in 3.11, where he describes the banishment of the philosophers, he never explicitly associates philosophy with his senatorial friends and victims Senecio, Rusticus, and the others (3.11.3). We would not even know from Pliny's letter that Musonius Rufus was an illustrious teacher of philosophy.[3] His relation to his philosopher son-in-law Artemidorus is described very much like Pompeius Julianus' to Euphrates (3.11.5, 1.10.8), as if it were simply another marriage alliance between an eminent Roman politician and a respected Greek philosopher, a trade of real power for symbolic capital. A Roman philosopher is too close for comfort, but a Greek philosopher can be admired as a philosopher from a safe distance.

> Si quando urbs nostra liberalibus studiis floruit, nunc maxime floret. Multa claraque exempla sunt; sufficeret unum, Euphrates philosophus. (1.10.1–2)

> If our city has ever thrived in liberal pursuits, now it is especially thriving. There are many illustrious examples; one ought to suffice, Euphrates the philosopher.

---

[2] On Socrates as the model philosopher in later philosophy, especially Stoic, see e.g. Epict. 1.2.33–36, Long 1988:160.

[3] Similarly, Seneca is mentioned only as a poet, not as a Stoic philosopher (5.3.5).

The letter opens by presenting Euphrates in a somewhat surprising context, as an example of the "liberal pursuits" that are flourishing more than ever in "our city." The general term "pursuits" or "studies" *(studia)* suggests the writings of Pliny and his friends, often called *studia* (e.g. 1.2.6, 1.3.3, 1.9.7), and may be most likely to call to mind the range of genres produced by the representative author-friend Saturninus: oratory, history, light verse, and letters, but not philosophy (1.16). Similarly, the additional designation *"our"* city to the more usual *urbs* evokes the characteristic idea of something shared between Pliny and his addressee, often a proprietary domain that they have especially in common: *our* friend Atilius, *our* part of Italy, *our* friend Saturninus, *our* Lake Como (1.9.8, 1.14.4, 1.16.1, 2.8.1 e.g.; Guillemin 1929:26). The special kind of literary pursuit shared by Pliny and his circle is exemplified by—a Greek philosopher! Only retrospectively do we realize that this example of Rome's flourishing literary studies may have something to do with the recall of the philosophers.[4]

This rhetorical tension between inclusion and exclusion typifies the status of East and West in the Roman Empire in Pliny's time, with the Greek East lagging behind the Romanized Latin West in incorporation into the Roman ruling class.[5] Pliny's hometown Comum, formerly in the separate province of Cisalpine Gaul, had become fully incorporated into Italy (thus *illa nostra Italia,* 1.14.4). The Gallic nobility's admission into the Senate had been achieved by Claudius (and celebrated by Tacitus, *Ann.* 11.24), and the prominence of Roman citizens from Spain is epitomized by the Spanish Trajan, the first non-Italian emperor (who is given the inclusive designation *"our"* emperor, *imperatore nostro* 1.17.1).[6] We might guess that like most of Pliny's correspondents, Attius Clemens is from the western half of the empire; Syme suggests Narbonensis (1958:802 n. 2). Westerners talk politely but condescendingly about the Greeks' cultural pride and political weakness (8.24), but the continuing rise of Greeks in the Roman ruling class may have

---

[4] The term *sub urbe nostra* at 5.6.4 distinguishes the climate that Pliny and the addressee know in common, as opposed to Pliny's own weather at Tifernum about which the addressee is worried. A similar *noster... nostra* at 4.22.7 contrasts the *moral* climate of Rome with that of the provincial town Vienne.

[5] Jones (1992:172) summarizes the evidence: "It seems that Vespasian admitted between six and thirteen new men of Eastern origin, Domitian perhaps as many as twenty-four and Trajan no more than thirteen and possibly as few as six." But the origins of about 55% of all senators are unknown (Hopkins 1983:200), and the rise in distinction of a few Eastern senators outweighs the small increase in numbers (Syme 1958:510).

[6] We would never know from Pliny that Trajan was Spanish (Syme 1958:95). Yet the Spanish Martial ventures to say *"our* regions of Spain" to Trajan (12.9.1 *nostros... Hispanos*).

been unsettling. "The customary and normal scorn of a Roman for any contemporary Greeks must now undergo some abatement or disguise."[7]

The letter opens, then, with a cosmopolitan gesture of inclusiveness. "Our" city can be exemplified by a Greek philosopher, and "our city" can mean both "the city of Pliny and Clemens" and "the city of Pliny, Clemens, and Euphrates." The opening rhetoric emphasizes both Italian clannishness and imperial cosmopolitanism, even reconciling these two impulses. The letter then shifts to the praise of Euphrates and of philosophy alone, described in opposition to Pliny's activities. Even the alien name Euphrates suits Pliny's purposes. This Greek philosopher, who lived in Syria, and came from Tyre (Philostr. *Vit. Soph.* 1.7.2, 1.25.5), bears the name of the river at the eastern edge of the Roman world.[8] This alien name is embedded once each (1.10.2, 5, 10) in the three sections of the letter, the opening laudatory sequence (1–4), the detailed description (5–8), and the final complaint (9–12). On the other hand, the only Roman name, redolent of Roman military greatness (Pompeius Iulianus), occupies a reassuringly central position (8).[9]

Pliny gives symbolic meaning to his first meeting with Euphrates. It was during his military service that the younger Roman politician met the older Greek philosopher: the young power of Rome meets the old wisdom of Greece. Elsewhere Pliny uses the practice of adolescent military service to exemplify the Roman ideals of obedience and the absorption of traditional laws and values from elders (8.14.5)—very different from the principles of Greek philosophy. Pliny was not touring the East at leisure to lap up alien wisdom, but he was on good Roman business, and he used his exposure to Greek ethical philosophy to reinforce the formative value of army service. Pliny mystifies the actual power relations between them by emphasizing how he "labored" to win Euphrates' affection, ignoring the clear benefits the philosopher could gain by establishing good relations with a rising young officer in the army of occupation. Such benefits are being rendered by this very letter, a publicity piece that bears the imprimatur of a high-ranking senator and guarantees that the philosopher combines authentic Eastern wisdom with loyal adherence to Roman government and values.

---

[7] Syme 1958:511. Pliny often uses the terms *philosophus* or *sapiens* with a condescending tone (e.g. 1.22.6, 7.26.4, 8.16.3); see Syme 1958:552–54.

[8] E.g. Tac. *Hist.* 5.9. The Euphrates and the Rhine can be paired in imperial panegyric contexts (Plin. *Pan.* 14.1; cf. Verg. *Georg.* 1.509).

[9] Pliny is quite capable of writing a long biographical letter with the subject named only once, as 1.22.1 *Titi Aristonis,* 3.5.1 *avunculi mei.* Other examples of the significant repetition of names are the lamenting repetitions of *Verginium* at 2.1.12, and especially the satiric-invective accumulations of Regulus' name, six times in 1.5, seven each in 2.20 and 4.2, and a remarkable 30 times in the collection (on repetitions for lament or invective see Trisoglio 1973:261 on 2.1.12).

The game of mutual benefits, which could be given this cynical interpretation, is represented by Pliny in the most honorific terms, through the interweaving of mutual flattery and reciprocal self-deprecation.

> Hunc ego in Syria, cum adulescentulus militarem, penitus et domi inspexi, amarique ab eo laboravi, etsi non erat laborandum. Est enim obvius et expositus, plenusque humanitate quam praecipit. Atque utinam sic ipse quam spem tunc ille de me concepit impleverim, ut ille multum virtutibus suis addidit! aut ego nunc illas magis miror quia magis intellego. Quamquam ne nunc quidem satis intellego; ut enim de pictore scalptore fictore nisi artifex iudicare, ita nisi sapiens non potest perspicere sapientem. (2–4)

> I made a profound and personal observation of this man in Syria, when I was on military service as a young man, and I worked at being loved by him, even though there was no need to work at it. For he is open and accessible, and filled with that humaneness which he preaches. If only I myself had come to fulfill the hopes he then formed for me, just as he himself has added a great deal to his own excellences! Or perhaps I am more astounded at those excellences now because I understand them more. And yet not even now do I adequately understand them; for just as in the case of a painter, carver, or sculptor only a craftsman can judge their work, so too no one but a philosopher can form an accurate view of a philosopher.

Pliny first praises Euphrates by saying that he had a thorough look at Euphrates' private life in Syria; presumably he found it thoroughly virtuous. He then modestly claims that he struggled to win Euphrates' affection: but no, he did not have to struggle. This ease then redounds to Euphrates' praise for his accessible "humaneness."[10] The reader can smile at Pliny's being modestly unaware that his easy access to Euphrates' affections also redounds to his own credit for having been a promising and virtuous young man (cf. Epict. 2.24.15). Pliny immediately expresses this self-praise in the modest form of Euphrates' great hopes for Pliny's future, praise which he shrugs off by framing it within a contrafactual wish ("if only I had fulfilled..."), and which he parries with corresponding praise of Euphrates' own self-improvement;

---

[10] Euphrates' *humanitas* suggests that he treats everyone as a *homo,* as a person, regardless of his own social superiority (though of course Pliny was superior in real status). Similarly, Pliny treats his ex-slave Zosimus with *humanitas,* and he brings out the meaning with an etymological echo (*...cui...* humanitas *exhibenda est...* homo *probus officiosus litteratus* 5.19.2–3); such laudatory lists for upper-class Romans generally use *vir,* not *homo* (e.g. 1.5.16, 1.7.3, 2.9.4, 2.11.5; Bradley and Arnold 1938:131 n. 2). Aulus Gellius says that the proper meaning of *humanitas* is "liberal education" (παιδεία) but it is popularly used to mean "affability" (φιλανθρωπία... *dexteritatem quandam benivolentiamque erga omnis homines promiscam,* 13.17). See also Trisoglio 1973 ad loc. *Humanitas* is an imperial virtue (6.31.14); the Good Emperor paradoxically combines opposites, *humanitas* with *divinitas* (*Pan.* 2.7) or with *maiestas* (4.6).

Euphrates' modestly vague "hope" for Pliny is replaced by Pliny's definite assertion of the "great increase in his virtues." Pliny then blunts the invidious possibility of such open praise of Euphrates by admitting that Euphrates' seeming "improvement" may simply derive from Pliny's erroneous judgment. Yet this self-deprecation is in turn couched in terms of self-praise: "perhaps it is only that I now have greater understanding of his virtues than before, [and thus I myself have become wiser and more virtuous, *and really fulfilled his hopes for me,*] since it takes a sage to recognize a sage." But this climactic point in the reciprocal praise is itself blunted by the (partial) confession that Pliny still doesn't recognize Euphrates' virtues (sufficiently), since only a sage can know a sage.[11]

Though overtly Pliny denies being a sage himself, the affirmation that a sage can truly recognize a sage nevertheless invites Pliny, Clemens, and us readers to share in the magic circle of sagacity in which anyone can participate who can understand and agree with Pliny's praise of Euphrates. Readers who are favorably disposed to accept this flattery of Pliny and Euphrates are rewarded by the suggestion that they too are sages, whereas hostile, envious readers are warded off by the suggestion that they are not wise or virtuous enough to recognize true praise. Thus the circle of praise concludes with the enticing suggestion that Euphrates is a perfect philosophical wise man, and that Pliny and his readers come just slightly short of being Stoic sages themselves. The circle is sealed by the echo in ring composition: *hunc... inspexi, ... perspicere sapientem.* Over the course of the ring the young Pliny's undefined "gazing" at the unevaluated "this man" takes on the specific meaning of the mature Pliny and readers' full intellectual comprehension of perfect philosophical wisdom and virtue, as embodied in the *laudandus* Euphrates.[12]

This rhetorical magical circle, however, runs the risk of pulling Pliny, Clemens, and the Roman reader entirely within the frame of values of this

---

[11] On self-fulfilling prophecies in the letters, see Trisoglio 1972:143. This characteristic trope of flattery as a ("seemingly") self-fulfilling prophecy recurs in a letter to his wife's aunt: "you used to prophesy that I would be the kind of person that I now *seem* to my wife to be" (*me a pueritia statim formare, laudare, talemque qualis nunc uxori meae* videor *ominari solebas,* 4.19.7). See also 1.2.6, 1.8.4, 1.14.1, 4.16.3. Rudd aptly describes this characteristically Plinian "boasting and humility... alternat[ing] in quick succession," producing a "kind of mental see-saw" (1992:32). Compare Quintilian's prayer to Domitian, *ut... me qualem esse credidit faciat* (*Inst.* 4 praef. 5). Quintilian recommends believing the stories of amazing memory feats in order that one may hope to do the same (11.2.51 *habenda tamen fides est... ut, qui crediderit, et speret*).

[12] The gaze into someone's character recurs at 4.17.4–5 *penitus inspexi* (of Corellius) and 10.86B *penitus inspecta est* (in a letter of recommendation). The importance of judging someone's character before entering into a close friendship was a commonplace, Cic. *de Amicit.* 86, Sen. *Ep.* 3.2.

itinerant Greek preacher, a frame of values in which philosophical wisdom and virtue mean everything and Roman political power means nothing. Hence Pliny inserts a penultimate simile which punctures the magical illusion, taking down by a notch the pretensions of Greek philosophy to know the true worth of all human values. The perfect, mutually guaranteeing communion of values between sage and sage is like that between craftsman and craftsman: painter, carver, plastic artist. This homespun analogy between the art of wisdom and the crafts, conventional in philosophy since Socrates, has a rather derogatory tone to the Roman ear. If the philosopher is the most threatening Greek cultural type to the Romans, the craftsman is perhaps the least threatening. Even the Greek Plutarch can say that no upper-class young man wants to be an artist after admiring works of art.[13] Thus Pliny's analogy suggests that just as we would not want to become a craftsman to admire the crafts fully, so too we would not want to become philosophers to admire Euphrates fully. Pliny would obviously not consider becoming an artist simply in order to achieve an expert's judgment on art. An artist is thought to create art in order to win not his fellow artist's approval but the general public's admiration. By analogy, the philosopher's function would be to convey something valuable to the audience, as if he were a glorified schoolteacher, rather than to make his (Roman) audience into philosophers.

> Quantum tamen mihi cernere datur, multa in Euphrate sic eminent et elucent, ut mediocriter quoque doctos advertant et adficiant. (5)

> But as far as I can judge, many features are so outstanding and illustrious in him that they arouse and attract even people of ordinary education.

This transition to Euphrates' actual teaching concludes the general evaluation of Euphrates with a diminuendo: even listeners of "average learnedness" are impressed by his "many illustrious qualities." In short, the potentially threatening image of the perfect communion of values between sages has been reduced to the more manageable image of an impressive lecturer. This slightly disparaging summary still depends on Pliny's own knowledge ("as far as I can discern"), but as we shall see, this has now become Pliny's special knowledge as an expert orator. Without insulting Euphrates, he cuts him down to size to introduce the specific list of his laudable qualities, the "many things" that "shine forth prominently."

---

[13] Plut. *Pericles* 2.1–2; cf. Epict. 3.23.25. Epictetus also compares the "art of listening" to a philosopher to the art of appreciating sculpture (2.24.7).

PRAISING THE TAME PHILOSOPHER

Pliny presents the list of Euphrates' qualities with seeming casualness, lurching back and forth from his speaking style to his physical appearance, then back to his speech and ending with his family. Although the entire section is laudatory, the praise is subtly muted. Pliny presents us with a non-threatening lecturer who can easily be assimilated to Roman values, and who does not challenge Roman supremacy: a tame philosopher.[14] His speaking is praised more for style than substance, his appearance displays, albeit in muted fashion, the rebarbative philosophic costume that Pliny mocks elsewhere (1.22.6), his moralistic diatribe is more appealing than attacking, and the description reaches its climax on a homey domestic note that obliquely subordinates the Eastern sage to his father-in-law, a leading Roman citizen.

The list of praises opens with Euphrates' teaching, and concentrates almost exclusively on style. Instead of a bold thinker who challenges the audience to consider all external power, money, and success as illusory and indifferent, we have a refined stylist, whose discourses are praised in terms similar to Pliny's praises of his friends' light verses and elegant letters. Even Plato is brought in not as the philosopher and commemorator of the uncompromising model Socrates, but for his stylistic excellence.[15] Although Pliny does confirm what we know from elsewhere, that Euphrates was a moral teacher on Stoic lines and not just a rhetorician like Isaeus (2.3), Euphrates' moral teaching is barely suggested behind general references such as the "humaneness" that he teaches (2) or the way he stirs even reluctant listeners (5). Not until after his physical description do we hear the only specifics about his teaching, that he attacks wrongdoing, not wrongdoers (7). Even this brief allusion to his doctrine comes almost as an elaboration of his appearance. Just as his clothing and facial hair are venerable, not repellent, so too his moral teaching is attractive, not aggressive. Pliny thus inverts Plato's account of the paradox between the philosopher's unimpressive appearance and his imposing message (Plat. *Symp*. 215B; cf. *Theaet*. 143E). Though Pliny does give us an impression of the moral slant of Euphrates' philosophy, he subsumes it under

---

[14] As Griffin puts it, "not only is he without the conventional Cynic defects (from the Roman point of view), but he is also without the conventional Stoic blemishes" (1996:199). Jones comments that "the philosopher from Chaeronea might not have been quite so presentable as these well-connected Syrians [Euphrates, Isaeus, and Artemidorus], or so considerate of Pliny's sensibilities," adducing Plutarch *de frat. am.* 479E (1971:61).

[15] *Platonicam illam sublimitatem et latitudinem,* 1.10.5. Socrates himself enters the collection only as a model for elegant dinner chitchat which will have to be limited to make room for good Roman *officia* the next morning (*Socraticis... sermonibus,* 3.12.1); at 5.3.2 Pliny is probably reading frivolous "Sotadic" verses, *pace* Gunderson 1997:224 n. 67 (mss. *Socraticos*).

familiar stylistic categories. Euphrates comes across as an orator who excels like Pliny and his friends, but in the moralizing genre traditional to Greek philosophy rather than in the more Romanized genres of oratory, history, or light verse. I do not think that the joke is on Pliny for being too superficial, as Fantham argues (1996:213). Pliny's slightly overemphatic praise of Euphrates' style is in keeping with the hint of irony at Euphrates' expense that runs throughout the letter. Surely Pliny knew about, but opposed, the total rejection of all externals preached by the more uncompromising Stoic and Cynic philosophers. There were enough bizarre aspects to Stoic doctrine, not to mention charlatans masquerading as sages, to lead a Roman, especially a rich and powerful Roman, to praise it only at a safe distance.[16]

The physical description of Euphrates continues the strategy of damning by faint praise. This time Pliny openly confesses this strategy by defending it. "Although these features might be considered accidental and superficial, they do win him the greatest degree of respect."[17] The four features he names are tallness, handsome facial features, long hair, and huge white beard. As his own comment suggests, Pliny is willfully missing the point of the philosophic garb, confusing accidental features with features that are superficial but purposeful. Tallness and handsome features have nothing to do with philosophy, but long hair and beard do indeed have something to do with philosophy, the beard in particular being the emblem of the philosopher (Zanker 1995:109). Epictetus argues at length for keeping one's beard as a natural growth of manliness (1.16.10–14; cf. Musonius fr. 21), and he would choose even death rather than shave it (1.2.29). Ordinary upper-class Romans did not wear beards until Hadrian's time, and even then they sported the well-trimmed beard of manliness, not the huge white beard of Eastern sagacity.[18] Euphrates' beard and long hair constitute a deliberate public statement that he obeys the dictates of reason and nature, not public convention and convenience. He comes to teach at Rome on his own terms, not the Romans'. Pliny carefully misinterprets this message by rolling Euphrates' entire appearance together into one striking, foreign package. Romans who misunderstand Euphrates' appearance in this way are at little risk of turning into hairy bearded men themselves. They can safely listen to his inspiring message as a quaint but stirring stopover on their Roman educational journey.

---

[16] The false display of philosophic dress and appearance is a commonplace, e.g. Sen. *Ep.* 5.2, Plin. 1.22.6, Quint. *Inst.* 12.3.12, Dio 66.13.1a, Epict. 4.8.15. Euphrates himself deprecates the mere display of philosophic garb at Epict. 4.8.17–20.

[17] Lilja compares Pliny's defense for describing Acilianus' appearance at 1.14.8 (1978:57), but there, in a marriage recommendation, Pliny's tone is not at all apologetic.

[18] See Zanker 1995:202, 218.

Pliny assigns the interpretation of Euphrates' appearance to two supposititious viewers, without indicating to which of the two views he himself subscribes. "Euphrates' features may be thought [by some people] to be accidental and superficial. [Among other people], however, they win him great respect." Is Pliny in the first or second group? He himself has listed Euphrates' physical features as part of his encomium, as if he is one of those fooled by exteriors. He then catches himself praising mere externals, and reasserts that they do, at least, add to his dignified presentation. Pliny is on neither side and on both sides, not fooled by external appearances but impressed by the whole performance. To this authorial pose we may counterpose letter 1.22, where Pliny scorns "those people" (*istis* 1.22.6) who flaunt their philosophical devotion by their appearance, as opposed to the Roman wise man Titius Aristo whose wisdom, like his name, combines the best of Greek and Roman, comprising both Roman law (2) and Greek unity of the virtues (7). We might be tempted to attribute the discrepancy to the versatility of Pliny's eulogistic talents, for which any feature, beard or no beard, mimes or no mimes (*Pan.* 46.1–3), can be grist for the rhetorical mill. But the tone of this section, slightly overstated and slightly underhanded, fits that of the entire letter. The gullible Pliny who falls for the long hair and beard, and cannot distinguish philosophical hair from just plain good looks, matches the gullible Pliny who falls in temporary awe of the perfect Stoic sage who is actually little more than a verbal artisan of moral virtue, or the entranced Pliny who needs to be reminded by the long-haired philosopher that the business of Roman administration is more important that whiling away whole days listening to Greek philosophical lectures about justice.[19]

Thus Pliny demotes his detailed account of Euphrates' teachings to a gloss on his appearance, continuing the sequence of oppositions that place Euphrates as the perfect mean between harsh and mild: severity without rebarbative grimness in his appearance, respect without terror, holiness of life but also geniality, attacking wrongdoing not wrongdoers, not criticizing but improving them (7). His words seem merely a part of his impressive appearance. The iron-clad logical chain of Greek ethics is transformed into a merely imposing performance that reinforces what Romans already know about morality. In place of the rigorous Socratic-Stoic challenge that the possessor of true wisdom cannot err we have the more comfortable Roman attitude about traditional values that can be reinforced by a persuasive authority figure. The summary of Euphrates' teaching, that he attacks vices, not people (7), sounds

---

[19] Pliny's emphasis on Euphrates' attractive neatness in his philosophic garb does, to be sure, match Epictetus' strictures against overdoing the philosophic carelessness about appearances to the point of dirtiness and unattractiveness, in order that one does not repel potential converts (3.22.89, 4.11.14).

not like the imposing moral challenge of an Epictetus, who routinely attacks the listener, but rather like the conventional pose of a mild Roman satirist.[20] Furthermore, very little specific Greek philosophical diction underlies the letter here or elsewhere, except for the generic term *philosophus* and its Latin version *sapiens*. Indeed, we can easily forget that Euphrates' teaching is taking place in Greek, so Romanized is the message. The omission is all the more striking since even in purely Roman letters Pliny likes to sprinkle in Greek phrases for special effects, such as the climactic μουσεῖον of 1.9.6 or the decisive last word of Corellius, κέκρικα (1.12.10). This Latinization reaches its climax at the end (10–11), first with the Greek philosopher's exhortation in favor of Roman politics, with impeccable Latin diction *(agere negotium publicum, cognoscere iudicare, promere et exercere iustitiam)*, and finally with Pliny's Romanized account of how Euphrates will give the final "polish and smoothness" to Clemens' education (11 *expoliendum limandumque;* compare, for example, Cic. *Fam.* 7.33.2 *limatulo et polito tuo iudicio).*[21]

Pliny's final praise of Euphrates' lecturing performance is again not far removed from satire: "even after he has persuaded you, you would want to keep on being persuaded." Too much praise of form tends to denigrate content, especially when the content is all-important, as in philosophy.[22] It somehow misses the point of the teaching that Pliny finds the style almost more moving than the message, so that he wants the style to go on even when

---

[20] For a few examples of the direct personal ridicule that Epictetus frequently aims at his listeners, see Epict. 1.10.3, 1.21.2, 2.21.22, 2.24.28, 3.1.31, 3.9.10. For the conventional defense that the satirist attacks only vices, not people, see Martial 10.33.1 *parcere personis, dicere de vitiis;* compare Mart. 5.15, 7.12, 10.5, and Thrasea's saying, *qui vitia odit, homines odit,* Plin. 8.22.3. The Stoics, to be sure, also spoke of the importance of reproving politely and attacking the vice, not the person (Sen. *de Ira* 2.10.7; cf. Epictet. 1.18.9, 1.28.9). But listening to a true philosophical lecture should be an agonizing experience, like a painful treatment in a doctor's office (Epict. 3.23.30 ἰατρεῖον, 3.23.37 ἠγονίασεν). Musonius Rufus' teaching seems to have come closer to reinforcing generally-held Roman values than did Epictetus' (see Bütler 1970:56).

[21] Merrill explains the judicial terminology (1912 ad loc.). It is instructive to compare Epictetus' less technical diction (and more scornful tone) in reminding a Roman senator of his duties (οὐκ οἶσθ᾽ ὅτι τὸν τοιοῦτον... δεῖ... ἀποδημεῖν ἄρχοντα ἢ ἀρχόμενον ἢ ὑπηρετοῦντά τινι ἀρχῇ ἢ στρατευόμενον ἢ δικάζοντα, 3.24.36).

[22] On the importance of content over style, see e.g. Seneca *Ep.* 108.6–7, 115.1–3, 18, Epict. 2.23.143, 3.23.21, 37, and Marcus Aurelius (Fronto *De Eloquent.* 2, 2.66 Haines). Quintilian (*Inst.* 10.1.81–84) contrasts the eloquent Plato, the Socratics, Aristotle, and Theophrastus with the old Stoics, whom he recommends for their subject matter, not for oratorical excellence, "at which, to be sure, they did not aim" (*rebus... acuti magis quam, id quod sane non adfectaverunt, oratione magnifici,* 10.1.83; cf. 11.1.33). The old Stoics were notorious for their unconcern for stylistic polish (e.g. Cic. *de Fin.* 4.78–79, *de Orat.* 2.159, 3.66, Epict. 3.2.13–16, 3.21.7; Griffin 1996:199). Yet Fronto the orator also includes Euphrates (along with Epictetus) in his catalogue of eloquent philosophers when trying to persuade Marcus that oratorical skill is important even for a philosopher (Fronto *de Eloquent.* 1, 2.50 Haines).

the message has reached its mark and is no longer needed. This epitomizes Pliny's Roman attitude to Greek philosophy: we already know the moral message, but it's nice to hear it so persuasively tricked out in syllogistic dress—as long as it *is* just the message we knew all along, that is. The Roman attitude to philosophical teaching is not that it is giving the basic logical framework to make the listeners into unerring Stoic sages, but that it is merely reminding them of the moral ideals they already knew. The gently teasing undertone of this trope appears clearly in a passage in Plato's *Protagoras* which may be Pliny's model here. Socrates claims, somewhat ironically, that Protagoras' long rhetorical performance entranced him in a magic spell so that he gazed at him for a long time, yearning to hear more (κεκηλημένος... ἐπιθυμῶν ἀκούειν, *Prot.* 328D; cf. Pliny 1.10.7 *attentus et pendens, et persuaderi... cupias*).[23] Pliny's Euphrates, like Plato's Protagoras, will simply hypnotize you into confirming the basic moral attitudes that everyone already knows.

The final Romanizing and somewhat denigratory touch in Pliny's laudation of Euphrates is that it ends not on philosophical teaching but on family (8): *Iam vero liberi tres, duo mares, quos diligentissime instituit.* ("And in addition, he has three children, two of them male, whom he has trained most carefully.") Our long-haired Greek philosopher has a good Roman wife and a good Roman family with the statutory three children (obtained the ordinary way and not, as with Pliny and some of his friends, by imperial fiat). The fact that our philosopher marries at all puts him on the safer side of the divide between the wild anti-Roman Cynic and the tame Romanized Stoic. Euphrates may have long hair and a beard, but he takes his anti-conventional leanings only so far. Though both the unmarried Epictetus and his married Roman teacher Musonius Rufus encourage their listeners to marry and fulfill their "natural" duties to family and society (Epictet. 3.21.5, Musonius fr. 13–15), more extreme Cynic branches set up the philosopher outside society as a divine messenger and scout who must remain unmarried (Epict. 3.22.23–24, 76).[24] Here as elsewhere, the founding figure Socrates set the tone for later trends in philosophy. Being both in the world but not quite part of it, he had an unphilosophic wife and conveniently young sons whom he dismissed from his deathbed in favor of his "real family," his philosophic companions (*Phaed.* 60A, 116C, Valer. Max. 7.2 ext. 1; cf. Epict. 2.22.29).

---

[23] Plato in turn seems to be parodying the Phaeacians' entrancement by Odysseus' long tale, in keeping with the Odyssean touches in the *Protagoras* (κηληθμῷ δ᾽ ἔσχοντο, *Od.* 11.334, 13.2).

[24] On the common ground between Stoicism and Cynicism see Diog. Laert. 6.104, Griffin 1996:194–96.

Euphrates, however, has shown proper Roman "diligence" in attentively training his children (designated by the statutory Roman term *liberi*)—at least two of them (or is it three?).[25] The diction tends towards neglecting the difference between the daughter and the sons, who are designated by the bland term "males" and may or may not be the antecedent of *quos,* the recipients of attentive, affectionate training. But the rhetoric puts the sons firmly in the center. The slightly ambiguous *quos* glosses lightly over the philosophic debate of whether daughters should receive "equal" education, as the Roman Stoic Musonius Rufus argued (fr. 3–4).[26] Pliny, the open-minded proponent of both modern cosmopolitan *humanitas,* "human(e)ness" (1.10.2) and of old Roman *virtus,* "man(li)ness" (1.10.3), would surely flaunt his liberal approval for girl's education.[27] But only someone as detached from the real upper-class world as a philosopher would seriously entertain the idea of giving young women the full oratorical, political, and military training for a career in oratory, politics, or warfare. Without having to give awkward details, Pliny suggests that with good philosophical open-mindedness Euphrates gave the boys *their* education, and presumably gave the girl *her* education.

Euphrates' wife, like her daughter, is elided out of the picture. These, perhaps the two most interesting members of the long-haired philosopher's household, his upper-class Roman wife and his educated daughter, are omitted as Pliny leapfrogs directly from the two sons to the father-in-law. Like the absence of Greek words, the absence of women in this letter might not seem surprising until we compare it to letters about other Plinian heroes, who are surrounded by female relatives. In Book 1 alone we have Corellius' daughter, wife, and sisters (and grandson), Mauricus' niece, Saturninus' wife, Aristo's wife and daughter, and Pliny's mother-in-law (1.4, 1.18.3). Why are Pliny's friends surrounded with so many women? Or rather, why does Pliny surround his friends with so many women? The answers will help explain the significance of Pliny's masculine description of Euphrates' family, and can be organized under three headings, first, the domestic touch, second, the centrality of the *laudandus,* and third, the benefits and disadvantages of kinship alliances.

---

[25] Ernout & Meillet 1959:355 s.v. *liberi:* "Le mot a une valeur technique et juridique." The use of the juridical term *liberi* rather than a neutral term such as *filii* or *pueri* or an emotive term such as *pignora* suggests that Euphrates' three children fulfill a traditional or even statutory obligation.

[26] Even Musonius says that girls should concentrate less than boys on mere dialectic, so as to prepare for women's indoor tasks such as wool-working (fr. 4). The philosophic debate, of course, goes back to Plato (*Rep.* 452–57). Socrates' own children were conveniently male.

[27] We can compare Saturninus' wife, whom he made "so learned and polished" (1.16.6), Pliny's wife "brought up and trained" by her aunt (4.19.6), and the educated late daughter of Fundanus (5.16.3). See Sherwin-White 1966:347 on 5.16.3.

The domestic touch is a counterpart to the depiction of public, political life in the letters. In opposition to the Senate, law court, or army, which are populated only by men, the private life of Pliny and his friends is signified by women, and the letters themselves incline towards the private. In the survey of genres represented by Saturninus, his wife comes up only in relation to the letters, which Saturninus claims she wrote. Letters are evidently the most feminine of the four genres oratory, history, light verse, and letters.[28] Many of Pliny's biographical and obituary letters emphasize the private, domestic side of the basic opposition between Rome and countryside, Senate and villa, and public and private (e.g. 1.12 Corellius, 1.22 Rufus, 3.1 Spurinna); this impression of domesticity is strengthened by the preponderance of women in the households. Thus, Pliny never tells us about his townhouse at Rome (Fantham 1996:202). Euphrates, by contrast, is being naturalized by Pliny's letter into the Roman political world. Even the mention of his family has more political than personal emphasis. The long-haired Eastern philosopher needs all the help he can get in order to appear in a traditional Roman guise; hence the reference to the Roman statutory three children, the prominent Roman citizen father-in-law, and the dynastic sons, whose lineage and education will probably combine to earn them political careers.[29]

A second difference between male and female relatives is the comparative centrality of a male character in a letter. A male surrounded by female relatives is set off more strongly than Euphrates with his male relatives. Solid Roman *patresfamilias* are the only male figures in their households, prominently in the center, with harmonious but dominant relations with loyal women who "never quarrel" with them (as at 8.5.1): submission masquerades as harmony. In the many letters illustrating life in the Roman villa, the principle "one villa, one man" prevails. We never find two roosters in one coop, but always the Roman Man surrounded by (slightly) subordinate women, (still more) subordinate slaves or tenants, and Other Roman Men passing through as guests or reporting in from afar through letters. Oedipal or fraternal tensions are absent. Pliny himself writes to only one male relative, his grandfather-in-law, and underlying tensions appear in their power relations, though we cannot tell how much of the tension is real personal difficulty and how much due to literary awkwardness in portraying

---

[28] It is not clear whether the letters in question were written in a female, male (Bardon 1956:198), or non-gendered persona (as Pliny's minor letters, e.g. 1.11, which shows little trace of the author's gender). Or the letters might not have existed at all outside of Pliny's imagination.

[29] Our guess as to how imminent their careers may be depends on the tense of *instituit* ("is training"? "has trained"? "trained"?). The picture is blurred, since only the outlines matter. Grimal claims that *instituit* means the children are still young (1955:575 n. 2).

the male relationship.[30] Certainly the overall gender balance is drastically different among the letters to relatives as opposed to the letters as a whole. Overall, there are 237-1/2 letters to about 100 different men and 9-1/2 letters to 7 different women. But among known relatives, there are 9 letters to 1 man (Fabatus), and 7 letters to 4 different women.[31]

The male-oriented description of Euphrates' family has the opposite effect. The alien philosopher is outclassed by his prominent Roman father-in-law, and perhaps even by his sons, who can combine the best of Eastern philosophy and Roman power politics. One might guess, for example, that his sons will not have huge beards—a bodily difference that would reflect a mental difference. Pliny slightly falsifies the relative status of Euphrates and Pompeius Iulianus, just as his initial picture of himself as a raw young Roman officer dancing attendance before the imposing elder philosopher had more than a little bad faith. He suggests that the marriage alliance is Iulianus' "most important" claim to greatness and fame; *cum cetera vita tum vel hoc uno magnus et clarus* (8) is an emphatic "especially," like the Greek ἄλλως τε... καί. But the sentence turns out to mean that Iulianus' real claim to fame is not that he was able to gain the higher-status Euphrates as his son-in-law, but that he willingly stooped to the lower-status Euphrates when he could have had a real political potentate (a *honoribus princeps*) like himself (a *provinciae princeps*). Though the authorial persona claims that the mixed marriage redounds to Iulianus' credit, the reader can see that it really redounds to Euphrates' credit, constituting the final and climactic step of the laudatory passage 1.10.5–8. Iulianus stooped to gain a sage, but Euphrates reached to gain a powerful political alliance—the same exchange of wisdom for power undertaken in the past when the young Pliny formed a friendship with the elder Euphrates, or in the present when Pliny, now a potentate himself, continues to patronize Euphrates by means of this letter.[32]

This mutually beneficial commerce of status reflects the function of the letters themselves, as mutually beneficial exchanges of cultural value, of symbolic capital. Pliny generously tells his friend to receive the "benefit" (9

---

[30] Pliny shows Fabatus respect "as for a father" (7.23.1 *parentis loco observo;* cf. 6.12.3 *ut... cum tuo filio*). Sherwin-White interprets it as personal difficulty, 1966:265, 368, 459.

[31] Some uncertainty arises from names such as Maximus which may belong to one or to several different addressees, and from possibly distant relatives, such as the unknown Plinius Paternus. One letter, 3.10, is addressed jointly to the husband and wife Spurinna and Cottia.

[32] Sherwin-White asserts that Iulianus, not otherwise known, is "not necessarily of high Roman rank" (1966:110 on 1.10.9). But for the purposes of this letter he is presented as if he were. Jones, on the other hand, speculates that Euphrates may have been more rich and powerful than Pliny reveals. "Local dignitaries were not merely showing respect for culture when they married their daughters off to philosophers: they were advancing their own positions" (1971:64).

frui) from the philosopher that Pliny himself cannot receive. Cultural exchange is not a zero-sum game; both sides of the exchange profit, Clemens by benefiting from the philosopher, and Pliny by having done a favor and being owed one in return. Yet the mutually beneficial exchange of cultural favors serves to reinforce cultural hierarchy. Roman politicians passing through Euphrates' hands for a philosophical touch-up job thereby assert their higher status, since they pass through philosophy as a temporary station between magistracies of political power while the non-citizen Euphrates is stuck in philosophy permanently.[33] Similarly, by "generously" giving Clemens the opportunity to be polished up by Euphrates, Pliny demonstrates his own higher status over Clemens. Clemens is otherwise unknown, but we can assume by that very fact that he is less powerful than Pliny the high-ranking senator, though the "polishing and smoothing" will probably serve to prepare him for political activities. Euphrates provides, as it were, the liberal arts component of Officers' Training Academy for Roman politicians. Indeed, Epictetus describes with scorn how Roman politicians casually visited his own school at Nicopolis—where they must have received an approach much less accommodating to political ambition than the approach Pliny attributes to Euphrates.[34]

The contrast between Roman power and Greek wisdom is emphasized by the final words of the laudation, with the slight oxymoron, *sapientia [princeps]* and the closing verb *elegit.*

> ... quod ipse provinciae princeps inter altissimas condiciones generum non honoribus principem, sed sapientia elegit. (8)
>
> ... that he, himself a leader of the province, chose for his son-in-law, among the loftiest ranks available to him, not a leader in honors but one in wisdom.

Roman power gave Iulianus the freedom to *choose* Euphrates. Ironically, although the free exercise of rational choice is the highest goal of philosophy (e.g. Epict. 1.4.14), this free choice now belongs to Roman power, not Greek wisdom. Pliny's Euphrates has abandoned the old Socratic-Stoic philosophical

---

[33] "[Pliny's] Greeks with single names would seem to be non-citizens," Sherwin-White 1966:244 on 3.11.5.

[34] Epictetus scorns students who only want to exchange mutual flatteries for their writings (2.17.35–40), or pseudo-philosophers who fawn over a senator in their audience (3.23.13) and hope that their speeches will impress the audience (3.23.19). Musonius Rufus used to say that if his listeners can merely relax and praise his speech, he has failed in conveying his moral message (Aul. Gell. 5.1.1; cf. Epict. 3.23.29). A real student must be ready to obey (2.21.10) and to feel agonizing distress about himself and his own failings (Epict. 3.23.37). One cannot experience Epictetus on a passing visit, between worldly obligations; philosophy takes time and devotion (3.9.11–14).

scorn of "indifferent" externals and follows Panaetius' variety of Stoicism in acquiescing to Roman dominance.[35] One wonders whether he had the opportunity to "choose out" a husband for his daughter, or whether again in his eagerness to establish a marriage connection to political power he was subject to a Roman groom who was "willing" to stoop to mere Greek wisdom for his marriage alliance.[36] But would a "real" philosopher care about his wife's social status, or that of his son-in-law? The Roman Iulianus is more philosophical about core values than is the Greek philosopher.

The concluding oxymoron pointedly contrasts "leaders in political honors" with this "leader in philosophy" or "prince of wisdom": *non honoribus* principem, *sed sapientia [principem]*. The paradox of the "leading statesman" in *philosophy* is only slightly softened by the *apo koinou* construction. The pointed contrast between wisdom and political honors suggests that our leading philosopher is *not* outstanding in "honors," at least in the Roman sense. By being subsumed into the Roman conceptual framework, the powerless Euphrates has been stripped of "honor," which he would have had as a Stoic sage had he stayed within the Greek cultural frame of reference. Yet Roman "honor" is not so stable a personal attribute as Pliny's rhetorical opposition implies, since political advancement is subject to the whims of a single "leading man" or *princeps*.[37] The picture of Iulianus, the *princeps* of the province, making the most rational choice to promote a meritorious inferior, forms a comforting parallel to Pliny's dependence on Nerva and Trajan, and formerly on Domitian. The reassuring picture of a solid meritocracy of power, like the concluding picture of Roman government as philosophy in action, is perhaps slightly overdone, as if to will away the underlying anxieties of upper-class subjects in a totalitarian hierarchy. The example of Pallas, the subject of perhaps Pliny's bitterest letters (7.29, 8.6), shows how insecure the imperial system has made the Roman politician's dominance over Greek upstarts.

---

[35] On Panaetius' efforts to de-emphasize the paradoxes of the "wise man" and to promote the positive ideals of justice through political activity, see Rist 1969:197–99, Sandbach 1975:127, Edwards 1997:27.

[36] At 4.19.8 Pliny imagines his aunt-in-law as "having chosen" him for his wife and his wife for him equally *(quasi invicem elegeris)*. He thereby idealizes his own marriage as between equally high-status members of the Roman upper class.

[37] *Princeps* is Pliny's flattering term for "emperor." He is chary of applying it to the "bad" emperors Nero and Domitian, in informal *damnatio memoriae*. The only exceptions are 4.11.8, for rhetorical point, virtually echoing the Vestal Virgin's thoughts (*ex contemptu principis*, "in contempt for the leading citizen"), and 10.60.1, Trajan's letter referring to Domitian. Letter 8.6 calls Claudius *princeps* throughout, in quoting or referring to the fulsome senatorial decree for Pallas.

The third reason for the contrast between the male relatives of Euphrates and the female relatives of so many other *laudandi* is the paradoxical disadvantage of male kindred, a disadvantage that can be suspected behind the workings of power and patronage in the Empire. Having only daughters may have been a successful alternative to childlessness, combining the absence of dynastic ambition with the possibility of political marriage alliances. Daughters and female relatives are also rhetorically useful for forming a contrast with male friends, political allies and protégés—a fictive kinship that is no less important than real kinship. Thus both Corellius' and Aristo's household portraits contain rising lists of intimacy that reach a climax with friendship: daughter, wife, grandson, sisters, true friends (1.12.3), slaves, wife, friend (1.12.7), wife, daughter, friend (1.12.9), wife, daughter, friends (1.22.9).[38]

Euphrates' family of three children, majority male, points in opposing directions, first, as ideal conformity to official Roman values, but second, as a subliminal message that this is not a man on the fast-track of imperial patronage, not a man to fear or rival. His sons may enjoy enough imperial patronage for political careers, perhaps at the cost of being childless themselves. Iulianus, on the other hand, seems to have only one daughter; hence the choice between a son-in-law with "honors" *or* one with wisdom. Perhaps he also has no sons, and this politically undistinguished son-in-law keeps him "safe" for receiving imperial patronage? Perhaps Clemens, or the typical Roman reader, knows no more about Iulianus' children than we do. The impression that the letter gives is all that matters.

I should emphasize that although I am painting a rather pathetic figure of a tame philosopher who has sold out his values and self-respect for Roman patronage, I do not mean entirely to refute Pliny's attractive picture of the distinguished and respected sage. Rather, I am aiming to show the opposite side of the coin, or perhaps the underside behind the façade, which can only be revealed by peeling through the various layers of Pliny's rhetorical persuasion, bad faith, and deliberate denials of the realities of politics and power. In part, Pliny's praise designedly falls short of the full praise of the ideal Roman politician, as shown for example in the complementary portrait of Corellius at 1.12, and in part, Pliny's effort to bestow maximum praise reveals his strain and suggests the negative side of the picture.

> Quamquam quid ego plura de viro quo mihi frui non licet? an ut magis angar quod non licet? Nam distringor officio, ut maximo sic molestissimo. (9)

---

[38] Pliny uses the motif of loving a friend "like a blood-relative" at 2.18.5 and 7.24.2.

> And yet why should I say more about a man from whom I am not allowed to benefit? Or is it in order that I may feel more anguish because I am not allowed? For I am occupied by duty, all the more annoying because it is so great.

After having brought the laudatory section to a neat epigrammatic conclusion, Pliny begins the final section of complaint and recommendation with the interrupting formula *quid plura?* The interruption is of course illusory. Pliny was not really intending to go on to complete his praises of Euphrates. As usual, an interruption motif occurs only after the prior section is complete, to give the impression of incompleteness.[39] The laudatory section is carefully shaped as a finished whole, but the gesture of breaking off in the middle implies that the laudation is just getting underway, that there is much more to say in praise of Euphrates, that the praise so far has been inadequate. As we have seen, much of the praise has indeed been rather muted or equivocal, and the gesture of interruption paradoxically both apologizes for, and reinforces this impression. Although Pliny implies that if he had not restrained himself then the praise would have been longer and stronger, nevertheless the fully rounded nature of the laudatory section suggests that Pliny has indeed already given Euphrates the best praise possible, that no greater qualities have been left unpraised. On the one hand, Pliny is giving a blank check of unlimited unstated praise so that we will not feel too consciously that Euphrates has been shortchanged, but on the other hand he is reinforcing the faintly satisfying impression that Euphrates has been praised only so much as to keep him in his place.

Pliny puts an original twist on the conventional formula by attributing the interruption to his own anguishing jealousy, thus making the formula serve as a transition device from the section of praise to the final section of complaint (to Euphrates) and recommendation (of Euphrates to Clemens). The entire laudatory section, we now learn, has been causing him distress, and the only reason to go on is the supposititious purpose that he might cause himself more distress over his lack, since he cannot profit from Euphrates now. Pliny glosses the interruption formula as jealousy, as if he is stopping the praise only because he has realized that the more he praises Euphrates, the more he will be tormented with jealous yearning. For a moment jealousy, that canonical Plinian vice, casts a shadow over the laudation, but only briefly (12 *neque... invideo*).[40] Jealousy violates the perfect epistolary circle of mutually beneficial exchange. Here jealousy interferes with the praise in a rather unconventional way. It is not that the speaker or audience envies the *laudandus*

---

[39] On the pose of suddenly interrupting oneself see Cic. *de Orat.* 3.203, Quint. *Inst.* 9.2.57.

[40] For jealousy as a canonical vice in the letters, see 2.8.2, 6.17.4, 7.26.2, 9.23.6. The opposite of the epistolary ideal of mutually beneficial exchange (e.g. 1.4.3) is to begrudge *both* oneself *and* other people some pleasure or benefit (1.15.3, 2.10.2).

such high praise, which is the normal problem of envy in laudation, but that the speaker envies that the audience may act on the praise and benefit from the *laudandus*. Pliny briefly pretends to envy the glory to Euphrates only because he envies the benefit to someone else. Pliny's temporarily irrational persona treats Euphrates' teaching as a possession that Pliny cannot buy, so he will not tell others how valuable it is; he treats it as a zero-sum game, rather than the mutually beneficial cycle by which Pliny always depicts cultural exchange. Only when the authorial persona comes back to his senses is he generously pleased for Clemens to enjoy what he himself cannot.

Pliny's painful longing, his jealousy of his imaginary self for what it might have had, is a most unphilosophical state of mind, and reinforces the almost comic reversal in which the Greek philosopher and the Roman politician argue about the value of Roman political activity, the Greek in favor and the Roman against. The authorial persona has sunk into an irrational, emotional fit of petulance, whereas Pliny's "real" views are put into the mouth of Euphrates, in a common Plinian strategy for self-praise. The real Pliny lets himself be detected behind the petulant complainer in the upstanding Roman diction *officio* (dutiful business), even *maximo* (greatest duty), performed at the dignified tribunal. The list makes a stark contrast with that in the prior letter, 1.9. There the tasks about which he complains are called "hollow" (*inania,* 3), "cold" (*frigidis rebus,* 3), and finally simply "business" (*negotio,* 6) and "efforts" (*labores,* 7) rather than noble duties, *officia.* The contrast is not one of chronology, or perhaps not only one of chronology, but rather is because in one letter Pliny is praising private literary work over semi-private legal work, and in the other he is implicitly praising public legal work over theoretical Greek philosophy.[41] Similarly, at 1.3.2–3 he praises literary labor over the private business of estate management.

Despite the touch of honorific diction, Pliny's account of his political tasks contrasts almost humorously with Euphrates' parallel and much more honorific account of the same tasks. Pliny's account dwells on the hollow externals: he sits in a fancy chair and pushes his pen. Euphrates' account, however, fills the externals with intellectual and moral worth: he makes findings and judgments, and advances and enacts justice. Accordingly, Pliny summarizes the two accounts with the striking terms "complaint" and "consolation." Pliny's complaint is in fact in a great deal of bad faith, only part of which the letter is designed to uncover to the reader. Pliny complains about having his time used up with useless politics; the reader is supposed to see, along with Euphrates (and Pliny's "real" views), that Pliny is nobly

---

[41] Letter 1.9 is generally dated before, and 1.10 after, the appointment to the prefecture of Saturn, by the description of the tasks (Mommsen 1869:37, Syme 1958:658, Sherwin-White 1966:108).

sacrificing his leisure for the valuable work of Roman government. We can also see, however, that Pliny is not performing public duty entirely out of self-sacrifice, but also out of greed for money, power, and status. Throughout the collection, his numerous complaints about public duties are tinged with this bad faith. Other ancient authors, whether arguing for or against political activity, decry this form of bad faith, political *recusatio*. For example, Plutarch castigates Pompey for pretending to yearn for leisure while actually being eager for his extraordinary appointments (*Pomp.* 30.6 εἰρωνείαν), and Epictetus (1.10.2–6) and Seneca (*Ep.* 22.10) attack those who pretend to yearn for philosophical detachment but are actually enticed by the power and wealth of politics.[42] Although Pliny tries to make his *recusatio* sound sincere, the rather implausible exchange of "complaint" and "consolation" threatens to push the under-meaning of the passage from bad to worse, from a disingenuous Pliny who knows perfectly well that politics is a noble enactment of philosophy, to a self-deceiving Pliny who cannot even confess to himself that he is really in politics for the power and wealth. It is lucky for Pliny that he is not talking to an Epictetus who would see through his pretence, but to a tamer kind of Stoic whose views can flatter the Roman politician.

Pliny uses the somewhat self-ironic term "complaint" *(queri)* as a rhetorical lever to hoist Euphrates' flattering views into authority by comparison with Pliny's more trivial "laments." But the slippery rhetorical ploy almost gets out of his control. "Complaint" is a generic term for the exaggerated laments of the poet-lover (e.g. Tib. 1.2.9, 1.4.71), which were hardly taken seriously by politicians dabbling in erotic verse (as Cicero's "complaints" about Tiro's denied kisses, 7.4.6, or Pliny's own "complaints" in light verse, 4.14.3 *querimur*). In the poetic game of the unhappy lover, "complaint" is little more than a conventional pose. Indeed, Seneca explicitly compares a politician's complaint in bad faith to a man's insincere "complaint" about a girlfriend (*sic de ambitione quomodo de amica queruntur, Ep.* 22.10).[43] Later in the collection, Pliny has found a more compelling reason to "complain" about his public duties, his wife's illness (6.4.1 *numquam sum magis... questus*).

Pliny nevertheless manages, in his final exhortation, to get the rhetorical upper hand and to put his philosopher back into a subservient, unthreatening position. Just as we have heard two versions of Pliny's political duties, we now hear two versions of the experience of studying with Euphrates. Pliny's supposititious experience which he would now be having, if not for politics, is

---

[42] Critiques of this trope of the false reluctance to hold power go back to Plato, *Rep.* 347C.

[43] In contrasting this kind of insincere pose to "good faith" (*bona fide,* 22.10), Seneca anticipates the modern psychological and political use of the term "bad faith" (e.g. Sartre 1994:55–67).

to "spend whole days in listening and learning," whereas the actual experience that he anticipates for Clemens is for Euphrates to give him a "polishing and filing." The first version gives Euphrates a loftier role, although the rather derogatory term *consumere* gives a self-ironic undertone to Pliny's persona with its excessive yearning for philosophy (cf. 1.9.3 *absumpsi*, "I have used up" days). Now Pliny has the self-irony firmly under control. Pliny the real author knows that it would indeed be a "waste of time" for a high-ranking senator to spend whole days listening to the Greek philosopher. Pliny apparently *is* persuaded that politics is the "best part of philosophy," since it is only of "this one thing" that he is not persuaded, that it is better to do philosophy at the office than to burn up whole days listening to the philosopher.[44] Even the authorial persona recognizes that he should be doing "real philosophy" at his Roman office; it is only out of sheer pleasure that he would prefer merely to hear Euphrates and learn with him. But his final description confirms the subordination of Euphrates, whose teaching becomes mere file and polish, superficial attractiveness added after the real construction work of Roman education is complete. These terms suggest literary "polish" (e.g. 1.8.3 *qua soles lima*), mere style and no substance.[45]

This final section of the letter firmly establishes the separation between the Roman politician and the Greek philosopher, between superior and inferior, that the opening lines threatened to dissolve. Pliny uses Euphrates' own authority to demonstrate that politicians are the real philosophers, clearly dividing between "us (philosophers) *ourselves* who teach" and those (politicians) who act (*agere negotium publicum... quaeque ipsi doceant in usu habere,* 10). Nevertheless, the letter ends with the two Romans Pliny and Clemens talking about the Greek philosopher, behind his back as it were, reducing his lofty wisdom to superficial spit and polish, and using him as an object of exchange between Roman equals (*amicis,* 12).

---

[44] In a final irony at Euphrates' expense, Pliny is *not* persuaded (11) by the persuasive (7) philosopher (Gesner 1739).

[45] For *lima* as literary polish, see Guillemin 1929:45.

THE DEATH OF CORELLIUS
PAIN AND LOSS, CONSOLATION AND GAIN (1.12)

Letter 1.12 introduces Corellius Rufus, one of the two senior statesmen and mentors (along with Verginius Rufus) whose obituaries appear in the opening books; in later books, on the other hand, obituaries tend to commemorate either lower-status figures (youths, women, and slaves) or less exemplary powerful old men (e.g. 5.16, 5.21, 8.16, 8.18). Pliny presents Corellius' death as the climactic moment which crystallizes the meaning of his entire life.[1] It also marks the transition from the Flavians to the adoptive emperors, as if it were representing the very day on which Domitian was assassinated and Nerva was proclaimed emperor, 18 September 96. Pliny's description shows Corellius engineering his suicide to be an explicit political act, though to be sure he mutes the impression of staginess by emphasizing Corellius' extreme pain. In refusing to die under Domitian, Corellius inverts the scenario of the "political suicide," such as that of Nerva's grandfather, who in the closing years of Tiberius' reign starved himself to death though in excellent health, as if protesting against Tiberius and his likely successor, Gaius (Tac. *Ann.* 6.26.1–2; cf. 6.48).[2] Thus Corellius' determination to endure until Domitian's death makes his suicide a commentary on the political shift from Domitian to Nerva.

---

[1] Compare Benjamin: "[someone's] life... first assumes transmissable form at the moment of his death," 1969:94. Other examples of final moments which embody the meaning of a person's life are Arria's *non dolet* (3.16.13) and Cornelia's modest flinch (4.11.9).

[2] On "political suicide" see Hirtzel 1908:181–86, Grisé 1982:68, 82–83, Plass 1995:108. By contrast, Classicus' death, if a suicide, demonstrated his guilt (3.9.5). Corellius' survival also inverts the panegyric motif of Tacitus' *Agricola,* that Agricola did *not* survive to see either Domitian's final horrible years or the dawn of the blessed new age which Agricola secretly prophesied (44.3–45.3).

This significant chronology, and therefore much of Pliny's interpretation of events, is artificially contrived.[3] We happen to know that Corellius outlived Domitian by many months, although the letter implies that he died immediately. We move straight from his wish to outlive Domitian "by even a single day" to Pliny's rapid narrative of his death (*ut... vel uno die supersim,* 8). "A god fulfilled his wish... he broke off his remaining ties to life (the disease had already grown worse) ... he escaped the unremitting disease. It was already the second, third, fourth day—he was refraining from food." Enough text intervenes between the "one day" (8) and the "second, third, fourth day" (9) to exonerate Pliny of outright lying, but the suggestion of falsehood is strong. We hear that Corellius obtained his wish to survive by "even one day," and then that he broke off his remaining ties with life; the disease *had* already grown worse *(increverat)*, presumably before Domitian's death. Then come the second, third, fourth day without food. One might be inclined to date Corellius' death to the end of September 96, right at the start of the New Age. We know from later letters, however, that Corellius was on a land commission appointed by Nerva (7.31.4), and that Pliny was consulting him regularly at the time of the Certus affair in mid-97 (9.13.4–6). Corellius' death, presented as if in the initial days of Nerva, probably occurred after Trajan's adoption in July 97 and possibly after his accession in January 98.

Why is Pliny so eager to gloss over one or even two years? Pliny's contemporaries would know the truth, posterity can deduce it, and Pliny even tells us Corellius' precise age. Evidently Pliny is casting a decent mist over the more troublesome aspects of the recent political transition. Corellius' death assures us that the government is secure and just, and even Pliny's grief and despair suggest the equal and opposite feelings, relief and celebration for the present state of affairs. It would not do to call attention to the uncertainties of the transition, not only the near-insurrection that was averted by the adoption of Trajan, or rather that led to it, but also the many disturbing features of the early days under Nerva.[4] The questions of who was involved in Domitian's assassination, who had been canvassed to become emperor, and how Nerva was chosen, had all been wrapped in a polite silence. Moreover, the opening part of Nerva's reign featured a feeble emperor, a vengeful senatorial reign of terror, an insubordinate imperial guard and prefect threatening Nerva and carrying out executions of Domitian's killers, and perhaps an impending armed revolt in the east (9.13.11, Dio 68.3.3). All this would hardly be an appropriate setting for Corellius' contented departure from life. On the other hand, by not putting the death explicitly under Trajan's rule Pliny gives the

---

[3] Sherwin-White 1966:113.

[4] The adoption "could have begun as a conspiracy, designed not to rescue Nerva but to supplant him," Syme 1958:35; Waters 1975:386.

impression that the current stable government dates back to Nerva's reign. Like the other letters of Book 1, this one offers implicit panegyric both to Nerva, the emperor at their dramatic date, and to Trajan, the emperor under whom they were edited and published. In the letters, as opposed to the *Panegyric,* Pliny praises the new regime of both Nerva and Trajan indiscriminately.

If we consider that chronological vagueness is fundamental to the letter, it is striking that Pliny gives us two fixed dates, although elsewhere he is sparing with such specifics, even dispensing with the age in some obituary letters (e.g. 3.21 on Martial). Here Pliny gives us the age both at death, 67, and at the onset of illness, 32. The fact that Pliny saw fit to include these two numbers invites us to speculate on their significance: perhaps Corellius was ill for half a lifetime, or a third of a century, or a generation, or during the prime of life.[5] More striking than the ages are the dates: illness about 62–63 C.E., death about 97–98. These are imperial dates: the first is the descent into Nero's final years of terror, with the end of Burrus' and Seneca's power and the renewal of the treason trials, and the second is the restoration of stable government under Trajan. Nero's reign of terror and the following civil war would have been the earliest period of political disaster still remembered and experienced by most high-ranking senators at the time of Trajan's accession. Nerva himself seems to have enjoyed his first political honors by participating in the bloody suppression of the Pisonian conspiracy.[6]

Corellius symbolizes the Roman state, which sank into fundamental disease, from its "feet" (4) or political foundation, in the last years of Nero, and ended its long illness with a "planned" death, the assassination of Domitian, or perhaps a pair of "planned" deaths. Although the worst disease of the state ended with the death of Domitian, the state did not fully recover until Nerva's death, which was "planned" in the sense that he was probably chosen emperor *because* he was old and near death. Pliny's description of the hereditary disease as something handed down from father to son *like property* reminds us that the basic disease of the Roman body politic was the hereditary principle itself, the idea that someone is designated for monarchy by line of descent (*morbi... per successiones... ut alia traduntur,* 4). Rome had been suffering

---

[5] Recorded ages at death can be "precise but not accurate" (Hopkins 1983:238, citing the *Testamentum Porcelli*). Also, the words *implere* and *complere,* as at 1.12.11 *implevit ... annum septimum et sexagensimum,* are used not only to indicate time but also "the completion... of a recognized stage of life (infancy, youth, old age, etc.)," Bodel 1995:458 on 5.16.2.

[6] Tac. *Ann.* 15.72; Jones 1992:195.

from this principle for about one long lifetime, 14–96 C.E., starting from the
critical moment when imperial power was first inherited.[7]

We could even identify the prime of Corellius' life, when he "conquered"
and "broke" the hereditary disease (5), with the reign of the first lasting non-
hereditary emperor, Vespasian, an island of stability within a third of a
century of hereditary misrule. It was from Vespasian that Corellius received
his consulship, followed by a legateship in Upper Germany in the early years
of Domitian, his last major honor under the Flavians. Corellius' disease is
accordingly described with political overtones: he had a "prejudicial" health
condition, and suffered from the "most undeserved tortures" (4 *iniqua
valetudine*; 5 *indignissima tormenta*).[8] Corellius' disease seems to have been
gout, a hereditary metabolic deficiency which can be only partially controlled
by a diet spare in meat and alcohol, as noted already in the Hippocratic treatise
Prorrhetikon.[9] The inevitable progression of this hereditary disease resembles
the inevitable degeneration of the Julio-Claudian and Flavian dynasties from
the relatively good beginnings under Julius Caesar and Augustus and under
Vespasian to the final years of Nero and Domitian.

The dating of Corellius' life invites a comparison with Nerva himself. Both
were born soon after 30, and matured under the hereditary crimes and follies
of Caligula, Claudius, and Nero. Like Nerva, who was honored after the
suppression of the Pisonian conspiracy (Tac. *Ann.* 15.72), Corellius must have
received his first major honors under Nero, perhaps in a less unseemly
context. Corellius' thirty-second year, which marks the outbreak of his
disease, also suggests the beginning of his physical and political prime, his
"green age" (*viridis aetas,* 5). A parenthetic note, that Pliny learned this from
Corellius himself, emphasizes that we are dealing with a time before Pliny's:
Pliny and his circle, "new men" from a younger generation, are untouched by
the hereditary vice contracted from Nero's reign or earlier. Corellius, like
Nerva, reached the consulship under Vespasian, and continued as a leading
consular under Domitian, though not so prominent as Nerva; we know of no
honors after his command in Upper Germany in the early eighties, in contrast
with Nerva's second ordinary consulship in 90. Corellius is neither a Veiento

---

[7] On the significance of 14 C.E. as the defining moment for the monarchy, see Syme
1958:369, Ahl 1984:61. Syme also suggests as cardinal dates 4 C.E. (368–70) or 37 C.E.
(269–70).

[8] To be sure, the metaphor of torture for painful illness is conventional (e.g. Sen. *Ep.* 30.14,
78.14; Bütler 1970:78).

[9] "Someone who has it by inheritance is not easily rid of it," ᾧ γὰρ ξυγγενές...
δυσαπάλλακτον, *Prorrhet.* 2.5; "[if] he is careful and diligent in his way of life," τὸν
τρόπον ἐστὶν ἐπιμελής τε καὶ φιλόπονος, 2.8. Compare Celsus *De Med.* 4.31; Jackson
1988:177–79. Pliny is careful not to blame Corellius for having this disease of immoral luxury;
contrast, for example, Mart. 9.93.9.

nor a Rusticus, neither an over-loyal collaborator nor an honored victim, but a moderate consular, charting the narrow course of prudence with honor that Pliny exemplified on the witness stand at 1.5.5–7. Though we can revere Rusticus and Mauricus, Pliny implies, we owe the "restored" empire to men like Corellius, Nerva, Trajan, and Pliny himself who survived with enough power and prestige to establish the new regime: it is indeed possible to be a "great man" and "of use to the republic" under bad emperors (Tac. *Agric.* 42.4).

The timing of Nerva's sickness, like Corellius', was crucial. Both stayed alive just long enough, a year or two, to fulfill the same vital function. Their prestige (3), which they managed to preserve even while serving under Domitian, ensured a successful transition to stable government, to an active and honorable Senate, and to Trajan. Nerva is to Trajan as Corellius is to Pliny, both being prominent elderly senators who kept their authority intact through the dark days of Domitian in order to deposit it into the young, healthy, and untarnished laps of Trajan the emperor and Pliny the senator.[10] Behind the inconsolable grief of Pliny, then, lies a celebration of the new era of stability made possible by Corellius (and Nerva), and inherited and established by Pliny (and Trajan). Deeper still, behind the confident celebration, lie unexpressed anxieties over the arbitrary distinctions on which the stable new order is founded. Can anyone emerge with clean hands from holding power under a Nero or a Domitian? How can the government under Trajan be more stable than before if the underlying system is the same?[11] What distinguishes Regulus the *captator* from Pliny the friend, who inherits Corellius' prestige and perhaps some of his property—or even from Trajan, who receives the Empire itself from the childless and grateful (or intimidated) Nerva?

THE PHILOSOPHICAL RECKONING OF GRIEF AND LOSS

The letter opens on its keynote ("the *severest deprivation* have I suffered"), which it immediately calls into question with a redefinition, "if the loss of such a great man is to be called a 'deprivation'" (*iacturam gravissimam feci, si iactura dicenda est tanti viri amissio,* 1.12.1).[12] Pliny reaches beyond language

---

[10] In fact, both Pliny and Trajan had more success under Domitian than Pliny is willing to admit (*Pan.* 44.1, Syme 1958:34), and the Senate actually had no more real power under Trajan than under Domitian (3.7.14, 3.20.12, 4.25.5).

[11] See 9.13.10, Tac. *Hist.* 4.8.2; Kennedy 1972:544.

[12] On rhetorical self-correction *(reprehensio),* see Cic. *Orat.* 135, Quint. *Inst.* 9.2.18. Some other instances of this typical Plinian trope are 1.14.5 *huic nostrae—ambitioni dicam an dignitati,* 2.1.10 *si tamen fas est... mortem vocare,* 3.9.28 *diligenter... temere dixi 'diligenter.'*

to express how great is his feeling of loss, beginning with an ordinary word for "loss" but then rejecting it, as if recognizing its inadequacy and feeling uneasy with the humdrum suggestion of mere financial loss, literally the "jettisoning" of excess cargo. Elsewhere, the redefinition of death can have a beatific tone, as when Pliny says that the death of the heroic Verginius Rufus can hardly be called death at all: "if it is right to call that a death by which not the life, but the mortality, of such a great man has been ended" (*si... fas est... mortem vocare, qua tanti viri mortalitas magis finita quam vita est,* 2.1.10).[13] But here the focus is on Pliny's own grief, and the beatific tone is kept well in the background.

Pliny's emphasis on his feeling of extreme loss reflects the awkward problem of grief with which he must deal throughout the letter. He is basically presenting a successful death, but he must avoid any sense of satisfaction, especially for a suicide, a death which might have been postponed. By contrast, Verginius Rufus' natural death allows for a greatly increased tone of satisfaction (2.1.1–7, 10–11, especially 2.1.1 *felicis,* 6 *felicitati*) and a more restricted expression of personal loss and grief (2.1.7–8, 10, 12). Yet such prominent, almost overprominent emphasis on grief and loss could make us wonder whether Corellius' death is really not a loss, not only to Corellius but also to Pliny. Pliny may even have profited from the will; the right of three children which he obtained about this time would make it even easier for him to inherit. But unlike the later obituaries (e.g. 4.2, 5.1, 7.24, 8.18) which concentrate on inheritance, Pliny's legal specialty, these obituaries of revered statesmen (1.12 and 2.1) leave no room for moralizing about mere cash. The will is an important diagnostic of a person's character, summing up the final meaning of a life in a single document, but only for more ordinary people, not for political heroes, whose entire life is the State.[14]

Pliny's political status is also unlikely to be harmed at this point by Corellius' death. Corellius has given crucial recommendations to Nerva to advance Pliny's career (4.17.7–8), but would he have had the same influence with Trajan? Moreover, Pliny is on the verge of reaching the consulship, and had probably become a consular by the time this letter was published. The

---

Catanaeus (1533) and Schaefer (1805) discuss Pliny's pose of finding the word *iactura* inadequate.

[13] Syme (1958:121 n. 2) suggests a verbal echo from Tac. *Agric.* 46.1, *quas neque lugeri neque plangi fas est.* The code words *tanti viri* (1.12.1, 2.1.10) connect the two political heroes Corellius and Verginius.

[14] Champlin (1991:10–11) comments on how the testament was viewed by the Roman elite as a true expression of the "last judgment" of the deceased *(supremum iudicium)* on his or her relatives and friends, and as a "mirror of people's characters" (Plin. 8.18.1 *testamenta hominum speculum esse morum*).

highest reaches of power function as a zero-sum game, with only so many magistracies, legateships, or positions among the *amici principis*. Once Pliny has enjoyed the patronage of the senior consulars and entered their ranks, it might even help him for them to die off. In any case, he can continue to enjoy patronage from Corellius' eminent son-in-law, probably either L. Neratius Priscus (perhaps the Priscus who is gracious to Saturninus at Pliny's request at 7.7–8) or his brother L. Neratius Marcellus (who helps Suetonius at Pliny's request at 3.8.1).[15] But such concerns over whether he might be helped or harmed by Corellius' death are highly unflattering. Pliny therefore emphasizes that his grief is personal and sentimental. Pliny's *amicitia* (7, 11) with Corellius is not just a political alliance but a real personal friendship, and Pliny is grieving over his lost mentor (12), not his lost patronage. An explicit discussion of patronage and its reciprocal obligations must be postponed for another occasion, when he explains his honorable repayment of favors to Corellius' relatives years later (4.17, 7.11). Though the obituary for Verginius shows that emphasizing patronage need not conflict with the presentation of sincere grief (2.1.8–9), in this letter nothing interferes with the vivid essentials: sickness and suicide, tyranny and restoration.

Pliny's abrupt announcement, "Corellius is gone" *(Decessit Corellius Rufus)*, expresses his pure grief, like the Homeric model for abruptness, κεῖται Πάτροκλος (4.11.12 = *Il.* 18.22). He then adds that it was a voluntary death, thereby launching a logical elaboration of his grief over the suicide. This logical discussion of suicide bristles with philosophical concepts: nature, fate, necessity, reason (1–3), and even the Latin term for philosopher, *sapientibus* (3).[16] The philosophical coloring presents an ideal Roman Stoic, opposed and superior to the ideal Greek Stoic of 1.10. Furthermore, by presenting Corellius as a Roman Stoic suicide, Pliny implicitly brings him into the ranks of opposition heroes from Cato to Rusticus. Corellius is a republican martyr in reverse. He did not heroically die rather than submit to tyranny, but he heroically stayed alive for the "republic" (1.12.11), to use his "clean conscience, reputation, and authority" (3) to help establish Nerva and Trajan, the new "republican" emperors. The list of strong reasons against suicide conveys to us how great was Corellius' pain, and thus how great was his heroism.

Both Corellius' decision to kill himself and Pliny's painful grief are potentially awkward rhetorical problems. Corellius' pain must be shown to be

---

15 For bibliography on Corellia's husband, see Raepsaet-Charlier 1987:238.

16 The philosophical term *summa ratio* (3) can be compared to the Stoic term for rational suicide εὐλόγως ἐξάγειν (Diog. Laert. 7.130; Grisé 1982:232). The philosophical justification of suicide in cases of pain and incurable illness goes back to Plato (*Laws* 9.873C); see Hirtzel 1908:85, 141.

severe enough so that he does not seem weak for succumbing to it. Pliny's pain, on the other hand, though showing the proper love and devotion, could seem trivial and cowardly if brought too closely into comparison with Corellius' real physical pain. Therefore, Pliny presents Corellius' pain most vividly in the central scene of perseverance (6–8), dramatizing how Corellius was indeed able to endure it "by force of mind" (*viribus animi sustinebat,* 5). By contrast, all mention of Corellius' pain is excluded from the death scene (9–10) and from the discursive prologue and epilogue, where the numerous words for pain all refer to Pliny's own pain of mourning.

Corellius' pain and Pliny's pain are delicately counterbalanced, between Corellius' relief and Pliny's "incurability" (2), between Corellius' severe repression and Pliny's effusive expression, between the final pains of death and the initial pains of a new life. In the opening section, Corellius' pain is displaced by a discussion of "reason" and "decision," concepts that recur at the death scene. "Supreme reason" forced Corellius to a "decision" (*summa ratio... consilium,* 3), making the suicide "necessary" in philosophical terms. Even after we have been told about Corellius' pain (5), Pliny implies that the disease had spread so far that death was imminent anyway. Corellius did not give in to pain; he merely stopped putting death off through extreme willpower once Domitian was dead and it was no longer necessary. The false suggestion that Corellius died at once reinforces this impression.

While excluding Corellius' pain from the opening lines, Pliny emphasizes his own pain as much as possible, suggesting a parallel with Corellius' real pain through vivid physical metaphors. The fact that it was suicide "turns my *pain* into a deeper *wound*," and the belief that he could have lived longer makes it an "*incurable* malady" (1 *quod dolorem meum exulcerat,* 2 *insanabilis* dolor).[17] The word for Pliny's "grief" (*dolor)* is the same as the word for Corellius' "disease" of the feet (4 *pedum dolore,* 6 *dolor... omnia membra pervagabatur*). Later, too, Pliny recognizes that he might be thought to be "weak"; the same word can describe the "old and weak" Corellius (*imbecillum* 12; *et imbecillus et senior* 4.17.6). Pliny is more afflicted by the pain (or "disease") than is Corellius. Corellius can keep his pain in check by mental will; neither his decision to prolong his life nor even his decision to end it was governed by his pain, but rather by his reason. Pliny portrays himself, on the other hand, as an irrational hostage to his emotional pain, not knowing any way to apply reason to keep it in control. This contrast between

---

[17] Such metaphors are conventional, to be sure. See, for example, 8.23.5 *quod... dolorem meum exulcerat,* Cic. *Fam.* 4.6.2 *tam gravi vulnere... illa... recrudescunt,* Iulius Victor 448.21 *...dolentem pauculis consolare, quod ulcus... cum plana manu tangitur, cruentatur.* On *exulcero* see Merrill 1912 ad loc.: "the word seems to be especially used of grief: cf. 8.23.5, 9.9.3, Sen. *Cons. ad Helv.* 1.3."

Corellius' rational control and Pliny's irrational pain recurs at the death scene, where Corellius final decision (κέκρικα 10) leads immediately to Pliny's endless lack and yearning *(desiderii)*.

Pliny's pain is in charge of his reason, and therefore his opening philosophically inflected arguments merely help to convince himself that his pain is incurable, in a parodic rendering of the conventionally "curative" powers of philosophy.[18] Pliny avoids the *consolatio,* a common epistolary genre, substituting the obituary letter in its place. With nothing else amiss in the ideal world under Trajan, Pliny prefers to revel in the one source of real grief, sickness and death, rather than to smother it up. The letter closest to a *consolatio,* 9.9, actually encourages and praises the addressee's grief as a sign of close and loyal friendship.

Nevertheless, Roman and philosophical attitudes deprecated extreme grief, which could even be a topic of satire, as in Regulus' mourning for his son (4.2, 4.7). The analogy between Corellius' physical pain and Pliny's mental pain does not reflect entirely well on Pliny. He therefore undercuts his philosophical argument, his anti-consolation, by punctuating the syllogism with the doubt-inducing terms *videtur* (1) and *creduntur* (2). Corellius' death (only) *seems* to be unnatural and unfated; it is (only) *believed* that he could have lived longer. We will soon be told that Corellius was in the last stages of terminal illness. The wonder is not that he died unnaturally early (1–2), but that he survived as long as he did, longer even than the "single day" past Domitian's death which was all he wanted. To the reader, the opening argument, and indeed the entire letter, have the opposite effect, convincing us that Corellius' philosophically reasoned and chosen death was proper and even necessary, as Pliny himself briefly concedes: reason serves in the place of necessity for philosopher-sages (*summa ratio, quae sapientibus pro necessitate est,* 3). As often, the shifting angles of Pliny's concessive rhetoric concede the point that the dominant voice pretends to deny.[19]

The dialogue on Corellius' suicide, then, alternates between Pliny's authorial voice that laments it and Corellius' philosophical counter-voice that considers it proper and necessary. This dialogue then takes on the form of a financial reckoning of accounts.[20] On one side are the "commitments" invested in living (*pignora,* 3), the "appraised value" of living (*pretia vivendi,* 4), his prestige, family, and friends. On the other side are the reasons (or "accounts")

---

[18] Elsewhere Fundanus *rejects* philosophical arguments which would console his grief (5.16.8); compare Sen. *ad Helv.* 17.3 *sanabunt, Ep.* 99.32 *remedium.*

[19] For example, at 1.10.3 Pliny concedes that he has indeed fulfilled Euphrates' high hopes for him. See Rudd 1992:32.

[20] Guillemin notes the influence of *suasoriae* on this trope (1929:54). On the "balance sheet" of life and death in suicide, see van Hooff 1990:122.

for death (*mortis rationibus,* 4), which are spelled out in Pliny's general narrative (4–6) and dramatized in the first deathbed scene (6–8).[21]

The credits on the side of the asset sheet for living are divided by the terms *praeterea* and *interque tot pignora* into three groups, first, Corellius' purely symbolic capital of conscience-reputation-authority, second, his kinship network of daughter-wife-grandson-sisters, and third, the climactic category, his true friends. Of the three items in the first group, the third, *auctoritas,* is marked out by its different adjective. One can have good or bad conscience and reputation *(optimam conscientiam optimam famam),* but *auctoritas,* "prestige," is always a good thing, of which one can only have more or less (maximam *auctoritatem).*[22] Harmful influence might be called *potentia,* but not *auctoritas,* which implies both the moral knowledge to make the right decisions and the influence to have them carried out. The terms might suggest a post-Domitianic setting, in which moral introspection *(conscientia)* and public reputation *(fama)* can be in consonance with each other and with the power to act *(auctoritas)*—the opposite situation from that of the secret interview in the first scene (6–8). Yet this honorific description of Corellius is not restricted to the New Age. Even under the Bad Emperor Corellius preserved his *auctoritas,* although it was fully displayed not in hypocritical silences in the Senate (8.14.8) but in scenes such as the secret interview (1.12.8) which reach down to moral bedrock. By preserving his reputation and moral influence with his "true" political comrades (*veros amicos,* 3), Corellius had enough influence to help establish the new order under Nerva and Trajan.[23]

The other two reasons to live, relatives and friends, are joined together through a slight ambiguity in the words *inter... pignora* (either *"in addition to* so many *kinship ties"* or *"among* so many *personal ties").* The friends are both a special category beyond the relatives and the epitome of personal relationship. Although the normal meaning of *pignora* is "relatives," the word can be used of friends (Stat. *Silv.* 2.1.200, *OLD* s.v. 4b), and its literal meaning, "a valuable pledge," could apply to the entire list of moral and

---

[21] Pliny avoids verbs such as *putare* or *existimare* that would match this idiom of "financial" reckoning, in favor of more decisive verbs such as *compulit, vincerentur, destinasse,* and finally the climactic κέκρικα in Greek, the proper language of philosophy. By contrast, Corellius' *cur... putas* (8) describes a supposedly imperfect attempt to evaluate Corellius' authoritative decision.

[22] Indeed, "bad conscience" appears in a legal text as a reason to kill oneself: those who kill themselves *mala conscientia* are not mourned (Neratius, *dig.* 3.2.11.3). Compare Plin. 1.5.8.

[23] See Trisoglio 1972:101: "Corellio Rufo, alto modello di dominio di sé e di odio alla tirannia, non solo è grande per sé, ma irraggia grandezza anche sugli amici."

personal ties that could make Corellius unwilling to die.[24] Pliny is both privileging and demoting kinship; he brings the relatives into the foreground only to dismiss them. Hence the list of relatives (daughter, wife, grandson, and sisters) has no clear logical shape, neither rising nor falling in preciousness.[25] All relatives are equally precious, but the emphasis falls on the friends. The two sickbed scenes dramatize this rhetorical balance, with the climactic emphasis twice falling on the true friend, Pliny.

Although the basic meaning of Corellius' death is political, Pliny has embedded the cold political message in the warm setting of personal relations. Beyond and above the political reasons for Corellius to wish to stay alive (his conscience, fame, and authority) are his personal obligations to his devoted family: he owes it to his political position, and he owes it to his family. Similarly, Seneca feels that his father (*Ep.* 78.2) and wife (104.3) are reasons for him to stay alive selflessly despite his own wishes.[26] Finally, at the climax of the list are his "true friends," who, though they embody his political reasons, are represented in personal terms, as kindred but even nearer, as it were.

Missing from this list of the "value" of living is the actual financial value. Corellius had power, kinship, friends, and of course *money* to enjoy in old age. Yet this is not a testamentary letter like 8.18 on the long endurance of Domitius Tullus, who kept going over his huge wealth with only his eyes (8.18.9), and Corellius is not even a Spurinna with a luxury villa equipped with silver and Corinthian bronze (3.1.9). Corellius' entire life has shrunk down to its political core, and his capital has shrunk down to basic political values and personal relationships. He has not retired from Rome in his old age like Silius Italicus, nor does he use his suburban villa as a place to write light verse like Spurinna.[27] Corellius lies sick right outside of Rome, as if ready to be carried to the Senate like the blind Appius Claudius to save the state with his bare *auctoritas*. Pliny's real inheritance from Corellius is *auctoritas,* not money.

---

[24] Elsewhere in the letters Pliny uses the word loosely to mean "personal guarantee" (2.4.2, 7.1.7, 8.4.7, 10.26.1); only in the *Panegyric* does he use the fossilized metaphor "relatives" (37.4, 39.5). A more technical term for "relatives" would be *propinqui* (3.8.1, 10.11.2). *Inter* is normally inclusive ("among"), but can refer to a group of lesser people "among" whom one is outstanding (*OLD* s.v. 4b).

[25] Compare 1.22.9 "wife, daughter, friends," 5.18.1 "wife, son," 8.23.7–8 "mother, wife, daughter" (twice). At 5.21.3 we find "brother, mother, sisters." The list at 1.12.3 may be influenced by typical rankings in wills: first children, then spouse, then siblings and other relatives, then friends (Champlin 1991:120, 127).

[26] The wife of the rather disreputable Domitius Tullus, on the other hand, seems to have given him the "will to live" more for enjoyment of what life remained than out of selfless duty to her (*et vivere volebat, sustentante maxime uxore,* 8.18.10).

[27] Spurinna is of course not portrayed in a hostile light; rather, he represents another ideal.

THE TWO SICKBED SCENES

At the core of the letter is a matching pair of sickbed scenes, a Domitianic scene displaying Corellius' heroic perseverance to live, and a briefer and indirectly reported Nervan or Trajanic scene displaying his equally heroic perseverance to die. The first scene is given greater length and dramatic emphasis, since the real point of the letter is Corellius' heroic survival, not his heroic suicide. We have already seen the political chronology of Corellius' disease, with a healthy rise to political adulthood in the Claudian and early Neronian periods, the onset of the disease around 63 C.E., a period of containment in the prime of life during the reigns of Vespasian and Titus, and the "unbelievable crucifying pains and most undeserved tortures" with the onset of old age, when the disease had spread from the foundation to every part of the body politic (perhaps age 50, 81 C.E., reign of Domitian). The stage is set for the first of the two scenes, vaguely set "in the times of Domitian": Pliny avoids specifying whether we are in the final years of terror. Domitian must be seen to be infected by the disease of hereditary succession from the beginning. Such a "thug" (8) should never have reached the throne, and Corellius and the other Good Senators have been holding out, grimly and bravely, for fifteen long years. Similarly, Regulus' crimes are loosely dated as having been committed "under Nero" and "under Domitian," 1.5.1, not in their closing years.

Every detail of the scene strengthens the impact of Corellius' climactic words. Pliny came to him outside the city (6), as to the philosopher Artemidorus (3.11), in exile, as it were, from the center of power. The episode demonstrates that despite their public faces, their private faces were appropriately anti-Domitianic, in keeping with the requirements of the new order under Nerva and Trajan.[28] Corellius was lying in bed, as if on his deathbed. Only his eyes move (*circumtulit oculos,* 8): is he paralyzed by the disease, like Domitius Tullus whose slaves even brushed his teeth (8.18.9), or is it by the political situation, which forces him to roll his eyes surreptitiously to check for secrecy? The physical and political diseases coincide. The slaves have withdrawn on their own. Under bad emperors, owners live in fear of their slaves (*Pan.* 42.2–4, Tac. *Hist.* 1.2.3); in Corellius' well-run household, slaves and master harmoniously thwart the long arm of Domitian's spy

---

[28] Riggsby notes the frequent association between the *cubiculum* and secret activity (1997:44). His suggestion that the Roman *cubiculum* can be seen as a "back region" or "backstage," where the verbal and gestural decorums of the official performance space can be violated, is illustrated by the fact that Corellius does not merely express treasonous thoughts but even calls the emperor *isti latroni* (8), "that thug there!"

network. It is "customary" for his more trusty associates to visit in this way (7 *habebat hoc moris, quotiens intrasset fidelior amicus*). In the dying Corellius' anti-Senate, customary procedures hold, with a senior consular regularly presiding over real decisions with real *auctoritas*. Political oratory is reduced to the bare necessities, to a style matching Regulus' ferocious eloquence (1.5.2). Even Corellius' trustworthy wife "used to absent herself" from these cabinet meetings. Or perhaps the imperfect means "(on this special occasion) *even* his wife *headed for the door*" (*quin etiam uxor... digrediebatur*; "si allontanava" Trisoglio 1973:213). If any meetings needed perfect secrecy, all the more so did this climactic meeting with Corellius' *most* trusted associate, the meeting at which Corellius goes straight to conspiracy.

The most intimate secret of the prior epoch can now be safely (or rather, profitably) broadcast in a published letter. A kind of pre-death *damnatio memoriae* demotes Domitian from highest to lowest, from the emperor to a vagabond thief who deserves to be executed. Why must Corellius tell Pliny this dangerous message? Simply to clear himself from the charge of collaboration with Domitian, or of greedily hanging on to a useless life? Is this an invitation to conspiracy in Domitian's final days, an invitation for Pliny to kill Domitian? Pliny's final comment sounds as if Corellius himself would have done it if he had been healthy: "had you given to this soul an equal body, he would have done what he was wishing" (8). But are we really to imagine that a leading senator would have killed the tyrant with his own hands?[29] At the most, a bold senator such as Valerius Asiaticus could boast that he wished he had killed the emperor (Dio 59.30.2). It would be especially unsettling to imagine Corellius among Domitian's assassins, who were later killed by the praetorians (Dio 68.3.3, Plin. *Pan.* 6.2, *epit. de Caes.* 12.8). Instead, the old Corellius can confidently wait for the young Domitian's death: for such a brigand-emperor, assassination is a natural death that cannot be postponed so easily as a physical disease. After all, Pliny does not openly say that Corellius wished to kill Domitian, but only that he wished for Domitian to die first.

One might therefore give the words a tamer meaning. "If Corellius had such absolute control over his body as he had over his mind, he would have accomplished, on his own, his wish to live indefinitely and survive Domitian *(fecisset quod optabat)*, but nevertheless the divinity was there to answer his wish." Still, the language does suggest that he wished for the assassination, and one could almost believe that Corellius was a spiritual leader, a force behind the scenes. "God hearkened and he obtained his wish." Did the conspirators

---

[29] *Occidisset* (Barthius in Cortius and Longolius 1734); *interfecturum fuisse* αὐτόχειρα *Domitianum, haud obscure innuitur* (Schaefer 1805); "...that Corellius would have conspired against, or with his own hand would have killed, the tyrant" (Merrill 1912).

consult him in preparing the murder and choosing Nerva for the succession? At the least his prayers brought about the deed, in one of the few instances of divine intervention in the letters.[30] Pliny's vagueness allows him to have it both ways, to assign to Corellius (and himself) spiritual credit for the benefits of the assassination without implicating them in the bloody deed. After all, a body equal to the omnipotent mind of Corellius would be not merely a healthy body, but a superhuman body. Such a body might well overcome the nearly insurmountable political difficulties involved in replacing a tyrant with a stable and just government, difficulties which Nerva accomplished better than did Galba, but certainly not perfectly.

Pliny hastens from one sickbed scene to the other, jumping over the troubled opening months of Nerva's reign; Corellius, like the state, is now "secure and free" (8). The second scene repeats and reverses the first. Pliny is the "only one," again the most intimate, trusted friend, summoned for a crucial deathbed conference, but this time he misses the event. Why does he emphasize his absence? Corellius' wife Hispulla is at the deathbed watch, with relatives and friends, and presumably slaves. Her first message reaches Pliny, "that Corellius had firmly decided to die, and was unmoved by her pleadings, or by their daughters', and that I was the only one left by whom he could be called back to life" (9 *destinasse Corellium mori nec aut suis aut filiae precibus inflecti; solum superesse me, a quo revocari posset ad vitam*). Next, a one-word sentence *(cucurri)*: the distinguished senator runs, perhaps for a great distance.[31] The unlikely scenario indicates how heavily the incident has been refashioned to give just the right emphasis, desperate hurry and failure. The reason for Pliny's failure, Hispulla's second message, is a bit of a surprise. It is too late for Pliny to do anything, not because Corellius is already dead, but because he has announced his final decision, as if a death-sentence, evidently his final utterance, missed by Pliny but transmitted by Hispulla.[32]

> Perveneram in proximum, cum mihi ab eadem Hispulla Iulius Atticus nuntiat
> nihil iam ne me quidem impetraturum: tam obstinate magis ac magis induruisse.
> Dixerat sane medico admoventi cibum: Κέκρικα, quae vox quantum
> admirationis in animo meo tantum desiderii reliquit. (10)

---

[30] Elsewhere too Pliny generally mentions the gods only in the context of a rescue, such as curing an illness (1.22.11, 7.19.11, 8.1.3; Bütler 1970:11). "Gli dei... hanno solo una funzione esornativa" (Trisoglio 1972:150 n. 5).

[31] As Niemirska-Pliszczynska (1955:112–14) notes, the asyndeton heightens the suspense in narration.

[32] "The utterance contrasts with his first: stately and philosophical Greek for pungent and political Latin, a lapidary word for a colourful pair of sentences, death for life..." (Hutchinson 1993:270).

> I had reached the vicinity when another messenger from Hispulla, Iulius
> Atticus, told me that not even I would get him to agree to our wishes, so
> determinedly had he stiffened his resolve more and more; at any rate, he had
> said to the doctor who was offering him food 'j'ai décidé,' an utterance which
> has left as much admiration as longing in my mind.

Pliny omits the moment of death itself, leaving vague the question of
whether he indeed arrived too late. We might at first wonder whether Pliny is
defending himself for missing Corellius' final moments. But Pliny's emphatic
portrayal of his absence has symbolic advantages. First, after the earlier near-
deathbed scene with its secret political colloquy, it is better to have Corellius
actually die in the bosom of his family. Yet Pliny must not be drowned out by
the throng of close kindred. Now he will be marked out as Corellius' most
important associate by his very absence: with all Corellius' 'friends and
relatives present, Pliny is still the only one whose advice might sway
Corellius. A repeat of the prior scene, with everyone but Pliny excluded, is
both unmotivated in a "free republic" and undesirable in putting too much
distance between Corellius and his family. As in the opening list of personal
"assets," Corellius' most important relationship is nominally with his family
but really with his political "friends," especially Pliny. This Pliny the trusted
advisor who is summoned to the deathbed is different from Pliny the authorial
persona, who would simply have repeated the pathetic pleas of family and
friends for Corellius to eat. Pliny the trusted advisor has such influence
precisely because his advice follows reason and not blind emotion, and he
would probably have voted for suicide, as Aristo's council would presumably
have done if his disease had been like Corellius' (1.22.10). For this reason too
Pliny must be kept away from the scene: urging one's mentor to suicide is too
impious to contemplate.

The absent Pliny symbolizes the bereft Pliny. He missed the climactic
scene, and he now "misses" the absent Corellius (*desiderii* 10, *caream* 11). But
absence need not be lack and longing; the utterance that he missed fills him
equally with admiration and longing (*quantum admirationis... tantum
desiderii,* 10). A similar distinction between painful grief and pleasant
celebration of the dead underlies Seneca's anti-consolation letters against
excessive mourning (e.g. *Ep.* 63.4, 99.23). The opposed responses of
admiration and longing correspond to Pliny's opposed personae. The
overemotional dependent feels longing; the confident senator who sees
through the overemotional response feels admiration.[33]

---

[33] Leach's comment (on 1.8) about Pliny's "awkward dialogue between public and private
selves" is also apt here (1990:31). As Hutchinson observes (1993:271 n. 25), "the expression
of Pliny's own, properly unconsoled, sorrow is not meant to make the reader think he does not
fully accept the rightness and greatness of Corellius' death."

Pliny's absence allows the powerful adult persona to take shape beneath the emotional surface, without presenting a harsh, cold face to the dying Corellius, or to the reader. The presence of Pliny, Corellius' closest associate, at the deathbed would have created a father-son dynamic. But the absent Pliny is not really a subordinate, obediently receiving deathbed wishes and commands. If his immediate sense of lack and longing is greater for his having missed Corellius' final moments, it also allows a more fully independent Pliny to emerge in the aftermath. Corellius' making his most difficult decision alone, without Pliny, is a model for Pliny himself to admire, and to emulate. Just beneath the helpless authorial persona lies a confident man who can make difficult, firm decisions on his own, without depending on colleagues' advice (for example, the decision to attack Certus, 9.13.6).[34]

Corellius' method of suicide, starvation, deserves attention. As we have seen, one awkward problem presented by suicide is that no matter how reasonable it may be, friends and relatives should not appear to be encouraging it. Thus, even the heroine Arria must be shown being dissuaded from performing suttee, and she proves her nobility by demonstrating that with her strong will she can overcome all obstacles, even smashing her head against the wall if need be (3.16.12). Dio's Seneca, on the other hand, comes off badly for encouraging his wife to die with him (62.25.1), as does Regulus, the proverbial *captator* who wants the rich man to die (at 2.20, and perhaps even his son at 4.2). Regulus almost encourages "physician-assisted suicide," still a controversial subject today for its contradiction with the basic Hippocratic principle, to do no harm. Corellius' doctor remains in the authorized, if somewhat ludicrous position of holding out food to "help" the dying man, while the impious possibility of connivance with suicide is avoided not only by the absence of Pliny but also by the presence of the relatives, the natural heirs who nevertheless bewail his hastened death and have summoned the doctor and Pliny to postpone it. Pliny's scenario would not be possible today, since improvements in forced feeding methods, not to mention analgesics, diagnostics, and treatments, would put the doctor in a much more problematic situation.[35]

Corellius needs no one to help him or even to connive in allowing him to die. Despite the opposition of so many strong people, he can enforce his strong will even with his enfeebled body, simply by shutting his mouth,

---

[34] "Another advantage of a dead man as model is that it avoided a personal dependency unseemly for the Roman aristocrat," Riggsby 1995:131 n. 15.

[35] On the current controversy, see for example Smith, who cites the Hippocratic oath (1997:68). In the *Historia Augusta,* Antoninus tells the ill Hadrian that allowing him to commit suicide would be parricide (*Hadr.* 24.9).

opening it only to say the one decisive word.[36] The paradox of weak and strong is captured by the oxymoron, *perseverantem constantia fugit* (Gesner 1739). "He bolted from the persistent disease, meeting it with inflexibility of his own, conquering it by flight." The tableau is vaguely ridiculous: the doctor's therapeutic expertise is reduced to the most basic task of holding out food, but he is clearly out of his league. Corellius needed not a doctor to hold up food, but a philosopher, or a Pliny, to understand that his refusal to eat was the correct decision. Yet since the family is showing pious opposition to Corellius' will, the unfortunate doctor had to be brought in to face this situation.[37]

A GREAT NEW CONSOLATION

With the central narrative section over, Pliny ends by returning to his opening deliberations; as usual, the opening returns with a difference. The question is the same: how much grief should one feel for an old and sick person who has correctly and rationally committed suicide? There are two main differences: first, the addressee and reader now know as much as Pliny did about the circumstances and reasons for the suicide, and second, the style and rhetorical presentation have changed. The final deliberations begin with a catalogue of three arguments of consolation, which, as we learn from the refrain *scio,* are "spoken" by Calestrio, as it were, or rather by that part of Pliny that knows Calestrio so well that he can voice Calestrio's arguments internally.

The beginning imitated the internal deliberations of Corellius on whether to commit suicide, but the ending imitates the epistolary form, being an internalization of a dialogue between Pliny and his addressee on whether to feel grief. Earlier, we saw Pliny deliberating on reason and necessity in dying, and weighing the arguments on both sides. Now that the narrative has been told, Pliny's authorial voice has fallen deeper into weak despondency, which is portrayed by the abandonment of rational argumentation to Calestrio's voice, and by the repetitive dirge-like quality of Pliny's voice. As Calestrio (and the reader) trot through the standard arguments for consolation, Pliny can only wail out "I know... I know... this too I know" (11). The repetitive quality of

---

[36] "The preference among Stoic suicides for... starvation seems to be due to the fact that the quality of persistent resolution... is better shown in such a death," Merrill 1912 ad loc.

[37] Slaves were compelled, on suspicion of murder and penalty of death, to prevent their master's suicide (Sherwin-White 1966:464–65 on 8.14). Corellius' self-starvation, like Italicus', protects his slaves and avoids having to remove them from the scene. Seneca the Younger mentions slaves reluctant to help their owner's suicide (*Ep.* 77.7), and the Elder gives a *controversia* on a slave who refused to give his sick owner poison (*Contr.* 3.9); compare also, for example, Suet. *Nero* 2.3, *HA Hadr.* 24.8.

lament continues for the rest of the letter: aside from repeated short words and rhetorical rhythms he repeats *doleo doleo, amisi... amisi,* and *numquam... numquam.*[38] Pliny is stuck in the endless cycle of grief, like Achilles going around and around the tomb with Hector's body.

We know, of course, that this aspect of Pliny's personality is only temporary, and that the eternally cheerful and optimistic persona will soon return, just as surely as the sprightly spring letter 1.13 follows on the heels of the mournful 1.12. The strong, independent persona will take over again, not on its own, but with the help of friends. The superficial persona of the weak Pliny will be replaced not with an independent Pliny, but with an interdependent Pliny. The letter elevates Pliny's friend Calestrio into the logical and authoritative position, in keeping with the epistolary setting which emphasizes mutual beneficial exchange among friends. What Calestrio will do for Pliny this time, helping restore him to his full rational self, Pliny will do for Calestrio or for another friend the next time. Pliny can do without Corellius, but he cannot do without friends; he still needs friends, but not any one friend.[39] Thus Pliny turns to a nominally equal-ranked friend, but one whose career is lagging behind Pliny's, and whose son, not he himself, will reach the consulship (Syme 1958:82, Sherwin-White 1966:419).

The reader must create the ending of the letter. Having spoken the conventional old tropes (in Pliny's impersonation) to no avail, Calestrio, or the reader, is instructed to create a new, more effective consolation for the "weak" Pliny. But Pliny implicitly gives us the clue to this consolation, which can be found by adding to the lines attributed to Calestrio the *opposite* of those attributed to Pliny. It is true that Corellius was old and sick, and, more importantly, that he left behind a prosperous family and above all a flourishing government. This recapitulation of the opening asset list makes explicit what the central narrative has revealed: the state is more important than anything, even than his family *(omnibus carior),* and its successful restoration is the main reason he can die in peace. Pliny claims to mourn as if for a "young and strong" man, acknowledging that we will reckon him to be "infirm" for so doing. The striking reversal of the real situation, as in the earlier play on *dolor, exulcerat,* and *insanabilis,* startles us into a correct understanding. We do not reckon the real Pliny to be infirm, but rather, only

[38] Trisoglio overemphasizes the "sincere emotion" expressed by the rhetorical device of repetition ("schietto sentimento," 1972:223). Other passages with mournful repetition are 2.1.12 *(Verginium... Verginium... Verginium)* and 4.21.2 *(angor... angor... angor).* Trisoglio (1973:1.261 on 2.1.12) cites numerous Latin examples of repeating a name to express lament or scorn. Compare Niemirska-Pliszczynska (1955:92–93): *repetitio affectum scribentis exprimit.* The connections between repetition, loss, and mourning loom large in psychoanalytic theory; see Bronfen 1993:104–07.
[39] This topic of consolation is stated most uncompromisingly by Seneca (*Ep.* 63.10–11).

his temporary persona. The real Pliny is everything the lost Corellius was, powerful, reputable, and wise, in addition to being young and healthy.[40] He has lost his witness, guide, and teacher, but has himself and his friends to be all this to each other; he will overcome his grief by imitating Corellius' rationality and force of will. Pliny only needs some time for this *consolatio* to become effective. The dramatic date of the letter is shortly after Corellius' death, since he still fears what he feared when his grief was "fresh," that he will live more carelessly now (*recenti dolore,* 12). Pliny has not yet started living the rest of his life.

The completion of the *consolatio* can be found by inverting Pliny's words. Pliny's fear implies its opposite. Once the fresh grief has passed, he will of course live carefully, perhaps *more* carefully, more rationally and prudently, since he will no longer be relying on another source of authoritative judgment, but will *be* one himself. This may be the "new and bigger" consolation that Pliny requests (13), the reminder that once the death pains of the sickly Corellius and the sickly republic have passed, the healthy Pliny can enjoy all the benefits, public and private, that Corellius had enjoyed (3), but in a healthy, "flourishing" republic (11). The death pains of Corellius are the birth pains of political restoration, but Pliny's use of a weak and pathetic persona avoids the tastelessness of celebrating life and health at the death of the sickly Corellius.

The final verbal echo (*sponte,* 1, 13) completes the full circle from the authoritative decisiveness of Corellius to the authoritative decisiveness of the real Pliny that is implied behind the infirm and negligent persona.[41] Corellius died "on his own," with independent force of will. Now (ineffective) consolations come to Pliny "on their own," from his prior reading and listening. The passive tone implies its opposite. Pliny will not return to his true self through passively receiving thoughts from his conversations and readings that strike him "on their own." He will have to understand *on his own,* and with his friend's help, the true meaning of Corellius' death, a meaning he has expressed for us in this very letter, if he could only see it for himself.

---

[40] The tone of restoration in the early books does not allow Pliny to mention the almost fatal illness he seems to have suffered about this time (10.5.1, 10.8.3, 10.11.1; compare 7.1).

[41] Merwald merely notes that the return of the opening words *sponte... dolorem* give a closing verbal assonance though the thought is different (1964:35). For numerous passages in which *sponte* is used for suicide, see Grisé 1982:295.

THE NEW FREEDOM OF SPEECH, ALONG WITH THE FREEDOM NOT TO LISTEN (1.13)

Pliny follows the grim obituary 1.12 with a bright, cheerful letter on literature. As so often in Book 1, politics lurks in the background; under the new regime, the flourishing of literature is a topic of panegyric (3.18.6, *Pan.* 47.1–3; Sherwin-White 1966:115). Pliny varies the celebratory tone, however, by overlaying a veneer of indignation, allowing him to indulge in some typically Roman yearning for the good old days, which he somewhat surprisingly places in the reign of Claudius.[1] In following up a pathos-filled obituary with a congratulatory letter on renewal, Pliny must not show too much self-satisfaction. Only indirectly does the letter point to Pliny as the ideal writer in the ideal New Age. Competing with this congratulatory subtext is a subtext of anxieties. The letter expresses and assuages two anxieties, anxiety over the ultimate value of literature and anxiety over the uneasy dependence of literature on the imperial political system. The first anxiety finds expression in the group of bored and scornful would-be listeners through whose point of view a recitation is described; the second is expressed through the slightly ominous appearance of the Emperor Claudius as the central exemplum for the Golden Age of literature.

The letter complements 1.10, the other letter celebrating the new flourishing of literature in the new age. There, Rome is *"blooming"* with "liberal studies" (1.10.1 *liberalibus studiis,* "pursuits befitting *free* people"); here, April is bringing a "bumper *crop"* of poets (*magnum proventum poetarum,* 1.13.1).[2] Letter 1.13 also matches 1.10 in selecting a somewhat marginal and even foreign genre to exemplify the new age of literature.

---

[1] "Pliny's golden age here, as in II.14.3, seems to be the time of Claudius if not Nero," Sherwin-White 1966:260 on 3.20.5.

[2] Murgia 1985:172.

Pliny's own genre, oratory, fails to convey the desired impression of a sharp break: under Domitian Pliny was a successful politician-orator, and now under Nerva and Trajan he is still a successful politician-orator. Hence Pliny cannot make an ostentatious literary rejection of the Flavian age as easily as can Tacitus the historian by saying that it is finally possible to write and publish freely (*Agric.* 3.1, *Hist.* 1.1.4). Philosophy, on the other hand, is the perfect example of the new "freedom" because of the banishment of philosophers in 93–94 and their recall under Nerva (*Pan.* 47.1).

Poetry is a more awkward case; as Pliny's catalogue of respectable Roman poets shows, it was cultivated not only by the Divine Julius, the Divine Augustus, and the Divine Nerva (whose posthumous deifications establish them as "Good Emperors"), but also by Tiberius (a mixed Good/Bad Emperor) and especially the Bad Emperor Nero (5.3.5–6). Literature was also patronized under the Flavians, for example through the literary competitions established by Domitian, whereas Trajan may have been more interested in sports than literature.[3] Still, Pliny sums up the difference between the Old Age of poetry and the New Age of poetry in his final words on the recent recitations: bored listeners walk out honestly and freely.[4] One is reminded of the descriptions of audience compulsion during Nero's recitations, with women giving birth, and people dying in their seats, or feigning death to escape the tedium (Suet. *Nero* 23.2, Tac. *Ann.* 16.5.2, Dio 62(63).15.2). Literature under compulsion implies an audience under compulsion. Not only was one forced to sit politely and cheer for Nero's own

---

[3] Plin. *Pan.* 81, Dio 68.7.3, Dio Chrys. 3.135–36; scholars have called him "Philistine" (Waters 1975:429) and "uncultured" (Sherwin-White 1966:565). But Cizek (1989:4) notes the literary flourishing under Trajan (especially Pliny and Tacitus). Aside from Pliny's effusive comments at *Pan.* 47, we hear of Trajan's patronage of the orator Dio Chrysostom and the sophist Polemo (Philostr. *Vit. Soph.* 488, 532 Olearius). Pliny also flaunts Trajan's casual mastery of Greek (6.31.12). See also Millar 1977:204 on the importance of oratorical skills for emperors. Perhaps after the highly pressured and dangerous literary patronage of Nero and Domitian, a period of relative neglect was healthy. In any case, the continuing practice of political advancement for oratorical skills would be patronage enough for literature (e.g. Plin. 10.4.4, 10.94.1).

[4] As opposed to "Bad" Emperors such as Tiberius and Domitian, who were denigrated for dissimulation, Trajan was praised for *simplicitas* (6.31.14, *Pan.* 4.6, 54.5, 84.1) as one of his imperial virtues. For private citizens, too, *simplicitas* is a canonical virtue among the "sincere" circle of Pliny and his friends (e.g. 2.3.5 *nihil aut sincerius aut simplicius aut melius;* 2.9.4 *quo nihil verius... simplicius... candidius... fidelius novi;* Guillemin 1929:53). In particular, *simplicitas* describes the "honest" criticism of one other's writings (3.10.4–5, 4.14.10), normally expressed through effusive praise, just as Trajan and the Senate express their "honest" feelings through effusive praise. Tacitus, as we might expect, uses the term ironically, of the *false* impression of unguarded casualness given by Domitian (*Hist.* 4.86.2) and Petronius (*Ann.* 16.18.1).

compositions, but audience behavior in general was politically charged.[5] Presumably while courtiers were reciting their fulsome praises of the emperor the audience felt equally compelled to sit and applaud. The grievances against Thrasea involved literature and praise, not performing at the Juvenalia performances, refusing to join the Senate's adulation of Nero after the deaths of Agrippina and Poppaea, and opposing the death sentence for Antistius Sosianus' satiric verses (Tac. *Ann.* 16.21, Dio 62.26.3; cf. 61.20.4).

Now that literature is free again, and free to flourish, the audience is also free not to attend.[6] In modern times, too, the lifting of tight censorship sometimes leads to a decreased interest in literature: former lackeys lose their compulsory audience, and even dissident writers lose some of the appeal they had from secretly voicing dangerous truths.[7] Pliny's complaint about uninterested audiences may partially reflect the problems writers were facing in making the transition from despotism to freedom. More importantly, however, it is a part of his continuing implied panegyric of the new regime. He suggests that since poets are no longer required to fill their works with imperial panegyric, audiences are adjusting to the more ordinary poetic fare of star myths and homosexual flirtations (as at 5.17 or 7.4). Or perhaps when poets do recite passages of open panegyric, audiences do not feel compelled to stay politely, but can walk out, not only "with dissimulation," like those faking death under Nero, but even "freely" (*alii dissimulanter et furtim, alii simpliciter et libere*, 2).

Behind the façade of praise, Pliny's opening description of the reciters is vaguely condescending, rather like his account of Euphrates the philosopher. A huge throng of poets is crowding forward ostentatiously, another nameless "someone" every day. Out of so many poets, is any one of them any good? Pliny never quite praises them singly or even collectively. He only says that literary pursuits in general are thriving, and that the "creative faculties" of poets push themselves forward for display even though people do not want to

---

[5] For example, Nero watched the audience's response to Britannicus' singing (*Ann.* 13.15.2), and bad emperors had people punished or executed for their behavior at the public shows (Plin. *Pan.* 33.3, Suet. *Calig.* 55.1, *Vitell.* 14.3, *Dom.* 10.1); see Veyne 1990:393, Barton 1993:63, Bartsch 1994:6–7, 14.

[6] Similarly, the freedom to leave early from a visit to the emperor is a topic of panegyric, *Pan.* 48.2.

[7] As Steiner comments, "the KGB and the serious writer are in total accord when they both know... that a sonnet... can be the power-house of human affairs" (1996:302). "'Censorship is the mother of metaphor,' notes Borges; 'we artists are olives,' says Joyce, 'squeeze us'" (299). "The external pressure of the overheated imperial cult [under Nero] required an extraordinary talent... For high or even ceremonial poetry, those days would not return" (Fantham 1966:182).

hear them. Perhaps next year will bring yet another crop of aspirants, as ephemeral as the annual produce or foliage. This year's crop is larger, but perhaps not better.

For those who know Pliny's career, the reference to leisurely seclusion (*secessum,* 6) dates the letter to Pliny's year off, 97 C.E., between his Domitianic prefecture of 94–96 and his Nervan-Trajanic prefecture of 98–100. Pliny makes the rhythm of his official life symbolize the new times. He is free to enjoy hearing and writing literature, and now literature itself is free to thrive and express itself under the new regime. Pliny himself is Mr. Literature: almost everyone who is fond of literary pursuits is also fond of Pliny (1.13.6). Even if we did not know the year from Pliny's career, the mood of renewal would suggest to us the first new spring of the new age, especially coming after 1.12 which seems to place Corellius' death soon after Domitian's assassination. The implied chronology is, September 96, death of Domitian and end of the old order; winter 96/97, the winter of disorder; April 97, the month of Rome's birthday, a new crop of talents.

The very term "poets" *(poetarum)* is slightly condescending. Pliny does not usually think of himself or his friends as poets, but as Roman gentlemen who write poetry, generally for mere relaxation (e.g. 5.3.2 *remissionis,* 7.9.9 *remitti,* 7.9.13 *remittatur*). Pliny's list of good Roman gentlemen whose dignity and reputation were not ruined by writing poetry (5.3) starts with eminent politicians such as Cicero and Brutus, but concludes with full-time poets such as Vergil and Ennius! Even for poets, poetry is not a Roman vocation but an avocation, as it is for himself (e.g. 7.4.4, 8.21, 9.25; cf. 7.9.9–14). Pliny inclines towards Latin words for poets, calling them people who write *carmina* or *versus,* or even using the lofty Augustan term *vates* in an explicitly "poetical" passage (8.4.5 *iure vatum... ego quoque poetice cum poeta*).[8] The Greek word lurking behind the Latin ending emphasizes the alienness of a not fully Romanized domain, as if we should say "a crop of maestros." Pliny can give a similar slant to the Greek *philosophia* vs. Roman *sapientia* (3.11.5–6) and, in a striking passage, *rhetor* vs. *orator* (4.11.1): Licinianus has been demoted from senator to exile, from lofty Roman orator to Greekling rhetor. Deprived of the toga, he must wear the Greek *pallium,* and it is almost a surprise that he is still using Latin to deliver his speeches (*"Latine" inquit "declamaturus sum,"* 3). We can even guess that some of the April poets may have recited in Greek, the language of Antoninus (4.3) and Caninius Rufus (8.4).

---

[8] Pliny uses Latin terms at (for example) 3.7.5 *carmina,* 3.21.2 *versiculis quos... composuit.* The only other use of the term *poeta* is at 3.15.1, where Pliny is echoing Acilius' words about Cicero "the encourager of *poets'* talents," to which Pliny adds protestingly that he reveres *poeticen*—in the fully Greek spelling.

Pliny's account of the audience's behavior continues the gentle satire at the poets' expense. Although Pliny himself was sitting earnestly in the audience, he reports the whole showy performance through the eyes of bored listeners who are themselves *not* present, but see it through the eyes of their messengers, presumably slaves going back and forth. The impressive entrance, hushed excitement, and grand preface are all things that can be avoided by a fashionably late arrival. Even the poetry itself is reduced to the merely physical rolling out of a fat scroll seen from afar by messengers who are only counting the minutes. One cannot help thinking that the exemplary story of the recitation under Claudius forms a contrast not only because the audience was shouting excitedly, but also because the reciter was a Nonianus, not one of a throng of nameless versifiers. Claudius entered suddenly not because he heard the shouting audience but because he was told that Nonianus was performing. The burst of applause fits what Quintilian tells us of Nonianus as a historian, "illustrious in talent and *thick with sententiae*" (*Inst.* 10.1.102). Apparently he followed the modern style of ending paragraphs with sententious quips, so that the audience will applaud every time the performer takes a breath, as Quintilian complains (8.5.14). What is needed to draw in the crowds again is Nonianus' counterpart, perhaps the sententious Tacitus, whom Pliny consistently identifies as the supreme prose writer of his time (e.g. 2.1.6, 7.33.1), or perhaps Pliny himself, the "imitator" of Tacitus (7.20.4), who always has enthusiastic audiences to spur his "worthy" efforts (e.g. 4.16.3).

Pliny's presentation of the crop of poets is concealed self-flattery, just as his presentation of the bored audience is concealed flattery of the new rulers and the new freedom. Letter 1.12 showed Pliny as a client/friend of Corellius; this letter shows him as a patron/friend of writers. Pliny attends not so much because he is enthusiastic about their writings as because he is doing them a favor with his benevolent accessibility. To Pliny, "spending" a whole month (*consumpsi,* 6) of his year out of office listening to new poetry is not "wasting" his time, but using it profitably in establishing networks of friendship and debts of gratitude that can be repaid, despite Pliny's denial (6), so long as he does not demand them back crassly. By contrast, those who behave badly, or do not hide their true scorn for the poetry, lose their friends while pretending to do them favors (6.17.3). Listening to recitations is an "obligation" (*officio,* 6) of an upper-class Roman patron, and thus comparable to the basic obligation of offering legal representation. Pliny uses the forensic terms of "standing by" a legal client (*adfui,* 6), or the opposite, "leaving someone in the lurch" (*nemini defui,* 5), to describe his attendance at recitations.[9] Even the emperor, the universal patron, can attend recitations to

---

[9] Compare, for example, 1.7.2 *adesse contra provinciam,* Quint. *Inst.* 6.2.4 *ut... non defuisse sibi advocatum sciat.*

encourage literature, for example Augustus in his "kind and patient" way (Suet. *Aug.* 89.3; *Tib.* 61.3) or Claudius in his half-crazy way (Plin. 1.13.3).[10] Pliny the indulgent, accessible patron of literature is following or setting the model for the Good Emperor, whose virtues are the opposite of the vices of the Bad Audience, alacrity and indulgence rather than "laziness and haughtiness" (*vel desidia vel superbia,* 1.13.5).[11] Just as the Emperor paradoxically reinforces his power over his subjects by showing his indulgence and equality, so too Pliny, the Emperor of Literature, reinforces his dominance over the nameless throng of talents by giving his time bountifully without demanding recompense, and by pretending to be their equal. The Good Emperor can paradoxically increase both his security and his leisure time by making himself more accessible to his "friends."[12]

When Pliny retreats to his villa and creates his own work of literature, he will *not* call in his debts by giving a recitation. This would destroy the bond-forming effect of exchanging favors, by immediately canceling one debt with its equal.[13] It would also bring Pliny down to the level of his poet-friends. In the opening books Pliny omits poetry-writing from his epistolary persona, perhaps because he is not yet writing verse (Sherwin-White 1966:289 on 4.14), but more likely because he needs to establish his serious status as an orator-politician in the early books before expanding his literary persona into the lighter genre of short poems, a stand-in for the genre of short letters in which he must also hope to excel.[14] Pliny's own rural retreat will not produce more grist for the mill of daily poetry readings attended by bored latecomers, but an eternal possession (as at 1.3.4) that will stay popular even when no longer new (as at 1.2.6). Pliny's talent and genre are great enough that he does not need to demand the favor of attendance at a recitation to publicize and

---

[10] On the emperor as the "literary patron of first resort" ever since Augustus, see Williams 1982:18. Claudius himself was an erudite historian; the evidence that he also wrote poetry is limited to a phrase in Seneca's *Apocolocyntosis* (*vos poetae,* 12.3); see Huzar 1984:625. Yet he was not prominent as a patron of literature (1984:650), and both ancient judgments and surviving fragments show him to have been a mediocre writer (Huzar 1984:627–35).

[11] On industriousness as a virtue of the new regime and of the new society, see, for example, 3.20.12, *Pan.* 44.7, 81–82, Dio Chrys. 3.55–85. On indulgence, see, for example, Plin. 10.2.1, 10.3A.1, 10.4.1, 10.5.1, *CIL* 6.1492 Trajan *(ab indulgentissimo imp); TLL* 7.1.1247.23–65 s.v., Veyne 1990:459 n. 265.

[12] On the good emperor's "bodyguard of love" see *Pan.* 49.2 *(non crudelitatis sed amoris excubiis... defenditur).* On the "leisure" of doing his tasks in person, see *Pan.* 48.1 *(quasi per otium).*

[13] Sen. *de Benef.* 2.21.2, 4.40.4–5; Guillemin 1929:59, Bourdieu 1977:5–6, 171, Derrida 1991:16, 37.

[14] "Pliny first mentions his hendecasyllables in the fourth book..., when he has firmly established his own record as orator, critic, and patron of... poets... Now he can let his hair down without loss of face" (Fantham 1996:217). Riggsby comments on the centrality of oratory for Pliny's self-presentation (1995:130 n. 12).

immortalize his work. Thus the relative absence of his recitations from the early books, like the absence of his poetry, may also reflect his self-image as a powerful politician and writer, rather than chronological reality.[15]

The actions of the poet and his various audience members all have subtle undertones of imperial propaganda, but the contrasting exemplum refers directly to a prior emperor, Claudius. So far we have had the earnest poet, dull but free, and the bad listener, indolent or haughty, with a thief's disguise or free person's openness, operating through slave-messengers who rudely come and go at his own will. The imperial resonances prepare us for the story of Claudius and Nonianus, presented as an exemplum of the Good Audience (and the Good Writer). Pliny explicitly sets the story one generation back, "in our parents' living memory" (*At hercule memoria parentum,* 3). In the preceding letter, too, Pliny uses a similar trope to emphasize that the outbreak of Corellius' disease belonged to the prior generation (1.12.4 *ut ipsum audiebam;* cf. 3.20.5 *supersunt senes ex quibus audire soleo...*). Writers of Pliny's time tended to think of imperial history in significant generations. In Pliny's letters we have Silius Italicus, the last of the Neronian consuls, whose death leads Pliny to the locus classicus for the passing of generations, Xerxes' bewailing that his great army will be dead in a century (3.7.13, Hdt. 7.45; cf. Sen. *de Brev. Vit.* 17.1, M. Aurelius *Med.* 4.32). In Pliny's own life, an "age" of changes has occurred since his professional debut (4.24.6 *si computes... vices rerum, aevum putes*). Tacitus uses an extremely long-lived British man to span the great literary (and political) divide from Julius Caesar to Vespasian (*Dial.* 17.3–4), whereas the opening of the *Annales* emphasizes that by Augustus' death a new generation had grown which had never seen the free republic (1.3.7). The story of Vespasian's dream of being weighed (Suet. *Vesp.* 25) must reflect the number games by which people "counterbalanced" Claudius and Nero with the Flavians, with 27 years for each, or about a generation. The emperors themselves liked to emphasize their New Age with all-too-frequent Secular Games "which no one had ever seen or would ever see" (Suet. *Aug.* 31.4, *Claud.* 21.2, *Dom.* 4.3, Tac. *Ann.* 11.11.1).

Claudius is here treated as the last "Good Emperor" within recent memory. Quintilian's complementary story of the death of oratory in the time of Domitius Afer (Plin. 2.14.9–11) may also date to Claudius' reign, though it may be more fitting to assign the story of forced applause to the reign of

---

[15] Indeed, his casual allusion at 2.10.7 to the excitement and pride he feels before an enthusiastic audience indicates that Pliny is already giving recitations of speeches at this period (*pace* Sherwin-White 1966:160, 201; see Mommsen 1869:105). Pliny's only clear disclaimer, here at 1.13.6, has a specific rhetorical function which may or may not be connected with reality. Letter 2.19 mentions his reluctance to perform specifically a forensic speech, and especially one bristling with legal subject matter.

Nero, the exemplary figure of false applause. The ideal age of decorum in senatorial elections seems to date to the same time.[16] It may be no coincidence that Pliny's two stories on the death of letters, of oratory (2.14) and probably of history (1.13, unless Nonianus was reciting his poetry), are attached to the authors Afer and Nonianus, who were not only leading writers of their time but also died in the same year, 59 C.E. Tacitus marks their deaths with a special joint obituary (*Ann.* 14.19), significantly placed just after a major turning point in Nero's reign, his matricide (14.1–13). After this crime Tacitus quickly passes to Nero's literary outrages, his own performances (14.14–15) and his punishing others for literary offenses, starting with the banishment of Antistius Sosianus in 62 for his satiric poetry (*Ann.* 14.48–49).

The deaths of these two leading writers were historically memorable and noteworthy because they occurred at a turning point, at the end of the good government of the *quinquennium Neronis* (Vict. *de Caes.* 5.2, *epit. de Caes.* 5.3) and just before the horrors of the Neronian reign of terror (and just before Pliny's birth).[17] Like Agricola's (*Agric.* 44–45), their deaths could be seen as fortunate. The leading representatives of literature did not live to see the literary abominations about to take place. Dio reports (62.19.4) that at the first unseemly performances people considered the dead fortunate, "since many of the leading men had died in that year" (59 C.E.).[18] After an entire generation framed by the Neronian and Domitianic reigns of terror, literature is finally recovering. The Vespasianic interval of respite is represented not by writers of old who were heard by "our parents," but by Pliny's "parents" themselves, his adoptive father Pliny the Elder who continued the history of Aufidius Bassus after the death of Nero, and his teacher, the orator Quintilian; both enjoyed abundant imperial patronage under the Flavians.

Pliny's description of his uncle's writings, which span both sides of Nero's worst years, reflects the cycles and vicissitudes of imperial reigns. After a brief first work, the next two have a pro-Claudian and perhaps anti-Tiberian slant. The *Life of Pomponius Secundus* marks a Claudian protégé (e.g. Tac. *Ann.* 12.27–28) who had been treated with hostility by Tiberius (*Ann.* 5.8),

---

[16] Sherwin-White 1966:260 on 3.20.5.

[17] We might mark the turning point at 62, when Thrasea stopped attending the Senate (Tac. *Ann.* 16.22.1; Syme 1958:558). To be sure, there were unseemly aspects to Afer's life that Pliny ignores: his early *delatio* (Tac. *Ann.* 4.52, 66), adulation of Caligula (Dio 59.19), and refusal to retire when his powers failed (Tac. *Ann.* 4.52, Quint. *Inst.* 12.11.3). Syme detects Tacitus' pride in his own historical writing in the praise of Nonianus over Afer (*Ann.* 14.19; 1958:338).

[18] Aufidius Bassus, another representative pre-Neronian writer, is paired with Nonianus as an outstanding newer historian, by both Tacitus (*Dial.* 23.2) and Quintilian (*Inst.* 10.1.103, with Bassus "a little older" than Nonianus). Bassus too seems to have died before the worst Neronian period (Sen. *Ep.* 30).

and the *Wars with Germany* was devoted especially to Claudius' father Drusus and no doubt also his brother Germanicus.[19] Next, his *Education of the Orator (Studiosus)* may have implicitly or explicitly praised the young Nero and his tutor Seneca, in the last years of Claudius' reign or the first years of Nero's (compare Quintilian *Inst.* 4 praef. 3–5). His next work, *Uncertain Speech (Dubius Sermo)* marks the interval of Nero's last years, when political "slavery" made a "freer" topic dangerous.[20] Uncertain speech is indeed a fitting title for times when speaking freely is impossible. Then, his continuation of Aufidius Bassus' *History* celebrates the new free times when such a work is again possible—perhaps in its preface, like those of Tacitus' *Agricola* and *Histories.* Certainly its contents celebrated all three Flavians, as the Elder tells us himself (*NH* praef. 20). Finally, the *Natural Histories* with its "lightness" (*levioris operae,* praef. 12) and its jocular teasing of Titus in the opening pages flaunts the Flavians' unpretentious, accessible camaraderie, and the corresponding political relaxation which can allow curiosity and erudition for their own sakes. Vespasianic traits seem also to be echoed in its unpretentious, practical outlook (praef. 16 *utilitatem*), its almost financial approach to collecting and saving facts (over 12,000, praef. 16), the diligent work required (praef. 18, Plin. 3.5.8), and the time-saving table of contents.[21] The overall plan echoes Vespasianic propaganda, with the unpretentious New Man gathering together and uniting the entire Empire of knowledge that has accumulated from prior generations, even to the edge of the Greek and non-Greek world (*NH* praef. 13), for the benefit and profit of present-day Romans.

At 1.13.3, then, Pliny is reaching back beyond Domitianic and Vespasianic patronage of the arts, beyond Nero's bizarre patronage and performance, to the last "free" time, in Claudius' reign. Pomponius Secundus can represent his literary recitations in the Claudian age as a republican political event in which he can "appeal to the people" against a censorious friend (*ad populum provoco,* 7.17.11); literature is free enough to be a substitute of sorts for free politics.[22] Vespasian's time is less suitable for Pliny to use as the Golden Age

---

[19] Tiberius was suspected of resenting the popularity of his dead brother (Tac. *Ann.* 1.33.2), and of ordering the death his more popular nephew (*Ann.* 3.16.1, Suet. *Calig.* 2). Syme suggests that Pliny wrote the book to honor the powerful Agrippina, Germanicus' daughter (1958:288).

[20] *Scripsit sub Nerone novissimis annis, cum omne studiorum genus paulo liberius et erectius periculosum servitus fecisset* (3.5.5).

[21] Serbat 1986:2095–96, Citroni Marchetti 1992.3249, 3296. Diligent labor at night was a conventional trope of prefaces, as a (disingenuous) disclaimer of talent, Janson 1964:160. Pliny's own boasts of laziness have the opposite effect, as a covert boast of his talent.

[22] By now, *provocatio* went not to the "people" but to the emperor who soon replaced praetorian courts (*RE* 23.2.2456 s.v. *provocatio*).

of poetry, since Vespasian's patronage seems to have emphasized prose.[23] Moreover, the banishment of philosophers and the execution of Helvidius Priscus for speaking too freely makes Vespasian's an unsuitable reign to praise for the free cultivation of letters. But above all, in his eagerness to denigrate Domitian, Pliny does not let even Titus or Vespasian escape lightly. Domitian was certainly a patron of poetry, and Quintilian even suggests that his youthful epic poetry makes him the supreme Roman poet (*Inst.* 10.1.91–92), but since he was a canonical Bad Emperor, poetry under him was tainted with adulation.[24] This may help account for the absence of Statius from Pliny's letters. Unlike Martial and Italicus, he died too early to recant through denigration of Domitian (Gamberini 1983:176 n. 3). Domitian's reign also saw such notorious executions for literary crimes as Rusticus' death for his praises of Thrasea and the elder Helvidius, and Herennius Senecio's for his biography of Helvidius.[25]

Pliny's picture of uninvited gate-crashing implies the denigration of the unfree times of Domitian or Nero by contrast. An uninvited appearance by a Bad Emperor at a recitation of poetry or history would surely be a terrifying event. Does the work have enough panegyric? Does it add enough irony or teasing to prevent the impression of forced praise?[26] Will the audience smile at the wrong time, or applaud loudly enough? Evidently these fears did not apply to the reign of Claudius, possibly because he was too absent-minded to notice or care. No doubt the entrance of one of the powerful ex-slaves or wives, who were said to run the empire in actuality, would have created a far more anxious stir. Presumably in the restored age of literary freedom, a sudden entrance by Nerva or Trajan would also cause no terror, but then again they are not scatter-brained enough for such a stunt.[27]

Pliny's flashback to Claudius reaches back past the crimes and indignities that Nero and the Flavians heaped upon literature and poetry, to a relatively pristine period when literature was free and honored. Claudius is also one of the three Julio-Claudians canonized as "divine," indicating a smooth transition

---

[23] On Vespasian's literary patronage, see Coleman 1986:3088 ("Vespasian had cultivated a Flavian atmosphere distinct from the idiosyncrasies of Nero's reign"). Aper's vigorous speech in the *Dialogus* on the danger and uselessness of poetry is set in Vespasian's reign. On Vespasian's patronage gift of 500,000 sestertii to the poet Saleius Bassus (*Dial.* 9.5), see D'Espèrey 1986:3052.

[24] On Domitian's literary patronage see Suet. *Dom.* 4.4, Coleman 1986:3095–3111.

[25] Suet. *Dom.* 10.3, Tac. *Agric.* 2, Plin. 7.19.5; Coleman 1986:3106. According to Plutarch, Thrasea himself had written a biography of Cato the Younger (*Cat. Min.* 25.1).

[26] Ahl 1984:59.

[27] Claudius boasted of ending the accusations for treason *(maiestas)* and literary crimes (Dio 60.3.6); the new regime under Nerva also boasted of putting an end to *maiestas* accusations (Dio 68.1.2).

without posthumous denigration or *damnatio memoriae*.[28] In any case, Pliny tends to treat Claudius as intermediate between Good Emperor and Bad. Although he appears in two of the worst positions in the whole collection, as the founding enemy of the opposition clan (in the Arria letter, 3.16) and as the emperor behind Pliny's most indignant invective (in the Pallas letter, 8.6), in this letter he is treated with relative respect. Indeed, even the other two letters present him in a relatively good light, considering the circumstances. In the Arria letter, Claudius is a silent figurehead against whom Scribonianus revolts and before whom Arria insults Scribonianus' wife. The immediate point is not whether Paetus was right in revolting or Claudius cruel in having him executed, but that Arria was noble in standing by her husband and killing herself. In the Pallas letter, Pliny carefully directs his indignation against Pallas, and almost more, against the Senate for being so obsequious to the ex-slave. He pretends that it was the Senate's initiative to vote him exorbitant honors and that the Senate had to be restrained by the more moderate Claudius. He ignores the possibility that the Senate was tacitly forced to go to obsequious extremes to allow Claudius to play the moderate while showing off the Senate's republican freedom: this is the imperial game perfected under Tiberius, according to Tacitus. Pliny summarizes the shameful roles in this charade by saying that Pallas was insolent, Claudius allowed it to happen (*patientiam,* 8.6.15), and the Senate was groveling. Claudius is clearly assigned the least damning vice, in accordance with his widespread representation as being too oblivious to notice or prevent the crimes of his ex-slaves and wives.

Pliny's anecdote of Claudius in the audience reflects this intermediate treatment of Claudius as worst of the Good Emperors and best of Bad Emperors. Even his title is intermediate in respectfulness, neither the official reverent Divus Iulius, Divus Augustus, Divus Nerva (5.3.5), nor the bare Domitianus or Nero (1.5.1), but the respectful title Caesar (often used in the *Panegyric* for Trajan, but only once for Domitian, quoted in the "flattering or mocking" last words of the Vestal Virgin (4.11.7).[29] Furthermore, the narration of the story subtly undercuts the laudatory point. Claudius' behavior reflects the denigratory tradition of his obliviousness and tendency to inappropriate action. He is walking in the imperial residence, and having heard a shout and having asked the reason, he is told that Nonianus is reciting (3). The imperial retinue is more aware of events than the emperor. Then he suddenly and unexpectedly bursts in. Emperors are not supposed to behave

---

[28] The two more recently deified emperors, Vespasian and Titus, were the only emperors succeeded by an immediate biological relative, who has the most to gain by avoiding denigration of the predecessor (*Pan.* 11.1).

[29] *Caesaris* at 1.18.3 might be Titus or Domitian, or it could be deliberately vague.

this way. They do not attend private events such as readings, or if they do they plan it carefully in advance to fit the needs of imperial dignity and propaganda. Claudius, not reared to be a ruler, forgets that he must always act as an emperor, just as Pliny must always act as a senator. He waxes eloquent in the Senate on the fast food of his childhood, and rushes up to join a banquet of Salian priests (Suet. *Claud.* 33.1, 40.1). Does the story prove that even the busy Claudius found time for recitations, or rather that Claudius was so aimless and idle that he could be expected to stroll into a recitation on any given day?

The main point of the story is that in those days Nonianus could draw an audience large enough and enthusiastic enough to make the strolling Claudius eager to come hear him. We might recall that Claudius himself was a historian, and though his speaking could draw mockery, at least it did not have to be said of him, as of Nero, that he was the first of the emperors to need borrowed eloquence (Tac. *Ann.* 13.3.2). Pliny's story makes Claudius seem better than Nero, but not so good as Trajan, who showed his accessibility in carefully arranged visits and banquets (Dio 68.7.3) rather than in eager and perhaps jealous impulses, and who was busy at the dramatic date of the letter (April–May 97) with military activities, not with wandering around Rome aimlessly.

The conventional picture of the weak, sickly, unmilitary Claudius makes a faintly amusing contrast with the opening interjection "by Hercules!" (*At hercule,* 3), especially since the active, military Trajan cultivated a resemblance to Hercules.[30] The choice of addressee, Sosius Senecio, may emphasize the implied contrast between Claudius and Trajan. Senecio was selected consul ordinarius for 99, the first year after Trajan's accession, he was a high-placed protégé of Trajan (cos. ord. again in 107), and like Trajan he was a military man.[31] Nerva, on the other hand, the reigning emperor at the dramatic date of the letter, shared certain traits with Claudius. Weak, sickly (Dio 68.1.3), and unmilitary, he was suddenly placed on the throne on the day of assassination, without official preparation, and never quite established a firm hold on power. Perhaps Claudius' unsettling similarity to Nerva helped shield him from receiving Pliny's mockery or contempt too openly. Only the different outcomes of their choice of adoptive successors allow for an explicit contrast in Nerva's favor (*Pan.* 7).

The balance between cheerfulness and indignation in the letter points both to political and to literary anxieties, to the uneasy political situation at the start

[30] 3.20.12, *Pan.* 14.5, 82.7, Dio Chrys. 1.84, Mattingly & Sydenham 1926, Trajan nos. 689–90, 699–702.
[31] Syme associates him with his father-in-law Frontinus as a supporter of Trajan's adoption (1958:35 n. 2, 53, 649–51).

of the New Age and to the uneasy position of the writer while literature is readjusting to the new "freedom."[32] Claudius at the penultimate moment before literature (and politics) fell into ruin makes a contrast with Nerva at a time when politics (and literature) are struggling to a restoration. At this moment in spring 97 the restoration is still fragile, with senators fearful of coming reigns of terror (9.13 in mid-97) and the praetorians close to revolt (*Pan.* 6, Dio 68.3.3). Writers are venturing forward, but the audience is reluctant, not making proper use of its new freedom and "telling stories" (*fabulis,* 2) instead of attending the recital. Perhaps it should be no surprise that talking about the still-unstable political situation is more gripping than listening to elegant poems on love pangs and star etiologies.

Yet the solid and confident image of Pliny and his friends points the way to the coming stability under Trajan. They create a stable, encouraging situation by enacting it. In both literature and politics, proper praise and promotion of merit is commonly said to create and encourage merit, as a self-fulfilling prophecy (e.g. 1.14.1, 4.16.3). Devoted supporters like Pliny form the stable kernel around which the coming period of prosperity can crystallize, just as Pliny and even more his friend Sosius Senecio form the backbone of political support upon which Trajan's regime will establish itself. Senecio is the highest-ranking addressee of Book 1, and is perhaps chosen to be the recipient of this letter more because he is a Trajanic patron of letters than because he is a man of letters himself. He is Plutarch's dedicatee in the *Lives* and elsewhere, but in Pliny receives only a recommendation letter requesting military patronage (4.4), in addition to this letter.

We might think of this letter, near the center of Book 1, as an alternate dedication letter, and aimed in the more usual direction, upwards on the scale of political status. It has less second-person engagement than any other letter in the book except 1.17, no direct address, no request, and no reference to the addressee's statements or views. Senecio might not even write back: here too Pliny suggests an alteration in the usual cycle of friendly favors. As Pliny looks downward to his circle of poet-friends, expecting no direct reward for his patronizing services, so too he looks upward to his connection in Trajan's inner circle without hoping for direct reward or exchange.[33] To make the full transition to stable government, hierarchical relationships are temporarily more important than reciprocal ones. Later in the corpus, and hence later into the new regime, Pliny portrays recitations with thriving audiences, and portrays himself as a frequent reciter as well as listener. Problems with

---

[32] Tacitus also speaks of the slow and difficult restoration of *studia* (*Agric.* 3.1).

[33] "The emperor ensured the loyalty of an inner circle of friends with his *beneficia* and thus granted them the resources to build their own clientèles whose loyalty was thus indirectly secured" (Saller 1982:78).

audiences are reduced to isolated instances, whether the unnamed rudely silent listeners or the unfortunate interjection by Iavolenus (6.15, 6.17). With Pliny's and Trajan's positions both secure, reciprocal relations can predominate again in the public literary arena.

The letter reveals literary anxieties still more openly than it reveals political anxieties. Pliny is in a year off from political office, with no guarantee of political patronage continuing under the new emperor or emperors. Perhaps for the rest of his life he will remain a praetorian senator in a relatively powerless Senate. The only meaningful activity of which he can be sure is literature; he must rely on literature to give his life meaning. A unifying thread throughout the letter is using time, spending time, wasting time. Many write poetry, few wish to hear it. Is listening to poetry a *waste of time?* Is writing poetry a *waste of time?* The Bad Listener *wiles away* with mere gossip the time that he *should spend* listening (2), and complains that he has *wasted the day*—precisely because he has not *wasted it.*

The Bad Listener is a doubly negative counter-exemplum for wasting time, as opposed to Pliny the Ideal Listener. The Bad Listener wastes the day outside (*tempus... conterunt,* 2) when he should be listening to the reading, and he wastes *every other day* even more so (4): "he complains that he has wasted the day *because he has not wasted it*" [unlike his usual days]. Pliny, on the other hand, makes the best use he can of his day of listening, as a solid supporter of literary renewal, even though he has more important things to do, and to write. We recall Pliny's complaints that typical upper-class favors at Rome make one "throw away the day" (1.9.3 *dies... absumpsi*). Pliny himself has "used up" in the city more time than he had allotted (*consumpsi,* 6).[34] Underlying all these allusions to using one's time is the paradigmatic example of Pliny's uncle, who did not spend an extra moment on sleeping, traveling, or even correcting a mispronunciation (3.5.12).

Poetry stands lower in the ranking of genres than the more Romanized and respectable genres of oratory or history (Syme 1958:93). Pliny regularly treats it as mere diversion from, and practice for, more serious genres. In praising poetry, Pliny is praising literature even in its least honorable form. Praise for poetry is praise for pure literature, for art for art's sake. If writing or listening to poetry is valuable, all the more valuable is oratory, which combines literary skill with political service, or history, which has information to teach. Accordingly, the eminently practical Elder Pliny wrote only practical works such as historical and informative treatises, and in the early books of letters Pliny presents himself as a writer of oratory only, aside from a commemorative biography for his friends Spurinna and Cottia, in

---

[34] With the shift from *conterere* to *consumere* Pliny distances himself from the masses (Merwald 1964:33).

honor of their son (3.10). Pliny can give a rather lighthearted frown at the rude audience practices because he is himself immune from them. He delivers his literary productions in the thick of trials and debates, where an interested audience is assured, not only at the Centumviral Court where hired claques prevail, but principally at the Senate, where his most important speeches are delivered.

We can assume that Pliny will go off to his retreat to write not light verse but serious speeches "which future generations will be able to compare to the pages even of Cicero" (3.21.5 = Martial 10.19.16–17). The relationship between Pliny and the poets of 1.13 reproduces the relationship between Pliny and Martial. Pliny's subordinates in political status and literary genre receive his patronage (and even money, 3.21.2); he either attends their readings during his time of *otium* in April of his year off, or reads their works late at night (3.21.5). Pliny will then go off to his retreat to write something more truly meaningful, something which his mere poet friends cannot match because they do not have the political rank to be chosen to conduct a major senatorial prosecution, for example. It goes without saying that *Pliny* does not deserve special praise, as his friends do (1), for writing despite bad audiences. We might even associate Pliny's *successus* of mid-97 (6) with the composition of his *de Helvidi Ultione,* which he must surely have written out in advance in accordance with his usual practice (9.36.2, 9.40.2) rather than later after an impromptu performance, as he claims (9.13.23). This speech shows that the ultimate value of Pliny's life of literature is that it creates political benefit (both for the State and for himself personally), as well as having worth, like poetry, as pure literature. One of the three advantages of attacking Certus in the Senate was in pushing himself forward (or as he more discreetly puts it, "pushing 'oneself' forward," 9.13.2 *se proferendi, OLD* s.v. *se* 3). It seems likely that the speech helped earn him the treasury post as Certus' successor (Sherwin-White 1966:499), along with Cornutus Tertullus (5.14.5), who supported Pliny in the senatorial debate (9.13.16). Similar Nervan-Domitianic imperial commendation had followed his prosecution of Baebius Massa in 93 (7.33.9), perhaps contributing to his promotion to a treasury post for 94–96. The Certus affair, as well as the Massa case, might actually have been undertaken with imperial encouragement. Much action behind the scenes remains murky in the events leading up to Trajan's adoption in October.

The political undertones of Pliny's literary activities suggest a response to Tacitus' *Dialogus,* which seems to underlie many of Pliny's programmatic discussions of poetry and oratory. Tacitus included a harsh attack on poetry for being less useful or prestigious than oratory while being just as dangerous; the speech in reply argued that poetry has greater lasting value (10, 12). Pliny maintains the hierarchy of oratory over poetry without disparaging poetry as a waste of time. The daily succession of poets might be people without access to Pliny's prestigious oratorical arenas, or they might be orators polishing up their style in their spare time. Judging from Saturninus and other friends of Pliny, most recited short poems that do not require the full-time commitment of large-scale poems (7.9.9; cf. Tac. *Dial.* 3.4). Above all, however, the new regime of liberty has ended the days when poetry was almost as dangerous as oratory (*Dial.* 10.5). For Pliny, however, oratory takes up the function of pure literary art, written in a "retreat" (1.13.6) that corresponds to Tacitus' description of the rural setting for writing poetry (*Dial.* 9.6, 12.1, Plin. 1.6, 1.9.6).[35]

A final paradox in Pliny's modest boast about his month in the lecture room is that this very letter was written during the month "spent" in the city in this way. Pliny does have a genre as brief and as polished as the poetry he has been hearing, that will be published and will bring him literary prestige just as poems can bring. But the letter guarantees its audience's attention, even for an imperial insider like Senecio who has even more political demands on his time than has Pliny and does *not* attend a month of readings in Rome; Pliny never suggests that *Senecio* should attend readings. Senecio, perhaps a stand-in for his imperial patrons, may not be able to attend readings, but he does want to know that they are taking place, and with no compulsion, as a sign of the beginnings of restored freedom. The suggestion that the busy rulers are taking care of public business banishes the specter of the oblivious Claudius sitting in the lecture room while the empire hurtles toward a Neronian disaster. The high honors that Senecio will have received by the time this letter is published allow the reader to relax in the supposition that stability has been restored for good under Trajan's rule, and to try to forget that this stability depends on the well-being and on the will of a single man.

---

[35] See Murgia 1985:181 on the many thematic links between the *Dialogus* and Pliny's Book 1.

PRODUCING THE NEXT DESERVING GENERATION
OF THE RULING CLASS (1.14)

Letter 1.14 shows Pliny in the role of marriage-broker. As a friend on both the groom's side and the bride's side (with Mauricus and the dead Rusticus), Pliny has the opportunity to indulge in lavishing praise on both sides; the letter combines obituary with recommendation. Being the link in this transaction between friends, Pliny can present his accustomed theme, the circulation of favors, as enacted and symbolized by the exchange of letters, and in this case by the exchange of a woman. As often, the abundant praise reflects back onto Pliny himself, and upward to the emperor. An ideal transaction of upper-class life suggests a portrayal of the ideal senator and the ideal emperor, who serve as models for each other, and whose ideal behavior enables the regeneration of the upper class.

Any letter to the Rusticus group inevitably has political overtones. Pliny's two letters to Mauricus (1.14 and 2.18) advertise his closeness to a symbol of the opposition group and portray its restoration to the Roman ruling class under the new regime. Letter 2.18 involves Pliny in the ruling-class education of Rusticus' sons, and 1.14 in the marriage of his daughter, which will produce the next generation of ruling-class men. Mauricus himself returns to become an intimate in the imperial circles of Nerva and Trajan (4.22). Under the "free" reigns of Nerva and Trajan, Mauricus' outspokenness is rewarded, not punished: the sequence of executions suffered by this opposition group under Claudius, Nero, Vespasian, and Domitian has come to an end in the New Age.[1]

---

[1] Rusticus himself almost joined Thrasea as a martyr under Nero (Tac. *Ann.* 16.26.3), and bore a scar as a memorial of his independent role as mediator during the Flavians' takeover (Tac. *Hist.* 3.80.2, Plin. 1.5.2). Mauricus himself tried to stir up a backlash against Neronian *delatores* in the opening days of the Flavians (*Hist.* 4.40.4).

Pliny's candidate Acilianus is from "that Italy of ours," North Italy, the "fatherland" (*patria,* 4) of Pliny and presumably of Mauricus and Rusticus. The very name Rusticus suggests the "rustic" qualities (*etiam rusticitatis,* 4), the restraint, frugality and severity which Pliny claims to be typical of the North. Pliny, like Tacitus, associates the rustic virtues of the North with olden times (Tac. *Agric.* 4.2, *Ann.* 3.55.3, 16.5.1, Sherwin-White 1966:117, 207). North Italy "still preserves" a great deal of the "ancient" rural qualities. The term "ancient" is common in the letters as a political compliment, and belongs to the ideology of "restoration" that runs throughout imperial history as a complement to the theme of the "New Age." The new emperor that brings in a new age, whether that of Augustus or Nerva-Trajan, simultaneously restores the ancient virtues of republican Rome.[2] For example, Pliny calls his colleague Cornutus Tertullus *antiquus* (5.14.3), a copy and model of ancient Roman virtue. The term is associated with imperial propaganda at 10.14, where Pliny calls Trajan's victory "most ancient," most like the victories of earlier times, at *Pan.* 83.5, where he calls Plotina "ancient," and at 7.33.9, where Nerva himself, before his accession, calls Pliny's behavior in the Massa case "similar to the ancients."[3]

It had long been conventional to admire the "ideal" earlier times, which could be dated at any time from mythical origins to as recently as the edge of living memory (as at 2.14.3, 9; 3.20.4), but the most prominent distinction between "now" and "earlier times" throughout the letters is the dividing line between republic and empire, whether it is dated from Augustus (e.g. *Ann.* 1.2–3) or Julius Caesar (e.g. Sen. *Ben.* 2.20.2, Tac. *Ann.* 13.3.2).[4] "People of old" had more political material to report (3.20.10), and Pliny's model Cicero embodies the end of the free republic (9.2), just as his Greek model Demosthenes embodies a similar end of Greek freedom under Philip and Alexander.[5] Pliny's letter to Mauricus gives the Golden Age of republican virtue a place: Cisalpine Gaul, a place that is more Roman than Rome. Rome itself has been corrupted by the influx of "foreign" urban vices, the opposite of the true Roman rustic virtues of restraint, frugality, and severity. The imperial vices at *Pan.* 82.9 are typical new urban vices: dice, sexual crime,

---

[2] Nerva used the coin legend *Roma renascens,* previously used in 68–69, probably under Galba (Mattingly & Sydenham 1926:227, 229). Moreover, Nerva's reissue coinage honored only Augustus, as the first imperial founder, unlike the many emperors thus honored by the Flavians and by Trajan (1926:302–04).

[3] Similarly *priscae frugalitatis,* of Aristo at 1.22.4.

[4] Béranger (1953:4 n. 3) gives citations on which was considered the first "emperor."

[5] Tacitus has Maternus connect Demosthenes' and Cicero's eloquence with their similar political situations, though in good panegyric style he emphasizes the civil strife of their times rather than the end of political freedom (*Dial.* 37.6). Compare [Longinus] *On the Sublime* 44.2–3, Bartsch 1994:110, 203.

luxury. The vices of Rome are the vices of the Bad Emperors, abundantly represented throughout Suetonius, whereas Pliny praises Trajan for shunning these Roman urban vices. Even Trajan's pleasures are rustic, hunting and sailing (*Pan.* 82.8).[6]

Ironically, this "homeland" of ancient Italian virtue was not even a part of Italy until its status was changed by Julius Caesar and Octavian, that is, from the opening years of the Empire.[7] It is no surprise that an imperial dynast has more power and more motivation to expand ruling-class privileges than does the conservative Senate (Chilver 1941:8–9, Hopkins 1983:188). Tacitus records Claudius facing senatorial opposition to admitting Gallic nobles to the Senate. Tacitus' version of his speech (*Ann.* 11.24) looks back to Caesar's citizenship grant to Cisalpine Gaul (11.24.3) and forward to a time when this expansion of privileges, in the best ancient tradition, will itself become an example (11.24.7)—evidently an allusion to expanding provincial opportunities under Trajan, and to Trajan himself, the first emperor from outside Italy. Pliny's praise of North Italy implies praise of Trajan. If the outermost district can be the true Italy of old republican times by "preserving" old-time Roman virtues, then the Spanish Trajan can be the ideal Roman and the restorer of republican virtue.[8]

This letter on the marriage of Rusticus' daughter implies praise of the new rulers. The very presence of Mauricus and Rusticus' children at Rome, participating fully in upper-class life, shows that freedom has been restored. Marriage and child-rearing are themselves topics of imperial praise. On Trajan's entrance procession in 99, women finally started taking pleasure in giving birth to citizens and soldiers (*Pan.* 22.3); under a Bad Emperor, people are unwilling to have children (10.2.2).[9] Sherwin-White wonders whether Pliny, widowed in 97, was half-expected to marry Rusticus' daughter himself (1966:117 on 1.14.1). But it is more natural to imagine that Pliny had already remarried, or at least had already made arrangements for his remarriage, so

---

[6] The characteristic *frugalitas* that Pliny attributes to North Italy (1.14.4) is an imperial virtue at *Pan.* 49.5; cf. 51.1.

[7] The people of the Transpadane region were given Roman citizenship by Caesar in 49 B.C.E. (Dio 41.36.3), and the provincial status of Cisalpine Gaul was abolished in 41 (Dio 48.12.5, Appian *BC* 5.3; Chilver 1941:10, Sherwin-White 1973:159).

[8] Syme (1958:27) comments on the paradox of how it was the innovating upstarts who promoted the values denoted by words like *antiquus* and *priscus*. "It was often the *homines novi* who, like Cato and Cicero, articulated most clearly the attitudes of their new social home... Tacitus and Pliny are the best examples" (Alföldy 1985:118). Compare Edwards 1993:17 (who gives as examples Horace, Seneca, the two Plinii, and Tacitus): "The moralising literature... was in general produced by writers whose claims to being authentic members of the Roman elite might be in some way open to question."

[9] The idea that children are no pleasure under a tyranny is a standard trope (e.g. Cic. *Fam.* 5.16.3, Sen. *Contr.* 2.5.1–4, Sen. *de Clem.* 1.13.5).

Mauricus could consult him without awkwardness on either side. Now that the New Age has begun, Pliny and Acilianus are arranging marriages for themselves and hoping for children, and Rusticus' children are able to enter the adult upper class through marriage or education.

Rusticus' children are still young, though Rusticus was already tribune in 66 and thus probably born before 36. His children, still teen-aged in 97 (ready for marriage and education), must have been born when he was over 45 years old. The timing resembles Pliny's own (age 36–40 at remarriage, 97–101; age 46 at wife's miscarriage, 107). The prospective groom, too, is over 35 years old, having already "run through" the *cursus* up to the praetorship (1.14.7), though he is "just a few years younger" than Pliny (*minor pauculis annis,* 3). The impression that this letter is from soon after Mauricus' return goes uneasily with the claim that Acilianus is a few years younger than Pliny but also of praetorian rank, or over 35. We could assume an early praetorship, a late letter date, or an exaggeration to describe Pliny at 36 and Acilianus at 35 in 97 C.E. (the ages Sherwin-White gives, 1966:117) as "a few years" apart. In any case, Pliny has clearly used a bit of stylization to create the impression of a praetorian senator, somewhat younger than Pliny, marrying Rusticus' daughter at the beginning of the new era.[10]

Apparently this is the point in the *cursus* at which marriage (or a second marriage) and especially child-rearing fit in. If we accept Syme's views on early marriage for senatorial men (in Augustus' time, usually in their early twenties, 1987:327), we might suspect a divorce, an "unpleasing phenomenon" that "Pliny refuses to admit" in his decorous pages (Syme 1968:73).[11] Sherwin-White (1966:117) speculates on a second marriage for Rusticus to account for the young children.[12] But Syme also observes a pattern of postponed marriage, at least for late Republican times.[13] In sum, either Acilianus the "new man" has waited until his political standing can bring him the most advantageous match, or perhaps he is entering a new match after a providentially childless first marriage.

---

[10] Bodel (1995) shows that letter 5.16 on Fundanus' daughter contains similar chronological stylization.

[11] Similarly, Parkin (1992:125) gives the mid-to-late twenties as a typical marriage age for Roman men, but the early twenties for the elite, especially the senatorial class.

[12] As Syme says (1987:328), "when an aristocrat marries very late, suspicion of an earlier wife cannot be suppressed." And as Treggiari says, "it may be postulated that as a man moves up the *cursus honorum,* he moves into successive 'brackets' as a potential husband or father-in-law" (1991:92).

[13] "At the capital a man might wait until he had made his mark in the courts of law or found influential patrons... Especially if he were a *novus homo"* (1987:325). Treggiari gives the upper-class men's marrying age as the late twenties to early thirties (1991:400).

Pliny virtually acknowledges the existence of the political "marriageability brackets" when he tells Mauricus that Acilianus has already "released" Mauricus from the need to campaign for him. Now that he is established as a senator, he can "buy" a more valuable marriage connection with his status, since he does have to factor in the "cost" of getting himself advanced up the ranks; by having served as quaestor, tribune, and praetor, he has *remitted* to his future in-laws the "cost" of canvassing for him (*necessitatem ambiendi remisit,* 7).[14] Conversely, the postponement of child-rearing may have been a political advantage for this "new man" in search of political patronage.

Despite the impression Pliny is eager to give in his election letters, the *cursus* was relatively uncompetitive up to the praetorship. For the twenty-odd slots in the lower *cursus* (20 *vigintiviri* plus emperor's candidates, 20 quaestors plus recently adlected senators) there were probably about 18 praetorships.[15] The real differences lay in receiving appointments in the years between offices, and in the consulship, where only about half of all surviving senators reached the approximately eight positions per year (Hopkins 1983:124, 129). Pliny himself received prestigious civilian prefectures before and after his consulship, and a successful military career would include major army commands. In emphasizing that canvassing is no longer necessary, Pliny gives us the impression that Acilianus' career is virtually over. In part this means that the consulship and other high appointments are more purely a matter of imperial patronage, but we are led to feel that there will be no higher career. Acilianus has gone as far as an ordinary new man can expect to go, and he might not go any further. Perhaps this makes him especially suitable for Rusticus' daughter. The daughter of the famous Stoic hero needs a husband who will have children, not one who will postpone them in favor of his future career. Someone as prestigious as Rusticus' daughter does need at least a low-ranking senator, but no more; the groom's money is more important than his lofty political prospects. Rusticus' daughter will not marry a Suetonius or a Pliny, or a Nerva, Trajan, or Hadrian. This will be a marriage of blood with money: the bride provides power and prestige, the groom wealth.

A marriage recommendation gives Pliny a perfect opportunity to depict an idealized network of kinship and friendship relations. At each step Pliny is at pains to portray a subtle combination, of equal, reciprocal emotional

---

[14] *Remisit* (1.14.7) suggests "waiving" a debt, as at 10.48 *remisit... remuneranda (OLD* s.v. *remitto* 13). The financial diction continues at 1.14.8 *debet... quasi praemium dari.*
[15] Hopkins (1983:157 n. 51) objects against this figure that it "is incompatible with the known competition at elections" (cf. Sherwin-White 1966:119), but the existence of any competition at all would lend itself to imperial praise, and would tend to be exaggerated to disguise the fact that the emperor virtually controlled everyone's political career.

attachments, together with hierarchies of influence and obedience. He camouflages systems of patronage under the guise of friendly ties of affection, encouragement, and advice, and correspondingly he camouflages the power and wealth that creates a member of the upper class under the guise of personal, moral qualities. This letter is about creating new members of the upper class, and the personal sketches of Pliny and Acilianus depict how a child makes the transition from being born into upper-class rank to achieving full upper-class power. The letter thus mystifies the hierarchies of power, disguising inherited power as earned merit.[16]

> Petis ut fratris tui filiae prospiciam maritum; quod merito mihi potissimum iniungis. Scis enim quanto opere summum illum virum suspexerim dilexerimque, quibus ille adulescentiam meam exhortationibus foverit, quibus etiam laudibus ut landandus viderer effecerit. Nihil est quod a te mandari mihi aut maius aut gratius, nihil quod honestius a me suscipi possit, quam ut eligam iuvenem, ex quo nasci nepotes Aruleno Rustico deceat. (1.14.1–2)

> You ask me to keep an eye out for a husband for your brother's daughter, a task which you properly assign to me more than anyone else. For you know how much I looked up to and loved that supreme man, with what exhortations he tended my younger years, indeed with what praises he caused me to seem to be worthy of praise. There is nothing greater or more rewarding that you could entrust to me, nothing nobler that I could undertake, than to chose the young man by whom it would be suitable for grandchildren to be born to Arulenus Rusticus.

Pliny's relation to Acilianus echoes Rusticus' relation to Pliny (Bütler 1970:103). In both cases, Pliny mystifies the power of a patron, by subsuming the power under the rubric of mutual friendly relations, while gently highlighting the hierarchy of authority. At every level of society, real hierarchy combines with a show of friendly equality. At one extreme, the emperor himself condescends to treat upper-class citizens as friendly equals (e.g. 6.31.2 *comitatem,* Pan. 49.4 *socialitas*), and at the other extreme, the upper-class citizen treats his slaves with "mildness" (1.4.4, 3.14.5) and even "paternal" affection (5.19.2).

Accordingly, Pliny's opening reference to Mauricus' request makes himself the lesser friend: Mauricus "imposes" on Pliny the duty of keeping an eye out for a groom. As Trisoglio notes (1973:218 n. 252), the word *iniungo* can have

---

[16] Compare the demystifying approach to patronage which Saller accurately describes at 1982:38 (though without entirely agreeing with it himself): "The patronal ideology and the concept of social cohesion have served to distract attention from the basic 'class structure'... the patronal ideology represents a false consciousness for the client and helps the patron maintain his superiority." Bütler comments uncritically about making young relatives of a "great man" worthy of their parents (1970:104).

a harsh tone, but as often in Pliny it implies his willing acceptance of a friendly obligation as if it is a command received from above (e.g. 2.18.1 from Mauricus, 6.16.3 from Tacitus). One might wonder, though, who is actually doing whom a favor. The answer depends on which side is marrying upwards, the bride or the groom, and is therefore obvious at the face value: power outweighs mere money, especially to this Stoic family which can afford to scorn money on account of its own high imperial connections. The relatively unknown Acilianus, whose shaky fame needs to be shored up with three other half-known relatives, will be outclassed by his bride, and their children will be known as "Arulenus Rusticus' grandchildren" (2). Conventional gender relations will be reversed: the groom is the cipher brought into the family to allow Rusticus and Mauricus to produce the next generation. Thus, Pliny is really doing Acilianus the favor, and Mauricus is doing Pliny the favor of allowing him to select the candidate for the honored position of nephew-in-law.

Pliny's diction does, to be sure, soften the impression that the lofty Mauricus is entrusting the big decision to Pliny. Mauricus has merely asked Pliny to "keep an eye out" for a groom, but Pliny rephrases this as being commissioned to "pick out" a young man worthy of fathering Rusticus' grandchildren (1 *prospiciam*, 2 *eligam*). Pliny goes on to describe the favor as if it is being rendered in opposing directions. It is both "most gratifying" (*nihil... gratius,* 2) and hence a favor from Mauricus to Pliny, but it is also "most noble" *(nihil... honestius),* and hence a return favor from Pliny to Mauricus, as if in return for Rusticus' patronage ("encouragement") to the young Pliny.

Pliny is of course not openly being given the power to choose the groom, but only the power to suggest a promising candidate. Mauricus, the bride's closest male relative, will make the final choice. Yet we can guess from the fact that Pliny is publishing the letter that Acilianus did marry the niece.[17] The body of the letter is therefore designed to convince Mauricus and the reader that he was the only possible winning candidate, the ideal combination of rustic virtue and Roman political success, of wealth and severity, with the good looks (and availability for marriage) of youth together with advanced senatorial rank. Mauricus will not have regrets, and in fact he did not have regrets, from this perfect match. One would have had to "search for a long time" for a groom if he had not been "prepared and as if prearranged by foresight" (3 *paratus et quasi provisus;* cf. 1 *prospiciam*). The unspecified preparation and foresight which mark out this candidate imply self-praise for

---

[17] Treggiari 1991:88; compare Della Corte 1967:19 n. 27 on 1.24, Williams 1968:23 on Horace *Epist.* 1.9. Syme's attempts to identify unsuccessful recommendations (1958:83, 1985:351) have not been universally accepted (contra, Sherwin-White 1966:179, 566).

Pliny, for it is actually Pliny who fashioned him, as Rusticus fashioned Pliny, and it is Pliny who, with the shared system of good Roman values, has recognized Acilianus' ideal suitability and is pointing him out to Mauricus.

> Qui quidem diu quaerendus fuisset, nisi paratus et quasi provisus esset Minicius Acilianus, qui me ut iuvenis iuvenem (est enim minor pauculis annis) familiarissime diligit, reveretur ut senem. Nam ita formari a me et institui cupit, ut ego a vobis solebam. (3–4)

> It would have been a long time in looking for him, if Minicius Acilianus had not been providentially (so to speak) ready, someone who loves me most imtimately as one young man to another (he is just a few years younger), but respects me as an elder. For he desires to be shaped and trained by me in the same way that I used to be by you two.

Pliny goes on to express the perfect union of opposites in Acilianus by the trope of the union of contrasting ages. Acilianus loves Pliny as youth to youth, but reveres him as youth to elder. The paradox attributes the perfect union of ages to Acilianus as well as to Pliny: just as Pliny is both youthful friend and senatorial elder, so too Acilianus is both distinguished senator (as Pliny's "equal" friend) and modest young protégé (as Pliny's junior).[18] The praise of the young Acilianus rebounds back onto the young-old Pliny, and onto the older Mauricus as well.

Pliny is thus doing a favor to his younger contemporary Acilianus by putting him forward as the groom to this illustrious and powerful family. The letter exemplifies the circulation of favors that is common in recommendation letters: the writer incurs a debt of gratitude from the addressee but earns gratitude from the person commended. We can presume that without this letter or some equivalent recommendation, Acilianus would not have been able to marry into this family. A recommender must pretend that the candidate deserves the favor even aside from the recommender's patronage.[19]

---

[18] The full version of the "union of ages" trope is used for Fundanus' daughter, who united elder, matron, and maiden (5.16.2). Macrinus' wife (possibly Acilianus' stepmother) also combined virtues of various ages (8.5.1), and at 6.26.1 Hadrian's nephew-in-law Fuscus Salinator has the characteristic virtues of a *puer (simplicitas), iuvenis (comitas),* and *senex (gravitas).* In another vein, when Pliny goes shopping for a teacher he gets to enjoy the pleasantness of a youth while receiving the respect due to a senator and orator (2.18.1), and the old Isaeus enjoys the harmless youthful pleasures of scholastic oratory (2.3.6). Compare Cic. *de Sen.* 38.

[19] Tacitus reveals the cold truth when he says that the good governor of Britain promotes by merit *rather than* by recommendation (*Agric.* 19.2), and that people observe a good start to a reign when promotions are based on merit, as Corbulo's (*Ann.* 13.6, 8). Similarly, in the good old days of senatorial elections, people won more often by merit than by patronage (Plin. 3.20.6 *saepius digni quam gratiosi praevalebant*).

In these delicate marriage negotiations the broker cannot openly reveal the circulation of favors, that the addressee is doing the author a favor by doing the candidate a favor and thus making the candidate grateful to the author (as e.g. 2.9.5, 6.8.9).[20] Thus Pliny pretends that he is also repaying a favor to Rusticus. Pliny is the perfect person to undertake the task of finding a groom for Rusticus' daughter, because Pliny owes his present position to Rusticus' encouragement, exhortations, even praises. His gratitude toward Rusticus is formulated in the characteristic combination of flattery and modesty. "By his praises, he made me (only) *seem to be* deserving of praise" (1 *quibus etiam laudibus ut laudandus* viderer *effecerit*)—a modest form of the trope of self-fulfilling prophecy, as at 1.10.3–4.

At each link in this chain of upper-class favors, Pliny naturalizes the artificialities of power.[21] People such as Rusticus, Pliny, Acilianus, and Rusticus' hypothetical descendants have power not because (or not merely because) they happen to be born into the wealthy aristocracy, but because they *deserve* it. The very word frames the letter: Mauricus *deservedly* (1 *merito*) enjoins Pliny above all others to look for a groom, and Pliny loves the young man most warmly as he *deserves* (10 *sicut meretur*). Pliny describes his patronage from Rusticus as mere encouragement and guidance which enabled him to *deserve* "praise," or in other words political power, and Acilianus has received from Pliny what Pliny received from Rusticus and Mauricus. He has been "shaped" and "instructed" into his current position of merit and high rank (4 *formari... et institui*).[22] A "new man" such as Acilianus or Pliny must have been in especially great need of such "shaping" to cross the boundary into the senatorial class; a descendant of the senatorial nobility, such as the young Piso, merely has to act in a way "worthy" of his ancestors (5.17.1 *dignum... maioribus suis*) so that his ancestral portrait masks (*imagines,* 5.17.6) may recognize and accept him as one of their own.

Pliny repeatedly stresses that the ideal senator deserves his position. He introduces the word that best expresses this claim, *dignitas,* in an ironic context, explaining how Acilianus' father deserved to be a senator even though he was not one. His father has consistently avoided our—shall I call it "office-

---

[20] Surviving accounts of marriage negotiations such as Tullia's third marriage (Cic. *Att.* 5.4, 5.13, 5.21, 6.1, 6.6, Treggiari 1991:127–34) or Claudius' fourth marriage (Tac. *Ann.* 12.1–2) indicate how awkward and delicate the negotiations could be.

[21] As Gleason puts it (1994:xxvii), cultures are "systems of euphemism that disguise the arbitrariness of asymmetrical social relations by presenting them as grounded in nature."

[22] These are some of the terms for "forming" a ruling-class member, somewhat comparable to the word "fashioning" in Renaissance English (Greenblatt 1980:2; compare Edwards 1997:30). Cf. *Pan.* 47.1 *mores... quam principaliter formas!* 83.7 *ita imbuit, ita instituit.* The chiastically embedded clauses, linking Pliny's greater friends to him and him to his lesser friends, is a characteristic trope in the letters, for example, 1.18.6, 1.24.4, 6.8.9, 7.23.1.

seeking" or senatorial *"worthiness"* (5 *ambitioni... an dignitati*)? The hint of self-deprecation allows Pliny to flatter Macrinus over his noble scorn of power, but the reader is of course supposed to see that the second term, *dignitas,* is the correct description of Pliny's and Mauricus' rank. The ideal senator does not so much seek out high political position as rise naturally to the position which his merits deserve, even displaying the requisite amount of modest refusal when appropriate. Later, Pliny says that Acilianus' very appearance includes a face suitable to the life of a free person, the bodily beauty of free birth, and even "a certain senatorial propriety" (*facies liberalis... ingenua totius corporis pulchritudo et quidam senatorius decor, 8*). As if in proof that Acilianus is "suited" to the high aristocracy which he has reached by birth and social climbing, his very body has the appearance of the upper class and even the Senate.

Pliny reinterprets the literal bodily "shaping" that comes from aristocratic leisure, diet, exercise, dress, and gesture as inborn qualities marking one out for political power. His appearance is "proper" for a senator (*decor, 8*) just as he is "proper" to beget Rusticus' grandchildren (*ex quo... deceat, 2*; the word *dig-nitas* comes from *dec-nitas, OLD* s.v.). Birth, appearance, and power all have a moral "rightness." Finally, Acilianus' climactic qualification, money, has the clearest aristocratic "propriety." As Pliny points out, the law ranks people by property, in particular through the senatorial property qualification of HS 1,000,000. Acilianus' father has the required money, or, more probably, far more than the required money (in Pliny's euphemism, "abundant resources," *amplas facultates, 9*). Acilianus therefore *deserves* the lofty rank of senator.[23]

> Patria est ei Brixia, ex illa nostra Italia quae multum adhuc verecundiae frugalitatis, atque etiam rusticitatis antiquae, retinet ac servat. Pater Minicius Macrinus, equestris ordinis princeps, quia nihil altius voluit; adlectus enim a divo Vespasiano inter praetorios honestam quietem huic nostrae—ambitioni dicam an dignitati?—constantissime praetulit. Habet aviam maternam Serranam Proculam e municipio Patavio. Nosti loci mores: Serrana tamen Patavinis quoque severitatis exemplum est. Contigit et avunculus ei P. Acilius gravitate prudentia fide prope singulari. In summa nihil erit in domo tota, quod non tibi tamquam in tua placeat. (4–6)

> His fatherland is Brixia, in our part of Italy that still holds onto and keeps a great deal of the respectful, restrained, and indeed rural ways of olden times. His father is Minicius Macrinus, a leading member of the equestrian class, since he did not want anything higher: for although he had been adlected by the Divine Vespasian to be among the praetorian senators he most steadfastly preferred an upright private life to this self-advancement—or shall I call it

---

[23] The topic of "worthiness," which Pliny develops here at length, is of course common in recommendation letters (Guillemin 1929:10).

worthy status?—of ours. He has as grandmother on his mother's side Serrana Procula, from the township of Patavium. You know the character of the place: still, Serrana is a paradigm of sternness even to the Patavians. Then there is his uncle, Publius Acilius, a man of almost unique seriousness, practicality, and loyalty. In short, you will find nothing in his entire household not to please you as much as in your own household.

The bulk of the letter is occupied with the actual commendation, arranged by hometown, relatives, career, appearance, and money. Acilianus' hometown, as we saw, is described according to "antique" and therefore republican ideal values which are "still" preserved in "our" part of Italy. By imagining all moral values to be deteriorating, Pliny can paradoxically depict the newest addition to Italy as having more authentic old values than the old Roman center: North Italy has had less time to deteriorate. Here as elsewhere, praise of Acilianus implies praise of Mauricus and Rusticus, of Pliny himself, and of the new imperial regime, especially Trajan, the emperor from the margin (Spain). The union of margin and center creates the ideal, just as North Italy embodies the union of old and young that is also exemplified by Pliny and Acilianus. The marginal figure at the political center combines rusticity and urbanity, rural and urban virtues, both modest self-restraint (*maxima verecundia,* 4) and energetic drive *(plurimum vigoris et industriae).*[24]

The sequence of relatives is rather surprising: father, maternal grandmother, and maternal uncle. As interesting as the people included are those absent. There is no mother, no siblings, no other uncles, aunts, or grandparents. Also absent is the bride herself, who disappears after the first sentence. Though Pliny of course does not need to describe or praise Mauricus' own niece to him, and though Pliny scrupulously avoids describing young women's appearances, still Pliny might have found occasion to allude to the bride's character or prospects for a harmonious marriage with Acilianus.[25] Elsewhere Pliny duly praises Saturninus' (possibly) learned wife (1.16.6), Fundanus' virtuous daughter (5.16.1–9), and the compatible (obedient) wife of a Macrinus (8.5.1), perhaps the father of our Acilianus. The bride's personal qualities, however, would distract from the political significance of the marriage arrangement. Right now Pliny is not so much seeking a groom for a virtuous or attractive bride, but rather a father for

---

[24] On industriousness in imperial propaganda on the new regime and the new society, see e.g. 3.20.12, *Pan.* 44.7, 81–82, Dio Chrys. 3.55–85; compare Vell. Paterc. 2.126.2 on Tiberius. *Industria* is especially a virtue of a lower-ranking assistant, 8.6.6 (Pallas), 8.23.5 (Junius Avitus), 10.26.2 (Rosianus Geminus), *Pan.* 19.4 (soldiers), 70.4 (provincial governors).

[25] For example, Cicero repeatedly worries about Tullia's prospects in her marriage with Dolabella (Cic. *Fam.* 2.15, 3.12, *Att.* 6.6, 6.9, 7.3); see Treggiari 1991:121. On Pliny's descriptions of personal appearance, see Lilja 1978:56, Leach 1990:21.

Arulenus Rusticus' grandchildren. After the wedding one could afford to praise her virtues, or even the harmony of their marriage, though the latter is best postponed until years later (as Macrinus', 8.5), unless in a private letter by the husband (to her aunt, 4.19, or to Calpurnia herself, 6.7, 7.5). At this point, it goes without saying that the bride has all the personal qualities that one could wish for. Her only quality significant enough to make it into the letter is the one that counts, her chastity, discreetly disguised in an indeterminate plural ("as if a reward for *young women's* chastity," 8).

The prominent groom's grandmother compensates, so to speak, for the feminine absence caused by the omission of the bride. It may be, of course, that the relatives Pliny mentions are the only ones Acilianus has (Sherwin-White assumes that the mother must be dead, 1966:118). In that case, both sets of grandparents, as well as his own parents, had exactly one son, perhaps to maximize the concentration of wealth and patronage in the family. Furthermore, given the disparity of ages in the typical marriage, the mother's mother is indeed the grandparent most likely to be alive for a 35 years-old man. But the rather surprising possibility that Acilianus' father is the Macrinus who lost his wife (in 107 C.E.) after 39 years reminds us that the lineaments of this, the first family described in detail in the letters, may be highly stylized. Perhaps the groom has had a stepmother since the age of six. Or perhaps that is another Macrinus, and our Acilianus' mother is still alive. In any case, Pliny is describing a typical network of political parentage and patronage by the father and the maternal uncle, the male stand-in for the mother, as at 2.9. The father is described exclusively by his political status, and even the uncle is given the moral attributes of the political life, *gravitas, prudentia,* and *fides* (6; cf. Aristo, 1.22.1 *gravius,* 3 *fides;* Mauricus 1.5.16 *gravis prudens,* 3.2.2 *gravitate prudentia*). Only the grandmother intrudes into this political framework, as if to remind us that this is not one of the typical recommendations for a senatorial or military post but for a marriage, and that the groom will not merely beget Rusticus' grandchildren but also live with the bride and raise the children.[26]

The grandmother not only intrudes into the political kinship structure, but even outshines her male associates. Her description is certainly more prominent than that of the very forgettable uncle, whose "almost unique" generic virtues (*gravitate prudentia fide prope singulari,* 6) make him indistinguishable from Pliny's other friends. It is almost more memorable

---

[26] It does not matter whether this is the Acilianus who dies, perhaps childless, at 2.16, but only that he *could* have been the ideal son-in-law, husband, and father. In political recommendations, most relatives mentioned are male, and there are no female relatives more distant than the mother (2.9 father, uncle, 2.13 father, step-father, mother, 4.4 uncle, 4.15 father, brother-in-law, 6.6 father, brother, 10.4 mother, father, stepfather, 10.87 father).

than the father's longer, more detailed biography, even though it really amounts to a single word, *severitas,* since it is livened by a touch of humor. "You know what Patavium is like; well, Serrana is a model of severity even to the Patavians." She is the relative with a name, not just the personal name Pliny gives twice, but a civic reputation. As Patavium is to Italy, so is Serrana to the Patavians. She epitomizes the moral significance of Acilianus' origin in North Italy, personally embodying the old Roman republican virtues that were lost during the Julio-Claudian and Flavian dynasties and are now being restored under the new regime of Nerva and Trajan. If moral deterioration is associated with modernity, Rome, and politics, then the perfect representative of republican virtue is this old Transpadane woman whose sex shields her from the infection of political vice even better than Macrinus' avoidance of ambition shielded him. Acilianus' maternal origin is even better than his "paternal origin" (his *patria,* Brixia), going back to the best of the best of the best, the best part of Patavium, which is the best part of North Italy, which is the best part of Italy.

After his grandmother, Acilianus' father is the next best, coming as close as a man can to antique virtue while still being a suitable father to a Roman senator. He is a "leading member" (*princeps,* 5) of the equestrians, a counterpart to the emperor who is the "leading member" of the Senate and state. The very fact that Vespasian adlected him to the Senate reminds us of the executions and civil wars which had depleted it. Acilianus' family had no share in the sorts of collaboration to which even Rusticus had to submit, acquiescing in Thrasea's execution and negotiating between Vitellius and the Flavian invading army (Tac. *Ann.* 16.26.3, *Hist.* 3.80.2). The term *constantissime,* "most firmly," gives the appropriate moral character to this *recusatio* of senatorial status. In refusing "office-seeking" *(ambitio)* and preferring "noble rest" *(honestam quietem)* he makes a striking contrast with Vespasian himself, who, in the ultimate office-seeking, fought his way to the top by civil war. The New Age, by contrast, began with Nerva's suitably modest choice between "rest" and promotion (10.58.7 *me securitatem omnium quieti meae praetulisse,* "that I valued everyone's freedom from trouble more than my own 'rest'"). With his "Vitellian scar" (1.5.2), Rusticus displayed on his own body a memorial of Vespasian's *ambitio,* whereas Acilianus, the representative of republican virtue, is infected with the Flavian taint as little as possible and is thus the ideal groom for Rusticus' daughter.

Acilianus' three relatives suffice to map out his "entire house" (6), which Mauricus needs to investigate. The wedding will unite not simply two individuals but two houses which will have to approve of each other, or rather, Mauricus will have to approve of Acilianus' house; it goes without saying that the rich but newly senatorial family from North Italy will approve of the famous family of the Stoic martyrs. Acilianus has nothing in his house for Mauricus to dislike, no morally reprehensible relative that could compromise his political position or force him into a conflict of obligations, and, as Pliny finally grudgingly adds, no impoverished relatives. We can assume that if Acilianus' grandmother has made a name for her severity in Patavium, she is also rich. It takes money to have a name, especially a name for not squandering money.[27] The money that Pliny does mention is Acilianus' father's (*esse patri eius...*, 9). With a Good Emperor to protect an inheritance and no siblings to divide it, the property can pass smoothly through Acilianus to Rusticus' descendants. Yet by postponing all mention of wealth to an apologetic afterthought, Pliny creates the impression that membership in the ruling class is a matter of character formation and inner worth, not money and patronage. Mauricus and Rusticus, the "joint addressees" of the letter (4 *vobis*, 9 *vos*), are ideal showpieces for this mystification of power, since they achieved their reputation through their strength of character, and as Stoic adherents they affect to scorn wealth. As Tacitus presents him, Rusticus was already revered for his character when he was praetor in 69 (*Hist.* 3.80.2 *propria dignatio viri*).

These model "households" of the ideal senator and of the ideal equestrian reflect imperial models. The ideal emperor must also have nothing displeasing anywhere in his "house" (*Pan.* 83.1). The reign of the well-meaning Claudius was ruined by his wives and ex-slaves, and the dynasty of Vespasian was ruined by his second son Domitian. The praise of Acilianus' house, epitomized in his grandmother, resembles Pliny's praise of Trajan's house, which is represented by his wife and his sister, herself a grandmother (of the woman who became Hadrian's wife by 101 C.E., *HA Hadr.* 2.10). Their virtues, moderation, frugality (*Pan.* 83.7), and simplicity (84.1), resemble Serrana's Patavian severity.[28] Whereas the Bad Imperial Household has an incestuous marriage (Claudius') or affair (Domitian's, 4.11, *Pan.* 52.3) with a niece, the ideal imperial household makes a marriage alliance through a niece with a promising young member of the ruling class (Acilianus, or, through Trajan's grandniece, Hadrian).[29]

Pliny's penultimate laudatory topic is Acilianus' appearance. Like the final topic, his wealth, this one requires an apology, though not so lengthy as the apology for mentioning wealth. We might wonder why Pliny adds the

---

[27] "To be parsimonious with effect and success, you need to have quite a lot of money" (Syme 1958b:19, on Agricola's family).

[28] Like her husband Trajan, Plotina was a provincial, probably from Nemausio (*HA Hadr.* 12.2). Coins of Plotina (*BMC* 3.82) have *Vesta* (525–28), *Fides* (1080–82), and *Pudicitia* (529).

[29] Nerva prohibited marrying one's niece (Dio 68.2.4), doubtless a piece of anti-Claudian and perhaps even anti-Domitian propaganda.

groom's appearance to the moral-political qualifications he has discussed so far, especially in writing to a family with Stoic leanings, for whom beauty is as meaningless as wealth, and not even defensible by an appeal to law, as is wealth. Pliny's apology, however, explains the obvious. The other qualifications are for Mauricus and his whole household; this one is for the bride, as if in "reward" for her chastity. The politically arranged marriage of blood with money will produce clear benefits for both households involved in the transaction, but what is in it for the bride? The political benefits hinge on the woman's cooperative obedience, on her chastity, but we must be shown that the bride is not being used, and her cooperation is not being taken for granted, for the sake of male political expediency.

Acilianus' appearance shows us what she is getting, a handsome groom. Beyond that, since the bride must not be represented as a completely unphilosophical fool deceived by mere appearances, his appearance betokens his moral worth, combining senatorial "dignity" and blushing modesty (the opposite of Domitian's shameless bloody complexion, *Pan.* 48.4 *impudentia multo rubore suffusa,* Tac. *Agric.* 45.3 *rubor quo se contra pudorem muniebat*). What she is really getting is a harmonious marriage, like Macrinus' (8.5), Pliny's (4.19, 6.7, 7.5), or Trajan's (*Pan.* 83).[30] Since the bride is neither married (like Pliny's or Trajan's wives) nor dead (like Macrinus' wife or Fundanus' daughter), it would be indiscreet to dwell on her personality or her future harmonious relations with the groom, and in any case the letter is about the groom, not about her. Hence Pliny lets the groom's morally meaningful appearance do the job of depicting the bride's satisfaction.

> Tu fortasse me putes indulsisse amori meo, supraque ista quam res patitur sustulisse. At ego fide mea spondeo futurum ut omnia longe ampliora quam a me praedicantur invenias. Diligo quidem adulescentem ardentissime sicut meretur; sed hoc ipsum amantis est, non onerare eum laudibus. (10)

> Perhaps you imagine that I have given in to my affection, and raised up these qualities of his higher than the facts allow. But by my honor I guarantee that you will find everything to be far greater than my commendations claim. I do love the young man most warmly, as he deserves; but this is itself the mark of a lover, not to overburden him with praises.

Pliny's closing comments deal with the problems of patronage and praise, the basic problems of the letters. Perhaps Pliny is praising his friend beyond what he "deserves," and is pushing forward an unworthy candidate to do him a favor and earn gratitude, at Mauricus' expense. If the letter does not reflect

---

[30] Pliny's rhetorical description of Trajan's marriage magically combines equality (*invicem... ex aequo... uterque vestrum, Pan.* 83.6) with wifely obedience (*obsequi gloria,* 83.7).

reality, the circle of mutually beneficial exchange is broken, and Pliny is benefiting at the expense of Mauricus and his niece, putting Mauricus in the role of the bad governor who grants promotions by recommendation *rather than* by merit (Tac. *Agric.* 19.2). Yet we may first note that Pliny's supposititious sin, *indulgentia (me... indulsisse amore meo,* 10), is an imperial virtue, perhaps the most characteristic imperial word in Book 10. Pliny indulgently dispensing favors to his lesser friends is a model for the emperor, whose chief public role was as the dispenser of benefits.[31] In showing how his own friendly indulgence results in fairness, Pliny is showing how the imperial system of favors distributed by one man's arbitrary decisions can be fair under an ideal emperor. Similarly, the numerous cases where the spirit of the law is chosen over the letter of the law demonstrate how arbitrary power can *improve* the law's fairness (e.g. 2.16 on inheritance, 4.9.17 on the punishment of Bassa).

Pliny shows how the problem of praise and the problem of patronage can together each solve the other problem, using two nuts, as it were, to crack each other. On the one hand, excessive praise leads to envious hostility, and on the other hand, exchanges governed by pure patronage bring about unfair promotion and favoritism. But Pliny's awareness that excessive praise defeats its own purpose leads him to make his praise "less than" the truth, and this restraint in turn causes a recommendation based on such moderate praise to have a fair and deserved result. Acilianus' recommendation demonstrates this principle. If Pliny's praise is excessive, Mauricus and his niece will be stuck with an unworthy groom, and whatever gratitude Pliny can earn from his lesser friend Acilianus will be more than counterbalanced by hostility from Mauricus, a powerful imperial intimate. Even the emperor must avoid appearing to give patronage undeservingly. Hence Pliny can put his gentleman's honor on the line, *fide mea spondeo,* even guaranteeing the future *(futurum ut... invenias).*[32]

Both Pliny and Acilianus stand to lose too if Pliny has been exaggerating and thereby causes Acilianus to marry too high. Pliny guarantees against Mauricus' losses by suggesting that it is also in Acilianus' and Pliny's own interests for the praise not to be excessive, not to be a "burden" (*non onerare eum laudibus,* 10): Pliny offers his own potentially ruined reputation as collateral against Mauricus' risks. And in fact, if we look behind the trite superlatives, Pliny has not really praised Acilianus so very much. Acilianus

---

[31] Saller 1982:32. Nerva's letter quoted at 10.58.9 exemplifies this ideology: "let people allow me to be available for fresh benefactions" *(me novis beneficiis vacare patiantur).*

[32] Similarly, in a recommendation of a teacher, Pliny puts himself as a "guarantor," *sponsorem* (3.3.6), for the candidate's personal life. See Guillemin 1929:5 for such juridical terms in recommendations.

simply has the basic conscientiousness *(plurimum vigoris industriae)*, decency *(maxima verecundia)*, and looks of a senator, along with wealth, presumably well beyond the statutory HS 1,000,000; we can well believe that Mauricus will discover more virtues in Acilianus. It is the high stakes of the permanent kinship connection, with all the personal and political disasters that could happen, that call for such an earnest pledge.[33]

Pliny's ultimate guarantee, the glue that holds together the cycles of friendship and of favors, is not Pliny's self-interest, not even Acilianus' merit, but the affection that is based on merit. Just as Pliny loved Rusticus *(dilexerim,* 1), he loves Acilianus *(diligo,* 10). Pliny loves Acilianus because he is deserving, and therefore Pliny's love is proof of Acilianus' merit. The same trope appears in a later letter of recommendation: Pliny's affection does not impair his judgment of his friend's virtues, but is *based* on his judgment (3.3.5). The cycle of affection by which Rusticus and Mauricus "formed" Pliny and Pliny "formed" Acilianus (1–4) is completed now with the union of Mauricus' and Acilianus' families. Just as that affection shaped the younger generation of the ruling class (Pliny and Acilianus), so too it will make the marriage transaction a genuine exchange of favors and merits in all parties' mutual self-interest. Pliny's letter stands balanced, in typical epistolary fashion, between past, present, and future, as a record of the past cycle of upper-class formation of "character," a means for the renewal and repayment of this past cycle through the present marriage transaction, and a promise of future benefits from the transaction, in particular through the creation of the future ruling class. The letter conceals networks of patronage and power in the guise of morals, merits, and mutual affection.

---

[33] A later recommendation uses a similar trope for combining restraint with hyperbole: when the addressee sees the candidate's true merits, he will think he is receiving, not bestowing a favor (7.22.3).

CREATING IMPERIAL MEANING OUT OF REPUBLICAN FORMS (1.23)

Letter 1.23 concerns a matter of political etiquette: may a tribune plead cases? Although magistrates were not supposed to initiate criminal proceedings, it seems to have been Pliny's idea to extend the ban to advocacy, though only for the tribunate.[1] It would be permissible, and probably normal, for Falco to plead cases during his tribuneship, but Pliny seems inclined to think that advocacy would impair the special sacrosanct nature of this magistracy. To plead cases would be "stripping the official power of its rank" (*potestatem... in ordinem cogi*, 1) and "resigning the magistracy, so to speak" (*quasi eiurato magistratu*, 3).

> Consulis an existimem te in tribunatu causas agere debere. Plurimum refert, quid esse tribunatum putes, inanem umbram et sine honore nomen an potestatem sacrosanctam, et quam in ordinem cogi ut a nullo ita ne a se quidem deceat. Ipse cum tribunus essem, erraverim fortasse qui me esse aliquid putavi, sed tamquam essem abstinui causis agendis. (1.23.1–2)

> You ask my advice whether I think you should plead cases during your tribuneship. It makes the biggest difference what you think the tribuneship is, a hollow shade and a word without honor or a sacrosanct power, one which should be stripped of its rank by no one, not even oneself. When I myself was tribune, perhaps I was in error in thinking that I was something, but I refrained from pleading cases as if I were something.

Pliny is here using one of his characteristic tropes, the productive self-delusion, the self-fulfilling belief. "Perhaps I erred *in supposing that I was*

---

[1] Sherwin-White 1966:140.

something" (erraverim fortasse qui me esse aliquid putavi).[2] Pliny uses this
trope elsewhere, about creating meaningful literature (by believing it *is*
worthwhile, one makes it worthwhile, 1.2.6, 1.8.4), and about forming an
upper-class gentleman (by praising him or having high hopes for him, one
makes him deserve praise or fulfill hopes, 1.10.3, 1.14.1). Only the first half
of the trope appears explicitly here: Pliny merely confesses that he may have
been in error *(erraverim fortasse).* Similarly, at 1.2.5 he wonders whether the
addressee will concur with "our error" of intending to publish the work, and
at the end he confesses that the booksellers may simply be flattering him with
a lie *(blandiuntur... blandiantur... mendacium;* cf. 7.4.10 *errant... errent).*

Pliny implies the same syllogism here. If you believe that the tribunate is
something (1)—or as he restates it, if I believe that *I* am something (2)—then
it will be something, it will have real value. Pliny needs the help of such logic
to build up real meaning out of insubstantial, symbolic raw materials, as if by
lifting oneself by one's own bootstraps. All these endeavors rest on insecure
foundations, whether creating lasting literary value out of an ephemeral
speech, or creating a ruling-class member who will "deserve" his wealth and
power, or making an obsolete magistracy from the early republic have real
sanctity and even power *(potestatem sacrosanctam,* 1). Although Pliny may
have borrowed this trope from a literary context, Catullus' thanks to Nepos
for having the faith that made his trifling poetry worth something, the
political context in this letter shows the trope in its most fundamental
meaning, so to speak: all other symbolic values rest on the stability of the
political system.[3] The political system most obviously secures for members of
the ruling class their wealth and power, and their ability to pass these things
on to newly formed members of the next generation. But it is also a
prerequisite for writers for the creation of literary meaning, not simply
because writing requires wealth, slaves, and education, but above all because
literature, especially Roman literature of the kind Pliny writes, needs a
centralized military and political dominance for its context, audience,
distribution, and lasting significance.[4] Yet the Roman imperial system rests on
a fiction, the fiction that the Republic is still functioning, that magistrates still
carry out meaningful duties, and that the Senate still makes meaningful
decisions, though now under the guidance of the princeps, merely a "leading

---

[2] As Trisoglio points out (1973:252 n. 427), the main point lies in the subordinate clause:
"Even though I may have been wrong, I supposed I was something."
[3] Note the similar wording, *me esse aliquid putavi* (1.23.2), *meas esse aliquid putare nugas*
(Catull. 1.3).
[4] The many exceptions, writers from the geographic or social margins such as Ennius,
Plautus, Josephus, or Epictetus, can be called exceptions that prove the rule, since their work
depends on contact with the dominant center.

citizen" who also has permanent tribunician power and permanent military command over the armed forces through his legates.

The tribunate thus symbolizes the problematic role of the senator, and encapsulates the overriding anxiety of Roman upper-class life. Is the tribunate a real power, or is it an "empty shade," a ghost after the death of the free republic? The words "empty shade" may be echoing a phrase from Lucan (2.303), with which Cato addresses *Libertas*—"Freedom," or rather, "The Free Republic."[5] Cato offers to follow the "name" of *Libertas* to the grave even when it is an "empty shade," thus foreshadowing his own death which will come immediately after the death of freedom.[6] Even compared to the other offices of the senatorial *cursus*, the tribunate has a special prominence, not only because of its ancient sacrosanct power, but also because it has become one of the central titles of the emperor. Tribunician power is the "term of highest eminence," to be used "for protecting the ordinary people."[7]

Indeed, a threatened emperor can use a tribune to protect his power against a show of independent power by the Senate. Thus, Vitellius appeals to a tribune to defend his own tribunician power when he is attacked by Helvidius (Tac. *Hist.* 2.91.3, Dio 64.7.2), and later a tribunician veto protects Vespasian's power when Helvidius proposes independent senatorial action over financial problems (*Hist.* 4.9.2). For the imperial fiction to work, it is necessary for there to be real tribunes with real sacrosanct power, so that there will still exist a Republican institution on which the emperor's power is grounded.[8] Conversely, senators who occupy the tribunate on their *cursus* get to play at emperor for a year, withdrawing from the turmoil of forensic competition and devoting themselves to offering aid to citizens in trouble, just as the Good Emperor devotes himself to distributing favors *(beneficia)* to citizens (as Nerva at 10.58.9). A tribune involved in a private lawsuit would parallel an emperor subjecting a court case or senatorial debate to his personal will. Pliny's letter skirts lightly over the real problem of a tribune being involved in a lawsuit, the problem of exerting unjust influence by his political prestige and power. Throughout his examples Pliny is careful to emphasize

---

[5] Guillemin 1929:119.

[6] It was a commonplace that Cato and the Republic died together, e.g. Sen. *de Tranquill.* 16.1.

[7] *summi fastigii vocabulum,* Tac. *Ann.* 3.56.2; *ad tuendam plebem,* Tac. *Ann.* 1.2.1. As Béranger comments (1953:101), "ironie désarmante: l'instrument de l'absolutisme était tiré de l'arsenal de la liberté." Trajan seems to have counted his years with tribunician power not from the start of his rule, as had been usual, but from December 10, as if he were entering an annual tribunate along with the ordinary tribunes, as Dio 53.17.10 and coin legends which give Trajan an additional year of tribunician power seem to indicate (Longden 1931, Niccolini 1932:159).

[8] Niccolini 1932:162. Accordingly, under Augustus not enough people could be found willing to hold the tribunate (Dio 54.30.2), so noticeably had it lost in power or gained in risk (Niccolini 1932:163).

the degrading of the office. People will *not* rise in respect, he will *not* be exerting the power to silence others, he *will* be interrupted with insulting attacks, and he will probably even ignore appeals for intercession and help. Just as the Emperor plays at not having power, the senator plays at having real independent power; both must use the traditional forms with great discretion. Thus it is precisely *because* the tribunate has lost all real power that the formalities of the office are so important.

The tribune under the empire is in a double bind. If he is insulted, he can endure patiently, in which case he will seem "ineffectual," or he can take vengeance, in which case he will seem "insolent." Similarly, if called on to intercede, he can keep his peace (*quiescerem sileremque,* 3), in which case he is virtually giving up his office. Pliny omits the other possibility, that he could try to intercede, but we can explain ourselves why that is unacceptable: if successful the intercession could bias the legal process. Two of Pliny's key terms here recur in allusions to the tribunate elsewhere: Pliny promised to defend a friend from the "insolence" of a tribune (*insolentiam,* 6.8.3), and Pliny himself received special commendation for keeping his "peace" during his own tribunate (*Pan.* 95.1 *quietis*), a commendation probably caused at least in part by his ostentatious avoidance of advocacy during his term of office. These passages illustrate the best way out of the dilemma. *Insolentia* must be avoided, whereas *quies* can be a virtue. A tribune must make cautious use of his powers so as not to be insolent, and must avoid awkward political situations which will make his *quies* seem like abandonment of his official powers. Clearly the letter is slanted towards avoiding advocacy, but even this solution will not entirely solve the tribune's problems; he will need to carry out his office with extreme discretion wherever he is. Tacitus shows us that a tribune's actions can incur imperial wrath as well as imperial favor, at least under a bad emperor. Nero would have killed Rusticus if Thrasea had not persuaded the latter not to intercede on his behalf (*Ann.* 16.26.3). Likewise, each senator, like the Senate as a whole, must perform the same balancing act, flattering the emperor by pretending to have independent (republican) power, while avoiding situations in which one might be called on to exert power in a politically sensitive context.

The emperor, too, must tread the same fine line. He must maintain the pretense of holding tribunician power, and must be able to intervene as if for the benefit of a citizen or of the public, without seeming to set the legal and political system out of balance by exerting "insolent" power. Yet an Emperor who tries to play the game of republican freedom too earnestly can be said to risk "giving up his office," like Pliny's "inert" tribune. Accordingly Vespasian complained that Helvidius was setting him back to the rank of a private citizen.[9]

Just as the tribune mimics the civil power of the emperor, the army legate mimics his military power, and a legate must exert even greater discretion than a tribune in carrying out his job adequately without overstepping his role. Pliny's addressee seems to have had an interesting term as tribune in the turbulent year of restoration, 97, if this Falco is the Murena whose intercession for Pliny's opponent, the illustrious Veiento, goes for naught, 9.13.19.[10] But his main career was military, like that of his father-in-law Sosius Senecio. Inscriptions show his legionary command, his participation in the first Dacian War, and his provincial governorships (*ILS* 1035–37, 1104– 05), and Pliny elsewhere recommends a friend to him for a military post (4.4). Falco's military career, including a command and decoration in the first Dacian war, was well underway when letter 1.23 was published.[11] Pliny's anxieties on how one should deal with a tribune's fictitious power parallel the greater anxieties on how one should deal with a general's power, one of the few official positions of real personal power in the empire.

Letter 1.23 has the same structure as 1.18 on Suetonius' dream.[12] "You ask me about legal pleading... it matters whether... when I was in a similar position, I... but you may be different." In 1.18, the flashback tends to dismiss Suetonius' anxieties, but in 1.23 it tends to reinforce Falco's anxieties. Suetonius' mere dream is not like Pliny's solid political obligation to *patria* and *fides* (1.18.4), whereas Falco's real political office is not merely an empty shade. Both letters use the foil of insubstantial, meaningless dreams and shades to claim solid value for political obligations such as advocacy (1.18) or the tribunate (1.23). Furthermore, the contrast with Pliny's own youth reflects indirect praise on the current regime. Both times, Pliny reaches back into his past under the *prior* regime, to his earlier career under Domitian. Even then Pliny was able to fulfill his obligations with discretion and thereby advance his

---

[9] Suet. *Vesp.* 15, *paene in ordinem redactus;* compare Plin. 1.23.4, *quasi eiurato magistratu privatum ipse me facere.* Similarly, Claudius complained to the Ostians that he had been "set back to the rank" of private citizen by not receiving an honorary reception (*in ordinem se coactum,* Suet. *Claud.* 38.1). Julius Caesar is said to have sarcastically challenged the tribune Pontius Aquila, who had refused to stand at Caesar's triumph, to ask for the Republic back again (Suet. *Jul.* 78.2).

[10] Just as Pliny sweeps away a tribune's possible intervention with a Homeric tag at 6.8.3, so Murena's ineffectual intercession at 9.13.19 results in Veiento's self-pitying Homeric tag (9.13.20). The tribune's antiquated, purely formal powers are as remote, and as easily parried, as poetic jabs and counter-jabs from Homer and the Trojan War.

[11] Syme (1958:650) identifies him from inscriptional evidence as one of the seven "younger Trajanic marshals" (the others being C. Iulius Quadratus Bassus, L. Minicius Natalis, C. Iulius Proculus, A. Larcius Priscus, L. Catilius Severus, and T. Iulius Maximus).

[12] Merwald 1964:27.

own prestige. If he was able to make advocacy and magistracy mean something even in that time, all the more can the rising younger generation represented by Suetonius and Falco behave successfully with dignity and discretion in the new age.

The opening lines bristle with terms for judgment and evaluation, concepts that proliferate throughout the letter, in accordance with the letter's goal of creating meaning and value out of insubstantial forms: *consulis an existimem te... debere... refert quid... putes.* This is the only letter in which an opening echo to a prior request for advice uses the word *consulis.*[13] We might suspect a pun on the title "consul," just as Pliny later puns on his office of augur.[14] The letter was probably published after Pliny's consulship (100) and perhaps before Falco's (108). In this, the first advice letter in the collection, we are shown the (soon-to-be) consular senator confidently giving advice to a younger colleague, who is rising in military prestige but still subordinate to the civilian Pliny by virtue of Pliny's authoritative judgment. The end of Book 1 shows Pliny out from under his dependence on senior statesmen such as Corellius (*testem rectorem magistrum,* 1.12.12) and Mauricus (*consilii ducem,* 1.5.10), and giving authoritative advice to his lesser friends Suetonius and Pompeius Falco.

Pliny's terms for evaluating the tribunate use a discreet ambiguity between the office, the officeholder in general, and Pliny in particular. Pliny suggests that the *office* may be "stripped of *office";* as Rusca notes, the idiom *in ordinem cogi* properly refers to a *person* deprived of office.[15] He then says that this should not be done by anyone, not even *one*self (*ne a se quidem*). The slightly illogical *se,* which does not refer back to anyone, avoids the hint of blame which the more logical *te* would carry, and effects a polite transition to Pliny himself (*ipse;* cf. 9.13.2 *se proferendi*). Falco must not be directly blamed for pleading during office, for the letter politely leaves that possibility open to him by the end. The transition to Pliny himself rephrases the basic question in a personal first-person form, no longer *quid esse* tribunatum *putes* (1) but me *esse aliquid putavi,* but the impersonal form returns at the recapitulation (*iterum dicam... quid esse* tribunatum *putes,* 5).

Pliny's shifting diction suggests a fusion of self and office. A tribune's behavior must preserve the dignity of the office and of himself, and the two are interdependent. The ruling class member derives his prestige from the prestige of the political forms he occupies, while bestowing on them their continuing prestige. This is perhaps nowhere more explicit than in the highly

[13] Elsewhere Pliny uses *rogas* 6.27, *quaeris* 4.10.2, 7.9, *deliberas* 7.18. These opening formulas are listed by Sherwin-White, 1966:6.
[14] 7.33.1 *auguror,* Murgia 1985:181; perhaps also at 4.15.5 *ominamur... augurari.*
[15] Rusca 1961:359.

personal office of the tribunate, whose "sacrosanct" power (*potestatem sacrosanctam,* 1) is connected with the sacrosanct *person* of the tribune.[16] Hence Pliny's list of possible conflicts of interest begins with theatrical rituals of rising and sitting that relate to the actual *body* of the tribune. The mutual cooperation of person and office in shoring up their prestige and power parallels the person and the office of the emperor, who holds the most sacrosanct office and who has the most sacrosanct body in the Roman empire. The Good Emperor bases his prestige on the prestige of republican offices and titles, while upholding, in turn, the prestige of these offices.

We can see the theatrical ritual of imperial power most clearly when it is being violated, as when Claudius harmed the prestige of his position by failing to maintain the distance required for personal sanctity. Stories told of his participating too closely in ordinary activities, even shoving with his own hands people who jostled him on the street (Suet. *Claud.* 38.2). By contrast, Trajan is praised for *not* having people shoved out of the way in imperial presumptuousness (*Pan.* 76.7 *adrogantiae principalis*). The tribune's power, and to a certain degree even the emperor's power, is symbolic and based on tacit agreement. In order that the power of the emperor and of the ruling class may not openly appear to be based on oppression and brute force, the symbolic power and sanctity of the old republican offices must be kept as high as possible.

> ... primum quod deforme arbitrabar, cui adsurgere cui loco cedere omnes oporteret, hunc omnibus sedentibus stare, et qui iubere posset tacere quemcumque, huic silentium clepsydra indici, et quem interfari nefas esset, hunc etiam convicia audire et si inulta pateretur inertem, si ulcisceretur insolentem videri. Erat hic quoque aestus ante oculos, si forte me adpellasset vel ille cui adessem, vel ille quem contra, intercederem et auxilium ferrem an quiescerem silerremque, et quasi eiurato magistratu privatum ipse me facerem. (2–3)

> ... first, because I thought it was unseemly that a person for whom everyone ought to rise and give way, should remain standing while everyone is sitting, and that a person who can order anyone at all to be quiet, should be assigned silence by the water-clock, and that a person whom it is forbidden to interrupt, should receive insults and seems passive if he endures it without retaliating, or overbearing if he retaliates. There was also this anxiety before my eyes, if by chance the man I was defending, or the man against whom I was pleading, had appealed to me, should I intercede and bring aid, or be inactive and silent, and as if resigning my office make myself a private citizen.

---

[16] Compare, for example, Suet. *Tib.* 2.4, 11.3. The tribunician power "allowed" the emperor to kill, as if for sacrilege, someone who offended him in deed or even in word (Dio 53.17.9). On the "sacrosanctity" of the tribunes, see Niccolini 1932:40–45.

Pliny's list of conflicts of interest gives four situations: standing, being silenced by the clock, being insulted, and being asked to intercede. The structure groups the first three together, introducing them with *primum* and following the grammatical parallelism of relative clause with governing infinitive. *"First,* I though it ugly... to stand... to be silenced... to be given insults and to seem inactive... or insolent... There was *also* this swirl of anxiety before my eyes... if... [then] should I intercede or keep quiet?" The possibilities are thus grouped as follows:

> I.a. stand. I.b. be silenced by clock. I.c. receive insult.
> (Ic.1. endure and seem inactive. I.c.2. avenge and seem insolent.)
> II. receive appeal. (II.1. intercede [and ??]. II.2. keep quiet and "resign office.")

The problematic occasions form a rising crescendo of anxiety, as Pliny penetrates from superficial, ritualistic aspects of the office to its core functions. As we move from *tribunicia sanctitas* to *tribunicia potestas,* we move from what is merely "not pretty" (*deforme arbitrabar,* 2) to the real source of anxiety (*aestus ante oculos,* 3).[17] The beginning of the list is almost nugatory: does it really matter whether all rise for him or he rises while all sit?[18] In any case, Pliny consistently portrays the role of the orator, which the tribune will be assuming, in ennobling rather than humiliating terms. In senatorial speeches Pliny receives polite, encouraging attention (2.11.14, 3.9.26, 4.9.10–12, 9.13.18). The absence of this attention makes a recitation of a speech seem inadequate (2.19.2; cf. Aeschines, 2.3.10). The supreme speaker can even turn an audience's hostility into respect (3.9.25, 9.13.18). In the age of claqueurs and operatic intonation (2.14.6, 12–13), oratory merely suffers from excessive enthusiasm, not insult: Pliny only reports the claqueurs cheering, not booing (2.14.6; compare the overenthusiasm at the Varenus proceedings, 6.5.5).

One wonders whether merely ritualistic challenges to the tribune's office would have been enough to make Pliny give up advocacy as a tribune. Yet even these challenges have an underlying significance: the respect accorded to an orator and that accorded to a tribune are incommensurable, based on opposite principles. A tribune's office demands respect; an orator must earn it. The ideal orator such as Pliny can fight his way through a hostile reception

---

[17] Trisoglio notes the ritualistic emphasis in the list of potential conflicts but misses the differentiation within the list: "L'epistolografo rievoca con pacato favore il rispetto quasi religioso che era riservato ai tribuni (2), però... si attiene rigorosamente agli aspetti protocollari senza trapassare a quelli più propriamente politici," 1972:16–17.

[18] We may compare Claudius' ostentatious apology for making tribunes stand in front of him, Suet. *Claud.* 12.2.

to command respect, but the other side of the coin is that an unworthy orator *can* be overcome by hostility and shouted down, as Veiento in the Senate (9.13.19). The tribune is like the emperor: a Good Emperor may be loved and admired, but even a Bad Emperor must be endured with a formal show of respect. Indeed, the refusal to offer the emperor such token forms of respect was a hallmark of the more extreme "opposition" members, starting with the tribune Aquila's refusal to stand at Caesar's triumph (Suet. *Jul.* 78.2), and continuing with Thrasea's walking out of the Senate (Tac. *Ann.* 14.12.1) and Helvidius' behavior which turned Vespasian into a "private citizen" (Suet. *Vesp.* 15). One might put a similar slant on Rusticus' behavior at Plutarch's lecture, refusing to interrupt the lecture when a letter from Domitian arrived, though Plutarch praises his self-command (*de Cur.* 522E). In short, the dangerous opponent refuses the emperor the automatic reverence that is owed to a sacred office, showing him only the respect he earns as a "leading citizen." And even a token form of opposition can have real significance: any deliberate violation of the public transcript of power threatens to undermine the existing power relations.[19]

Since respect for the emperor and the tribune are not earned, but claimed as a right of office, they must avoid roles that give even the appearance of bringing them into open public competition for respect and authority. Hence even something as mechanical as a water-clock would put the tribune's or emperor's sacred authority at risk. If he needed more time to speak, it would be unseemly to have to beg for it (as at 7.6.11), it would put an undue restriction on his authority to be cut off early, and it would be an undesirable display of raw power to seize more than is allotted to private citizens. The third item in Pliny's list is intermediate between the token problems I.a and I.b, and the real problem II. Being insulted violates not merely what "should be," as with standing (*oporteret*), or "could be," as with silencing (*posset*), but is a basic religious violation of sacrosanct status (*nefas*).

Yet as we have seen, the exchange of attacks is simply part of the fundamental competition for authority and respect that a pleader undergoes in any legal case, the opposite side of the coin from the respect won by the ideal orator, even if the prevalence of invective has had to be reduced under authoritarian imperial conditions (Tac. *Dial.* 40.1, 41.4). Indeed, the tribune's dilemma is merely an intensification of any orator's dilemma in dealing with competition and invective in the hierarchical, unfree state. If one endures insults without striking back one would seem helpless, but if one responds aggressively one would seem insolent (2 *si inulta pateretur inertem, si*

---

[19] "A single act of successful public insubordination... pierces the smooth surface of apparent consent... It is now public knowledge that relations of subordination, however immovable in practice, are not entirely legitimate" (Scott 1990:205, 215).

ulcisceretur insolentem videri)—and might also run political risks. We can compare Pliny on the stand at 1.5.5: should he acquiesce spinelessly in Regulus' attacks on Modestus, and risk losing his client's case, or should he counterattack vigorously and incur political danger? Pliny is of course not advising that one should never practice advocacy, even under a Bad Emperor, and he is not even firm about dissuading the tribune from practicing advocacy, as the ending shows. Rather, he is emphasizing that the ritualistic, republican, and imperial undertones of the tribunate make the delicate balancing act of any politician still more delicate, even in the new age of "freedom."

The fourth and climactic problem is what to do if a client, or worse, an opponent, appeals for intercession. Since Pliny's practice of avoiding advocacy was apparently rare, and since he does not firmly exclude that option for Falco, we do have to consider what the tribune-advocate *should* do in such a situation. Guidance is provided by the structural imbalance: "should I intercede <and consequently —??>, or should I keep quiet and consequently 'abdicate' from office?" The consequences of the first choice are evidently too awkward even to contemplate, especially if it is the opponent appealing for aid. If one's client appeals, one risks asserting unfair influence, which is bad enough, but if one's opponent appeals, one risks violating one's basic pledge of honor *(fides)* to one's client and is practically guilty of collusion *(praevaricatio)*.[20]

Conflict between obligations, a fundamental threat to an honorable gentleman's reputation, must be banished from the letters. Examples of the finesse required to avoid it are at 1.7 (pleading against the Baetici) or 5.1 (sitting in judgment over one's own inheritance, but then voluntarily paying it back). The tribune clearly stands intermediate between the ordinary, non-sacrosanct politician and the super-sacrosanct emperor. Any politician must cautiously avoid prevarication based on ties of obligation with the opponent's side, as when friends of the Classicus defendants approach Pliny secretly between sessions (3.9.25). The Good Emperor too must refrain from being involved in either side in disputes or litigation (as the impartial Augustus at Suet. *Aug.* 56.3), though he can flaunt his fairness (as Pliny in 5.1) by judging a case that involves a possible conflict of interest ("I am no Nero," 6.31.9). Elsewhere the emperor shows how the ideal tribune should behave if he does practice advocacy and receives an appeal. In the disgraceful exchange of invective between Nepos and Celsus, senators implored Trajan to be *propitious* to one or both parties, as if using his Olympian powers over the circus mob *(propitium Caesarem ut in ludicro aliquo precabantur,* 6.5.5). If

---

[20] The symmetry is somewhat contrived for rhetorical point; in practice, only the defendant appeals for tribunician *auxilium* (Niccolini 1932:121).

both sides appeal to the emperor, or to a tribune arguing a case, the conflict of obligation is sharpest. Evidently by doing nothing "Caesar" maintained his sacred dignity and impartiality; his self-restraint did not make him a "private citizen," as Pliny fears for Falco. Clearly the tribune-advocate must keep quiet in such a situation.

By contrast, when Veiento hints that a tribune should come to his aid, Murena (perhaps Falco) "at once" responds to the call, though in vain (9.13.19). This demonstration that the tribune has no real power to influence legal or political decisions shows why it *is* safe for him to intercede, as long as he does not have a personal conflict of interest. We can easily imagine that Murena does not really support Veiento's view. He gives up after one formulaic intervention ("I permit you to speak, *most illustrious* Veiento," 9.13.19) while Veiento keeps on struggling against the outcry until he finally must nurse his wounded pride with a trivializing Homeric tag (9.13.20): like old Nestor, the prime of his power has passed.

The closing line of Pliny's exemplum repeats the notion that the tribune should "resign" his office rather than risk a conflict of obligations. Pliny preferred to be available "to *all* as tribune rather than to *some* as advocate." Pliny cannot be tribune to all if he is advocate to some, since he would have to refuse to be tribune to his clients and opponents. The delicate opposition between tribune and advocate manages to exalt the tribunate without denigrating the role of advocate. Though the advocate has real power, the tribune occupies a symbolically more exalted position precisely because his power, weak but sacrosanct and redolent of the free republic, is available to all citizens.

Pliny's conclusion returns to the beginning with a verbal echo and an explicit acknowledgment of the ring composition *(iterum dicam)*. The proleptic *tu* highlights the transition back to the addressee (cf. 1.18.5 *tu quoque*). "But you—I'll say it again—'it makes the greatest difference what you suppose the tribunate is,' what role you are taking on." As usual the ring composition returns to the start with a difference. Using a characteristic epistolary structure, Pliny opens in the present, swings back to the past, and returns to the present but in the new light of the past, and with a clearer sight onto the future. This structure underlies nine letters in Book 1 alone, letters 1, 2, 5, 6, 8, 12, 18, 21, and 23. For example, in 1.12 the intervening account of Corellius' illness and death makes the return of Pliny's inconsolable grief seem temporary and points the way to real consolation, and in 1.18 Pliny's own dream shows by contrast how Suetonius' anxious wish for a delay is less necessary, though more easily fulfilled.

In 1.23 Pliny returns to the same evaluative question of what the tribunate is, whether it is nothing or something, an empty shade or a sacrosanct power.

In the opening version, the alternative was heavily weighted towards the
second of the pair, towards considering the tribunate important, by means of
the excessively dismissive first choice ("...name without honor") and the heavy
moral coloring of the second choice ("sacrosanct... it is proper..."). But in the
concluding version, despite the intervening argumentation in favor of
avoiding advocacy, the two choices are much more evenly balanced. The first
choice is now perfectly acceptable, even to a "wise man." It may indeed be
wiser to continue one's normal legal activities if one cannot carry out the
theatrical performance (or the farce) of the "sacrosanct tribune" to the fullest.
Anyway, the highly connected military careerist Falco will not be roaming
around offering tribunician intercession to all and sundry; a discreet
performance or two in the Senate will suffice to justify his obligatory year on
the *cursus* on his way to a military command.

The structure of Pliny's intervening argumentation has already shown the
way to reconciling the tribunate with advocacy: ignore the trivial violations of
tribunician ritual (I.a–b), respond to forensic interruption and abuse with
dignified restraint as any proper orator would (I.c), and if necessary, "make
yourself a private citizen" rather than interceding if it would cause a clear
conflict of interest (II). The evenly balanced ending releases Falco from
feeling obliged to avoid advocacy, while leaving the flattering impression that
he did avoid it. The very fact that he asked for advice from a Pliny shows that
he already inclines toward avoiding advocacy. To ask advice means that one
would be willing to accept it; hence Pliny does not consult Corellius when he
is determined to attack Certus (9.13.6). The corollary of the principle of
binding advice is that when giving advice one should leave an escape, if
possible, so as not to force the questioner to choose between following
unwelcome advice and offending a high-ranking advisor. As in 1.18, Pliny's
self-ironic close undercuts the self-flattery of the central flashback and leaves
open the droll possibility, stronger in 1.18 than in 1.23, that all his ponderous
moralizing will count for nothing.

In accordance with its new function, the recapitulation is actually altered,
despite Pliny's announcement that he is repeating *(iterum dicam)*.[21]

> Plurimum refert, quid esse tribunatum putes, inanem umbram et sine honore
> nomen an potestatem sacrosanctam... (1)
> Sed tu (iterum dicam) plurimum interest quid esse tribunatum putes, quam
> personam tibi imponas; quae sapienti viro ita aptanda est ut perferatur. (5)

---

[21] For other announced recapitulations, compare 1.5.16 *ut idem saepius dicam,* 3.11.8 *illuc
enim unde coepi revertor,* 3.16.13 *quod initio dixi,* 4.22.7 *longius abii,* 6.11.3 *repetam enim,*
6.27.5 *ut supra scripsi,* 6.33.11 *iterum dicam,* 9.34.2 *iterum dicam.*

It is of *the greatest import* what you reckon the tribunate to be, an empty shadow and a mere word without honor, or a sacrosanct power...

But as for you, I'll say it again, it makes the *biggest difference* what you reckon the tribunate to be, what role you are taking on yourself: since a man who is wise should fit his role to himself in such a way that he may carry it off to the end.

Aside from the changed ending, with the indirect question omitted ("whether it is... or..."), the introductory verb is changed, from *plurimum refert* ("it matters a great deal") to a close synonym, *plurimum interest* ("it makes a great deal of difference," or literally "there is a great deal *in between* the two possibilities"). Such elegant variation is of course characteristic of Pliny, but it would seem strange that precisely when Pliny omits the alternate indirect questions he should choose a verb which suits them literally ("there is a great deal of difference *between* the two possibilities of what you think the tribunate is, [*whether* you think... *or*...]").[22] The reason may be that the opening indirect question is not so much a real alternative as a way to launch a detailed argument for the second possibility, that tribunician power *is* sacrosanct and should not be infringed, whereas here at the end Pliny is finally offering the two choices to Falco as real alternatives, which he does not need or wish to spell out again in less slanted terms than he did at the opening. When he was arguing for the importance of the tribunate he said it was of "the greatest importance"; now that he seems to be genuinely offering two possible views he says there is the "biggest difference" between them.

Although he omits a more balanced restatement of the two views, Pliny does suggest to us how we should rephrase the alternate questions, by introducing the image of the mask. "It makes the biggest difference what *mask* you are putting on yourself." The tribunate is more than an empty shade and name, but less than a sacrosanct power; it is a mask, or rather a variety of masks, depending on what view one takes of it, on what role one plays as tribune. Pliny has already suggested the theatricality of political roles by saying that his choice was between "displaying" himself as tribune or as advocate (*me... exhibere*, 4; cf. *OLD* s.v. 3). Each position in the ruling class is a mask, all the more so because of the imperial charade in which the emperor pretends not to have supreme unconstitutional power, and the Senate

---

22 Some examples of Pliny's very frequent elegant variation are 3.11.1 *officia amicorum... extollat, meum meritum... praedicatione circumfert,* 3.11.8 *me... laudibus cumulat;* 6.17.1 *indignatiunculam... apud te... effundam,* 6.17.6 *indignationem... prodidi;* 8.19.1 *solacium... doloris levamentum;* 8.21.1–3 *severitatem... graviora... seria;* 8.21.4–5 *satietatis... taedium.* The first two examples occur in ring composition. Quintilian mentions elegant variation at *Inst.* 10.1.7.

and magistrates pretend to have real republican power.[23] The advocate must carry his role through to the end, the tribune must carry his role to the end of his year in office (as Murena put on a good show of it at 9.13.19), and the emperor must carry his role to the end of his life. Suetonius aptly reports that Augustus, the inventor of the fiction of imperial republicanism, asked on his deathbed whether he seemed to have played the theatrical role well to the end (Suet. *Aug.* 99.1 *mimum vitae commode transegisse;* Dio 56.30.4). By contrast, the Bad Friend Regulus gives himself away by "changing masks" (2.20.8 *mutat personam*), just as the Bad Emperor Domitian gave himself away (4.11.13 *gaudio proderetur*) by letting slip his mask of virtuous moral censor and exulting in guilty relief.[24]

The proper wearing of the political mask must be done by a "wise man" (*sapienti viro,* 1.23.5). The term *sapiens,* which can translate φιλόσοφος (e.g. Val. Max. 7.2 ext. 4), is only slightly demoted here from a technical term to a mere adjective by the noun *viro.* The Stoic philosopher also wears masks. Although he knows that power, money, kinship, and all external goods are comparatively worthless, he still preaches involvement in the world of such conventional ties and political obligations. Pliny's Euphrates who calls Roman politics the summit of philosophy is merely a Romanized exaggeration of the real thing. Indeed, the theatrical metaphor is a favorite Stoic illustration of how the wise philosopher acts *in* this world without fully being a part of it.[25] Philosophy will not tell the wise man how often to visit his mother (Epict. 3.24.22), or how much to be willing to grovel to the rich or powerful (1.25.17), but it will tell him do all these things with reason, propriety, and above all, detachment, as an actor merely playing a role. The philosopher combines carefulness and tranquillity when he undertakes action (Epict. 2.5.2, 7 ἐπιμελές... ἀτάραχος). A discreet senator "puts on" the worn-out republican roles in the same way that the philosopher "puts on" all the roles of social and political life, sometimes following conventional behavior and sometimes differing from it, but always keeping an awareness that it is only a performance, and always guiding that performance by his higher principles.

---

[23] Compare 4.25.5, where senators' votes, which are hardly more than a charade in the imperial system, become an open "farce" when some senators write frivolous and obscene comments on the secret voting tablets *(ista ludibria,* scaena et pulpito *digna).*

[24] Seneca contrasts the wise man, who always plays the same role, to ordinary people who are always changing their masks (*Ep.* 120.22; see Edwards 1997:34).

[25] E.g. Diog. Laert. 7.160 (Ariston), Epict. 1.25.10, 4.1.165, 4.7.13, *Encheir.* 17, M. Aurelius *Med.* 3.8, 12.36; Sen *Ep.* 77.20. O. Hense traces this theatrical metaphor in the diatribe tradition back to Bion of Borysthenes by way of Teles (1889:xci–xcix); see Teles fr. 2 p. 3.3, p. 11.5, fr. 6 p. 40.4 Hense, and Gill 1988:192. "The actor, as Erving Goffman remarks... can preserve an inner autonomy, 'holding off the ceremonial order by the very act of upholding it'" (Barton 1993:134).

The tribune cannot respond to insult with the instinct of the vigorous advocate, but must first consider how it may reflect on the office of the tribunate. On the other hand, he also cannot mechanically answer an appeal as tribune without first considering his obligations as advocate. Even Pliny's own solution, to act as tribune to all, is only an easy way out that does not solve the real anxiety, but only hints at the real solution, the delicate balancing act between republican pretense and imperial discretion. Pliny cannot offer Falco a neat solution, for Falco's problem is merely an exacerbated form of every politician's problem from the lowest advocate all the way up to the emperor. Both choices are acceptable, but both need to be carried out with caution. The republican forms may be mere masks, but the mask will only show if it slips off. Yet the better the emperor wears his mask, the easier it is for the Good Senator to carry out his side of the charade.

ESTABLISHING FRIENDLY TIES AND HIERARCHIES
SUETONIUS (1.18, 1.24)

PLINY'S DREAM: BRAVERY UNDER THE PRIOR REGIME

In letter 1.18, a "masterpiece of genteel, natural, and courteous style" (Trisoglio 1973:232), Pliny responds to Suetonius' bad dream. Pliny and Suetonius are apparently pleading a case together, with Pliny as the leading member of the team (Sherwin-White 1966:128), able with his superior skill and authority to discover some "feint" (*aliquam stropham,* 6), and to "plead" Suetonius' "case" for him (*agamque causam tuam,* 6). Anxiety is the explicit subject of the letter, Suetonius' anxiety about pleading his case soon after his bad dream. Suetonius' anxiety serves as a foil for Pliny's confidence, both in the present when Pliny can either reassure Suetonius or obtain a delay for him, and in the past when Pliny overcame a similar anxiety of his own. Pliny's past experience, ostensibly a mere exemplum, is actually the main point of the letter, being described in much greater detail than the current and relatively unimportant case of Suetonius. Counterbalancing the first and last sections, in which Pliny agrees to seek a delay, is the large central section in which he reassures Suetonius by describing his own frightening dream which turned out lucky.

Will Pliny persuade Suetonius? Or will Suetonius write back continuing to request a delay? Pliny and Suetonius knew what happened, but the reader must guess, since the events of such a minor legal case are not, and probably were not, general knowledge. Trisoglio, responding to Pliny's dominant persona, seems to assume that Pliny was successful, since he dwells admiringly on Pliny's rhetorical technique in persuading Suetonius.[1] But behind the dominant

---

[1] "Pliny gives the dream an optimistic interpretation, lightheartedly dismisses the oppressive cloaks of the dream, opposes not theory against theory but case against case, and achieves the efficacy of giving a command without provoking the usual reaction to a command" (1973:233).

persona we can recognize Pliny's self-irony, his recognition that the persuasion will fail. The giveaway is the final line, the usual position for Pliny's self-ironic undercutting (e.g., in Book 1 letters 2, 7, 9, 15, 18, 20). Having presented a self-flattering example, Pliny confesses that his own situation was different from Suetonius', since Pliny could not have postponed his suit even if he had wanted. The confession both gives Suetonius a face-saving excuse and shows that Pliny's example does not really prove what it pretends to prove.

> Scribis te perterritum somnio vereri ne quid adversi in actione patiaris; rogas ut dilationem petam, et pauculos dies, certe proximum, excusem. Difficile est, sed experiar, καὶ γάρ τ' ὄναρ ἐκ Διός ἐστιν. Refert tamen, eventura soleas an contraria somniare. (1.18.1–2)

> You write that you have been thoroughly terrified by a dream and that you are scared that something untoward may happen to you in the lawsuit; you ask me to seek a delay and get you released for a few short days, at least one day. It is not easy, but I will try, "for in sooth every dream is from Zeus." Yet it makes a difference whether you usually dream what comes to pass, or the opposite.

Looking back over the letter, we can see that Pliny's persuasion was never very likely to succeed. Suetonius' words, echoed by Pliny's opening, indicate extreme terror, not openness to persuasion. Suetonius has been "thoroughly terrified" by a dream, the contents of which Pliny seems not to know; he feels that something "untoward" may happen to him; and he requests a delay, "a few short days, at least one day." The term for extreme terror, *perterritus,* is rare in Pliny, going against the general tone of confident security under the new regime. Other examples of terror are Pliny's fear for his ill wife (6.4.4 *exterret*) or friend (7.1.1 *terret*), the legal or political fears of Regulus (1.5.8 *exterritus*) and Nominatus (5.13.2 *perterritum*), and, of particular relevance here, the dreams of Curtius Rufus (7.27.2 *perterrito*) and of Fannius (5.5.6 *expavit*) and the ghost seen by the (fearless) philosopher Athenodorus (7.27.4 *magis terribile*). Suetonius has been completely terrified far beyond normal anxiety and nervousness over speeches (2.11.11 *sollicitudo... metus*), readings (5.12.1 *vererer*), or electoral campaigns (2.9.1 *anxium... inquietum;* 6.6.1–2 *sollicitudinis... metu*). Fear, like regret or envy, is a canonical vice in Pliny, who boasts of being fearless against Certus (9.13.8) and Massa (7.33), and of being brave and fearless during the volcanic explosion, like his uncle (6.16, 6.20). Only on behalf of others is fear honorable.[2] Pliny freely confesses his solicitude for his friends' physical, legal, or political well-being; here the

---

[2] In accordance with conventional ideas about friendship, some kinds of unacceptable behavior, especially unrestrained pleading and soliciting, become honorable when done on behalf of a friend (Cic. *de Amicit.* 57).

sensible Roman differs from the severe Stoic. Supernatural causes also make fear pardonable, as if it were an expression of religious reverence. Not only the nameless owners of the Athenian haunted house but also good Roman politicians such as Curtius Rufus and Fannius feel fear at the supernatural. It requires an unnaturally imperturbable Greek philosopher to signal calmly to a ghost to wait, and to continue writing while the chains clank over his head (7.27.9).

The style of Suetonius' echoed report illustrates his extreme fear. His repeated request for a delay sounds almost desperate: "a delay... a few short days... certainly the next day." Most other "echo" openings are brief and to the point (e.g. 1.8, 1.14, 1.23), but this one seems to aim at stylistic characterization (his wife's letter at 6.7.1 seems similarly characterized). Suetonius is begging for a delay, any delay, preferably several days, but even one day would help. The diminutive *pauculos* also characterizes: the next letter concerning Suetonius (1.24) has no fewer than four diminutives *(agellus, viteculas, arbusculas, praediolum)*, of which the last three have an emotive tone of humorous condescension. We could imagine the diminutive *pauculos* as representing Pliny's amused condescension, or Suetonius' terrified wheedling, or both. Yet, although fear of the supernatural might be forgiven with a smile, it is not very admirable to be rearranging public business because of private supernatural fears; only the superstitious Regulus consults diviners *(haruspices,* 6.2.2) about the outcome of a case. Perhaps the most famous illustration of the situation is the taunt to Caesar: "Break up the Senate till another time,/ When Caesar's wife shall meet with better dreams" (Shakespeare *Julius Caesar* 2.2.98–99 = Plutarch *Caesar* 64.3). Under Tiberius and Claudius, dreams real or fictitious were even used as reasons for executing people (Dio 60.14.4, 62.15.7, Tac. *Ann.* 11.4.2, Suet. *Claud.* 37). Pliny will not get Suetonius a delay by telling the truth ("my colleague Suetonius has had a bad dream"), but by some "dodge" (1.18.6).

If Pliny will be telling white lies to the judge, perhaps Suetonius is also lying to Pliny? A dream is the most unprovable of events, and even without dreams to scare him Suetonius is excessively cautious and diffident (5.10); a pun on his name Tranquillus, Mr. Calm, may lurk in the background.[3] But Pliny portrays his relations with his friends as based on absolute honor, and thus the initial echoing characterization of Suetonius' sheer terror assures Suetonius (and the reader) that the dream is accepted as authentic. Law cases are nerve-racking, as Pliny repeatedly says, and a frightening dream is natural beforehand; even Pliny has suffered from one. Furthermore, Pliny appears to

---

[3] *Tranquillitas* can serve as a translation for the philosophical ideal of εὐθυμία, Cic. *de Fin.* 5.23; compare Sen. *de Tranquill.* 2.3, *de Ira* 3.6.3. On Suetonius' "diffidence" see Syme 1958:91.

take the dream seriously as an omen. He promises at once to seek a
postponement, justifying the attempt with Homeric authority (1.18.1): "for
indeed a dream is from Zeus" (that is, from Iuppiter Optimus Maximus,
1.7.1).

Yet the Homeric authority takes away more than it gives. At best, Greek or
poetic authority is used merely to reinforce traditional Roman values, as in
protecting one's friend (6.8.3 = *Il.* 1.88) or not boasting over the dead (9.1.3
= *Od.* 22.412), but it can easily slide into mere jesting, as in Pliny's numinous
nod (1.7.1, 1.7.5 = *Il.* 16.250, 1.528) or his comparing his "divine" speech to
Vulcan's armor (6.33.1 = *Aen.* 8.439). Homeric authority is especially
slippery in this case, since the first dream in the *Iliad* is deceptive (2.6–15),
and Penelope's famous speech distinguishes between true and false dreams
(*Od.* 19.560–67). Pliny changes this distinction to make it more respectful and
encouraging to Suetonius, distinguishing not between true and false, but
between dreams that come true and dreams for which the opposite comes true.
He even makes this a matter of individual habit: it depends on whether you are
accustomed to dreaming things that come true or the opposite. Pliny is not so
much discussing the science of dreams as making a transition to the personal
example that should persuade Suetonius, while also giving him a face-saving
excuse if he is not persuaded. Elsewhere in the letters we never hear of
dreams that predict the opposite, but only of dreams that come true (5.5, 7.27)
or, at best, are averted. The slave's ominous dream meant that Pliny *would
have* been executed if Domitian had not been killed (7.27), and his uncle's
dream of Drusus' ghost suggests the conventional supernatural *threat* from an
angry ghost which the Elder averted by writing the history of the German
wars.[4] By the conventional Roman interpretation, omens portend harm, which
may be averted by expiation.

Pliny's theory of the lucky bad omen displays the virtuosity of the expert
orator who can turn almost anything to his argument; just as unfavorable
evidence can be explained away, bad omens can be argued into good omens.
He can even cite Homer against Homer, arguing first that dreams matter (*Il.*
1.63) and then that they should not interfere with politics (*Il.* 12.243), an
argument he reverses with Roman proverbial wisdom ("when in doubt, don't
do it").[5] Perhaps if Suetonius were as skillful an orator as Pliny he would not

---

[4] Sallman 1984:586.

[5] The parallel version in Cicero (*Off.* 1.30) has a moral tone that underscores the relative
banality of Suetonius' request: "they say not to do anything which you doubt whether it's *right
or wrong*" *(quod dubites aequum sit an iniquum)*. Ancient writers on dreams normally
distinguished between meaningful and empty dreams, not between dreams that come true and
dreams whose opposites come true (e.g. Cic. *De Div.* 2.127–28, Artemidorus 1.12, 4 praef.,
Suet. *Aug.* 91.1, Hor. *Sat.* 1.10.33; Van Lieshout 1980:195–200). But in narrating Pompey's

need to fear bad dreams. Pliny implicitly compares his oratory with Suetonius': "I will 'conduct' this 'case' of yours, in order that you may be able to conduct that [actual] case when you want" (6). In order to argue for his client successfully, Suetonius must call in another lawyer, presumably a superior one, to argue for him. But the self-irony keeps the implied self-flattery in check. Pliny may be able to manipulate the legal system to obtain a special favor for Suetonius, but he cannot persuade Suetonius to give up his desire for a postponement. Suetonius has already thought about it and he does "think it safer" (5); he obviously does not "tend to" dream of good luck in reverse; and he will no doubt seize on the concluding proverbial advice, to do nothing, in order to confirm his own hesitations.

> Mihi reputanti somnium meum istud, quod times tu, egregiam actionem portendere videtur. Susceperam causam Iuni Pastoris, cum mihi quiescenti visa est socrus mea advoluta genibus ne agerem obsecrare; et eram acturus adulescentulus adhuc, eram in quadruplici iudicio, eram contra potentissimos civitatis atque etiam Caesaris amicos, quae singula excutere mentem mihi post tam triste somnium poterant. (2–3)

> When I think back on my dream, I think that that one which is scaring you is a sign that the lawsuit will turn out outstandingly. I had undertaken the case of Junius Pastor, when my mother-in-law appeared to me in my sleep, clasping me by the knees and pleading with me not to argue the case. Furthermore, I was about to argue the case while still quite a young man, I was about to argue in front of the full fourfold judicial board, I was about to argue against the mightiest men of the state, indeed associates of the Caesar, any one of which reasons could have unnerved me after such a grim dream.

Pliny's contrasting example reflects praise not only onto himself but also onto the new emperors. Pliny's own dream, unlike Suetonius', was not frivolous, because he had real obstacles to overcome. The first two of the three named obstacles reflect well on himself: he was still young, and he was about to plead in a special joint session of all four panels of the Centumviral court. But the third obstacle reflects badly on the prior regime. Pliny was about to plead before the most powerful men of the state, even "friends" of the emperor. Under a bad regime one could enter the Centumviral court with a mere civil case and depart on trial for one's life (5.1.7). Suetonius' extreme fears are all the more groundless, Pliny implies, now that there are no longer reasons for lawyers to dread political disasters coming out of a case. As Pliny puts it, Suetonius merely fears "something contrary" (*quid adversi,* 1). We can

---

deceptive dream Lucan says that dreams prophesy the opposite (*contraria visis/ vaticinata quies,* 7.21–22, cited by Merrill 1912).

guess, by contrast with Pliny's genuine personal fears at the time of *his* bad dream, that the worst that can happen is that Suetonius will lose his case and perhaps fail in his duty to his client *(fides)*.

In alluding to the dangerous days of old, Pliny uses the naked, ominous term *potentia* (*potentissimos*, 3) rather than a gentler euphemism such as *auctoritas*.[6] In those days leaders had raw power; now they have "prestige" and "influence." We cannot be sure whether this debut was under Titus, and therefore at about age 18 to 20, or under Domitian.[7] Pliny's tone seems rather hostile for Titus, but the term "Caesar" seems too honorific for Domitian (elsewhere only in the last words of the Vestal Virgin Cornelia, 4.11.7). Furthermore, unless he dreamed about his "mother-in-law" before he was actually married, the reign of Titus seems too early for a marriage (10.2.2). Yet Titus appears elsewhere in the letters only as an object of fear for the unjustly harassed Bassus (4.9.2), and is even used as a negative exemplum in one of his two appearances in the *Panegyric* (11.1; contrast 35.4). On the other hand, Pliny might be using the term *Caesaris amicos* (3) to refer to a semi-official status, not merely the "friends of Domitian" but the Privy Council. Perhaps Pliny's average reader was no more certain of the date than we are, despite his boast that the trial made him famous (4). Whether under Titus or the first years of Domitian, the tone is slightly ominous. An advocate ran personal risk only under the prior regime (1.5.4, 5.1.7–8), not under Nerva and Trajan.

Pliny's dream was clearly more than an idle fright, as Suetonius' seems to have been. Rather, it was a nightmarish expression of the political anxieties of the age. In prior times, "friends" of the emperor (1.18.3 *Caesaris amicos*) might try to win a case through unfair influence, or even to use a case to carry out revengeful attacks. Now, Titinius Capito uses his "friendship with the leading citizen" (*amicitia principis*, 1.17.2) to carry out his campaign of vengeance against Nero by the harmless and even honorable method of erecting a public statue of Nero's victim Silanus. Inheritance, the probable subject of this dangerous case of Pliny's at the Centumviral court, is a panegyric topic in distinguishing Good and Bad Emperors (*Pan.* 43); Trajan himself boasts that he can judge his own ex-slave's inheritance case fairly (6.31.9). The Good Emperor allows the ruling class to maintain its collective existence by being able to pass on its wealth to relatives and friends.

---

[6] "The pejorative synonym of 'auctoritas'... is 'potentia'" (Syme 1958:413). The term has a pejorative or negative context in all but one of the occurrences in Pliny (3.7.4 *sine potentia*, 3.9.9 *ne potentissimi... elaberentur*, 9.5.2 *ne gratiae potentium nimium impertire videantur*, *Pan.* 83.6 *non potentiam tuam sed ipsum te reveretur*). The exception is at 4.4.1 *(disertum, quod apud me vel potentissimum est)*. Quintilian discusses how to use *figurae* to avoid risks in pleading against *personae potentes* (*Inst.* 9.2.68).
[7] Sherwin-White 1966:128.

Pliny's dream does not so much illustrate the *habit* of having bad dreams turn out good, as the *ability* to turn bad into good. As he finally advises, "see whether you *too* might *turn* your dream into good" (5). The ominousness of the dream parallels the ominousness of the case itself, which Pliny turned to his own good. It was precisely the danger of the case, especially the political danger, that made it "open up the door of fame" (4). A flagrant imperial opponent wins glory only at the cost of his life, but a discreet opponent can win glory safely. We can guess that Pliny had already calculated that the case would not really bring down imperial wrath onto his head. Another of Pliny's moments of political bravery, in the Massa case, paired him with Herennius Senecio (7.33). By emphasizing his connection with Senecio Pliny gets to portray himself both as a close ally of Domitian's famous victim and as a proponent of a safer style of bravery. Perhaps if Herennius had restricted himself to such safe bravery and not flaunted his opposition with useless gestures such as refusing to accept higher office or publishing a eulogy of the elder Helvidius Priscus (7.19.5), he too would have survived. Pliny did not make Herennius' over-officious gesture of persisting in the prosecution into the penalty phase (Sherwin-White 1966:446 on 7.33.5), but rather, rescued Herennius once he had gotten himself into this hole (7.33.8). By contrast, it is the Elder Pliny's literary discretion under Nero (3.5.5) that serves as a model for Pliny.

In bravely overcoming his mother-in-law's dream-supplication, Pliny becomes mentally prepared, so to speak, to overcome the risks of the case and win fame. The dream gives him psychological practice in facing uncertainty and crisis. If his mother-in-law had actually supplicated, he would no doubt have had to obey, putting *pietas* to family above *fides* to client. But the fact that it is only a dream, that she did *not* supplicate, shows us that this case has the ideal balance of risk and safety, enough risk to win glory but enough safety to come out of it successfully, like the later affairs of Massa (7.33) and Certus (9.13). One might almost suspect that here, too, another factor in addition to the ideal balance of danger and safety was implicit imperial patronage, patronage of which Pliny gives us a glimpse in the two later events. Pliny's behavior in the Massa case merited commendation from the not-yet-emperor Nerva in the best imperial style (7.33.9 "congratulations for *our era*") and may have contributed to his appointment to a treasury prefecture in 94; his speech against Certus probably contributed to his prefecture appointment in 98. In the shifting winds of imperial patronage, the perfect balance of imperial favor and honorable senatorial behavior must have been difficult to attain, especially in transitional years. All of Nerva's reign, along with the start of Trajan's, would have seemed transitional at the time, as

would Titus' reign and the start of Domitian's.[8] Thus, we cannot assume that
just because Pliny was opposing "friends of Caesar" he was not acting to win
imperial patronage. If the case was in Titus' reign, it could have involved
political factionalism connected with Titus' "inheritance" of his father's
"friends"; if it was in Domitian's reign, then it could have been connected with
the corresponding transition from Titus to Domitian. Bassus' varying fortunes
give us a glimpse of the risks during such realignments (4.9.2). Pliny's uncle
did not live long enough past Vespasian's reign to show how well he would
have managed the transitions.

We see, then, that Pliny did not really dream *contraria,* the opposite of
what was going to happen. He did not dream that he would lose the case. His
dream only presented the dangerous aspects of the case in heightened form,
and the illusory aspect of the dream mirrored the illusory political dangers of
the case. His mother-in-law only *seemed* to beseech him not to argue the case;
in reality she saw, or could have been persuaded to see, that the opportunity
for advancement outweighed the apparent dangers. Similarly, Pliny only
seemed to be opposing the emperor; in reality he probably gained imperial
patronage by conducting the case with honor and success, as in his later
politically charged cases. In this period of Roman history, opening up people's
ears and the door to fame, means opening the *right* ears and the *right* doors,
winning popularity not with the common citizen but with the imperial inner
circle (*illa actio mihi aures hominum, illa ianuam famae patefecit,* 4).

As in 97, the young Pliny saw an opening that was safe enough that he
could expect it to win him imperial patronage, but dangerous enough that not
everyone would be willing to try; the danger increases the potential benefit.
The details are lost. Perhaps Pliny helped a new emperor restrain the
ambitions of certain of his predecessor's "friends," or perhaps simply the
show of political freedom was useful for a new emperor. A young politician
like Pliny may have been the perfect tool for this use. Having a weaker
network of political connections than that of an older politician, he would be
willing to take forensic risks to strengthen his links with the imperial center—
an honorable version of what Bad Senators do, *delatores* such as Regulus,
Mettius Carus, or Baebius Massa. In his later years, with less status to gain and
more to lose, Pliny, like Regulus, shifts to defense cases.[9] His last major
prosecutions were "assigned" to him before his consulship, against Priscus in
late 98, and against Classicus probably in September 99 (Sherwin-White
1966:59). These final prosecutions can also be seen as politically "transitional"

---

[8] Indeed, Pliny implies that Domitian's last years already seemed transitional at the time
(1.12.8).
[9] Fantham 1996:205. In the late republic, too, orators generally shifted from prosecution to
defense by age 40 (David 1992:538, 595).

affairs, as I am suggesting for the Pastor case of 1.18.3. Later in Trajan's reign, less glory and greater risk would be obtained by prosecuting governors appointed under Trajan, as opposed to the Nervan governors Priscus and Classicus, who probably governed in 97–98 (Syme 1958:70, 103).

Pliny dismisses his prior fears with another Homeric line, this time not a mere tag but a well-known line from a pivotal scene, with Hector about to breach the Greek wall and set fire to the ships, not to be dissuaded from this disastrous step by a bad omen.[10] Although the original Iliadic context is hardly encouraging, the Greek gives a feeling of remoteness, almost of levity, to the risk. Pliny often uses Greek to lighten the tone at a serious moment (e.g. 1.7, 2.20.12, and even Trajan at 6.31.12).[11] Here he even drops into Greek syntax, introducing the Homeric quotation with a Greek participle to supply Latin's missing past active participle.[12] The ensuing explanation pulls the quotation back into the Latin orbit of serious political values, and away from the ancient Greek military bluster of Hector. Pliny first translates "fatherland" from Greek to Latin, and then he supplants it with the solid Roman concept *fides,* the loyalty of an advocate to a client (*nam mihi patria, et si quid carius patria, fides videbatur,* 4). Hector may go wrong on the battlefield with excessive patriotic bluster, but one can never go wrong standing by one's *honor.* The somewhat startling *contrast* between country and honor, and Pliny's suggestion that something could be dearer than country, highlights both Pliny's awkward position under shifting imperial regimes, and his special problem as a purely civilian administrator who made it to the upper reaches of power.[13] People such as Pliny and Suetonius like to think of their lives of power and exploitation as lives of loyalty and serving. But it is not so clear what (or whom) they are serving. A military commander such as Sosius Senecio, or Verginius Rufus, or Trajan himself, can imagine that he is preserving or extending the Roman Empire. Regardless of who is emperor, a commander serves the State. The varying meanings of *imperium* (military authority, monarchical power, territorial empire) make the pretense easier.[14]

---

[10] The figure of Hector, who rejects his wife's and mother's entreaties at *Iliad* 6 and 22, is also well suited for Pliny's rejection of his mother-in-law's entreaties.

[11] Hector's famous line (also quoted by Cicero, *Att.* 2.3.4) had already been subjected to parody by the comic poet Metagenes: "One omen is best, to come to the aid of one's *dinner,"* Athen. 6.271A. Two other lighthearted Homeric tags appearing in Pliny also had a history of parodic use: *Il.* 16.250 (Plin. 1.7.1, Athen. 8.350D), *Il.* 8.102 (Plin. 9.13.20, Athen. 10.444E).

[12] Niemirska-Pliszczynska suggests *'ratiocinatus' verti potest* (1955:51); Merwald notes the parallel passage at 1.23.4 *his rationibus motus* (1964:27).

[13] Schaefer and Ernestius comment on the startling metaphor of *patria* for *fides (duriusculum,* Schaefer 1805).

[14] On the meanings of *imperium* see Richardson 1991:5.

Verginius Rufus could boast that he vindicated *imperium* not for himself but for the "fatherland" (*patriae*, 6.10.4 = 9.19.1). Did he bestow *supreme power* (and the right to choose the Supreme Leader) onto the state? Or did he rescue the *Empire* for the state, keeping it from crumbling under civil war and the attendant foreign invasions? Both meanings are suggested, and equated: the stability of the imperial government and of the territorial empire are interdependent.[15]

For non-military men such as Pliny and Suetonius, however, the question of loyalty is both more and less pressing.[16] A military leader must be loyal if his skill is to be useful rather than dangerous to the emperor, but his loyalty is more easily defined, as obedience to the emperor. His position, though risky, is relatively clear: he must obey orders. Hector's dilemma between strategy and glory is less likely for a Roman general. Whereas Hector is both a leading warrior and a leading policy-maker, the ideal Roman general leaves the major decisions to the emperor, sacrificing all, glory and even safety, to obedience. Only when he must make on-the-spot decisions in the field must he operate independently and try to second-guess the emperor. A civilian politician, on the other hand, is nominally free and only unofficially bound to follow the emperor's wishes in all his decisions. Pliny wishfully pretends that *fides* is enough to guide him through difficult political decisions; in reality his various obligations to friends, clients, and patrons can conflict with each other or with his overriding obligation to the universal patron, the emperor. But if Pliny needed the lodestar of *fides* to help him serve the Bad Emperor and rise in power without sacrificing his honor, the contrasting situation of Suetonius implies praise of the new regime. Suetonius presumably did not have a dream of a close relative beseeching him to give up the case because of his own political danger, but merely some ill-omened vision that suggested that he might lose the case. He is not considering abandoning the case, but merely needs a day or two to get over the bad omen and his aggravated stage fright. Pliny had to weigh *fides* against the well-being of himself and his family, but Suetonius' decision involves neither *fides* nor safety; a delay will not betray his client, and a loss will not endanger himself. On the other hand, the case will not open the door to fame for Suetonius, as Pliny's did for him. Pliny's

---

[15] Rudich calls Verginius' epigram "nearly as ambiguous as its author's historical behavior" (1993:216). *Imperium adseruit* (τὸ κράτος... περιεποιήσατο at Dio 68.2.4) may echo the (metrically unusable) early imperial propaganda term *vindicare* (Caes. *BC* 1.22.5, Aug. *Mon. Anc.* 1.2), and thus pun on Vindex, whose name attracted puns (Tac. *Ann.* 15.74.2; Suet. *Nero* 45.2; cf. Plin. *NH* 20.160 *Iulium Vindicem adsertorem... a Nerone libertatis*): Verginius boasts that he and not Vindex was the true vindicator. Compare the coin title, possibly under Vindex, *Hercules adsertor* (Sutherland and Carson 1984:207 n. 49).

[16] Syme notes that Pliny is one of only three non-patrician consulars between 70 and 120 *known* not to have commanded a legion (1958:68 n. 4).

equestrian friend will continue his slow and cautious political rise through loyal dependence on his patrons while Pliny continues his illustrious career with high-profile senatorial cases and direct patronage from the imperial circle. Not until Suetonius' towering rise and precipitous fall in the early years of Hadrian will he experience the greater benefits and dangers that come from direct contact with the center of imperial patronage.

NO REGRETS: REAL ESTATE AND THE CIRCULATION OF SYMBOLIC CAPITAL

Pliny's letters are a presentation of his friendships, and the glue that holds together the network of friends is gift-exchange, the exchange of favors. It is fitting, then, for Book 1 to end with a cash transaction, since this illustrates how the crassest financial transaction can be transformed into abstract values of friendship, gratitude, tranquillity, and even literary value. The seller, location, and price are all omitted from the letter, since its sole function is to illustrate the higher values of the deal. In letter 1.19, by contrast, the numerical amounts of 100,000 and 300,000 are necessary to show that Pliny is really giving not mere money but political status.

Pliny's letter is worth money: it will reduce the sale price, and Pliny strongly suggests that Suetonius would have bought the estate at the higher price. We might even try to estimate the letter's cash value by comparing land prices in Pliny: HS 100,000 for his nurse's *agellus* which has since decreased in value (6.3.1), 700,000 (reduced from 900,000) for a 5/12 share of an inheritance sold to Corellia (7.11), 3,000,000 for an additional property (formerly worth 5,000,000) at Tifernum (3.19.7), and 400,000 in annual income at Tifernum (10.8.5). Suetonius' prospective purchase has a villa, vineyards, orchards, and a pathway, much like Pliny's luxury estates but on a smaller scale; it is an *agellus* or *praediolum,* whereas the larger estates are called *agri* or *praedia.* We might guess a sale price of 100,000–500,000, and perhaps the letter will lower the price by 5–10% or HS 5,000–50,000.

> Rogo cures, quanti aequum est emat; ita enim delectabit emisse. Nam mala emptio semper ingrata, eo maxime quod exprobrare stultitiam domino videtur. In hoc autem agello, si modo adriserit pretium, Tranquilli mei stomachum multa sollicitant, vicinitas urbis, opportunitas viae, mediocritas villae, modus ruris, qui avocet magis quam distringat. (1.24.2–3)

> Please see to it that he buys it at a price that is fair; for in that way he will be happy that he bought it. For a bad buy is always thankless, and especially because the owner thinks that he is being reproached by it for his stupidity. This bit of property has much to appeal to the appetite of my friend Tranquillus, so long as the price shows favor: the proximity of the City, the convenient

access to the road, the modest size of the country-house, and the limited amount
of farmland, enough to divert him rather than distract him.

What will the seller get for this lost money? He will gain *gratia.* If he
lowers the price, the sale will not be "thankless" (*ingrata,* 2). Suetonius will
"owe" Pliny, and Pliny will "owe" Hispanus (*quantum esset ille mihi ego tibi
debiturus,* 4)—and Hispanus will similarly be in debt to his friend the seller.
Since each link of this chain is already a bond of friendship, all these favors
will be repaid with other favors, whether in cash, social duties, literary
advice, legal help, or political patronage, the favors we have seen circulating
throughout Book 1. The buyer's friend and the seller's friend are each taking
a cut out of the sale price, to be repaid in social obligations.

Pliny conceals the price cut by calling the reduced price the "fair" price
(*quanti aequum est,* 2) that prevents a "bad deal" *(mala emptio),* and by giving
the transaction emotional overtones. Suetonius will "rejoice" *(delectabit),* the
purchase will not be "without favor" *(ingrata),* and he will not feel "stupid"
(exprobrare stultitiam) if the price "smiles at him" *(si... adriserit),* since many
factors "stir his appetite" *(stomachum multa sollicitant,* 3, a fuller form of
multa sollicitant, 3.19.1). The emotional tone intensifies with Pliny's
anticipatory description of the scholar enjoying his estate. He only needs
enough land to be able to lighten his head, refresh his eyes, creep along the
boundary, tread down a single path, know every vine and count every tree
(4). The diminutives *(viteculas, arbusculas, praediolum)* bestow emotional
warmth, as well as a touch of condescension.[17]

Suetonius is less rich than Pliny, and perhaps than the seller and Hispanus
as well. The real reason he is buying a "modest" estate is not that a larger one
would interfere with his studies but that he cannot afford it. This one estate
will serve for income and for leisured luxury near Rome, combining the
functions of Pliny's two estates at opposite ends of the Tiber, one for income
and one for literary leisure. A rich landowner like Pliny owns more vines
than he can know, more trees than he can count, and more land than he can
stroll around.[18] The condescending description of Suetonius' tidy little estate
hides the outrageously vast sizes of the great estates of Pliny and his set.

---

[17] To be sure, Pliny occasionally uses diminutives in the villa letters purely for emotional
warmth, without condescension (2.17.29 *villula;* 5.6.21, 27 *areola;* 23, 36 *sipunculus;* 23, 40
fonticulus; 38 *zothecula;* see D'Agostino 1931:94).

[18] Seneca, by contrast, condemns the greed that "calls a long journey through one's own
properties 'possession'" (*Ep.* 90.39). Although de Neeve warns us against making
assumptions about the price of land and therefore the sizes of holdings (1985:99), we might
guess that Pliny's Tifernum estates alone, with an income of HS 400,000 (10.8.5), may have
been thousands of *iugera,* or in the range of 5–20 miles in circumference, more than a casual
stroll around.

Evidently an important difference between Suetonius the scholastic-equestrian and Pliny the orator-senator is money. It is easier to create an equestrian, as at 1.19, than to create a senator, which requires not only imperial patronage but also larger sums of money. Thus, Pliny's favor, which buys Suetonius' indebtedness at the cost of a debt to Hispanus, reinforces his superiority over Suetonius.[19]

The first book of letters ends where it began, with no regrets (*paenitentiae,* 4). Suetonius will enjoy his farm with no regrets, just as Pliny will publish the letters with no regrets (*paeniteat,* 1.1.2). The same word describes Pliny's regret-free munificence to Comum (1.8.8) and literary leisure away from Rome (1.9.5), and the idea underlies many other letters: in repudiating present anxieties, he imagines looking back without regret. Pliny will not regret the purchase of slaves (1.21), or the publication of a self-flattering speech (1.8), or a gift to a hometown friend (1.19). He has no regrets over his legal and political decisions about Regulus (1.5), the Baetici (1.7), or "friends of Caesar" (1.18). He will *not* live his life after his mentor's death so negligently as to leave him with regrets (1.12). And under his patronage, Suetonius will be able to argue a case (1.18) or buy an estate (1.24) under conditions that will cause him no regrets.

It is at cardinal moments in the upper-class life of Pliny and his friends that Pliny emphasizes the absence of regrets. The purchase of an estate or of slaves provides the material conditions for their lives; literary publication and legal or political activities provide status and meaning; and the ruling-class cycles of death (1.12) and replenishment through marriage or promotion (1.15, 1.19) provide the human continuity. Pliny wishes his and his friends' lives to be evaluated through their decisive moments, just as in the imperial government, political decision has been mostly reduced to the decisive moment at which one emperor succeeds another. Selection of a Good Emperor will ensure that Rome and the empire will have no regrets for the remainder of his reign: Nerva was missed after his death precisely because his foresight in choosing Trajan ensured that he would not be missed (*desiderandus quod prospexerat ne desideraretur, Pan.* 10.6). Furthermore, the rule of the Good Emperor ensures that the cardinal activities of the upper-class gentleman can proceed in tranquillity, with no regrets. Under the Good Emperor the rich can enjoy their estates safely (*Pan.* 50), friends can trust the loyalty of their friends (42.2), slave-owners can control their slaves safely (42), literary men can conduct their studies safely (47.1), heirs can inherit securely (43), and men and women are even more willing to have children (10.2.2, *Pan.* 22.3, 27.2). By contrast, under a Bad Emperor people *regret* that they were ever born

---

[19] "A client, by publicizing his patron's *beneficia,* also advertised his own inferiority," Saller 1982:127.

(*ut... sui parentumque paeniteat, Pan.* 27.2). Indeed, Suetonius' literary estate, rather than his marriage, will procure him the statutory children that he needs in order to profit from his friends' wills: Pliny lists his erudition and devotion to studies as prime qualifications for the grant (*eruditissimum... studia,* 10.94.1).[20] The purchase of the estate, which is well "dowered" (*his dotibus,* 1.24.4), is a metaphorical marriage for the "scholastic lord of the household" (*scholasticis... dominis,* 4).[21]

Pliny is doing for Suetonius the same thing he did at 1.18, helping a lesser protégé become established in the cardinal activities of aristocratic life. In both instances, Suetonius' debut in upper-class life is a pale reflection of Pliny's own position. His diminutive farm is far smaller and cheaper than Pliny's vast estates and luxury villas, and his ordinary case has neither the risk nor the prestige of the young Pliny's case at the Centumviral Court. Suetonius needs the experienced and influential Pliny to get him the delay that will let him plead his own case successfully, though he does not really need the delay. We might also wonder whether he really needs Pliny's help in getting a "fair price" for the estate. If the estate is endowed with so many features, the fair price may be the price he would get without Pliny's intervention. If the estate will cause no regrets at a low price, perhaps it should cause no regrets at the higher price. Pliny does not say Suetonius does not have enough money, but that a bad deal will seem to reproach him for his stupidity. The less experienced Suetonius needs Pliny's expert help mainly to make sure he is not being duped.

In concluding with a second letter concerning the anxious Tranquillus, Pliny counteracts the tone of modest subservience earlier in the book. In the dedication letter and the literary letters 1.2 and 1.8 he needs advice and encouragement to publish at all, and the character portraits of Euphrates, Corellius, and Aristo put Pliny at least superficially in a reverent and inferior position. Other letters flaunt his close relations with his great model and rival Tacitus (1.6, 1.20), the heroes of the prior age Rusticus and Mauricus (1.5, 1.14), and the members of the imperial inner circle Sosius Senecio and his son-in-law Pompeius Falco (1.13, 1.23). The Suetonius letters place into the foreground what lies elsewhere in the background, the fact that the letters celebrate not only the secure grounding of the Roman empire under its first Good Dynasty, but also Pliny's entrance to full political manhood in the New Age. Behind the anxious scholar, finally secure as "lord" of his estate (2

---

[20] Literary studies are a standard qualification for political advancement: e.g. 2.13.6–7, 3.2.3, 4.24.4 (Pliny himself), 7.22.2, 10.4.4. Literary achievements appear frequently in recommendation letters of Cicero (e.g. *ad Fam.* 13.3, 12, 16, 22) and Fronto (e.g. *ad Amicos* 1.1–5, 1.280–90 Haines).

[21] Pliny uses the same metaphor of his villa, 2.17.29 *tot tantisque dotibus villulae nostrae.*

domino, 4 *dominis*) we can also see the confident high-ranking senator, with enough wisdom and authority to maintain his own political and financial status with no regrets. Behind both lies the "lord" of the empire, the emperor, on whose well-being everyone's depends, and who is therefore the ultimate source both of security and of anxiety.

CONCLUSION: A PERSONAL NOTE

Many writers on Pliny speak of his personality with a certain degree of admiration: considerate, humane, and generous, perhaps vain but at least with a touch of modesty. For example, Bütler's book, still the most recent full-length work that studies Pliny's values and attitudes, tends to accept Pliny's claims at face value and therefore to reflect the image that Pliny has so carefully created. I have tried to read critically and skeptically, and to search for false poses, bad faith, self-interest, and hypocrisy in every letter, in every line. Clearly I do not accept Pliny's picture of himself. What, then, do I think of Pliny the man? To answer honestly, I should also ask what I think of myself, for modern life, especially academic life, is disconcertingly similar to Pliny's in many ways. Cultivating circles of "friends" and patronage relationships for mutual benefit, writing letters of recommendation, publishing for symbolic capital, living off the labors of others, and so on: many of the anxieties and hypocrisies are parallel, and I have used my own experiences to understand the reality behind Pliny's façade—perhaps I have used them too much.

Of course, there are basic distinctions: Pliny lived off the labor of many hundreds of slaves in forty-room mansions; Pliny probably killed the slaves caught enlisting in the army, as well as many Christians (10.29, 10.96); the chance survival of Book 10 tells us things that Pliny may not have liked the general reader to know.[1] Yet I would probably not have done any better had I been born into his place, nor have been able to create writings such as his. And perhaps Pliny would have considered the structural flaws in my life as severe as those in his. In any case, the flaws of Pliny were essentially the flaws of his position in upper-class society. Friendship and generosity tended, then as now, to be infected with self-interest and self-promotion; adulation and

---

[1] Pliny and Trajan prefer to use euphemisms such as *animadvertendum* (10.30.2) and *duci... puniri* (10.96.3), apparently for the death penalty.

mutual flattery drove out honesty; the upper-class villa did indeed waste vast resources; and little of the endless production of literature with which so many men occupied so much of their time was of lasting value.

Yet his letters remain, all the more fascinating when seen as a conscious and disingenuous attempt to shape his public image. We need not admire Pliny the man to admire his literary skill, which a critical reading can help us appreciate, as I hope I have shown. We need not accept his values, either, to learn from him. His very struggle to harmonize the conflicts in his upper-class life give us valuable first-hand insight into the workings of one of the richest and most literate ruling classes the world had ever known.

APPENDIX: MARRIAGE AND CHILD-REARING
AMONG THE ROMAN ELITE

Since I am assuming that Pliny and his circle voluntarily limited their child-rearing, I would like to discuss in one place the possible motives and methods for this practice. I deliberately use the term "child-rearing" rather than "child-bearing" so as not to prejudge the question of how families were kept small, whether by avoidance of conception, by abortion, by disposing of infants, or by a combination; it is also the term Pliny uses, perhaps for the same reason (1.8.11 *educationis, Pan.* 26.5 *educandi*).[1]

From a practical point of view, we should note that the contraceptive and abortifacient plants that were known in antiquity have been shown to be somewhat effective (Riddle 1992). We should also not exaggerate the difficulty of aiming to have few or even a single child in an age of high infant mortality. Since most infant mortality occurs in the first few years, parents could wait several years after a birth, to see if the child survived the critical period, before deciding whether to try for another child. If we take, for the sake of example, 35 years as a possible life expectancy for the Roman elite, Hopkins' figures show that 60% of those alive at age one will survive to age 40 (1983:74). And with advantages of nutrition, avoidance of contagion (e.g. 5.6.2), and perhaps medical advantages, the Roman ruling class may well have had a higher life expectancy than other classes in the Roman world, or even than twentieth-century societies without access to modern technology.

Although the ancient writers themselves mention the topic frequently, their attention tends to be directed at childlessness rather than small families in

---

[1] Seneca's *controversia* on a childless woman during a tyranny mentions the alternatives of abortion or (probably) contraceptive techniques (*quaedam... elisere conceptos, quaedam fecunditatem suam moratae sunt,* 2.5.2). Another pleader attributes the childlessness to the absence of sexual relations (five years of anxious nights spent in planning to kill the tyrant, 2.5.4).

general, in accordance with the profusion of their invective against the figure
of the *captator,* whose schemes are mainly directed against the childless. This
is presumably the thought behind Pliny's casual allusion to "the rewards of
childlessness in this age" (4.15.3 *orbitatis praemia*).[2] But the role of the
captator reflected social and political pressures that functioned in more subtle
ways, and that tended to keep upper-class families small as well as keeping
some upper-class men childless. If we try to identify these pressures, we can
probably discount the importance of the "tedium and work" of child-rearing
(1.8.11) that Pliny mentions, at least for the Roman elite whose numerous
slaves did the tedious work. A small child could be said to know its nurse
better than its father (e.g. Sen. *Ep.* 99.14, Quint. *Inst.* 6 praef. 8). The more
substantial costs of a young man's upper-class education are also not likely to
have been a major impediment to those in the upper reaches of the ruling
class. A greater problem would have been the danger that having too many
children would divide up the family inheritance too much. On the other hand,
a young man from a wealthy but "new" family may have helped his chances of
attracting patronage by postponing child-rearing. The longer such a man
stayed childless, the longer his patrons could expect a major inheritance as a
return for their patronage if he died young; the senator that Pliny promotes as
a groom to Rusticus' daughter may be the same Acilianus who dies at 2.16,
leaving property to Pliny.[3]

Perhaps the strongest clue that having children could discourage patronage
is offered by the sequence of "adoptive" emperors from Nerva to Marcus
Aurelius: being unburdened by dynastic succession was evidently advantageous
for receiving political patronage at the highest level. The shift from Republic
to Empire, from dynastic aristocratic groupings to monarchical patronage,
meant that the best way to rise in power was to be totally loyal, without
independent networks of kindred. Childlessness made one safer to be lifted by
imperial patronage to positions of power; both Pliny himself and his uncle
may have been helped in their rise from provincial gentry to the inner circles
of imperial patronage by being childless.[4] A successful New Man can afford to

[2] Compare 1.8.11, 10.2.2. See Champlin 1991:87–102, and 201–02 for a list of ancient
references. Champlin argues from the lack of concrete evidence that the cruder form of *captatio*
denounced by ancient writers was rare (100–02). Still, the evidence only shows that "probably
well over... 90 percent... of testators followed the dictates of duty or natural affection"
(1991:101): perhaps as many as 5% did not. Champlin himself recognizes that "the social and
demographic pressures... existed; they need not have been heavily abused" (101).
[3] The reason for limiting reproduction generally given by ancient sources is to consolidate
money and power (e.g. Polyb. 36.17, Mart. 5.38, Plut. *Cato Min.* 25, Muson. Rufus 15b;
Parkin 1992:119, Hopkins 1983:78–97).
[4] "Such was the infertility of *novi homines* at Rome, few of them had consular sons" (Syme
1958:228). Syme notes that "two notable figures of power, makers of emperors," Mucianus

eschew the statutory benefits of children, since his additional imperial patronage will make it up, as Pliny caught up with Calestrius Tiro through Domitian's patronage (7.16.2). The emperor functions somewhat like a *captator,* doling out presents of political power which will return to the emperor (him or his successor) on the death of the recipient. On the other hand, a politician with children to inherit his power after him would threaten to form an independent political base that will limit the emperor's freedom in dispensing patronage. For example, senators' sons could expect to become senators themselves, leaving the emperor fewer places to use as rewards to loyal followers.[5]

Not all successful men with few or no children would need to have planned for small families in order to achieve success. The effects of even a small amount of intentional limitation of upper-class family size could have been compounded by a sort of natural selection by which men who happened to have few or no children tended in fact to be more successful. And if childlessness is ideal, daughters are almost as good, allowing one to make useful marriage alliances while avoiding the political threat of building one's own family dynasty. One might half-seriously suggest that if upper-class infants were exposed, it was the *male* infants.[6] Corellius is an ideal instance, with a single daughter, a powerful son-in-law (either L. Neratius Priscus or L. Neratius Marcellus), and a male grandchild to carry on the "burden" of the *imagines* (3.3.6; apparently Corellius Pansa, consul ordinarius in 122).[7]

These social and political pressures to restrict child-rearing were in almost unresolvable tension with the constant rhetorical and legal encouragement to increase it.[8] The neatest solution was the loophole allowing the emperor to grant the *ius trium liberorum* as an act of patronage even to childless men. Pliny himself probably represents a typical successful strategy: marry (and if necessary remarry) early, secure the *ius trium liberorum,* and yearn publicly

---

and Licinius Sura, have no known relatives, wives, or descendants (791). "Trajan, like so many members of the new imperial aristocracy, had no son, not even a daughter" (233). Vespasian, by contrast, was the rare and frightening phenomenon of an emperor "with grown sons" (Tac. *Hist.* 4.8.4 *iuvenum liberorum patrem;* compare Philostr. *Vit. Apoll.* 5.35).

[5] Syme comments on the intense competition for the consulship caused by the fact that so many consulships had to be set aside for consular descendents (1958:69).

[6] The usual assumption is the opposite for lower-class infants (e.g. Gardner 1986:157), though McLaren considers both possibilities (1990:34, 53).

[7] Raepsaet-Charlier 1987:238.

[8] A powerful senator was not so likely to be challenged for his hypocrisy as the childless Greek philosopher urging marriage, in Lucian's story: "fine, Epictetus, then let me marry one of your daughters" (οὐκοῦν, ὦ Ἐπίκτητε, δός μοι μίαν τῶν σαυτοῦ θυγατέρων, *Demonax* 55).

for real children (8.10.3, 10.2.2).[9] Similarly, Suetonius had his "unlucky" marriage to show for himself when Pliny petitioned Trajan on his behalf (*parum felix matrimonium,* 10.94.2). Of course, Pliny's yearnings might not have been entirely insincere; the patronage pressures to postpone child-rearing may well have acted at least partly against his personal desires.

The details of Pliny's marital history must be pieced together from scattered passages, the most important of which is letter 10.2. We hear of a dream about his mother-in-law at the time of his first prominent case (1.18.3), and he includes a letter to his mother-in-law Pompeia Celerina, probably the same woman (1.4; cf. 3.19.8, 6.10.1, 10.51.1). In 97, at the time of his speech in vindication of Helvidius, his wife had recently died (9.13.4). In 98, when Trajan had granted him the "right of three children," he mentions his two marriages as evidence for his desire for children (10.2.2). And his wife Calpurnia is first mentioned in book four (about 104–105), in letters to her grandfather and to her aunt (4.1, 4.19). Although Sherwin-White has argued for three marriages on the evidence of 10.2, the simplest interpretation is that Pliny married his second wife Calpurnia in 97 or 98, shortly after his first wife died in 97.

> eoque magis liberos concupisco, quos habere etiam illo tristissimo saeculo volui, sicut potes duobus matrimoniis meis credere. Sed di melius, qui omnia integra bonitati tuae reservarunt; malui hoc potius tempore me patrem fieri, quo futurus essem et securus et felix. (10.2.2)

> And all the more do I [now] desire children, which I wanted even in that most grim era—as you can well believe from my two marriages. But the gods [have granted something] better, since they preserved everything unharmed for your goodness. I had rather that I become a father at this time especially, when I was going to be both safe and happy.

Sherwin-White objects that a parenthetical reference to the "grim era" is awkward and unlike Pliny's style (1966:559). But the "two marriages" refer back to both parts of the sentence, to the present marriage with its present desire for children, and to the past marriage with its past desire for children. Even more telling is the tone of the conclusion, which confidently announce that he is about to become a father, and that he preferred it this way, for his fatherhood to be postponed so that he could become a father under the good Trajan and did not have to endure being a father under the Bad Emperor. In a bold reversal of the situation, Pliny turns his thanks for the grant of substitute

---

[9] The publication of the miscarriage letters 8.10–11 advertises that Pliny is still trying (Gamberini 1983:177 n. 6).

rights for the childless into thanks for being about to become a father under the goodness of Trajan's reign.[10]

Being married was evidently an advantage for an aspirant to the "right of three children," a compromise for the sake of appearance, making it seem that the grant was simply to prevent people from being punished for natural misfortune beyond their control. Pliny's first marriage, and his rapid remarriage in accordance with the demands of the Augustan marriage legislation, demonstrate that he has tried and will continue to try to have children the real way.[11]

The only plausible argument for assuming an unmarried Pliny at 98 is Calpurnia's absence from books 1–3. But 4.19, which is often taken as a letter celebrating a new marriage, actually suggests a marriage of some time, with Calpurnia memorizing his speeches and setting his verses to music. Perhaps Pliny deliberately excludes matters such as marriage and poetry-writing from the introductory books 1–3 with their serious, political, and masculine emphasis. Even Sherwin-White, who believes that letter 10.2 does not refer to Calpurnia, acknowledges that "Pliny may have... married Calpurnia at the earliest possible moment for legal reasons, without writing a literary letter about her until she was old enough to be of interest" (1966:264).

---

[10] More recently Raepsaet-Charlier has also interpreted letter 10.2 as implying that Calpurnia is Pliny's second wife (1987:170 s.v. Calpurnia).

[11] On the appropriateness of awarding the "right of three children" to a married man, see Allain 1901.1:47. Martial denounces a married man who spends his time in Rome seeking the right of three children instead of having children (8.31; compare 2.92, 9.66). On remarriage, see Ulpian *Tituli* 14, Treggiari 1991:74. Ummidius Quadratus, who would already have been a father "if the god had given the nod," may have had a son later, if the Ummidius Quadratus who had married Marcus Aurelius' sister was his son (7.24.3 *si deus adnuisset pater;* cf. *HA M. Antoninus* 7.4, Sherwin-White 1966:431).

BIBLIOGRAPHY

Ahl, Frederick M. 1984. "The Rider and the Horse: Politics and Power in Roman Poetry from Horace to Statius, with an Appendix by J. Garthwaite." *ANRW* 2.32.1:40–124.

Alföldy, Géza 1988. *The Social History of Rome.* Transl. D. Braund and F. Pollock, Baltimore: Johns Hopkins University Press.

Allain, E. 1901-1902. *Pline le Jeune et ses héritiers.* 4 vols. Paris: Fontemoing.

Baldry, H. C. 1952. "Who Invented the Golden Age?" *CQ* n.s. 2:83–92.

Bardon, Henry 1956. *La littérature latine inconnue, tome II: L'époque impériale.* Paris: Klincksieck.

Barton, Carlin A. 1993. *The Sorrows of the Ancient Romans: The Gladiator and the Monster.* Princeton: Princeton University Press.

Bartsch, Shadi 1994. *Actors in the Audience: Theatricality and Doublespeak from Nero to Hadrian.* Cambridge MA: Harvard University Press.

Beard, M., A. K. Bowman et al. 1991. *Literacy in the Roman World. JRA* Supp. 3, Ann Arbor.

Benjamin, W. 1969. *Illuminations.* Transl. H. Zohn, New York: Schocken Books.

Béranger, Jean 1953. *Recherches sur l'aspect idéologique du principat.* Basel: F. Reinhardt.

Bodel, J. 1995. "Minicia Marcella: Taken Before her Time." *AJP* 116:453–60.

Bourdieu, Pierre 1977. *Outline of a Theory of Practice.* Transl. R. Nice, Cambridge and N.Y.: Cambridge University Press.

Bourdieu, Pierre 1991. *Language and Symbolic Power.* Ed. J. B. Thompson, transl. G. Raymond and M. Adamson, Cambridge MA: Harvard University Press.

Bradley, G. G. and T. K. Arnold 1938. *'Bradley's Arnold' Latin Prose Composition.* Ed. J. Mountford, London: Longman's.

Bradley, Keith 1994. *Slavery and Society at Rome.* Cambridge and N.Y.: Cambridge University Press.

Bronfen, Elisabeth 1993. "Risky Resemblances: On Repetition, Mourning, and Representation." In S. W. Goodwin and E. Bronfen, eds., *Death and Representation.* Baltimore: Johns Hopkins University Press, 103–29.

Bütler, Hans-Peter 1970. *Die geistige Welt des jüngeren Plinius: Studien zur Thematik seiner Briefe.* Heidelberg: Carl Winter Universitätsverlag.

Catanaeus, I. M. 1533. *C. Plinii Caecilii Secundi Novocomensis Epistolarum Libri X. Eiusdem Panegyricus Traiano Dictus Cum Commentariis Ioannis Mariae Catanaei.* Paris.

Champlin, Edward 1991. *Final judgments: duty and emotion in Roman wills, 200 B.C.–A.D. 250.* Berkeley: University of California Press.

Charlesworth, M. P. 1937. "Flaviana." *JRS* 27:54–62.

Chilver, G. E. F. 1941. *Cisapline Gaul: Social and Economic History from 49 B.C. to the Death of Trajan.* Oxford: Clarendon Press.

Citroni Marchetti, Sandra 1992. "Filosofia e ideologia nella 'Naturalis historia' di Plinio." *ANRW* 2.36.5:3248–3306.

Cizek, Eugen 1989. "La littérature et les cercles culturels et politiques à l'époque de Trajan." *ANRW* 2.33.1:3–35.

Coleman, K. M. 1986. "The Emperor Domitian and Literature." *ANRW* 2.32.5:3087–3115.

Corbeill, Anthony 1996. *Controlling Laughter: Political Humor in the Late Roman Republic.* Princeton: Princeton University Press.

Cortius, Gottlieb and Paullus Daniel Longolius 1734. *Caii Plinii Caecilii Secundi Epistolarum Libri Decem cum Notis Selectis.* Amsterdam.

Cugusi, Paolo 1983. *Evoluzione e forme dell'epistolografia Latina.* Roma: Herder.

Curtius, E. R. 1953. *European Literature and the Latin Middle Ages.* Transl. W. R. Trask, New York: Pantheon Books.

D'Agostino, V. 1931. "I diminutivi in Plinio il giovane." *Atti, Accademia delle Scienze di Torino* 66:93–130.

D'Arms, John H. 1981. *Commerce and Social Standing in Ancient Rome.* Cambridge MA and London: Harvard University Press.

David, Jean-Michel 1992. *Le patronat judiciaire au dernier siècle de la république romaine.* École Française de Rome: Palais Farnèse.

Della Corte, Francesco 1967. *Svetonio: eques romanus.* Firenze: la nuova italia editrice.

De Neeve, P. W. 1985. "The Price of Agricultural Land in Roman Italy and the Problem of Economic Rationalism." *Opus* 4:77–109.

Derrida, Jacques 1992. *Given Time I: Counterfeit Money.* Transl. Peggy Kamuf, Chicago: University of Chicago Press.

D'Espèrey, Sylvie Franchet 1986. "Vespasien, Titus et la littérature." *ANRW* 2.32.5:3048–86.

De Ste. Croix, G. E. M. 1981. *The Class Struggle in the Ancient Greek World from the Archaic Age to the Arab Conquests.* Ithaca: Cornell University Press.

Dixon, Suzanne 1993. "The Meaning of Gift and Debt in the Roman Elite." *EMC* 37 n.s. 12:451–64.

Döring, M. 1843. *C. Plinii Caecilii Secundi Epistolae, mit kritisch berichtigtem Text erlautert von Moritz Döring.* Freiberg: Engelhardt.

Duncan-Jones, Richard 1974. *The Economy of the Roman Empire: Quantitative Studies.* Cambridge and N.Y.: Cambridge University Press.

Duncan-Jones, Richard 1990. *Structure and Scale in the Roman Economy.* Cambridge and N.Y.: Cambridge University Press.

Edwards, Catherine 1993. *The Politics of Immorality in Ancient Rome.* Cambridge and N.Y.: Cambridge University Press.

Edwards, Catherine 1997. "Self-scrutiny and Self-transformation in Seneca's Letters." *G&R* 44:23–38.

Ellis, Simon P. 1991. "Power, Architecture, and Decor: How the Late Roman Aristocrat Appeared to His Guests." In Elaine K. Gazda, ed., *Roman Art in the Private Sphere: New Perspectives on the Architecture and Decor of the Domus, Villa, and Insula.* Ann Arbor: University of Michigan Press, 117–34.

Ernout, A., and A. Meillet 1959. *Dictionnaire étymologique de la langue Latine: Histoire des mots.* 4th ed., Paris: Klincksieck.

Fantham, Elaine 1996. *Roman Literary Culture: From Cicero to Apuleius.* Baltimore: Johns Hopkins University Press.

Fell, Martin 1992. *Optimus Princeps? Anspruch und Wirklichkeit der imperialen Programmatik Kaiser Traians*. München: Tuduv.

Franklin, James L. Jr. 1991. "Literacy and the parietal inscriptions of Pompeii." In Beard, Bowman et al. 1991, 77–98.

Gamberini, F. 1983. *Stylistic Theory and Practice in the Younger Pliny*. Hildesheim: Olms.

Gardner, Jane F. 1986. *Women in Roman Law and Society*. Bloomington and Indianapolis: Indiana University Press.

Garnsey, Peter 1968. "Trajan's Alimenta: Some Problems." *Historia* 17:367–81.

Garnsey, Peter 1988. *Famine and Food Supply in the Greco-Roman World: Response to Risk and Crisis*. Cambridge and N.Y.: Cambridge University Press.

Garnsey, Peter 1996. *Ideas of Slavery from Aristotle to Augustine*. Cambridge and N.Y.: Cambridge University Press.

Genovese, Eugene D. 1974. *Roll, Jordan, Roll: The World the Slaves Made*. N.Y.: Pantheon Books.

Gesnerus, I. M. 1739. *C. Plinii Caecilii Secundi Epistolarum libri decem; eiusdem gratiarum actio siue Panegyricus: cum adnotationibus perpetuis Io. Matthiae Gesneri*. Leipzig: Casparus Fritschius.

Gill, Christopher 1988. "Personhood and Personality: The Four-*Personae* Theory in Cicero, *de Officiis* I." *Oxford Studies in Ancient Philosophy* 6:169–99.

Gleason, Maud W. 1994. *Making Men: Sophists and Self-presentation in Ancient Rome*. Princeton: Princeton University Press.

Greenblatt, Stephen 1980. *Renaissance Self-Fashioning: From More to Shakespeare*. Chicago: University of Chicago Press.

Griffin, Miriam 1996. "Cynicism and the Romans: Attraction and Repulsion." In R. Bracht Branham and Marie-Odile Goulet-Cazé, eds., *The Cynics: The Cynic Movement in Antiquity and its Legacy*. Berkeley: University of California Press, 190–204.

Grimal, P. 1955. "Deux figures de la *Correspondance* de Pline: le philosophe Euphratès et le rhéteur Isée." *Latomus* 14:370–83.

Grisé, Yolande 1982. *Le suicide dans la Rome antique*. Montréal: Bellarmin.

Guillemin, Anne-Marie, ed. 1927–1928. *Pline le Jeune, Lettres I–IX*. 3 vols. Paris: Les Belles Lettres.

Guillemin, Anne-Marie 1929. *Pline et la vie littéraire de son temps*. Paris: Les Belles Lettres.

Gunderson, Erik 1997. "Catullus, Pliny, and Love-Letters." *TAPA* 127:201–31.

Harris, William V. 1989. *Ancient Literacy*. Cambridge MA: Harvard University Press.

Hense, Otto 1889. *Teletis Reliquiae*. Leipzig: Teubner.

Hirtzel, Rudolf 1908. "Der Selbstmord." *Archiv für Religionswissenschaft* 11:75–206.

Hopkins, Keith 1983. *Death and Renewal: Sociological Studies in Roman History, vol. 2*. Cambridge and N.Y.: Cambridge University Press.

Horsfall, Nicholas 1991. "Statistics or states of mind?" In Beard, Bowman et al. 1991, 59–76.

Humphreys, S. C. 1981. "Death and Time." In S. C. Humphreys and H. King, eds., *Mortality and Immortality: The anthropology and archaeology of death*. London: Academic Press, 261–83.

Hutchinson, G. O. 1993. *Latin Literature From Seneca to Juvenal*. Oxford: Clarendon Press.

Huzar, Eleanor 1984. "Claudius—the Erudite Emperor." *ANRW* 2.32.1:611–50.

Jackson, Ralph 1988. *Doctors and Diseases in the Roman Empire*. Norman OK and London: University of Oklahoma Press.

Janson, Tore 1964. *Latin Prose Prefaces*. Stockholm: Almquist and Wiksell.

Jones, Brian W. 1992. *The Emperor Domitian*. London and N.Y.: Routledge.

Jones, Christopher P. 1971. *Plutarch and Rome*. Oxford: Clarendon Press.

Kaster, Robert A. 1997. "The Shame of the Romans." *TAPA* 127:1–19.

Keller, O. 1887. "Zu Plinius epist. 1,5,14." *Archiv für Lateinische Lexikographie und Grammatik*, 4:139–40.

Kennedy, George 1972. *The Art of Rhetoric in the Roman World, 300 B.C.–A.D. 300*. Princeton: Princeton University Press.

Kienast, Dietmar 1968. "Nerva und das Kaisertum Trajans." *Historia* 17:51–71.

Krenkel, Werner 1984. *Plinius der Jüngere: Breife in einem Band, herausgegeben von Werner Krenkel*. Berlin und Weimar: Aufbau-Verlag.

Kudlein, Fridolf 1991. *Sklaven-Mentalität im Spiegel Antiker Wahrsagerei*. Forschungen zur Antiken Sklaverei Bd. 23, Stuttgart: Franz Steiner Verlag.

Leach, Eleanor Winsor 1990. "The Politics of Self-Presentation: Pliny's *Letters* and Roman Portrait Sculpture." *CA* 9:14–39.

Lilja, Saara 1978. "Descriptions of Human Appearance in Pliny's Letters." *Arctos* 12:55–62.

Long, A. A. 1988. "Socrates in Hellenistic Philosophy." *CQ* 38:150–71.

Longden, R. P. 1931. "'Tribunicia Potestas': A Note." *JRS* 21:131–33.

MacMullen, Ramsey 1974. *Roman Social Relations, 50 B.C. to A.D. 284*. New Haven: Yale University Press.

Markus, Hazel and Susan Cross 1990. "The Interpersonal Self." In Lawrence A. Pervin, ed., *Handbook of Personality: Theory and Research*. New York and London: The Guilford Press, 576–608.

Mattingly, Harold and Edward A. Sydenham 1926. *Roman Imperial Coinage, vol. 2: Vespasian to Hadrian*. London: Spink and Son Ltd.

McKay, A. G. 1975. *Houses, Villas, and Palaces in the Roman World*. Southampton: Thames and Hudson.

McLaren, Angus 1990. *A History of Contraception from Antiquity to the Present Day*. Oxford: Clarendon Press.

Merrill, E. T. 1912. *Selected Letters of the Younger Pliny*. London: Macmillan.

Merwald, Günter 1964. *Die Buchkomposition des jüngeren Plinius*. Diss. Friedrich-Alexander-Universität, Erlangen-Nürnberg.

Millar, Fergus 1977. *The Emperor in the Roman World*. London: Duckworth.

Mommsen, T. 1869. "Zur Lebensgeschichte des jüngeren Plinius." *Hermes* 3:31–139.

Murgia, Charles E. 1985. "Pliny's Letters and the *Dialogus*." *HSClP* 89:171–206.

Mynors, R. A. B. 1963. *C. Plini Caecili Secundi Epistularum Libri Decem*. Oxford: Clarendon Press.

Niccolini, Giovanni 1932. *Il tribunato della plebe*. Fondazione Guglielmo Castelli vol. 6, Milan.

Nichols, John 1980. "Pliny and the Patronage of Communities." *Hermes* 108:365–85.

Nicholson, John 1994. "The Delivery and Confidentiality of Cicero's Letters." *CJ* 90:33–63.

Niemirska-Pliszczynska, Joanna 1955. *De elocutione Pliniana in epistularum libris novem conspicua*. Lublin.

Parkin, Tim G. 1992. *Demography and Roman Society*. Baltimore: Johns Hopkins University Press.

Plass, Paul 1995. *The Game of Death in Ancient Rome: Arena Sport and Political Suicide*. Madison: University of Wisconsin Press.

Raepsaet-Charlier, Marie-Thérèse 1987. *Prosopographie des femmes de l'ordre sénatorial (Ier–IIe siècles)*. Leuven: Peeters.

Ramage, E. S. 1989. "Juvenal and the establishment: denigration of predecessor in the 'Satires.'" *ANRW* 2.33.1:640–707.

Richardson, J. S. 1991. "*Imperium Romanum:* Empire and the Language of Power." *JRS* 81:1–9.

Riddle, John M. 1992. *Contraception and Abortion from the Ancient World to the Renaissance.* Cambridge MA: Harvard University Press.

Riepl, Wolfgang 1913. *Das Nachrichtenwesen des Altertums, mit besonderer Rücksicht auf die Römer.* Leipzig and Berlin: B. G. Teubner.

Riggsby, Andrew M. 1995. "Pliny on Cicero and Oratory: Self-Fashioning in the Public Eye." *AJP* 116:123–35.

Riggsby, Andrew M. 1997. "'Public' and 'private' in Roman culture: the case of the *cubiculum.*" *JRA* 10:36–56.

Riggsby, Andrew M. 1998. "Self and Community in the Younger Pliny." *Arethusa* 31:75–98.

Rist, J. M. 1969. *Stoic Philosophy.* Cambridge: Cambridge University Press.

Rudd, Niall 1992. "Stratagems of Vanity: Cicero, *Ad familiares* 5.12 and Pliny's letters." In T. Woodman and J. Powell, eds., *Author and audience in Latin literature.* Cambridge and N.Y.: Cambridge University Press, 18–32.

Rudich, Vasily 1993. *Political Dissidence under Nero: The Price of Dissimulation.* London and N.Y.: Routledge.

Rusca, L. 1961. *Plinio il Giovane: Lettere ai familiari.* Trad. e note di L. Rusca, Milano: Bibl. Universale Rizzoli.

Saller, Richard P. 1982. *Personal Patronage Under the Early Empire.* Cambridge and N.Y.: Cambridge University Press.

Sallmann, Klaus 1984. "Der Traum des Historikers: Zu den 'Bella Germaniae' des Plinius und zur julisch-claudischen Geschichtsschreibung." *ANRW* 2.32.1:578–601.

Sandbach, F. H. 1975. *The Stoics.* New York: Norton.

Sandys, John Edwin 1927. *Latin Epigraphy: An Introduction to the Study of Latin Inscriptions.* 2nd ed. revised by S. G. Campbell, Cambridge: Cambridge University Press.

Sartre, J.-P. 1994. *Being and Nothingness.* Transl. H. E. Barnes, New York: Gramercy Books.

Schaefer, Gottfried Heinrich 1805. *C. Plinii Caecilii Secundi Epistolarum libri decem et Panegyricus ex recensione Jo. Matthiae Gesneri.* Revised by Schaefer, Leipzig.

Scott, James 1977. "Patronage or Exploitation." In Ernst Gellner and John Waterbury, eds., *Patrons and Clients in Mediterranean Societies.* London: Duckworth, 21–39.

Scott, James C. 1985. *Weapons of the Weak: Everyday Forms of Peasant Resistance.* New Haven: Yale University Press.

Scott, James C. 1990. *Domination and the Arts of Resistance: Hidden Transcripts.* New Haven: Yale University Press.

Serbat, Guy 1986. "Pline l'Ancien. État présent des études sur sa vie, son oeuvre, et son influence." *ANRW* 2.32.4:2069–2200.

Sherwin-White, A. N. 1966. *The Letters of Pliny: A Historical and Social Commentary.* Oxford: Clarendon Press.

Sherwin-White, A. N. 1973. *The Roman Citizenship.* 2nd edition, Oxford: Clarendon Press.

Smith, Wesley J. 1997. *Forced Exit: The Slippery Slope from Assisted Suicide to Legalized Murder.* New York: Random House.

Stampp, Kenneth M. 1969. *The Peculiar Institution: Slavery in the Antebellum South.* New York: Alfred Knopf.

Steiner, G. 1996. *No Passion Spent: Essays 1978–1995.* New Haven: Yale University Press.

Sutherland, C. H. V. and R. A. G. Carson 1984. *Roman Imperial Coinage.* 2nd edition, London: Spink.

Syme, Ronald 1930. "The Imperial Finances under Domitian, Nerva, and Trajan." *JRS* 20:55–70.

Syme, Ronald 1958. *Tacitus.* 2 vols. Oxford: Clarendon Press.

Syme, Ronald 1958b. *Colonial Elites: Rome, Spain and the Americas.* London: Oxford University Press.

Syme, Ronald 1968. "The Ummidii." *Historia* 17:72–105.

Syme, Ronald 1985. "The Correspondents of Pliny." *Historia* 34:324–363.

Syme, Ronald 1987. "Marriage Ages for Roman Senators." *Historia* 36:318–32.

Townend, G. B. 1960. "The Sources of Greek in Suetonius." *Hermes* 88:98–120.

Traub, Henry W. 1955. "Pliny's Treatment of History in Epistolary Form." *TAPA* 86:213–32.

Treggiari, Susan 1991. *Roman Marriage: iusti coniuges from the Time of Cicero to the Time of Ulpian.* Oxford: Clarendon Press.

Trisoglio, Francesco 1972. *La personalità di Plinio il Giovane nei suoi rapporti con la politica, la società e la letteratura.* Memorie dell'Accademia delle Scienze di Torino, Classe di Scienze Morali, Storiche e Filologiche, ser. 4 no. 25, Torino.

Trisoglio, Francesco 1973. *Opere di Plinio Cecilio Secondo.* 2 vols. Torino: UTET.

van Lieshout, R. G. A 1980. *Greeks on Dreams.* Utrecht: HES Publishers.

Van Dam, Harm-Jan 1984. *P. Papinius Statius, Silvae, Book II: A Commentary.* Leiden: E. J. Brill.

van Hooff, Anton J. L. 1990. *From Autothanasia to Suicide: Self-killing in Classical Antiquity.* London and N.Y.: Routledge.

Veyne, Paul 1967. "Autour d'un commentaire de Pline le Jeune." *Latomus* 26:723–51.

Veyne, Paul 1990. *Bread and Circuses: Historical Sociology and Political Pluralism.* Transl. B. Pearce, London: Penguin Press.

Vinson, M. P. 1989. "Domitia Longina, Julia Titi, and the literary tradition." *Historia* 38:431–50.

Vogt, A. 1933. "Vorläufer des Optimus Princeps." *Hermes* 68:84–92.

Wallace-Hadrill, Andrew 1988. "The Social Structure of the Roman House." *PBSR* 56:43–97.

Ward-Perkins, J. B. 1988. *Roman Architecture.* New York: Rizzoli International.

Waters, K. H. 1975. "The Reign of Trajan, and its Place in Contemporary Scholarship (1960–72)." *ANRW* 2.2:381–431.

White, Peter 1974. "The Presentation and Dedication of the *Silvae* and the *Epigrams*." *JRS* 64:40–61.

Williams, Gordon 1968. *Tradition and Originality in Roman Poetry.* Oxford: Clarendon Press.

Williams, Gordon 1982. "Phases in Political Patronage of Literature in Rome." In B. K. Gold, ed., *Literary and Artistic Patronage in Ancient Rome.* Austin: University of Texas Press, 3–27.

Winterbottom, M. 1964. "Quintilian and the Vir Bonus." *JRS* 54:90–97.

Woodman, A. J. 1975. "Questions of Date, Genre, and Style in Velleius: Some Literary Answers." *CQ* 25:272–305.

Zanker, Paul 1995. *The Mask of Socrates: The Image of the Intellectual in Antiquity.* Transl. A. Shapiro, Berkeley: University of California Press.

Zelzer, Klaus 1964. "Zur Frage des Charakters der Briefsammlung des jüngeren Plinius." *WS* 77:144–61.

INDEX

adrogantia, 61, 201
analogy, linked, 11, 182, 185 n. 22, 222
antiquitas, 178
Appian, 179 n. 7 (*BC* 5.3)
Aristotle, 16 n. 3 (*EN* 8.4 1157A15), 60 n.
  15 (*Problem.* 29.951B1), 74 n. 43
  (*Rhet.* 3.11.6 1412A21)
Artemidorus (friend of Pliny), 152
Artemidorus (writer on dreams), 214 n. 5
  (1.12, 4 praef.)
Athenaeus, 34 n. 16 (6.267E–270A), 219 n.
  11 (6.271A, 8.350D, 10.444E)
Athenodorus, 212
auctoritas, 89, 102, 150
Augustine, 60 n. 15 (*Confess.* 4.2)
Augustus, 6, 53, 79, 165, 167, 178, 197 n.
  8, 208; 220 n. 15 (*Mon. Anc.* 1.2)
Aulus Gellius, 134 n. 34 (5.1.1), 88 n. 70
  (12.9.1), 123 n. 10 (13.17), 23 n. 25
  (17.9.2)
(M.) Aurelius, 91 n. 78 (*Med.* 3.4), 17 n. 4
  (3.4.2), 208 n. 25 (3.8), 167 (4.32), 17
  n. 4 (8.2), 17 n. 4 (8.53), 17 n. 4
  (11.19), 208 n. 25 (12.36)
Aurelius Victor, 168 (*de Caes.* 5.2)

bad faith, 29, 51, 105, 114, 116, 122, 133,
  139 (and throughout)
(Aufidius) Bassus, 168–69
(Julius) Bassus, 216
beard, 127
boasting, modest, 13, 20, 22, 48, 60 n. 14,
  116, 123, 185, 195

(Julius) Caesar, 178–79, 202, 213; 220 n.
  15 (*BC* 1.22.5)
Callimachus, 10 (*Epigr.* 21.4), 10 (*Hymn*
  2.105–13)
Calpurnia, 9, 139, 213, 232–33
captatio, 12, 42, 55–58, 145, 230
Cato the Elder, 29 n. 1 (*Agr.* 10.1)
Cato the Younger, 170 n. 25, 197
Catullus, 15 n. 2, 36; 20–21 (1), 196 (1), 37
  n. 22 (16.4)
Celsus, 144 n. 9 (*De Med.* 4.31)
(Publicius) Certus, 8, 87, 142, 175, 206
children and childlessness, 12, 42, 94–97,
  107, 130, 135, 179, 181, 223, 229–33
chronological artificiality and stylization, 8–
  9, 141, 180
Cicero, 18, 22 n. 20; 219 n. 11 (*Att.* 2.3.4),
  27 (5.16.2–3), 27 (5.21.5), 24 (5.21.9),
  27 (6.2.4–5), 24 (6.3.1–2), 27 (6.3.3),
  24 (6.4.3), 24 (7.1.2–4), 24 (8.12.5),
  23 (10.11.1), 23 (10.18.1–2), 23
  (11.4a), 24 (11.6.2), 23 (11.9), 16 n. 3
  (*de Amicit.* 27–32, 51, 69), 212 n. 2
  (57), 19 n. 12 (66), 124 n. 12 (86), 214
  n. 5 (*de Div.* 2.127–28), 129 n. 22 (*de
  Fin.* 4.78–79), 213 n. 3 (5.23), 39
  (5.53), 214 n. 5 (*de Offic.* 1.30), 60 n.
  15 (2.51), 129 n. 22 (*de Orat.* 2.159),
  70 n. 35 (2.239), 129 n. 22 (3.66), 35
  n. 18 (3.155), 137 n. 39 (3.203), 184 n.
  18 (*de Sen.* 38), 16 n. 3 (*Fam.* 2.4.1),
  148 n. 17 (4.6.2), 179 n. 9 (5.16.3),
  129 (7.33.2), 65 n. 24 (8.15.1), 224 n.
  20 (13.3), 17 n. 4 (*Muren.* 61), 145 n.

12 (*Orat.* 135), 23 n. 25 (*Phil.* 2.7), 17 n. 4 (*Tusc. Disp.* 5.53, 81)

(Caecilius) Classicus, 59, 204, 219

Claudius, 161–72, 201

Columella, 29 n. 1(3.3.8)

comparative, diminutive, 20, 103

complaint, 138

Comum, 31–33

conflict of obligations, always resolved, 25, 79, 117, 190, 200–01, 204, 220

Corellia, 11 n. 19

Corellius Rufus, 102, 141–59, 167, 206, 231

Cornelius Nepos, 20–21; 22 (*Atticus* 16.3–4)

cubiculum, 32, 152

Curtius Rufus, 26 n. 30 (3.7.15)

dedication letters, 15–21, 42, 173

delatio, 56, 66, 218

deliciae, 33

Demosthenes, 22 n. 20, 178, 88 (*Olynth.* 2.9)

denigration of prior emperors, 24, 27, 64–65, 137, 169–70

diminuendo, optimistic closing, 43, 46

Dio, 179 n. 7 (41.36.3), 179 n. 7 (48.12.5), 201 n. 16 (53.17.9), 197 n. 7 (53.17.10), 79 n. 53 (54.23), 197 n. 8 (54.30.2), 79 (55.8.2), 208 (56.30.4), 52 (57.19.2), 63 n. 21 (58.11.3), 168 n. 17 (59.19), 153 (59.30.2), 170 n. 27 (60.3.6), 52 (60.13.2), 213 (60.14.4), 52 (60.15.5), 70 (61.14.2), 163 (61.20.4), 52 (62.13.4), 213 (62.15.7), 168 (62.19.4), 156 (62.25.1), 163 (62.26.3), 162 (62(63).15.2), 95 n. 5 (63.22.6), 197 (64.7.2), 69 (64.19.1), 70 (64.19.3), 63 (64.20–21), 127 n. 16 (66.13.1a), 60 n. 13 (67.3.3–4), 68 (67.13.2), 170 n. 27 (68.1.2), 172 (68.1.3), 190 n. 29 (68.2.4), 220 n. 15 (68.2.4), 142 (68.3.3), 153 (68.3.3), 173 (68.3.3), 115 (68.7.3), 162 n. 3 (68.7.3), 172 (68.7.3)

Dio Chrysostom, 172 n. 30 (1.84), 166 n. 11 (3.55–85), 187 n. 24 (3.55–85), 162 n. 3 (3.135–36)

Diogenes Laertius, 49 n. 12 (6.55), 130 n. 24 (6.104), 147 n. 16 (7.130), 208 n. 25 (7.160)

distinctio, 5, 7, 57–60, 66, 88, 145, 218

Domitian, 24, 55, 61–66, 76, 81, 85, 87, 89, 94, 141–43, 152–53, 162, 169–70, 190–91, 199, 216–18

Domitius Afer, 167

Domitius Tullus, 152

Drusus, 41

emperor, terms for, 65; *Caesar,* 171, 216; *divus,* 171; *dominus,* 36, 49, 52, 66, 225; *dux,* 90; *imperator,* 65; *optimus,* 65, 73; *pater patriae,* 6, 96; *princeps,* 6, 133–35, 189

envy, 43, 98–99, 104, 107, 117 n. 14, 137

Epictetus, 230 n. 8

114 n. 7 (1.2.12), 127 (1.2.29), 120 n. 2 (1.2.33–36), 134 (1.4.14), 53 (1.7.32), 129 n. 20 (1.10.3), 49 n. 12 (1.13), 127 (1.16.10–14), 129 n. 20 (1.18.9), 129 n. 20 (1.21.2), 208 n. 25 (1.25.10), 114 n. 7 (1.25.15), 208 (1.25.17), 129 n. 20 (1.28.9)

208 (2.5.2, 7), 114 n. 7 (2.6.8), 134 n. 34 (2.17.35–40), 134 n. 34 (2.21.10), 129 n. 20 (2.21.22), 130 (2.22.29), 17 n. 4 (2.22.35), 129 n. 22 (2.23.143), 125 n. 13 (2.24.7), 123 (2.24.15), 129 n. 20 (2.24.28)

129 n. 20 (3.1.31), 129 n. 22 (3.2.13–16), 114 n. 7 (3.7.31), 129 n. 20 (3.9.10), 134 n. 34 (3.9.11–14), 114 n. 7 (3.9.18), 2 (3.15.8), 49 n. 12 (3.19.5), 130 (3.21.5), 129 n. 22 (3.21.7), 130 (3.22.23–24, 76), 128 n. 19 (3.22.89), 134 n. 34 (3.23.13, 19, 29, 37), 30 n. 14 (3.23.17–26), 129 n. 22 (3.23.21, 37), 125 n. 13 (3.23.25), 129 n. 20 (3.23.30, 37), 208 (3.24.22), 129 n. 21 (3.24.36), 114 n. 7 (3.24.44–49)

208 n. 25 (4.1.165), 208 n. 25 (4.7.13), 127 n. 16 (4.8.15), 2 (4.8.17–20), 127 n. 16 (4.8.17–20), 128 n. 19 (4.11.14)

208 n. 25 (*Encheir.* 17), 17 n. 4 (34), 17 n. 4 (fr. 25)

epistolary structure, significant use of, 22, 31, 43, 48, 50, 82, 157

epitome de Caesaribus, 168 (5.3), 53 (12.1), 95 (12.4), 100 n. 18 (12.4), 106 n. 29 (12.4), 153 (12.8)
Eutropius, 115 (8.4)

(Calpurnius) Fabatus, 52, 94, 132
fashioning of an upper-class person, self-fashioning after the emperor, 6, 49, 53, 55, 88, 115, 145, 177–78, 181, 185, 190, 197
Fronto, 224 n. 20 (1.280–90 Haines), 101 n. 20 (1.308), 2 (2.50), 129 n. 22 (2.50, 66), 110 n. 32 (2.58)

gods, 74
Golden Age, 34, 39, 50
Greek words, phrases, and quotations, 14, 23, 32, 36–37, 55, 70, 87, 119, 121, 129, 164, 205, 219

Hadrian, 17, 190, 221
Hector, 218–20
Helvidius Priscus (elder), 53, 66 n. 25, 68, 197
Helvidius Priscus (younger), 120
Herennius Senecio, 68, 217
Herodotus, 167 (7.45)
Hesiod, 34 n. 15 (*Op.* 92, 114)
hierarchy of power, reinforced through friendly exchange, 12, 115, 134, 140, 166, 223
Hippocrates, 144 n. 9 (*Prorrhet.* 2.5), 144 n. 9 (2.8)
Historia Augusta, 18 n. 8 (*Hadr.*), 190 (2.10), 17 n. 6 (11.3), 190 n. 28 (12.2), 71 (16.10), 156 (24.8–9), 233 n. 11 (*M. Antoninus* 7.4), 71 (27.7)
Homer, 214 (*Il.* 1.63), 214 (1.88), 214 (1.528), 214 (2.6–15), 219 n. 11 (8.102), 52 (12.243), 214 (12.243), 214 (16.250), 219 n. 11 (16.250), 147 (18.22), 52 (22.91), 6 n. 10 (*Od.* 2.47), 34 (4.566–68), 130 n. 23 (11.334), 130 n. 23 (13.2), 214 (19.560–67), 64 (22.412), 214 (22.412)
Horace, 4; 39 (*Epod.* 16.41), 29 n. 2 (*Odes* 1.1.33–37), 10 (2.20.4), 118 (3.29.12), 214 n. 5 (*Sat.* 1.10.33), 118 (2.6.23–39, 59–62)

imperial virtues, 6; *comitas,* 102 n. 21, 182; *felicitas,* 39 n. 26, 103; *frugalitas,* 179 n. 6; *humanitas,* 123 n. 10; *indulgentia,* 57, 103, 166 n. 11, 192; *industria,* 166 n. 11, 187; *moderatio,* 61, 190; *providentia,* 89; *securitas,* 52 n. 19, 166, 189; *simplicitas,* 162 n. 4, 190
internalization of friendly relations, 43–44, 104, 157
Iulius Victor, 24 n. 26 (448.5–9), 19 n. 12 (448.16–17, 32–33), 148 n. 17 (448.21), 37 n. 25 (448.30)
Ius Trium Liberorum, 94, 113, 231

Juvenal, 112 n. 4 (1.127–33), 114 n. 8 (1.134–38), 113 n. 5 (3.186–89), 60 n. 13 (4.8–10), 66 n. 26 (4.38), 20 n. 14 (4.85–86), 29 n. 2 (7.178–83), 34 n. 14 (7.183), 26 (11.162–64), 29 n. 2 (14.86–95, 140–72), 57 n. 6 (16.51)

letter exchange, as symbol of friendly exchange of favors, 3, 133, 177
literary value, anxieties over, 21, 29, 39, 44, 117, 174
Livia, portico of, 79
[Longinus], 178 n. 5 (*On the Sublime* 44.2–3)
Lucan, 197 (2.303), 214 n. 5 (7.21–22)
Lucian, 230 n. 8 (*Demonax* 55)
Lucretius, 37 (1.832)

Martial, 10 (1.91), 57 n. 6 (2.65), 233 n. 11 (2.92), 114 n. 8 (3.60), 59 n. 12 (4.16), 10 (4.27), 114 n. 8 (4.68), 57 n. 6 (4.70), 22 n. 23 (4.89.6–7), 10 (5.10), 129 n. 20 (5.15), 230 n. 3 (5.38), 26 n. 30 (5.44), 26 (5.78.27), 96 n. 9 (6.3), 59 n. 12 (6.38), 59 n. 12 (6.64.11), 26 (6.71.2), 129 n. 20 (7.12), 113 n. 5 (7.86), 233 n. 11 (8.31), 113 n. 5 (8.64), 233 n. 11 (9.66), 144 n. 9 (9.93.9), 22 n. 23 (10.1), 129 n. 20 (10.5), 90 n. 75 (10.6.2), 59 n. 12 (10.19), 175 (10.19.16–17), 129 n. 20 (10.33.1), 112 n. 4 (10.70), 62 n. 18 (11.27.7), 66 n. 26 (11.33.1), 90 n. 75 (12.8.6), 121 n. 5 (12.9.1), 26 (14.203)
(Baebius) Massa, 175, 217

(Iunius) Mauricus, 61, 81, 87, 89–91, 177–85

Mettius Modestus, 63, 72–76, 86

munificence, 93–110

Musonius Rufus, 2, 129 n. 20, 134 n. 34, 131 (fr. 3–4), 130 (fr. 13–15), 230 n. 3 (fr. 15b), 127 (fr. 21)

mystification of power structures, 122, 182, 185, 190

Narnia, 52

Nero, 8, 34, 53, 65, 143, 162, 168

Nerva, 9, 53, 60, 94–96, 141–45, 172, 223

Nestor, 205

New Year, restoration imagery connected with, 81

(Servilius) Nonianus, 165, 167, 172

Otho, 55, 73, 96

Ovid, 79 n. 53 (*Fasti* 6.639–46), 48 n. 10 (*Her.* 4.1, 18.1), 34 (*Metam.* 1.107), 50 (1.135), 35 n. 19 (3.407), 48 n. 10 (9.530), 48 n. 10 (*Trist.* 3.3.88)

Pallas, 62 n. 19, 90 n. 76, 108, 135, 171

paradox or union of opposites, 33, 38, 41, 61, 118, 123 n. 10, 156, 165, 184

Perusia, 52

philosophy, 71, 79, 119–40, 147, 208

Philostratus, 230 n. 4 (*Vit. Apoll.* 5.35), 60 n. 13 (7.6), 122 (*Vit. Soph.* 1.7.2, 1.25.5)

Pindar, 34 (*O.* 2.61–62)

(Calpurnius) Piso, 8, 63, 68

Plato, 126; 147 n. 16 (*Laws* 873C), 130 (*Phaedo* 60A, 116C), 130 (*Prot.* 328D), 139 n. 42 (*Rep.* 347C), 43 n. 36 (440A), 131 n. 26 (452–57), 126 (*Symp.* 215B), 126 (*Theaet.* 143E)

Pliny the Elder, 17–18, 32 n. 7, 40–41, 168–69, 214; 15 n. 2 (*NH* praef. 1), 19 (praef. 1–3), 169 (praef. 12, 13, 16, 18, 20), 63 n. 23 (praef. 31), 41 (7.188–90), 52 (18.35), 220 n. 15 (20.160)

Pliny the Younger, 60 n. 14 (1.1.1), 43 n. 34 (1.1.2), 102 (1.1.2), 119 (1.2.2), 79 (1.2.3), 196 (1.2.5), 21 (1.2.6), 43 n. 34 (1.2.6), 43 (1.2.6), 166 (1.2.6), 166 (1.3.4), 32 (1.4.2), 182 (1.4.4), 122 n. 9 (1.5), 110 (1.5), 171 (1.5.1), 216 (1.5.4), 204 (1.5.5), 24 (1.5.7), 150 n. 22 (1.5.8), 212 (1.5.8), 22 n. 20 (1.5.12), 7 (1.5.15), 9 (1.5.15), 188 (1.5.16), 206 n. 21 (1.5.16), 176 (1.6), 40 (1.6.1), 43 n. 34 (1.6.3), 204 (1.7), 219 (1.7), 214 (1.7), 117 (1.7.1), 119 (1.7.1), 87 n. 68 (1.7.2), 165 n. 9 (1.7.2), 25 (1.7.3), 140 (1.8.3), 43 (1.8.4), 87 n. 68 (1.18.4), 61 n. 17 (1.8.5), 229–30 (1.8.11), 36 n. 20 (1.8.12), 63 (1.8.14), 9 (1.8.17), 40 (1.8.17), 138 n. 41 (1.9), 140 (1.9.3), 174 (1.9.3), 129 (1.9.6), 176 (1.9.6), 43 n. 34 (1.9.7), 121 (1.9.8), 71 (1.10), 79 (1.10), 161 (1.10.1), 51 n. 16 (1.10.2), 185 (1.10.3–4), 6 n. 8 (1.10.8), 9 (1.12), 136 (1.12), 62 n. 20 (1.12.3), 167 (1.12.4), 218 n. 8 (1.12.8), 83 n. 64 (1.12.11), 56 (1.12.12), 66 n. 25 (1.13.3), 12 (1.13.6), 81 n. 58 (1.14.1), 89 (1.14.3), 5 n. 5 (1.14.4), 11 (1.14.4), 121 (1.14.4), 6 n. 8 (1.14.5), 66 n. 25 (1.14.5), 145 n. 12 (1.14.5), 89 n. 74 (1.14.6), 62 n. 18 (1.14.8), 127 n. 17 (1.14.8), 88 (1.14.9), 18–19 (1.15), 11 (1.15.3), 137 n. 40 (1.15.3), 101 (1.16), 121 (1.16), 37 (1.16.5), 9 n. 16 (1.16.6), 131 n. 27 (1.16.6), 187 (1.16.6), 12 (1.17.1), 121 (1.17.1), 216 (1.17.2), 12 (1.17.4), 8 (1.18), 52 (1.18), 199 (1.18), 231 (1.18.3), 43 n. 34 (1.18.5), 205 (1.18.5), 11 (1.18.6), 185 n. 22 (1.18.6), 223 (1.19), 11 (1.19.3), 101 (1.19.3), 110 (1.20), 74 n. 43 (1.20.13), 86 (1.20.13), 68 (1.20.14), 71 (1.20.15), 75 (1.20.15), 87 n. 68 (1.20.22), 33 (1.20.23), 43 n. 34 (1.21.2), 121–22 (1.22), 188 (1.22.1), 102 (1.22.3), 178 n. 3 (1.22.4), 62 n. 20 (1.22.5), 126–28 (1.22.6), 136 (1.22.9), 151 n. 25 (1.22.9), 155 (1.22.10), 43 n. 34 (1.22.11), 154 n. 30 (1.22.11), 111 (1.23), 91 (1.23.3), 219 n. 12 (1.23.4), 213 (1.24), 11 (1.24.4), 185 n. 22 (1.24.4)

83 n. 64 (2.1), 146 (2.1), 41 (2.1.2), 83 (2.1.4), 5 n. 5 (2.1.6), 165 (2.1.6), 122 n. 9 (2.1.12), 158 n. 38 (2.1.12), 126

(2.3), 33 (2.3.4), 162 n. 4 (2.3.5), 184 n. 18 (2.3.6), 202 (2.3.10), 88 (2.4.3), 68 (2.5), 121 (2.8.1), 137 n. 40 (2.8.2), 17 (2.9), 19 (2.9), 188 (2.9), 43 n. 36 (2.9.1), 212 (2.9.1), 162 n. 4 (2.9.4), 185 (2.9.5), 43 n. 34 (2.9.6), 137 n. 40 (2.10.2), 39 n. 27 (2.10.4), 167 n. 15 (2.10.7), 212 (2.11.11), 202 (2.11.14), 61 (2.11.15), 37 n. 22 (2.11.21), 37 (2.11.21), 61 (2.11.22), 62 n. 20 (2.11.24), 90 (2.13.5), 224 n. 20 (2.13.6–7), 178 (2.14), 202 (2.14), 168 (2.14.9–11), 7 (2.15), 31 (2.15), 188 n. 26 (2.16), 192 (2.16), 230 (2.16), 34 (2.17), 37 (2.17.8), 39 (2.17.15), 224 n. 21 (2.17.29), 32 (2.17.20), 32 n. 7 (2.17.22–24), 32 (2.17.23), 83 n. 61 (2.17.24), 50 (2.17.26), 37 (2.17.27), 11 (2.17.29), 222 n. 17 (2.17.29), 183 (2.18.1), 184 n. 18 (2.18.1), 136 n. 38 (2.18.5), 167 n. 15 (2.19), 202 (2.19.2), 55–58 (2.20), 89 (2.20), 122 n. 9 (2.20), 63 (2.20.2), 48 n. 11 (2.20.5), 78 (2.20.5), 9 n. 16 (2.20.6), 208 (2.20.8), 219 (2.20.12), 43 n. 34 (2.20.14)

44 (3.1), 78 (3.1.4), 32 (3.1.7–9), 151 (3.1.9), 8 (3.1.11), 6 n. 8 (3.2.2), 88 (3.2.2), 188 (3.2.2), 73 n. 224 n. 20 (3.2.3), 40 (3.3), 52 (3.3.1), 193 (3.3.5), 192 n. 32 (3.3.6), 231 (3.3.6), 43 n. 34 (3.3.7), 60 (3.4.4, 8), 61 n. 17 (3.4.5), 43 n. 34 (3.4.9), 169 (3.5), 122 n. 9 (3.5.1), 39 n. 27 (3.5.4), 41 (3.5.4), 217 (3.5.5), 32 n. 7 (3.5.8), 41 (3.5.8), 66 n. 25 (3.5.9), 174 (3.5.12), 116 (3.5.15), 40 (3.5.17), 6 (3.6.4), 33 (3.6.4), 8 (3.7.2–3), 216 n. 6 (3.7.4), 164 n. 8 (3.7.5), 35 n. 19 (3.7.8), 167 (3.7.13), 30 (3.7.14), 42 (3.7.14), 145 n. 10 (3.7.14), 11 (3.7.15), 110 (3.7.15), 144 n. 2 (3.9.5), 216 n. 6 (3.9.9), 81 n. 57 (3.9.16), 20 n. 17 (3.9.21), 68 (3.9.21), 61 (3.9.21–23), 204 (3.9.25), 202 (3.9.25–26), 145 n. 12 (3.9.28), 162 n. 4 (3.10.4–5), 120 (3.11), 152 (3.11), 206–07 (3.11.1, 8), 88 n. 72 (3.11.2), 71 n. 37 (3.11.5), 164 (3.11.5–6), 126 n. 15 (3.12.1), 74 n. 41 (3.13.1), 23 (3.13.2), 101 n. 20

(3.13.5), 47 (3.14), 182 (3.14.5), 164 n. 8 (3.15.1), 26 n. 30 (3.15.3), 171 (3.16), 66 n. 25 (3.16.7), 156 (3.16.12), 141 n. 1 (3.16.13), 206 n. 21 (3.16.13), 48 n. 10 (3.17.3), 74 n. 41 (3.18.1, 3), 61 n. 17 (3.18.4), 82 n. 60 (3.18.4), 7 (3.18.6), 161 (3.18.6), 221–22 (3.19), 116 n. 12 (3.19.2–3), 39 (3.19.5), 51 (3.19.8), 178 (3.20.4, 10), 167 (3.20.5), 7 (3.20.6), 184 n. 19 (3.20.6), 62 n. 20 (3.20.9), 23–24 (3.20.10–12), 145 n. 10 (3.20.12), 166 n. 11 (3.20.12), 172 n. 30 (3.20.12), 187 n. 24 (3.20.12), 142 (3.21), 175 (3.21), 164 n. 8 (3.21.2)

232 (4.1), 98 (4.1.6), 43 n. 34 (4.1.7), 55–58 (4.2), 71 (4.2), 122 n. 9 (4.2), 35 n. 19 (4.2.5), 164 (4.3), 38 (4.3.5), 199 (4.4), 216 n. 6 (4.4.1), 22 n. 20 (4.5), 40 (4.6), 95 (4.6.2), 117 (4.6.2), 55–58 (4.7), 71 (4.7), 61 (4.7.3), 81 (4.7.3), 61 n. 16 (4.7.5), 73 (4.7.5), 87 (4.7.5), 109 (4.7.6), 6 n. 8 (4.8.3), 22 n. 20 (4.8.4), 18 n. 9 (4.8.5), 43 n. 34 (4.8.6), 66 n. 25 (4.9.1), 218 (4.9.2), 216 (4.9.2), 202 (4.9.10–12), 192 (4.9.17), 7 (4.9.19), 200 n. 13 (4.10.2), 63 (4.11), 190 (4.11), 164 (4.11.1), 60 n. 13 (4.11.5–9), 85 n. 66 (4.11.6), 171 (4.11.7), 216 (4.11.7), 135 n. 37 (4.11.8), 141 n. 1 (4.11.9), 147 (4.11.12), 80 (4.11.13), 208 (4.11.13), 37 n. 22 (4.11.14), 65 (4.11.14), 98 (4.13), 33 (4.13.3–4), 6 (4.13.5), 94 (4.13.5), 96 (4.13.5), 139 (4.14.3), 37 n. 22 (4.14.5), 162 n. 4 (4.14.10), 230 (4.15.3), 200 n. 14 (4.15.5), 43 n. 34 (4.16.3), 124 n. 11 (4.16.3), 165 (4.16.3), 60 n. 13 (4.17), 124 n. 12 (4.17.4–5), 148 (4.17.6), 102 (4.17.8), 56 (4.17.8–9), 89 n. 74 (4.17.10), 37 (4.18.1), 188 (4.19), 232–33 (4.19), 52 (4.19.1), 131 n. 27 (4.19.6), 124 n. 11 (4.19.7), 135 n. 36 (4.19.8), 158 n. 38 (4.21.2), 100 (4.22), 20 n. 14 (4.22.3), 58 n. 7 (4.22.4), 65 (4.22.4), 62 n. 18 (4.22.5), 8 (4.22.6), 61 (4.22.6), 121 n. 4 (4.22.7), 206 n. 21 (4.22.7), 224 n. 20 (4.24.4), 167 (4.24.6), 7 n. 14

(4.25), 145 n. 10 (4.25.5), 208 n. 23 (4.25.5)

25 (5.1), 204 (5.1), 88 n. 72 (5.1.3), 215–16 (5.1.7–8), 164 (5.3), 126 n. 15 (5.3.2), 66 n. 25 (5.3.5), 120 n. 3 (5.3.5), 171 (5.3.5), 162 (5.3.5–6), 61 n. 17 (5.3.8), 214 (5.5), 32 n. 7 (5.5.5), 212 (5.5.6), 41–42 (5.5.7), 33–35 (5.6), 222 n. 17 (5.6), 229 (5.6.2), 121 n. 4 (5.6.4), 37 (5.6.25), 32 (5.6.41), 43 n. 34 (5.6.46), 93 (5.7.3), 23 (5.8.4), 213 (5.10), 105 n. 28 (5.11.1), 94 n. 3 (5.11.2–3), 212 (5.12.1), 212 (5.13.2), 178 (5.14.3), 175 (5.14.5), 97 n. 12 (5.14.8), 187 (5.16.1–9), 8 (5.16.2), 184 n. 18 (5.16.2), 131 n. 27 (5.16.3), 118 (5.16.8), 149 n. 18 (5.16.8), 163 (5.17), 185 (5.17), 62 n. 18 (5.17.3), 151 n. 25 (5.18.1), 37 n. 22 (5.19.1–2), 6 (5.19.2), 96 (5.19.2), 182 (5.19.2), 123 n. 10 (5.19.2–3), 33 (5.19.9), 58 n. 8 (5.20.5), 151 n. 25 (5.21.3)

56–59 (6.2), 68 (6.2), 64 (6.2.1), 213 (6.2.2), 8 (6.2.4), 221 (6.3.1), 43 n. 34 (6.3.2), 139 (6.4.1), 212 (6.4.4), 61 (6.5.5), 202 (6.5.5), 204 (6.5.5), 212 (6.6.1–2), 59 n. 9 (6.6.5), 188 (6.7), 213 (6.7.1), 112 (6.8), 198–99 (6.8.3), 214 (6.8.3), 40 (6.8.6), 184 (6.8.9), 185 n. 22 (6.8.9), 220 (6.10.4), 206 n. 21 (6.11.3), 133 n. 30 (6.12.3), 174 (6.15), 22 (6.16), 212 (6.16), 183 (6.16.3), 82 n. 60 (6.16.8), 174 (6.17), 165 (6.17.3), 137 n. 40 (6.17.4), 207 n. 22 (6.17.6), 89 n. 74 (6.19.4), 22 (6.20), 48 n. 11 (6.22.1), 98 (6.25.3), 47 (6.25.4), 184 n. 18 (6.26.1), 200 n. 13 (6.27), 206 n. 21 (6.27.5), 102 n. 21 (6.31.2), 182 (6.31.2), 36 n. 20 (6.31.3), 18 (6.31.9), 204 (6.31.9), 216 (6.31.9), 61 n. 17 (6.31.11), 20 n. 14 (6.31.12), 219 (6.31.12), 162 (6.31.12, 14), 26 (6.31.13), 61 (6.31.13), 89 (6.31.13), 123 n. 10 (6.31.14), 22 n. 20 (6.33), 214 (6.33.1), 206 n. 21 (6.33.11), 100 n. 18 (6.34.2)

159 n. 40 (7.1), 212 (7.1.1), 117 (7.1.3–6), 112 n. 4 (7.2), 114 n. 7 (7.3.3), 163–64 (7.4), 41 n. 30 (7.4.4), 139 (7.4.6), 21 (7.4.8), 117 (7.4.8), 196 (7.4.10), 188 (7.5), 203 (7.6.11), 101 (7.7), 112 n. 4 (7.7), 101 (7.8), 164 (7.9), 200 n. 13 (7.9), 10 (7.9.5–6), 176 (7.9.9), 43 n. 34 (7.9.16), 43 n. 34 (7.10.3), 221 (7.11), 11 (7.11.1), 12 (7.11.3), 100 (7.11.4), 11 (7.14.1), 102 n. 21 (7.15.3), 231 (7.16.2), 94 n. 3 (7.16.4), 43 n. 34 (7.16.5), 169 (7.17.11), 200 n. 13 (7.18), 94 (7.18.2), 88 (7.18.5), 170 n. 25 (7.19.5), 217 (7.19.5), 154 n. 30 (7.19.11), 11 (7.20.3), 165 (7.20.4), 58 (7.20.6), 39 (7.21.4), 224 n. 20 (7.22.2), 193 n. 33 (7.22.3), 94 n. 3 (7.23.1), 133 n. 30 (7.23.1), 185 n. 22 (7.23.1), 136 n. 38 (7.24.2), 233 n. 11 (7.24.3), 38 (7.25.3), 33 n. 9 (7.25.4), 25 (7.26), 117 n. 14 (7.26.2), 137 n. 40 (7.26.2), 122 n. 7 (7.26.4), 212–14 (7.27), 41 (7.27.7), 68 (7.28.1), 108 n. 31 (7.29), 108 n. 30 (7.29.2), 22 n. 20 (7.30), 142 (7.31.4), 94 n. 3 (7.32), 99 (7.32.1), 212 (7.33), 217 (7.33), 22 (7.33), 111 (7.33.1), 165 (7.33.1), 200 n. 14 (7.33.1), 85 n. 66 (7.33.9), 175 (7.33.9), 178 (7.33.9)

33 (8.1.2), 154 n. 30 (8.1.3), 33 (8.2), 51 (8.2), 88 n. 72 (8.2.1), 164 (8.4), 33 n. 9 (8.4.3), 38 (8.4.3), 43 n. 34 (8.4.5), 132 (8.5.1), 187–88 (8.5.1), 184 n. 18 (8.5.1), 108 n. 31 (8.6), 135 n. 37 (8.6), 171 (8.6), 187 n. 24 (8.6.6), 62 n. 19 (8.6.12), 66 n. 25 (8.8.6), 232 (8.10–11), 94 n. 3 (8.10.2), 43 n. 34 (8.10.3), 52 (8.11.3), 47 (8.14), 20 n. 14 (8.14.2, 10), 122 (8.14.5), 150 (8.14.8), 24 (8.14.8–9), 39 n. 26 (8.14.10), 25 (8.14.21), 49 (8.16), 96 (8.16.2), 117 (8.16.2), 37 n. 22 (8.16.2–3), 23 (8.16.3), 122 n. 7 (8.16.3), 89 n. 74 (8.17.2), 151–52 (8.18), 146 n. 14 (8.18.1), 57 n. 4 (8.18.4), 35 n. 19 (8.18.11), 49 (8.19), 207 n. 22 (8.19.1), 164 (8.21), 207 n. 22 (8.21.1–5), 25 (8.22), 129 n. 20 (8.22.3), 148 n. 17 (8.23.5), 187 n. 24 (8.23.5), 151 n. 25 (8.23.7–8), 121 (8.24), 37 n. 22 (8.24.5)

3 (9.1.1), 66 n. 25 (9.1.1), 64 (9.1.3), 214 (9.1.3), 178 (9.2), 22 n. 20 (9.2.2), 23 (9.2.2–3), 41 n. 30 (9.3.1), 43 n. 35 (9.3.2), 216 n. 6 (9.5.2), 83 n. 61 (9.5.3), 102 (9.9), 149 (9.9), 73 n. 40 (9.9.2), 25 (9.12), 117 n. 15 (9.12), 57 (9.12.1), 9 (9.13), 78 (9.13), 87 (9.13), 142 (9.13), 175 (9.13), 217 (9.13), 199–200 (9.13.2, 19–20), 232 (9.13.4), 61 n. 17 (9.13.4), 8 (9.13.4–5), 74 (9.13.4–5), 60 n. 13 (9.13.5), 89 n. 74 (9.13.6), 102 (9.13.6), 156 (9.13.6), 204–07 (9.13.6, 19), 52–53 (9.13.7–8), 212 (9.13.8), 66 (9.13.10), 27 (9.13.10–12), 56 n. 3 (9.13.11), 88 (9.13.11), 117 (9.13.11–12), 51 n. 17 (9.13.13), 84 (9.13.16), 86 (9.13.17), 202–03 (9.13.18–19), 219 n. 11 (9.13.20), 7 n. 12 (9.13.23), 83 (9.13.23), 30 (9.14), 43 n. 34 (9.14), 97 n. 12 (9.15.1), 40 (9.16), 220 (9.19.1), 30 (9.19.3–6), 83 n. 64 (9.19.5), 51 (9.20), 47 (9.20.2), 43 n. 34 (9.21.4), 37 n. 22 (9.22.2), 137 n. 40 (9.23.6), 164 (9.25), 88 (9.26.9), 16 n. 3 (9.30.2), 25 (9.30.4), 38 (9.30.4), 206 n. 21 (9.34.2), 32 n. 7 (9.36.2), 116 (9.36.2), 175 (9.36.2), 32 (9.36.4), 51 (9.37), 97 (9.37.2), 47 (9.37.2–3), 32 (9.40.2), 41 (9.40.2), 175 (9.40.2) 85 n. 66 (10.1.2), 232–33 (10.2), 39 n. 26 (10.2.2), 179 (10.2.2), 216 (10.2.2), 224 (10.2.2), 230 n. 2 (10.2.2), 90 (10.4.1), 162 n. 3 (10.4.4), 224 n. 20 (10.4.4), 9 (10.5.1), 159 n. 40 (10.5.1), 103 (10.8), 94–95 (10.8.1), 100 (10.8.1), 9 (10.8.3), 159 n. 40 (10.8.3), 221–22 (10.8.5), 33 (10.8.9), 159 n. 40 (10.11.1), 39 n. 26 (10.12.2), 178 (10.14), 187 n. 24 (10.26.2), 227 (10.29–30), 62 n. 20 (10.30.2), 81 n. 56 (10.35), 12 (10.51.2), 52 n. 19 (10.52), 89 n. 74 (10.54.1), 76 (10.58), 103 (10.58), 39 n. 26 (10.58.7), 52 n. 19 (10.58.7), 189 (10.58.7), 115 (10.58.7–9), 192 n. 31 (10.58.9), 197 (10.58.9), 135 n. 37 (10.60.1), 89 n. 74 (10.61.1), 76 (10.65), 39 n. 27 (10.66.2), 76 (10.72), 65 (10.75.2), 89 n. 74 (10.77.1), 52 n. 19 (10.82.1), 124

n. 12 (10.86B), 106 n. 29 (10.93), 162 n. 3 (10.94.1), 224 (10.94.1), 232 (10.94.2), 227 (10.96.3), 39 n. 26 (10.102.1), 89 n. 74 (10.108.2), 52 n. 19 (10.111), 100 n. 18 (10.116), 94 n. 3 (10.120.2) 74 n. 41 (*Pan.* 1.2), 103 (1.2), 52 n. 19 (2.2), 74 n. 41 (2.7), 123 n. 10 (2.7), 61 n. 17 (3.2), 7 n. 12 (4.1), 103 (4.1), 123 n. 10 (4.6), 162 n. 4 (4.6), 102 (5.5), 96 (6.1), 9 (6.2), 153 (6.2), 172–73 (6–7), 96 (7.4), 52 n. 19 (8.1, 4), 61 (9.2–4), 20 n. 14 (9.3–5), 9 (10.1), 61 (10.3–4), 96 (10.6), 223 (10.6), 171 n. 28 (11.1), 216 (11.1), 90 n. 75 (12.1), 122 n. 8 (14.1), 172 n. 30 (14.5), 187 n. 24 (19.4), 90 (20.4), 90 (20.5), 61 (21), 96 (21), 102 (21.2), 107 (22.3), 179 (22.3), 224 (22.3), 52 n. 19 (24.1), 61 n. 17 (24.2), 88 n. 72 (25.2), 89 n. 74 (25.4), 96 (26.3), 107 (26.5), 229 (26.5), 97 n. 11 (26.6), 52 n. 19 (27.1), 106 (27.1), 224 (27.2), 97 (27.3–4), 88 n. 72 (27.4), 98 (28.3), 106 n. 29 (28.5), 96 (28.7), 106 (28.7), 163 n. 5 (33.3), 89 n. 74 (34.2), 64 (34.3), 52 n. 19 (34.5), 64 (35.1), 216 (35.4), 64 (36.1), 151 n. 24 (37.4), 151 n. 24 (39.5), 3 (42), 224 (42), 88 n. 72 (42.1), 47 (42.2–4), 152 (42.2–4), 64 (42.4), 216 (43), 224 (43), 145 n. 10 (44.1), 3 (44.2), 85 (44.2), 3 (44.5–7), 63 (44.6), 79 (44.6), 166 n. 11 (44.7), 187 n. 24 (44.7), 3 (45.2), 128 (46.1–3), 162 (47), 5 n. 5 (47.1), 224 (47.1), 3 (47.1–3), 166 n. 12 (48.1), 62 n. 18 (48.4), 191 (48.4), 61 (49.1), 166 n. 12 (49.2), 179 n. 6 (49.5), 223 (50), 3 (50.4), 100 (50.5), 117 (50.5), 52 (50.5–7), 179 n. 6 (51.1), 190 (52.3), 64 (52.4), 88 (52.4), 64 (52.5), 64 (53.3, 5–6), 61 (54–56), 162 n. 4 (54.5), 102 (55.4), 104 n. 25 (56.2), 102 (57.1), 33 (59.2), 20 n. 14 (60.4), 74 n. 42 (60.5–7), 48 n. 11 (66.3), 52 n. 19 (68.2–4), 187 n. 24 (70.4), 102 n. 21 (71.6), 52 n. 19 (72.7), 89 n. 74 (75.5), 3 (76), 20 n. 14 (76.3), 61 (76.7), 201 (76.7), 36 n. 20 (77.4), 61 n. 17 (77.9), 20 n. 14 (78.1), 52 (80.1),

88 n. 72 (80.1), 162 n. 3 (81), 166 n.
11 (81–82), 187 n. 24 (81–82), 178–79
(82–83), 172 n. 30 (82.7), 190–91 (83–
84), 216 n. 6 (83.6), 162 n. 4 (84.1), 3
(85.1), 18 (88.1), 65 (88.6), 7 (88.10),
74 n. 41 (88.10), 41 (89), 65 (89.2), 85
(92.4), 18 n. 8 (94.5), 91 (95.1), 198
(95.1)
Plotina, 178, 190
Plutarch, 213 (*Caesar* 64.3), 230 n. 3 (*Cato
Min.* 25), 170 n. 25 (25), 69 n. 32 (*de
Curios.* 522E), 203 (522E), 126 n. 14
(*de frat. am.* 479E), 60 n. 13 (*Numa*
10.8), 70 n. 34 (*Otho* 1.2), 125 n. 13
(*Pericles* 2.1–2), 98 n. 13 (*Phocion* 9),
139 (*Pomp.* 30.6)
poetry, 9, 30, 36, 162–65, 174
political activity, justification of the worth
of, 115, 137–38, 196
Polybius, 230 n. 3 (36.17)
(Murena) Pompeius Falco, 17, 199, 204,
206
Pompey the Great, 24, 139
Pomponius Secundus, 169
praise, justification of, 96, 101–08, 191–93
Priscian, 66 n. 26 (*Gramm.* 3.506.1–3)

quies, 78, 91, 189, 198
Quintilian, 23 n. 25 (1.1.29), 169 (4 praef.
3–5), 124 n. 11 (4 praef. 5), 230 (6
praef. 8), 165 n. 9 (6.2.4), 75 n. 44
(6.3.86), 74 n. 43 (8.2.21), 165
(8.5.14), 35 n. 18 (8.6.6), 145 n. 12
(9.2.18), 137 n. 39 (9.2.57), 114
(9.2.60), 216 n. 6 (9.2.68), 74 n. 43
(9.2.78), 20 n. 18 (9.3.19), 7 n. 13
(9.3.65), 207 n. 22 (10.1.7), 93 n. 1
(10.1.21), 33 n. 11 (10.1.46), 129 n. 22
(10.1.81–84), 170 (10.1.91–92), 165
(10.1.102), 168 n. 18 (10.1.103), 116
n. 13 (10.3.22–24), 41 n. 30 (10.3.27–
28), 75 n. 46 (10.7.14), 59 n. 11
(10.7.32), 43 n. 36 (10.44.10), 22 n. 20
(11.1.15–22), 129 n. 22 (11.1.33), 88
n. 69 (11.1.49), 124 n. 11 (11.2.51),
127 n. 16 (12.3.12), 59 (12.9), 61 n. 16
(12.9.8–13), 68 n. 28 (12.9.9), 37 n. 24
(12.10.31), 37 (12.10.34), 8 (12.11.1–
7), 168 n. 17 (12.11.3), 41 n. 30
(12.11.7), 112 n. 4 (12.11.18)

recusatio, 7, 60, 102, 139
regret, 16, 22–27, 43, 62, 66, 80, 84, 90,
97, 104–05, 113, 116–17, 223
(M. Aquilius) Regulus, 4, 8–9, 35, 42, 55–
91, 109, 114, 122, 149, 152, 156, 207,
212–13
relatives, friends compared to, 135, 150,
155
repetition, rhetorical, 122, 157
reprehensio (self-correction), 145 n. 12, 185
restoration panegyric, 3–8, 24–27, 52–53,
55, 61–67, 79, 81, 83, 88–90, 95–97,
120, 143–45, 159, 161, 163, 172–73,
177, 179, 188, 215–16, 223–24
ring composition, 13, 76, 107, 124, 157,
159, 199, 205, 223
role-playing, upper-class life compared to,
207
(Arulenus) Rusticus, 69–70, 190, 198, 202

Sallust, 68 n. 28 (*Hist.* 2 fr. 37D), 89 n. 73
(*Jug.* 31.15)
Saturnalia, 53
(Pompeius) Saturninus, 100–02, 121, 132
Scribonianus, 171
self-fulfilling prophecy, 21, 42, 100, 123,
173, 185, 195
Seneca the Elder, 34 n. 13 (*Contr.* 2.1.13),
47 n. 7 (2.1.26), 179 n. 9 (2.5.1–4),
229 n. 1 (2.5.2, 4), 157 n. 37 (3.9)
Seneca the Younger, 29 n. 2 (*ad Helv.*
12.4), 149 n. 18 (17.3), 85 n. 66
(*Apocol.* 1.1), 34 n. 15 (4), 39 (4.1), 85
n. 66 (4.1), 166 n. 10 (12.3), 16 n. 3
(*de Benef.* 1.1.9–1.2.3), 178 (2.20.2),
115 (2.21.2), 166 n. 13 (2.21.2,
4.40.4–5), 49 n. 12 (3.12.6), 49 n. 12
(3.24.2), 6 n. 10 (3.35.1), 37 n. 22
(3.35.1), 25 n. 28 (6.33.1), 112 n. 4 (*de
Brev. Vit.* 2.4), 111 n. 1 (3.1), 24 n. 27
(5.2–3), 167 (17.1), 179 n. 9 (*de Clem.*
1.13.5), 85 n. 66 (2.1.4), 49 n. 12 (*de
Ira* 1.15.3), 129 n. 20 (2.10.7), 213 n. 3
(3.6.3), 213 n. 3 (*de Tranquill.* 2.3),
197 n. 6 (16.1), 91 n. 78 (17.1), 17 n. 4
(*de Vita Beata* 7.4), 124 n. 12 (*Ep.* 3.2),
127 n. 16 (5.2), 43 n. 36 (6.4), 16 n. 3
(7.8), 31 (15.1), 48 n. 10 (15.1), 139
(22.10), 168 n. 18 (30), 144 n. 8

(30.14), 62 n. 18 (40.13), 49 n. 12
(47.19), 16 n. 3 (48.2–3), 35 n. 17
(55.6), 34 n. 14 (55.7), 82 n. 60
(55.11), 48 n. 10 (58.37), 155 (63.4),
158 n. 39 (63.10–11), 157 n. 37 (77.7),
208 n. 25 (77.20), 151 (78.2), 144 n. 8
(78.14), 46 (80.9), 29 n. 2 (86.4–11),
34 n. 14 (86.8), 29 n. 2 (90.9), 36
(90.39), 222 n. 18 (90.39), 17 n. 4
(92.29), 230 (99.14), 155 (99.23), 149
n. 18 (99.32), 151 (104.3), 10 n. 17
(104.9), 49 n. 12 (107.1–5), 129 n. 22
(108.6–7), 129 n. 22 (115.1–3, 18), 29
n. 2 (115.8–9), 17 n. 4 (115.18), 24 n.
27 (118.1–2), 208 n. 24 (120.22)

Septicius Clarus, 15–25

Serrana Procula, 188–89

Shakespeare, 213 (*Julius Caesar* 2.2.98–99)

shame and blushing 61, 80, 90, 117, 191

significant names, 14; 65 (Regulus), 73
(Modestus), 178 (Rusticus), 214
(Tranquillus)

Silius Italicus, 8, 167

slavery, 23, 29, 35, 38, 45–52, 94, 116–17,
152

Socrates, 120, 125, 126, 128–30

solving two problems by joining them, 30,
108–09, 112, 192

Sophocles, 35 n. 17 (*Phil.* 17–19)

Sosius Senecio, 172–73, 176

(Vestricius) Spurinna, 32 n. 7, 78–80

Statius, 170; 60 n. 13 (*Silv.* 1.1.36), 34 n.
14 (1.2.156–57, 1.3.5–8), 34 n. 13
(1.3.15–17, 48), 35 n. 19 (1.3.35–36,
47–57), 150 (2.1.200), 34 n. 13
(2.2.15, 52–53), 35 n. 19 (2.2.63–69,
85–93), 34 n. 14 (3.5.83), 60 n. 13
(5.3.178)

Suetonius, 17 n. 6, 19, 211–225; 167 (*Aug.*
31.4), 204 (56.3), 166 (89.3), 214 n. 5
(91.1), 208 (99.1), 169 n. 19 (*Calig.* 2),
26 n. 30 (16.3), 52 (41.2), 163 n. 5
(55.1), 202 n. 18 (*Claud.* 12.2), 89 n.
73 (14), 167 (21.2), 172 (33.1), 213
(37), 199 n. 9 (38.1), 201 (38.2), 172
(40.1), 167 (*Dom.* 4.3), 170 n. 24
(4.4), 60 n. 13 (8.3–4), 163 n. 5 (10.1),
68 (10.3), 170 n. 25 (10.3), 62 n. 18
(18.1), 61 n. 17 (23.2), 23 n. 25 (*Jul.*
56.6), 199 n. 9 (78.2), 203 (78.2), 157

n. 37 (*Nero* 2.3), 162 (23.2), 70 (34.4),
26 n. 30 (34.5), 220 n. 15 (45.2), 96 n.
9 (*Otho* 10.2), 201 n. 16 (*Tib.* 2.4), 201
n. 16 (11.3), 115 n. 11 (24.2), 7 n. 12
(29.1), 166 (61.3), 115 (*Tit.* 8.1–2), 17
n. 4 (10.1), 53 (*Vesp.* 6.3), 53 (15), 66
n. 25 (15), 199 n. 9 (15), 203 (15), 167
(25), 163 n. 5 (*Vitell.* 14.3), 69 (16), 63
(17), 19 n. 11 (*de Poetis* fr. 40)

supplication, 52, 77, 217

symbolic capital or cultural capital, 11, 99,
114, 117

Tacitus, 4, 22; 68 (*Agric.* 2), 170 n. 25 (2),
162 (3.1), 173 n. 32 (3.1), 178 (4.2),
71 (4.3), 119 n. 1 (4.3), 184 n. 19
(19.2), 192 (19.2), 8 (42.4), 90 (42.4),
145 (42.4), 7 n. 12 (42.5, 43.4), 168
(44–45), 144 n. 2 (44.3–45.3), 83 n. 64
(44.5), 24 (45.1–2), 62 n. 18 (45.3),
191 (45.3), 146 n. 13 (46.1)
178 (*Ann.* 1.2–3), 197 n. 7 (1.2.1), 167
(1.3.7), 90 n. 76 (1.6), 115 n. 11
(1.12–13), 169 n. 19 (1.33.2), 47
(2.30.3), 169 n. 19 (3.16.1), 107
(3.25.1), 178 (3.55.3), 197 n. 7
(3.56.2), 168 n. 17 (4.52, 66), 168
(5.8), 141 (6.26.1–2), 141 (6.48), 213
(11.4.2), 167 (11.11.1), 121 (11.24),
179 (11.24), 168 (12.27–28), 172
(13.3.2), 178 (13.3.2), 184 n. 19 (13.6,
8), 90 n. 76 (13.14.1), 163 n. 5
(13.15.2), 56 (13.43.3), 168 (14.1–13),
70 (14.9.1), 203 (14.12.1), 168 (14.14–
15), 168 (14.19), 47 n. 4 (14.44.2–3),
49 n. 13 (14.45), 168 (14.48–49), 52
(14.60), 143–44 (15.72), 220 n. 15
(15.74.2), 178 (16.5.1), 162 (16.5.2),
52 (16.17), 162 n. 4 (16.18.1), 163
(16.21), 168 n. 17 (16.22.1), 189
(16.26.3)
176 (*Dial.* 3.4), 170 n. 23 (9.5), 175–76
(9–10, 12), 5 n. 5 (15.3, 38.2, 21.6),
167 (17.3–4), 168 n. 18 (23.2), 85 (37–
41), 178 n. 5 (37.6), 24 (40–41), 203
(40.1, 41.4)
162 (*Hist.* 1.1.4), 60 n. 13 (1.2.2), 47
(1.2.3), 152 (1.2.3), 17 n. 4 (1.15.3),
26 n. 30 (1.50.1), 81 n. 56 (1.55–56), 8
n. 15 (1.84.4), 197 (2.91.3), 26 n. 30

(2.96.2), 70 n. 34 (3.55), 63 (3.67), 53
    (3.72), 53 (3.78), 69–70 (3.80.1–2),
    189–90 (3.80.2), 71 (3.81.1), 63
    (3.85), 56 (4.8.3), 230 n. 4 (4.8.4), 197
    (4.9.2), 81 n. 56 (4.39), 62 n. 18
    (4.40.1), 56 (4.42.1–4), 63 (4.42.2–4),
    83 n. 63 (4.42.5), 70 n. 34 (4.47), 162
    n. 4 (4.86.2), 122 n. 8 (5.9)
Teles, 208 n. 25 (fr. 2 p. 3.3, p. 11.5, fr. 6
    p. 40.4)
Terence, 113 n. 5 (*Phorm.* 40–49)
Thrasea Paetus, 4, 68, 171
Thucydides, 81
Tiberius, 95, 162, 168, 213
Tibullus, 34 n. 16 (1.10.7)
Titus, 19, 170, 218

union of ages, 8, 184

Valerius Maximus, 130 (7.2 ext. 1), 208
    (7.2 ext. 4)
Velleius Paterculus, 187 n. 24 (2.126.2)
Vergil, 39 (*Aen.* 6.639), 39 (6.669), 214
    (8.439), 122 n. 8 (*Georg.* 1.509)
Verginius Rufus, 41, 83, 146, 220
Vespasian, 52–53, 69–70, 144, 169
Vestal virgin, 69, 141, 171
villas, 4, 29–36
(Iulius) Vindex, 95, 220
virtuous circle, 10, 15, 39, 43, 50–51, 58,
    89, 108, 110, 122, 184
Vitellius, 52–53
Vitruvius, 23 (5 praef. 1)

wealth, attempt to transform into higher
    value, 3, 30, 36, 39, 106, 221
women, portrayal of, 51, 131–36, 187–88,
    190–91

zero-sum game, 10, 22, 30 n. 3, 134, 138,
    147